D1554059

In Search of Modern Portugal

In Search of Modern Portugal

The Revolution & Its Consequences

Edited by
Lawrence S. Graham & Douglas L. Wheeler

THE UNIVERSITY OF WISCONSIN PRESS

Published 1983

The University of Wisconsin Press
114 North Murray Street
Madison, Wisconsin 53715

The University of Wisconsin Press, Ltd.
1 Gower Street
London WC1E 6HA, England

Copyright © 1983
The Board of Regents of the University of Wisconsin System
All rights reserved

First printing

Printed in the United States of America

For LC CIP information see the colophon

ISBN 0-299-08990-8

Contributors

Nancy Bermeo
Department of Goverment, Dartmouth College, Hanover, New Hampshire

Thomas C. Bruneau
Department of Political Science, McGill University, Montreal, Canada

Charles Downs
Department of City and Regional Planning, University of California, Berkeley, California

José Medeiros Ferreira
Faculdade de Ciencias Sociais, Universidade Nova, Lisbon, Portugal

Tom Gallagher
School of Peace Studies, University of Bradford, Bradford, United Kingdom

Lawrence S. Graham
Department of Government, University of Texas, Austin, Texas

John R. Logan
Department of Sociology, State University of New York, Albany, New York

Bill Lomax
Department of Sociology, University of Nottingham, University Park, Nottingham, United Kingdom

Alex Macleod
Department of Political Science, University of Quebec at Montreal, Montreal, Canada

Harry M. Makler
Department of Sociology, University of Toronto, Toronto, Canada

Walter C. Opello, Jr.,
Department of Political Science, University of Mississippi, University, Mississippi

Ben Pimlott
Department of Politics and Sociology, Birkbeck College, University of London, London, United Kingdom

Paulo de Pitta e Cunha
Lisbon, Portugal

Jean Seaton
Department of Social Studies, Polytechnic of the South Bank, London, United Kingdom

David L. Raby
History Department, Erindale College, University of Toronto, Mississauga, Canada

Joyce Firstenberg Riegelhaupt
Anthropology Department, Sarah Lawrence College, Bronxville, New York

Douglas L. Wheeler
Department of History, University of New Hampshire, Durham, New Hampshire

Contents

Part 3. Altering the Structures of the State: The Problems of Institutionalizing Change

Part 4. The Limits of Change in a Dependent Nation

Tables

Acknowledgments

The preparation of edited volumes of papers, which frequently bear the authorship of a single editor, seldom is the work of only one person. Such is the case with this compilation. Just as members of the International Conference Group on Modern Portugal have come together in recent years to share and compare research and scholarship, as well as ideas, theories, and points of view, so they have combined efforts in bringing together these papers from a recent conference—papers that they believe best represent up-to-date thought on this nation of vital mutual interest. A number of Group members have given their time and talents to this project. Douglas L. Wheeler (University of New Hampshire) more than any other single person warrants mention, as chairman of the Conference Group and organizer of the 1979 conference, and as a historian with an ongoing interest in Portugal. I am pleased that not only did he agree to take on the task of writing the concluding chapter to place these papers in proper historical perspective but that also he was willing to join me as co-editor to help me finish this book while I was in Yugoslavia for research. Joyce F. Riegelhaupt (Sarah Lawrence College), who for years shared responsibilities with Douglas Wheeler as co-chair of the Conference Group, consented to write the introduction. In addition to these two scholars, Harry M. Makler (University of Toronto) and Stanley G. Payne (University of Wisconsin) deserve acknowledgment for time spent reading these papers. Had it not been for the willingness of all four to review all of the conference papers and to offer suggestions regarding inclusions, exclusions, and editing, this project could not have come to completion.

I should also like to thank the staff of the Institute of Latin American Studies (University of Texas at Austin), especially Mary Moran and Max Hosmanek. Without their assistance in typing, proofing, and completing other related chores, my work as editor would have been impossible.

Lawrence S. Graham

Acronyms

AD	Democratic Alliance (Aliança Democrática)
ANP	Popular National Action (Acção Nacional Popular)
CAP	Confederation of Portuguese Agriculture (Confederação de Agricultura Portuguêsa)
CDS	Social Democratic Center (Centro Democrático Social)
CFE	Portuguese State Railways (Caminhos de Ferro do Estado)
CGT–N	General Confederation of Portuguese Workers–Intersindical (Confederaçâo Geral dos Trabalhadores–Intersindical)
COPCON	Continental Operations Command (Comando Operacional do Continente)
CR	Council of the Revolution; Revolutionary Council (Conselho da Revolução)
EEC	European Economic Community
ELP	Portuguese Liberation Army (Exército para a Libertação de Portugal)
FPLN	Patriotic Front for National Liberation (Frente Patriótica de Libertação Nacional)
GNR	Republican National Guard (Guarda Nacional Republicana)
INSCOOP	Antonio Sérgio Institute for the Cooperative Sector (Instituto António Sérgio do Sector Cooperativo)
MDP/CDE	Popular Democratic Movement (Movimento Democrático Popular)

MES	Movement of the Socialist Left (Movimento da Esquerda Socialista)
MFA	Armed Forces Movement (Movimento das Forças Armadas)
MIRN	Independent Movement for National Reconstruction (Movimento Independente para Reconstrução Nacional) (see PDP)
MRPP	Movement to Reorganize the Party of the Reorganizativo Proletariat (Movimento Reorganizativo do Partido do Proletariado)
NORMA	Office of Studies for the Development of Enterprises (Sociedade de Estudos para o Desenvolvimento de Empresas)
PCF	French Communist Party (Parti Communiste Français)
PCI	Italian Communist Party (Partito Comunista Italiano)
PCP	Portuguese Communist Party (Partido Comunista Português)
PDP	Party of the Portuguese Right (Partido do Direito Português) (grew out of MIRN)
PIDE	International Police for the Defense of the State (Polícia Internacional de Defesa do Estado) (secret police)
PPD	Popular Democratic Party (Partido Popular Democrático) (see PSD)
PRP	Revolutionary Party of the Proletariat (Partido Revolucionário do Proletariado)
PS	Socialist Party of Portugal (Partido Socialista)
PSD	Social Democratic Party (Partido Social Democrata) (grew out of the PPD)
SAAL	Mobile Local Support Service (Serviço Ambulatório do Apoio Local)
SEAP	State Secretariat for Public Administration (Secretariado de Estado para a Administração Pública)
SEDES	Society for Economic and Social Development (Sociedade para o Desenvolvimento Económico e Social)

STAL	Union of Workers in Municipal Administration (Sindicato dos Trabalhadores da Administração Local)
TAP	Portuguese State Airways (Transportes Aéreos Portugueses)
UDP	Popular Democratic Union (União Democrática Popular)
UGT	General Union of Workers (União Geral dos Trabalhadores)
UN	National Union (União Nacional)

In Search of Modern Portugal

Joyce Firstenberg Riegelhaupt

Introduction

In the early morning hours of Thursday, April 25, 1974, the Portuguese people, and the rest of the world, were awakened to the news that the longest standing authoritarian government in Western Europe had been toppled. The revolt of the captains, later known as the Armed Forces Movement (MFA), had in the course of just a few hours abruptly ended fifty years of corporatist dictatorial rule under António Oliveira Salazar and, after 1968, Marcello Caetano. The Portuguese revolution, the revolution of the flowers, of carnations, brought a euphoria to the country and smiles to the faces of the Portuguese. In early May a foreign reporter was told by a Lisbon lawyer, "We have made a considerable anatomical discovery this April: the Portuguese have teeth." The foreigner, thinking that the lawyer was referring to the ferocity of the revolution, replied with some confusion that surely it had been the mildest of revolutions. "No," the lawyer explained. "What I mean is that you can see us smile." As the reporter then observed, not only had the teeth of the Portuguese made their appearance, but so had their tongues. "This has been," he reported, "the revolution not of the gun, but of the word."[1]

While the smiles may have faded in the years since that Thursday morning, the words have not ceased. For what happened and did not happen in the course of the Portuguese revolution has been seen by both scholars and the Portuguese themselves to have important ramifications for the course of political action and the possibilities of rapid social change (revolutionary change) in a western society in the last quarter of the twentieth century.

The Portuguese Revolution: Symposium Results

The papers in this collection, prepared for the International Conference Group on Modern Portugal meeting in Durham, New Hampshire in June 1979, attempt to place the revolution of April 25 and its aftermath in a perspective that combines analyses of the internal sociohistorical conditions of Portugal with those of the international events of the mid–nineteen-seventies. Taken in their entirety, the essays demonstrate that an understanding of the social and political processes that Portugal experienced during the revolution must include a comprehension of the Portuguese experience throughout the last century, the particularities of the international context, and especially the developments that had occurred in Portugal's relations with both Europe and Africa since the early nineteen-sixties.

If these papers speak to both the internal and international dimensions that influenced the course of change in Portugal, they also address the question of whether or not April 25 was, in fact, a revolution either in intent or in practice. It is interesting to note the different emphases given by those who experienced living in Portugal from 1974 to 1976 and those who look back on those years from a broader perspective. Downs and Bermeo describe the actual events in *commissões de moradores* (neighborhood commissions) and worker-controlled firms, and others, like Lomax, discount these very developments as unimportant and overestimated. How does one reconcile the two different conclusions without seriously questioning the scholarship of the authors?

Such diverging viewpoints suggest that the experience of the Portuguese revolution speaks to a larger issue, one that is powerfully felt within Portugal but that has not been easily translated into formal party politics, a smoothly running constitutional government with an effective bureaucracy, and a successful economy. For at a minimum the Portuguese revolution, whether or not intended by the soldiers who allowed it to occur, was about freedom and human dignity. These are the concerns that dominate in Bruneau's study of public opinion after the revolution and in Pimlott and Seaton's paper on the media and the revolution.

For those who did not know the silence of the Portuguese people over the decades of the Salazar regime it is perhaps difficult to evaluate the meaning of the opportunity to speak. The endless meetings that took place after the revolution had occurred, the inevitable (?) dismay with the endless talk, and the seeming impossibility of accomplishing the smallest changes—all of these were critical aspects of the revolutionary process which were not neatly codified into voting patterns or electoral politics.

Perhaps a starting point for another type of analysis of the long-term impact of the revolution will be found, not so much in the formal institutional changes that have been accomplished, but in the cultural forms of discourse and exchange that may have been much more radically altered. One cannot escape being struck by the changes that have occurred in language and by the removal of the restrictive patterns of deference that had characterized this previously highly stratified society. It is not clear to me, as an anthropologist, whether such changes can be neatly surveyed in a public opinion poll; a careful reading of the results that Bruneau and his colleagues obtained is warranted.

Because the Bruneau and the Pimlott and Seaton papers deal with the larger context of the revolution and with the broader transformations that have taken place in Portuguese society, they have been placed at the beginning of the volume (Part 1). Before entering into conflicting interpretations of the revolution and into analyses of particular revolutionary phenomena, we need to look at the country as a whole and try to understand how its public opinion has been molded.

The disparity between elite political actors' perceptions of the people and the reality that the people perceived comes across in the important essay that Pimlott and Seaton have written about the role of the media, and particularly the press, in the revolutionary situation. It provides an excellent insight into the power of the media to construct a reality for the participants, and the limitations of that power. As they correctly point out, the Portuguese people under the Salazar regime had little doubt about the ideological role of the media. Even relatively uneducated peasants did not believe what they read or what they heard on the news. In the early years of the colonial wars in Africa I heard villagers reinterpret the news constantly. If there was one underlying theme it was that the government (i.e., the media) never told the truth. Such skepticism did not vanish with the end of the Estado Novo (New State). Pimlott and Seaton show that while the media had a catalytic effect after April 25, there were limitations to its persuasive power over mass opinion. Newspapers have a very limited circulation in Portugal, and despite the fact that their circulation and numbers proliferated after the revolution they remained largely an urban source of information. Here, too, Pimlott and Seaton hit on a theme that is important in other essays: the disparity between events as they occurred and were perceived in the greater Lisbon area and their reception elsewhere in the country. They point quite clearly to the dominant, and ultimately mistaken, view that "he who controlled the television networks came close to controlling the public response to political events." For, as they reveal, "televised propaganda had no more magical, hypnotic effect on its audience after the coup d'etat than it had before the event. Indeed there is strong evidence that control of, or influence over, radio and television did the far left remarkably little good in 1975."

Pimlott and Seaton also provide us with the beginnings of an analysis of the metaphors of dissent and of the intellectual revolution (particularly evident in literature) that had preceded the political changes. If, in American English, "freedom" has been reduced to a cliché, and if "freedom of speech" has become part of a litany, we must not necessarily assume that these words have the same meaning in another society. Few papers in this collection take the symbolic meaning of change as the question for analysis. However, I would urge the reader to look beyond the changes that took place in formal institutional structures; such structures often disappeared overnight as the whole edifice of the corporate society seemingly crumbled away, only to be "reincarnated" the next day under different names and the same bureaucrats. The Portuguese experience may force analysts to break away from the conventional assumptions that institutional change is the hallmark of a revolutionary experience, and that there will be a one-to-one correlation between meaning and structure.

Interpreting the Revolution: Countervailing Viewpoints

The essays in parts 2 and 3 are most closely integrated by questions of success and failure in structuring a new Portugal, and by concern with the internal structure of Portuguese society. As the reader explores these essays, the volatile nature of the first two years of transition, whether viewed as revolutionary or not, will become apparent. Many of the papers focus on the rapidity of the changes and the swerves in direction that the Portuguese government experienced from the end of the Caetano-Salazar regime to the constitutional governments that came into power after April 1976. It was this series of events that caught the eyes of immediate observers as well as of the international community. (For a chronology of significant events, 1968–1980, see pp. 15–18.)

In the first few years the questions for Portuguese society seemed to be, How far left? and, Which left? In the years since the implementation of the 1976 constitution the question has become, How far to the right will Portugal move?[2] Elections in October 1980 for the National Assembly confirmed the existence of a large conservative constituency. Yet these results, which gave the center-right Democratic Alliance a clear majority in the assembly, must be contrasted with the results of the December 1980 presidential election. The reelection of General António Ramalho Eanes demonstrated that, while the Portuguese left is currently divided, no government can function in Portugal without taking political forces of the left into account. If open support cannot be obtained, at a minimum the left's tacit support is essential to avoid a political stalemate.

Among those authors who lived in Portugal during the first two years after the revolution, as well as those who have analyzed the revolutionary process from a distance, the tendency to want to slow down events—or to ignore swerves and directions that did not culminate in structural change—is quite apparent. Such tendencies may account, in part, for the disparity among the Gallagher, Lomax, Logan, Downs, Bermeo, and Makler chapters. Within these essays, and within the very sources that the different authors have used to develop and document their arguments, is often hidden an issue that cannot be discounted in the study of any revolutionary society, and particularly in the study of a contemporary situation—namely, the political ideology of the analyst. The scholarship that has been produced about Portugal should provide ample material for the intellectual historians of the future to demonstrate the impossibility of a "value-free, consensus type of analysis" produced by disinterested scholars. The careful reader will easily discern those who see themselves as "disinterested" and those who clearly represent particular viewpoints and are concerned that one outcome or another did not prevail. But I would like to suggest that even the "disinterested" observers had a stake in how events in Portugal evolved. Unfortunately, the mask of "science" obscures the commitment of many of the authors, and the reader will often have to interpolate and compare one work with another in order to resolve what may appear to be blatant contradictions. This collection of papers speaks thus not only to the immediacy of the Portuguese case, but to larger theoretical issues in the analysis of social processes.

David Raby's paper places the issue of populism and the continuity between political actors of the left, like Delgado and Otelo, in perspective. Raby quite correctly points out that the political climate that characterized Portugal under Salazar was one of fear and intimidation, which was more effective in demobilizing popular resistance than all the repressive activities of the PIDE (the secret police) and the GNR (the Republican National Guard). It is only through an understanding of that climate (which provided Delgado with his rallying cry: he wanted "the country to stop being afraid") that one can get a sense of the repressive atmosphere that was Portugal. That is why freedom, personal liberty, and the opportunity to speak and—as important—to let others speak were so critical to the people. Portuguese society was one in which, except for the powerful elite, "*a gente tem medo*" [people were afraid] of everything and everyone. Raby also guides the reader toward an analysis of the discourse used by Delgado and later by Otelo. He reveals an enduring difference between such political leaders (rare individuals) who spoke directly to the people and the countless politicians and political parties, who, continuing in the Salazarian mode, always spoke of what was best for *o povo* (the people). It was *o povo*, the disembodied masses, who organized at the grass roots level, creating serious problems for the organized political parties, particularly and paradoxically for the parties of the left.

Tom Gallagher sees the events of April 25, 1974, as a coup d'etat with few, if any, enduring revolutionary implications. He provides us with a historical analysis of the relative weakness of the right's ability to organize itself as a political party, despite its enduring attraction to certain sectors of Portuguese society. In the "standstill polity" that Salazar intentionally established politics remained taboo; it was a polity built on a personal autocracy, and no secular party of the right was permitted to emerge. In fact, no political parties existed. Gallagher describes the coopting of civilian rightists to the largely fictitious corporatist program, which was constructed on an integralist (and hence appealing) vocabulary. He traces the possibilies for organization that existed for the right after 1974, and points to several constituencies which could have been mobilized. Gallagher concludes his essay by forecasting a militant right-wing recovery in Portugal; he sees its seeds in the revival of a fascist youth movement and in a growing Salazar cult.

Looking at the role of the left in Portugal, Lomax questions even more strongly than Gallagher the "revolutionary" nature of the country after 1974. In his paper he examines the social reality that lay behind the political rhetoric. He attempts to demonstrate that neither politics nor ideology make a revolution; a revolution, for Lomax, can only be built on the economic and social conflicts extant within a society. Pursuing a most controversial argument, he states that the economic and social conflicts that did erupt in Portugal after April 25 were conflicts about the just ordering of a capitalist society, and were not conflicts which would lead to the formation of a socialist state.

Despite its leftist ideology and the illusion of a march toward socialism, April 25 was necessary as a step in the rational transformation of Portuguese capitalism. Lomax suggests that if the MFA had not existed its invention might have been necessary, for the Caetano regime was increasingly unable to provide a climate for capitalist development; that the Portuguese Communist Party was not the mobilizer of the working class against the capitalist society; and that the creation of "popular power" (see Downs and Bermeo) on the revolutionary left embodied more rhetoric than reality. In fact, to Lomax it is a radical illusion to see the manifestations of popular power as representing fundamental anticapitalist, collective consciousness. On the contrary, he argues, "they were often inspired by long-standing aspirations toward private ownership."

The last chapter in Part 2, the Logan essay, does not engage in the polemics concerning whether or not a revolution really took place in Portugal. What it does is to document the rise of political consciousness within the unions from 1968 to 1974, and then to discuss worker mobilization during the next three years. Through his analysis of the interaction between urban labor and the newly formed political parties, Logan answers the question of the role of urban labor during these years. Without some knowledge of the formation of the labor union movement it is difficult to understand the less structured and more spontaneous movements to establish popular control over urban housing and worker control over industry and commerce.

Whether or not the rhetoric of both the left and the right obscured the true nature of events, careful observers like Downs, Bermeo, Opello, and Graham attempt in their papers to deal with the issues involved in institutionalizing change in a modern bureaucratic society. None of these authors confuses ideology with reality, and all give us original and valuable contributions in which the actors (neighbors, workers, and bureaucrats) who are struggling to make social change are constantly encountering state, party, and international constraints.

Of interest to all who are concerned with social changes in the modern state should be the Downs essay, which gives us the first case studies in English of attempts to make grass roots changes through neighborhood commissions, and the Graham and Opello essays, each of which analyzes tensions between political institutions and the needs of the populace. Opello and Graham demonstrate the weight of continuity both in policy and personnel that survived all the changes during the revolutionary period. Opello, in examining the patterns of local government since the revolution, finds that at the parish level the mayors and the presidents of parish boards are still the administrative representatives of the state at the local level, despite the fact that they are now elected in competitive, open elections. Moreover, he finds that the parishes are still dependent on the national government for more than 65 percent of their income. Thus the financial as well as the administrative constraints that existed under the Salazar government continue to plague local government.

Graham demonstrates more clearly than most of the authors do the issue alluded to earlier: while "buildings and offices are often the same, [and the] legal precepts utilized . . . show little change," the very social bases of organization have been changed. The rigid hierarchy has vanished, and the old standards and expectations, with "their emphasis on order, deference, regulation, and control, are gone." To this observer, these fundamental changes in social structure and culture are changes in the very discourse within which social relations occur: between bosses and workers, men and women, children and parents. It is precisely in all of these domains, in which hierarchy and authority precluded freedom, that one finds the continuing revolutionary impact of April 25.

Lomax's foreign observer, probably an Englishman or an American who had never been in Portugal before 1974, might doubt that the revolution had ever taken place, but I doubt whether any member or student of that society would agree with that conclusion. Nevertheless, there can be no doubt about the fact that the revival of the Portuguese right, and the inability of the left to completely dismantle the economic foundations of the old society, imposed limits on the extent of revolutionary change. It is in this regard that we must consider the role of the industrial bourgeoisie—those who owned and ran small, medium, and large private firms in Portugal. This part of the equation, which is missing from the earlier treatments of urban labor, residents' commissions, and worker control, is discussed by Makler. In his paper we see issues of labor and management that have continued to be pressing problems for Portuguese society and the Portuguese state.

International Constraints on the Portuguese Revolution

While the first three parts of the book focus on the internal dynamics of Portuguese society, Part 4, including papers by Medeiros Ferreira, Macleod, and Pitta e Cunha, looks at the constraints imposed upon the direction of the Portuguese revolution by Portugal's position as a dependent nation within the larger international context. From his experience as foreign minister in the First Constitutional Government, Medeiros Ferreira brings the perspective of one centrally involved in the shaping of Portuguese foreign policy in 1976 and 1977. His paper summarizes the foreign policy considerations that shaped Portuguese actions abroad during the critical phases of the revolution. Having given the background, he discusses the options and outlooks that have characterized Portuguese foreign policy since the revolutionary period. For him 1974 represents a decisive break with the past and the initiation of a new course for Portugal as a European state.

But influence between centric and dependent nations does not always flow in a single direction. Macleod and Pitta e Cunha introduce important complementary considerations. In different ways, each calls attention to the interaction between internal and external affairs that today makes Portugal an inseparable part of the larger European setting. The Macleod essay argues that the course of the Portuguese revolution affected the direction of Eurocommunism, particularly in Italy and France. The difficult positions that the Italian and French Communist parties were placed in at different times as the "hard line" of the Portuguese Communist Party evolved are made evident. Moreover, by looking at three different Communist parties Macleod is able to demonstrate the degree to which, even in their most international aspects, each party must take into account the internal situation in which it finds itself.

Pitta e Cunha clearly draws attention to the incompatibility of the 1976 constitution's definition of the Portuguese economy with the constraints that will be imposed by Portugal's forthcoming membership in the European Economic Community. Such contradictions, as well as the International Monetary Fund loan commitments that Portugal has entered into, cannot help but internally restructure Portuguese society, regardless of political party platforms. Portugal seems to have no choice but to proceed with its integration into Western Europe.

Every volume must have its cut-off date. Pitta e Cunha's paper carries the reader up to the limits of the time period dealt with in this volume: the end of the year 1980. For all of its problems and uncertainties, Portugal did indeed come a long way during the 1970s. As the country enters the 1980s, it is on a trajectory far different from that on which it entered the previous decade.

Wheeler's chapter concludes the volume by placing the revolution in a broad historical perspective—a perspective that is vital to understanding the revolution, but one that Wheeler feels has been lacking in many of the analyses of it. His chapter examines recent historical research that has been done by other scholars, focusing on historical papers given at the Conference Group Meeting but not included in this collection. In addition, Wheeler discusses the importance of using government archives in research to fully understand the prologue to Portugal's most recent revolution.

An Assessment of This Collection

No volume of collected papers from one conference can possible cover all of the critical issues raised by the events in modern Portugal. In this collection the possibilities and limitations of rapid social change in a contemporary western society, within the Euro-American sphere of influence, have been analyzed. The enduring issues of the role played by the state, the attempted organization of political parties and elections, and the roles played by *o povo* as subjects and as actors have all been looked at. If there is a gap in the collection it is in the lack of essays on conditions and events in rural Portugal, and on the consequences of decolonization in Africa for Portuguese society.[3]

Although numerous preliminary, and many polemical, works on the process of agrarian reform in the south of Portugal have appeared,[4] thorough analyses of the impact of April 25 on the northern peasantry and the southern agriculturalists have yet to appear in either English or Portuguese. The Lisbon-centered, industrial orientation of many of the programs and policies of the successive Portuguese governments has obscured critical questions about the agrarian situation. There is, to date, very little information on what peasants in the north participated in, either before or after April 25. Much of what has been written about the Alentejo and the occupation of latifundia lands has focused on the role played—or not played—by the Communist party, and too much of the material on the north has stressed only the *jacquerie* response of the peasants. In each instance the Portuguese agriculturalist (peasant, sharecropper, tenant, or landless laborer) is too often viewed as a passive participant waiting to be led by either of the twin evils—the Portuguese Communist Party in the south, the clergy and the notables in the north. As events have shown, the social issues of land reform, land ownership, and the right to a decent living, and the economic issues of increasing agricultural productivity have been among the most intransigent problems with which the successive provisional and constitutional governments have had to deal.

While Portugal's authoritarian and repressive dictatorship was replaced by an extremely open and competitive political system, the structural changes that might have ensued have not always been accomplished. Between the writing of a constitution and the transformation of society lie the realities of the last quarter of the twentieth century. The world economic situation that the New Portuguese Republic has encountered has not been propitious: the oil embargo and OPEC policies have seriously affected the Portuguese economy; Portuguese workers who found employment in the rest of Europe now find those opportunities increasingly rare, and unemployment, along with inflation, has risen dramatically; agricultural production remains low; and the dissolution of the centuries-old colonial empire has brought thousands of former colonists (*retornados*) to a homeland many had never seen before. However, unlike a Chile, an Iran, or a Nicaragua, violence has yet to become the means by which the Portuguese attempt to redesign their society; to date, neither the left nor the right has replaced the carnations with guns.

Notes

1 Richard Eder, "Portuguese Revolt: Smiles, Arguments and Meetings, *New York Times*, May 14, 1974.

2 Article 1 of the 1976 Portuguese constitution states that "Portugal is a sovereign Republic based on the dignity of the human person and on the popular will and pledged to a transformation into a classless society." Article 2 affirms that Portugal is "a democratic state in transition to socialism."

3 Both the Portuguese military and the consequences of decolonization for Portuguese society have been topics of interest for Kenneth Maxwell. See in particular his chapter "Portugal and Africa: The Last Empire," in Prosser Gifford and Roger Louis, eds., *The Transfer of Power in Africa* (New Haven, 1980).

4 See notes 48 and 49 to chapter 5 for a listing of these sources.

Joyce Firstenberg Riegelhaupt

The Sequence of Events: The Temporal Setting

Time, as lived in, is rarely as programmatic and consistent as scholars would want it to be—and the rapidity of events in the first two years of the Portuguese revolution offered no exceptions. Yet as the historians Wheeler and Raby point out, the microfocus often obscures the long-term continuity of a situation. In chapter 15 Wheeler calls attention to the fact that some analysts see the constitution of 1976 as having brought into being a third republic, rather than a second republic as other proponents have argued (p. 351). In the short run, however, the reader will notice that certain dates are repeatedly mentioned in these essays as signifying sharp changes of direction in the social and political processes that were unfolding in Portugal. The following outline is designed to provide a ready reference that can be used to keep the sequence of events in mind as different (and sometimes conflicting) views of the revolution are presented.

1968–1973: The Failure to Restructure the Old Regime

The events of 1968 are crucial to an understanding of the background of the revolution. Converging within this twelve-month period are a number of momentous phenomena: the selection of Marcello Caetano as new premier following the disabling illness of António Salazar, awareness that the colonial African wars begun in

1961 could continue indefinitely, acceleration of development in Portugal through increased foreign investment, and continuing emigration of Portuguese workers to Western Europe. For the next six years nothing is resolved. Salazar dies in 1970, and Caetano proves to be an ineffectual ruler. In Africa guerrilla warfare increases; the regime is unable to win a decisive victory, but is unwilling to accept the independence of the colonies. On the mainland dissatisfaction with the dictatorship grows, as evidenced by waves of illegal strikes, isolated acts of violence, and the emergence of political opposition in the early 1970s.

1974: The Year of the Revolution

FEBRUARY. Publication of the book *Portugal and its Future*, by General António Spınola brings into the public discourse the issue of Portugal's inability to win its African wars and the failure of its colonial policies.

MARCH 16. An abortive revolt by several military units takes place in the region around Caldas da Rainha.

APRIL 25. A successful revolt led by a group of junior officers, known as the Armed Forces Movement (MFA), overthrows the Caetano regime.

MAY 16. The First Provisional Government takes office, with Palma Carlos as premier and General Spínola as president. Spínola appears as the unifying public figure heading the Junta of National Salvation.

JULY 8. The First Provisional Government collapses as a consequence of its attempt to reconstruct a moderate version of the previous ruling elite.

JULY 17. The Second Provisional Government takes office, with Vasco Gonçalves as premier; Spínola remains president.

SEPTEMBER 28. Spínola, alarmed at the events that have been occurring in the preceding weeks, calls upon the "silent majority" to demonstrate on September 28 against the "anarchy" that is, in his view, characterizing Portugal. Barricades are placed in the streets and in roads leading into Lisbon, but the called-for demonstrations of the right fail to materialize. By September 30, Spínola has resigned as president. Costa Gomes becomes president and the Third Provisional Government comes to power. The military become more closely allied with the popular direction of events. The Third Provisional Government rules until March 1975.

1975: The Radicalization of Revolutionary Forces

In these twelve months Portugal moves to the brink of revolutionary upheaval and violence. The first six months are marked by the increasing control of the revolution by the left, especially after March

11. In July and August the revolution peaks. Thereafter the revolutionary coalition disintegrates. Internal MFA dissension, coupled with the inability to form a viable leftist government, leads to intervention by military moderates. By the end of the year military and civilian left-wing leaders have been displaced from power.

MARCH 11. An abortive right-wing coup by Spínolist military officers leads to the collapse of the Third Provisional Government. Spínola flees to Spain. The Fourth Provisional Government decrees large-scale nationalization of private monopolies.

JULY 16. The collapse of the Fourth Provisional Government takes place. Fear is expressed by President Costa Gomes that the "revolution is taking place at too fast a pace." The months of July and August witness increasing land occupations in the south of Portugal and violent mob actions in the north of the country. The headquarters' of the Communist party in various towns are ransacked. The country is ruled by a triumvirate of Costa Gomes, Vasco Gonçalves, and Otelo de Carvalho.

AUGUST 8. The Fifth Provisional Government is installed, with Vasco Gonçalves continuing as premier. The MFA becomes sharply split into a pro-Communist party wing, a group of officers associated with Melo Antunes and called the "Nine" (who produce a moderate-left position paper), and the extreme left led by Otelo.

SEPTEMBER 6. Vasco Gonçalves, prime minister of the Second through Fifth Provisional governments is forced to resign by Costa Gomes. As the "hot summer" progressed he had been under increasing pressure from the "Nine" and factions allied with Otelo.

SEPTEMBER 19. The Sixth Provisional Government takes office, with Admiral Pinheiro Azevedo as premier. It is hoped that he will moderate between socialist and Communist interests, but instead his policies increasingly alienate the left.

NOVEMBER 25. Moves by leftist officers around Lisbon prompt the mobilization of a counter coup which, as Downs argues in chapter 7, "eliminate the possibility of the left and popular forces coming to power." As a result of these events the Communist party loses its control of the ministries of labor and agriculture, and is replaced at the most senior level of government by Socialist party members.

1976: The Consolidation of Democratic Government

Following the consolidation of control by military moderates led by General António Ramalho Eanes, Portugal moves away from revolutionary conflict toward electoral competition and democratic politics. Three events stand out in this process: legislative elections in April, presidential elections in June, and ratification of a new constitution. This constitution is accepted with the understanding that it is a transitional document, reflecting the balance between left and right forces in the Constituent Assembly. Articles 286 and 287 make provisions for reopening the discussion of the country's constitutional framework in 1981.

1976–1980: The Constitutional Governments

In the years since 1976 there have been six constitutional governments: a minority Socialist government headed by Mário Soares; a Socialist/Social Democratic Center coalition government under Soares; three nonpartisan "technocratic" governments appointed by President Eanes (including one headed by Portugal's first woman prime minister, Maria de Lurdes Pintasilgo, of the Catholic left); and, beginning in the spring of 1980 (as Portugal approached two more rounds of elections in the fall), a center-right coalition government headed by Premier Francisco Sá Carneiro. Sá Carneiro, it should be noted, had served as an Acção Popular (government party) member of the National Assembly under Marcello Caetano. In October 1980 the center-right coalition wins the National Assembly elections, but Presidents Eanes is reelected in December, overwhelming General Soares Carneiro, the center-right candidate. With Sá Carneiro's unexpected death on the eve of the presidential election and Ramalho Eanes' reelection, Portugal enters 1981 with the same tentative accommodation between left and right political forces that had existed under all the Constitutional governments—with conservative forces dominant in the National Assembly and the president representing a wider national constituency.

PART 1
PUBLIC OPINION: CAUSE OR CONSEQUENCE OF REVOLUTIONARY CHANGE?

1 *Thomas C. Bruneau*

Popular Support for Democracy in Postrevolutionary Portugal: Results from a Survey

The demise of long-lived authoritarian rule, the dissolution of empire, and the formation of a liberal democratic political system provide material for a generally positive view of recent developments in Portugal. Today the country is undergoing a process of modernization whereby its political, economic, and social systems are being transformed from archaic models decreed legally in the early 1930s into models more common to contemporary Europe. While there has been general agreement since the coup of April 1974 that a rightist authoritarian model would no longer suffice, consensus about what should replace it has been notably lacking. For a while it appeared as though a communist mobilizational model would predominate, but that alternative has been discredited; today it commands little internal support, let alone external sufferance.

Portuguese politics currently operate within the framework of a liberal democratic system in which the views and attitudes of the population carry influence. To appreciate the nature of these attitudes, the results of a survey conducted in March 1978 will be reported and conclusions drawn about the level of popular support for the regime.[1]

The Political Setting

Before presenting these data some comprehension of the previous authoritarian regime and of the revolutionary process initiated by its demise is essential. The primary legacy of nondemocratic, noninnovative government has been a complete lack of structures upon which to build a democratic system.[2] The Armed Forces Movement (MFA) and the parties and groups that became involved in overthrowing the old regime eliminated previously existing structures and sought to replace them with alternative systems. As the issue of a new regime was so broad, so open, and ultimately so abstract, a dynamic process resulted that must be termed revolutionary both in its momentum and in its impact on society and economics. A key actor in this process was the Portuguese Communist Party (PCP), which had concrete goals and strategies to attain them. Its prominence jointly with the MFA encouraged the emergence of other groups and parties, many with international support, which contested its strategy. The opposition of political and military forces to the PCP strategy led to a number of dramatic events, with the result that in early 1976 there began to emerge the elements of a civilian regime in which the attitudes of the population were represented.

In the armed forces the elements who assumed prominence were MFA moderates. They have been committed to leaving power and have structured the military and civilian arenas of power accordingly. They have also redefined the role of the armed forces within the lines of NATO, and have reasserted traditional military hierarchies and training. The armed forces are to be professional, small, and apolitical. So far they seem to be succeeding in attaining these goals.

In the political party arena the formation of new parties, groups, and movements slowed down during 1975 and 1976. By the time of the election of the Constituent Assembly on April 25, 1975, there were twelve parties contesting in the elections, with four clearly predominant. These patterns have continued. While there are a number of other smaller parties, none of them has been significant in terms of voting strength.[3]

In civilian politics, military moderates assured the promulgation of the new constitution on April 2, 1976 (thereby providing a charter for a civilian system), guaranteed the elections for the Assembly of the Republic on April 25, and held the presidential election that June. Elections to the Assembly showed results similar to those for the Constituent Assembly a year earlier (see table 1.1), with the Socialist Party (PS) winning 35 percent in 1976, the PPD (precursor of the PSD, the

Social Democratic Party) winning 24 percent, the PCP 14 percent, and the rightist Social Democratic Center (CDS) almost 16 percent. On the basis of these results the PS formed a minority government and attempted to govern.

In the presidential election the candidate of the MFA moderates, General Ramalho Eanes—who had been the military head of the group that put down the attempted leftist coup of November 25, 1975—won with some 61 percent of the vote, versus the 16 percent for Major Otelo Saraiva de Carvalho—the flamboyant military leftist—and only 7 percent for the PCP candidate, Octavio Pato. The position of the president proved to be extremely important in the light of the Socialist party decision to form a minority government and as a consequence of constitutional provisions.

The results of the four crucial elections in the 1974–1976 period can be seen in table 1.1 in which the parties have been grouped according to the general strategic/ideological orientations relevant to 1975 and 1976, when the pivot of politics was the role of the PCP. Two main

TABLE 1.1
Portuguese Elections, 1975–1976,
with Parties Grouped by Strategic/Ideological Orientations
(in percentages)

	Elections			
Party Group	Constituent Assembly 4/25/1975	Assembly of the Republic 4/25/1976	Presidency 6/27/1976	Local Governments 12/12/1976
Group A: opposed to the PCP[a]				
PS	37.9	35.0	Ramalho Eanes 61.5	33.2
PPD/PSD	26.4	24.0		24.3
CDS	7.6	15.9		16.6
PCP-ML	—	0.3		0.4
MRPP	—	0.7		0.6
AOC	—	0.3	Pinheiro de Azevedo 14.4	—
PDC	—	0.5		—
PPM	0.6	0.5		0.2
Subtotal	*72.5*	*77.2*	*75.9*	*75.3*
Group B: PCP and affiliates[b]				
PCP	12.5	14.6	Octavio Pato 7.6	—
MDP/CDE	4.1	—		17.7
FSP	1.2	0.8		—
Subtotal	*17.8*	*15.4*	*7.6*	*17.7*

TABLE 1.1 (continued)

	Elections			
Party Group	Constituent Assembly 4/25/1975	Assembly of the Republic 4/25/1976	Presidency 6/27/1976	Local Governments 12/12/1976
Group C: leftist, populist, changing relations to the PCP[c]				
UDP	0.8	1.7		—
MES	1.0	0.6		—
FEC	0.6	—	Otelo	—
PUP	0.2	—	16.5	—
LCI	0.2	0.3		0.1
PRT	—	0.1		0.01
GDUP	—	—		2.5
Subtotal	*2.8*	*2.7*	*16.5*	*2.6*
Blank/null	6.9	4.8	1.3	4.4
Total voting	91.7	83.3	75.4	64.6
Abstentions	8.3	16.7	24.6	35.4

[a]Group A:
PS—Partido Socialista (Socialist Party of Portugal)
PPD/PSD—Partido Popular Democrático (Popular Democratic Party)/Partido Social Democrático (Social Democratic Party)
CDS—Centro Democrático Social (Social Democratic Center Party)
PCP-ML—Partido Comunista Português-Marxista Leninista (Communist Party of Portugal-Marxist Leninist)
MRPP—Movimento Reorganizativo do Partido do Proletariado (Movement to Reorganize the Party of the Proletariat)
AOC—Aliança Operária Camponesa (Worker-Peasant Alliance)
PDC—Partido da Democrácia Cristá (Christian Democratic Party)
PPM—Partido Popular Monárquico (Popular Monarchist Party)
[b]Group B:
PCP—Partido Comunista Português (Portuguese Communist Party)
MDP/CDE—Movimento Democrático Popular (Popular Democratic Movement)
FSP—Frente Socialista Popular (Popular Socialist Front)
[c]Group C:
UDP—União para a Democrática Popular (Union for Popular Democracy)
MES—Movimento da Esquerda Socialists (Movement of the Socialist Left)
FEC—Frente Eleitoral de Comunistas (Communist Electoral Front)
PUP—Partido del Unidade Popular (Popular Unity Party)
LCI—Liga Comunista Internacionalista (International Communist League)
PRT—Partido Revolucionário dos Trabalhadores (Workers' Revolutionary Party)
GDUP—Grupos Dinamizadores de Unidade Popular (Dinamizing Groups of Popular Unity) (created to promote Otelo's candidacy)

points can be readily surmised from these results. First, the distribution of votes for the three ideological groups was generally stable during the period; excluding the presidential election, votes for the PS and PSD decreased somewhat, while those for the CDS increased. Second, the number of abstentions increased significantly from 8.3 percent to 35.4 percent in local government elections; this could have been anticipated, as the very low rate in 1975 was a result of the novelty of elections as well as of the polarized situation of the country at that time. By the end of 1976 a certain level of stability had been attained. Coupled with this factor was the perception that local elections are less important than national elections.

While Portugal has a functioning liberal democratic regime in place, there are a number of serious socioeconomic problems. With the coup of April 25, 1974, and the subsequent revolutionary process much was expected and even more promised, as people believed they would enjoy all the positive aspects of the past with the added benefits from the three Ds of the MFA: decolonization, democracy, and development. Instead, they found that the first of the three Ds resulted in some 600,000 refugees making demands on the state and competing for scarce jobs, while Portugal lost the economic benefits from colonies that had absorbed goods and provided cheap raw materials. The second granted a great many opportunities to participate in civil affairs, but it also produced extravagant promises and rhetoric that became increasingly hollow and at odds with the real situation. The last D, if considered as economic development, has yet to materialize, and it is unanimously recognized that the economic situation is serious.[4]

In general, then, the revolution and the political system emerging from it have left something to be desired. In addition to the problems of decolonization, which can be blamed on the post-coup governments, there were also setbacks created by the rapid increases in petroleum prices after 1973 and by the world recession, which has severely limited the possibilities of emigration. However, a population accustomed to order and stability finds it difficult to comprehend such factors, and it is particularly disconcerting to the Portuguese to have to come to terms with the fact that Portugal is now a small European country rather than an empire spanning three continents.

The military has become linked more and more closely with NATO and no longer formally exercises direct political power. However, MFA elements in the armed forces retain power in two quite different but interrelated ways. The first, and most important, is through the presidency of MFA General Ramalho Eanes, who was supported by the Socialist Party, the Social Democratic Party, and the Social Democratic Center Party in the presidential election in June 1976, and won with some 61 percent of the vote. Not only does he have the support of the armed forces in general and the main remnants of the MFA in particular, but his rule has also been legitimated through nationwide elections. In the constitution promulgated in 1976, the president is granted extensive powers to form and dissolve a government, to veto laws, and to declare war and a state of siege. Thus the system, despite the basis of power in the parliament, is semipresidential in character.

The MFA also retains power through the continuation of the Council of the Revolution. The council was formally recognized in the constitution (pursuant to a pact between the MFA and the main parties, signed in February 1976) in order to guarantee a continuing progressive orientation in the government. While the council's function is supposed to lapse in 1981, it presently has extensive powers to assist the president, supervise the government, and judge the constitutionality of legislation. The CR is not popularly elected. Constituted from within the armed forces, it gives representation to those elements in the MFA that have survived the transition from revolution to democratic regime.

The Portuguese political system is very much a hybrid. While government is presumably based on parties in the Assembly of the Republic, in effect the president has extensive powers, and he in turn is closely related to the CR. The council functions somewhat unclearly as a balance or flywheel to offset pressure from the right. It plays this role not so much because of its structured relationship to the system, but because of personal relationships with the president and contacts between members of the government and the armed forces. A negative implication of this indirect system in which the president and the CR have extensive powers is that the political parties need not compromise as much as they might if they held all the power to form governments. There is, then, a certain tentative aspect to the system which allows the parties leeway and does not oblige them to act responsibly. With power ultimately located at some other level, the parties, as represented in the assembly, may simply fulfill unimportant, ancillary functions, as the National Assembly did under the Estado Novo (New State).

What is more, the present political parties are poorly equipped to fulfill their representational and governing roles in Portugal. The only party that existed in fact before the coup of April 25 was the Communist party, which survived clandestinely and in exile, with the result that it is dogmatic and largely Stalinist. It might be argued that the Socialist party antedated the coup, but it was founded only in 1973 in the Federal Republic of Germany, and had not developed by April 25. The other main parties, the Social Democrats and the Center Democrats, were founded after April 25.

A number of implications arise from the fact of delayed party development. The parties are weakly structured, lacking in cadres, and still without elaborated goals, ideologies, and programs. In fact the Socialist party, after the Communist party the most organized, is still headed by old liberals or descendents of old liberals, and is extremely unstable with regard to middle-level cadres. All of the parties but the Communist are in flux internally, with competition among their leaders and the middle-level personnel. The party system has lacked a central point or fulcrum: between 1976 and 1980 each party acted more in reaction to the other parties than for any other reasons. If there was a fulcrum it was in the Communist party, which does have an organization, an ideology, and well-prepared cadres. Furthermore, while receiving a consistent 13 or 14 percent of the vote in the national elections, the PCP enjoys considerably more support in certain regions (such as the Alentejo) and in certain sectors of the economy. Its union organization, the Confederação Geral dos Trabalhadores–Intersindical (CGT–IN), controls some 217 unions of a total of 490.

While the Communist party no longer dominates the political arena as it did in 1975, it maintains a definite presence and controls a substantial number of votes and structures. During the period 1975 through 1979 the other parties were forced to define themselves in relationship to the PCP. Probably the main reason that the PS remained for so long the party with the biggest electoral support is that it seemed to be the only viable option to the PCP, and thus received extensive domestic and international support. Even in this position of opposition to the PCP, however, the Socialists and the Social Democrats have defined themselves as much more to the left than either their cadres or their action would suggest. The predominance of the Communist party at a particular period, and its strength in important economic sectors, have tended to push the political spectrum to the left as other parties have situated themselves slightly to its right. The PCP's continuing position on the left has been one factor in making agreement among the parties difficult to obtain: the PCP must appear to be uncompromising and faithful to its doctrine and its constituency; it apparently cannot allow itself to be included in coalitions.

In reviewing the results of the elections in 1976, it becomes clear that, with the exception of the Socialist party, which had fairly broad support, each party had regional bases of support (see appendix 1.1). The implication of this for our purposes is that the four main parties can survive and in fact draw votes from supporters of the PS. Something of this nature occurred in the municipal elections in Evora in November 1978, in which the PS dropped to third place behind the PCP and the PSD. In short, it would appear that no single party is likely to win a majority; coalitions are in theory inevitable, but the PCP is unlikely to participate.

The tentative nature of the political institutions also holds for the fundamental charter, the Constitution of 1976. The constitution was formulated by the representatives to a constituent assembly, who had been elected on April 25, 1975; it was approved by all the deputies except those of the Social Democratic Center. The constitution combines many elements of Western democratic experience, and is an eclectic and elaborate document in which the revolutionary gains made following April 25, 1974, are presumably consolidated. At one point it assumes responsibility for "assuring the transition to socialism through the creation of conditions for the democratic exercise of power by the working classes." At another it states that "the development of the revolutionary process imposes, on the economic plan, the collective appropriation of the principal means of production." In order to allow time for consolidation a provision was written in to prohibit its amendment before 1981 (five years after its promulgation); amendments after that time require a positive vote by two-thirds of the assembly. The constitution was formulated during a period of revolutionary fervor (when even the deliberations of the constituent assembly seemed somewhat beside the point) by parties still defining themselves in relationships to the PCP. It is a very advanced and all-inclusive document.[5] It guarantees precisely those structural modifications which can be called into question, and indeed have been, as internal and international realities become better understood. It is, in short, a document that is advanced for a country at Portugal's level of development under which the population, through parties and interest groups, can influence government.

Another important factor that contributes to decreasing confidence in the government and in the legitimacy of the constitution is the substantial number of tasks under the direct control of the state. It would be difficult enough to govern in the face of socioeconomic crises, decolonization, and new political institutions even if the role of the state was not substantial. However, in Portugal the state has been traditionally central, through the corporative system and in terms of investment policies. After the revolution this role increased considerably as the banks and insurance companies were nationalized, bankrupt firms were absorbed, and the technocrats and managers of the previous regime's monopolies fled the country. Today the state sector is huge, with some 45 percent in overall investment (as opposed to 18 percent in 1973), yet the system of public administration is left over from the colonial era, in which efficiency and competition were not necessary considerations. While the role of the state is great, its ability to enact policies is extremely limited, resulting in poor policy implementation and general inefficiency. Ironically enough, the standard text for public administration is Marcello Caetano's *Manual de Direito Administrativo*, which is now in its tenth edition. The old administrative system remains while the many projects and plans for the short- and middle-terms come and go. One might be impressed with the data and aspirations indicated in government plans, but they seem to have little to do with actual policies.

The combination of these factors has created a situation in which the survival of a particular government can become a question of the survival of the whole regime. Much was promised and embodied in the constitution, but both party government and the administrative system have demonstrated severe limitations in their ability to govern. As a result, the population has maintained its reserve in supporting the new political structures, and the president has been forced to assume more power than he was intended to have or than he personally desired. The political dynamics from which this situation arose may be best illustrated by reviewing the instability of Portugal's governments since the First Constitutional Government took office in July 1976.

The results of the April 25, 1976, elections to the Assembly of the Republic gave the PS 107 deputies, the PSD 73, the CDS 42, and the PCP 40. Despite the minority position of the Socialist party, it decided to govern alone in a parliamentary system requiring at least a majority to pass legislation and to remain in office. An alliance with the Communist party was eschewed both for reasons of international concern (it was a period of growth for Eurocommunism) and because much of the justification of the Socialist ascent to power rested in that party's opposition to the Communists during the high tide of the revolution in 1975. Some of its sister parties encouraged the Socialists to form a coalition with the Social Democrats but others did not. The PS avoided a coalition in part because of the animosity between Mário Soares (General Secretary of the PS) and Sá Carneiro (president of the PSD), but chiefly because of the expectation that popular support for the PSD would evaporate if it was not in power. The Socialist government survived for some sixteen months by looking for support from the left on some issues and from the right on others. However, as the difficult problems of the society and the economy became clearer this strategy became less viable.

By the late summer of 1977 the Communist party was advocating the collapse of the Socialist government on the agrarian reform issue. What finally brought it down were the fundamental issues of the general state budget, the plan for 1978, and the requirement of the International Monetary Fund (IMF) that the government have broad political and social support in Portugal before negotiating a $50 million loan (which would open the way for a large loan of $750 million). The need for a loan (to cover a balance of payments deficit) highlighted the serious economic situation in the country, and in return for their support the other parties demanded participation in the Socialist government. The Socialist party, calculating that coalitions were unlikely (if not impossible) without its participation, refused its support, and the government was defeated on a vote of no-confidence 100 to 159, on December 9, 1977.

The collapse of the First Constitutional Government was followed by a period of slightly less than a month of intense negotiations concerning the formation of another government (the IMF negotiation was in abeyance). For the PS, the same obstacles to forming a coalition with either the PCP or the PSD pertained as before; what is remarkable is that a coalition was formed between the PS and the presumably rightist CDS, which had even opposed the constitution. The arrangement was not called a coalition, but rather a Socialist government with the participation of some Social Democratic Center elements (three ministers and several secretaries of state). However, it was a coalition and functioned as such. It was felt again in the PS that the PSD would see its support evaporate if it was out of power.

The program of the Second Constitutional Government was approved in February 1978 only by the Socialist and Social Democratic Center parties. But when Sá Carneiro consolidated his power in PSD, it became evident to the CDS that involvement in a government which of necessity had to implement unpopular policies could erode its power base on the right in favor of the PSD. At this point the CDS escalated its demands for changes in the cabinet; the PS refused, thereby causing the disappearance of a government majority in the assembly. The president acted rapidly in exonerating Mário Soares of his position as prime minister in July 1978.

Following the negative experiences of the First and Second governments, and with the continuation of Portugal's serious economic problems, the president increased his role: he called on an independent, Nobre da Costa, to form the Third Constitutional Government with other independents. The parties were little involved in the formation of this government, which took place in August, and when its program was presented in the assembly on September 14 only the PSD and some independents supported it. The Third Constitutional Government, however, remained in office until November 21, 1978.

By this time it was becoming increasingly clear that the options for formation of a government were three-fold: a coalition of parties, which seemed impossible; a government initiated by the president; or general elections. The president formed the Fourth Constitutional Government as he had the third, but this time with further consultation, at least with the PS, PSD, and CDS. Since the other options seemed even less attractive to the parties, and as extensive consultation did take place, the Fourth Government under the leadership of Carlos Alberto de Mota Pinto, took office in December 1978. It resigned in June 1979 in the face of two censure motions which brought together the Socialists and the Communists. While the split was in part along left/right lines, in fact there were tremendous difficulties within the government and its general popularity was quite low.

As neither a coalition nor a government initiated by the president proved viable, he appointed an interim prime minister (Lourdes Pintassilgo) in August 1979, dissolved the Assembly of the Republic, and prepared for mid-term parliamentary elections. These were held on December 2, 1979. The outcome was: PS, 27 percent of the vote; Democratic Alliance (PSD, CDS, and PPM [Popular Monarchist Party]), 43 percent; and APU (United Popular Alliance of the PCP and the MDP [Portuguese Democratic Movement]), 19 percent. This resulted in a government with the Democratic Alliance having 121 deputies, the PS 74, and the APU 47. In the regular elections on October 5, 1980, the results were similar.

Public Opinion and Attitudes Towards Government

From this background describing the recent evolution of the Portuguese political system and its economic context, we can turn to the results of the 1978 survey to gauge the attitudes of the population concerning the new liberal democratic regime. These attitudes are important because this is a system in which attitudes are registered in votes. Thus there is a possibility that parties having thinly veiled antidemocratic platforms might capitalize on the discontents of the population, come to power, and change the system in such a way that the structures of representation no longer function for most of the people—as was the case between 1926 and 1974.

Table 1.2 indicates the voting intentions of the persons in the survey sample. While those indicating a party preference conformed to voter preferences revealed in past elections, the total of 58 percent who indicated no party, no response, and "don't know" could swing an election in any direction. We must look beyond the data on party

TABLE 1.2
For Which Party Would You Vote Today (1978)?
(percentage of respondents)

PCP	8 (19)[a]
CDS	9 (21)
PS	15 (37)
PSD	7 (17)
UDP	1 (2)
Other right-wing party	1 (2)
Other left-wing party	1 (2)
None	13
Don't know	30
No response	15

[a]The percentages in parentheses are calculated on the total number of those indicating a party.

preference, therefore, to discover the popular appreciation of the regime and of the gains from the revolution of April 25, 1974.

In answer to a question concerning what people are proudest of in Portugal, respondents ranked their first, second, and third priorities according to the distribution reflected in table 1.3. What emerges most clearly is pride in historical and cultural factors, and a low regard for the results of the revolution of 1974, such as the new government (only 4 percent were proud of this), the constitution of 1976 (10 percent), and decolonization (6 percent). These findings are similar to the results of a survey done in 1973, which posed a similar question. At that time a total of 4 percent of the respondents mentioned the political system, while a total of 18 percent mentioned the government and authority.[6] If anything, then, the government is held in even less regard today than in the past. We might note in table 1.3, however, that a total of some 23 percent gave the revolution of April 25 as a response. But when we asked specific questions about the results of the revolution, we found something less than enthusiasm. In general people are aware of changes, and in response to a question on change in the country, 72 percent indicated awareness of change, 11 percent indicated no awareness of change, and 17 percent did not respond. (It's interesting to note that the lower the social class, the less awareness of changes.)

When asked about the details of change, and whether change has been for the better or worse, the sense of the responses was negative indeed, as indicated in table 1.4. While there is a positive evaluation for politics and liberty, most other changes in national life are evaluated negatively—particularly general social and economic factors. Lest the positive evaluations regarding salaries deceive us, we must look to the responses to a question on the impact of the revolution on the individual's own situation. Had the individual's life changed for better or worse? Fifty percent indicated no change, 25 percent indicated that change had been for the worse, 18 percent thought that it had been for the better, and only 6 percent did not respond. In what ways life had changed for better or worse are shown in table 1.5. Again the responses were mixed, but except for liberty of expression, the balance is negative as the cost of living counters the improvement in salaries. The overall trend is clearly negative concerning the results of April 25.

TABLE 1.3
What Should Portuguese Be Proud Of?
(percentage of respondents)

	Priority			
National Characteristic	1st	2d	3d	Total
Contribution to civilization	10	6	2	18
Government	1	1	2	4
Discoveries	14	8	4	26
Revolution of 25 April	15	6	2	23
Literature	1	2	4	7
Qualities of our people	5	8	8	21
Religious life	3	2	2	7
Constitution of 1976	1	6	3	10
Artistic wealth	—	1	5	6
Decolonization	1	2	3	6
Armed forces	1	3	5	9
Nothing	12	2	2	16
No response	37	53	58	

TABLE 1.4
Has Change Been for the Better or Worse?
(percentage of respondents)

Aspects of National Life	Better	No Change	Worse	Don't Know
Morals	10	15	47	28
Politics	33	7	26	34
The economy	3	6	61	30
Salaries	44	8	25	23
Religion	5	48	20	27
Education/teaching	11	17	40	32
Housing	8	15	52	25
Liberty	51	4	21	24
Development/progress	16	23	28	34
Production	5	9	48	38
No response	30	36	24	—
Average	19	15	37	29

Maybe this mixed, but generally negative, evaluation is best illustrated by the responses to a question on decolonization (table 1.6). Thus while independence for Portugal's colonies was clearly favored by most, there was equally strong disagreement with the manner in which it was handled by the postrevolutionary governments.

In order to appreciate how people perceived the general situation in the country, we asked whether they thought the society was undergoing a crisis. Some 63 percent responded that there was a crisis, 5 percent indicated that there was not, 28 percent did not know, and only 4 percent did not respond. Clearly, then, there is a general sense of a crisis in the society. In asking about the nature of this crisis, an overwhelming number of respondents specified economic factors, such as lack of jobs (30 percent), the economy in general (29 percent), and the increase in the cost of living (26 percent). There is not, however, much agreement on how to resolve the crisis and how to promote progress in the country, as can be seen in table 1.7. Obviously no simple solution to Portugal's problems is perceived; the most frequent response is that people should work more.

Our respondents did not feel that the postrevolutionary governments have been effective in resolving the generally felt problems. This attitude is indicated in a number of items in the survey. When asked

TABLE 1.5
What Has Changed in Personal Life?
(percentage of respondents)

Change	Better	Worse
Salaries	53	3
Liberty of expression	23	1
Return from colonies	—	9
Cost of living	—	51
Unemployment	—	18
Everything better	7	—
Everything worse	—	16

TABLE 1.6
What Should Portugal Have Done Concerning the Colonies?
(percentage of respondents)

Continued to fight	2
Granted independence, as it was done	9
Granted independence, but guaranteeing rights of the Portuguese	59
Created a federation	6
Don't know	22
No response	2

whether they thought the First Constitutional Government (July 1976 to December 1977) had ruled properly, 5 percent of the respondents thought that it had governed properly, 68 percent thought it had not, 25 percent did not know, and only 1 percent did not respond. Such a response, of course, would be a terrible indictment of any government. However, in analyzing the data from a survey done in December 1978, just after the Fourth Constitutional Government was formed, we find that the First enjoyed more confidence than the other postrevolutionary governments (table 1.8).[7] With 31 percent having much or some confidence in the First Constitutional Government, it ranks higher than the other three, indicating a decreasing confidence.

Because of the problems contemporary with and created by the revolution of April 25, 1974, and the inability of postrevolutionary governments to resolve them, the New State has begun to look better to the people. The evidence can be seen in table 1.9 concerning attitudes toward governments before and after April 25: some four years after that date, the 35 percent who favored for the old regime contrasts to the 21 percent who favored the postrevolutionary governments. What is particularly dramatic is the low 9 percent for Mário Soares, who had then been in office for more than a year and a half; this rating is barely above the 8 percent for Vasco Gonçalves, who is held by

TABLE 1.7
What Should Be Done to Stimulate Progress and Better Living Conditions?
(percentage of respondents)

Have only one person rule	11
Reduce number of rich people	17
Decrease population	1
Workers should work more	33
People should participate more	18
Don't know	16
No response	4

Table 1.8
What Confidence Have You Had in the Postrevolutionary Governments to Resolve Portugal's Problems?
(percentage of respondents)

Constitutional Government	Much	Some	Little	None	Don't Know/ No Response
First	9	22	12	24	33
Second	3	20	16	28	33
Third	6	20	11	25	38
Fourth (newly formed)	6	21	6	20	47

Table 1.9
Which Government or Regime Governed the Country Best?
(percentage of respondents)

Salazar	7
Caetano	28
P. Carlos (1st Provisional Govt.)	1
V. Gonçalves (1st–5th Provisional govts.)	8
Pinheiro de Azevedo (6th Provisional Govt.)	3
Mário Soares (1st, 2d Constitutional govts.)	9
Don't know	31
No response	13

many to have been responsible for the haphazard process of decolonization and the economic problems arising from nationalizations. In looking at responses to an open-ended follow-up question, the reason for preferring the old regime (for some) and that of Vasco Gonçalves (for others) over that of Mário Soares was clearly the economic factor. While the government of Mário Soares was given credit for guaranteeing the constitution, promoting liberty, and the like, those who expressed their preference on constitutional grounds were of an order of only 10 percent of the respondents, whereas the economic preference for earlier government was on the order of 50 percent.

While table 1.10 can be understood as suggesting that the population realizes what political parties are for, and table 1.11 suggests that the people think political parties are necessary for democracy, table 1.12 shows that they still do not think parties are useful for bringing benefits to the country. The data are supported by responses to the question in table 1.13 concerning the institutions necessary to a democratic Portugal: political parties decrease in importance in comparison with the presidency. This finding is corroborated by table 1.14, which shows who the respondents think really runs the country. We find that 50 percent felt that the president and the Council of the Revolution govern, while some 40 percent felt that the prime minister and the Assembly of the Republic govern.

In light of the above it is clear that there is not a great deal of support for the parties or for the governments, and that as they did earlier the people look to more indirect, somewhat removed, structures of authority. This pattern is borne out by responses to an open-ended question concerning the principal qualities to be desired in the leaders of the country (table 1.15). What is most impressive is the low percentage of references to some aspect of democratic or popular control; a leader could possess most of the indicated characteristics or qualities without functioning in a democratic manner at all.

Table 1.10
What Are the Most Important Objectives for Political Parties?
(percentage of respondents)

	Priority		
Objective	1st	2d	Total
To take power	5	2	7
Express popular will	14	9	23
Defend democracy	21	16	37
Link people and government	14	20	34
Political awakening	2	3	5
Make demonstrations	1	3	4
Don't know/no response	43	47	

Table 1.11
How Necessary Are Political Parties for Democracy?
(percentage of respondents)

Very necessary	33
Slightly necessary	25
Not necessary	15
Don't know/no response	27

Table 1.12
Do Political Parties Bring Benefits for the People?
(percentage of respondents)

Bring many benefits	10
Bring some benefits	38
Do not bring benefits	25
Actually counteract benefits	13
Don't know/no response	14

Conclusions

There are a number of conclusions that can be drawn from this short discussion and analysis. Portugal, after fifty years of dictatorship, does indeed have a liberal democratic system in place. However, for historical and structural reasons the direct or immediate link between the wishes of the population and the government has not functioned effectively. Many serious economic and social problems have not been confronted, and the president has been forced to assume a larger role in governing than intended.

The population has been mildly supportive of Portuguese democracy, but it is clear that it does not identify yet with the structures of the present regime, and that it is unhappy with the results of democracy. Given the long period under the old regime, the people learned not to expect much from politics, and are now probably coming to terms with

Table 1.13
Which Institution Is Necessary If Portugal Is to Be Democratic?
(percentage of respondents)

President of the Republic	24
Neighborhood groups	2
Political parties	18
Organized armed forces	5
A single party	5
Other	2
Don't know	40
No response	4

TABLE 1.14
Who, or What Institution, Really Governs the Country?
(percentage of respondents mentioning)

President of the Republic	39
Cabinet	20
Assembly of the Republic	14
Prime Minister	26
Council of the Revolution	11
Other	1
None	2
Don't know	30
No response	3

the unfulfilled promises made since 1974. Their expectations should be reasonably easy to satisfy—a point which was illustrated by the response to a question on what the objectives of the government in the near future should be (table 1.16). When we remember that the country was at war during the thirteen years before the coup overthrew the old regime because of that war, we can comprehend the overwhelming support for peace. The other responses are reasonably evenly distributed, and liberty is rather far down on the list.

In viewing the historical and survey evidence together, we can probably conclude that the liberal democratic regime will continue, but that the particular form of the structures of power will change. The political parties, in the context of a representative parliamentary system, have not demonstrated their abilities to govern. Conflicts have concerned all types of issues, with the personal and the societal mixed indiscriminately, and only in rhetoric have solutions been offered to resolve the Portuguese "crisis." There is reason to fear that the failure of the parties under the present arrangements will further decrease the legitimacy of the constitution and of the regime. Thus issues of everyday politics increasingly become issues concerning the regime itself, and it is possible that the electorate would support a nondemocratic alternative that promised to provide what the population clearly desires:

peace and economic growth. This negative option need not be adopted, and one must recognize that President Eanes, by making politics somewhat more indirect, has taken steps necessary to maintain the democratic regime.

Popular support for a democratic system in Portugal probably still does not exist if this system is identified with the governments that have come and gone since April 25, 1974. People are looking for concrete benefits that they were told were denied to them by the New State, but which were promised to all after the revolution. If anything, the situation is now more difficult in Portugal: postrevolutionary governments simply have not governed well, and have not provided the benefits so eagerly sought. However, the basic elements of the democratic system are in place and can be made increasingly operable with some competence on the part of those in power. The new institutions will themselves change in relationship to the issues that are confronted. As the system is further defined, the concrete benefits to the population will likely increase and popular support for democracy will be nurtured. In this way the institutions of the liberal democratic regime will be established in the culture of the population as they are implemented in the activities of the elite.

TABLE 1.15
What Are the Principal Qualities a Person Governing This Country Should Have?
(percentage of respondents mentioning)

Honesty	23
Courage/firmness	14
Competence	12
Dedication to the people	11
Intelligence	7
Unaligned to party	6
Energy	5
Sincerity/coherence	5
Democratic attitude	5
Don't know/no response	51

TABLE 1.16
What Should Be the Most Important Objective of Government?
(percentage of respondents)

Peace	45
Equality	14
Order/stability	11
Socialism	10
Development	10
Liberty	4
Don't know	5
No response	1

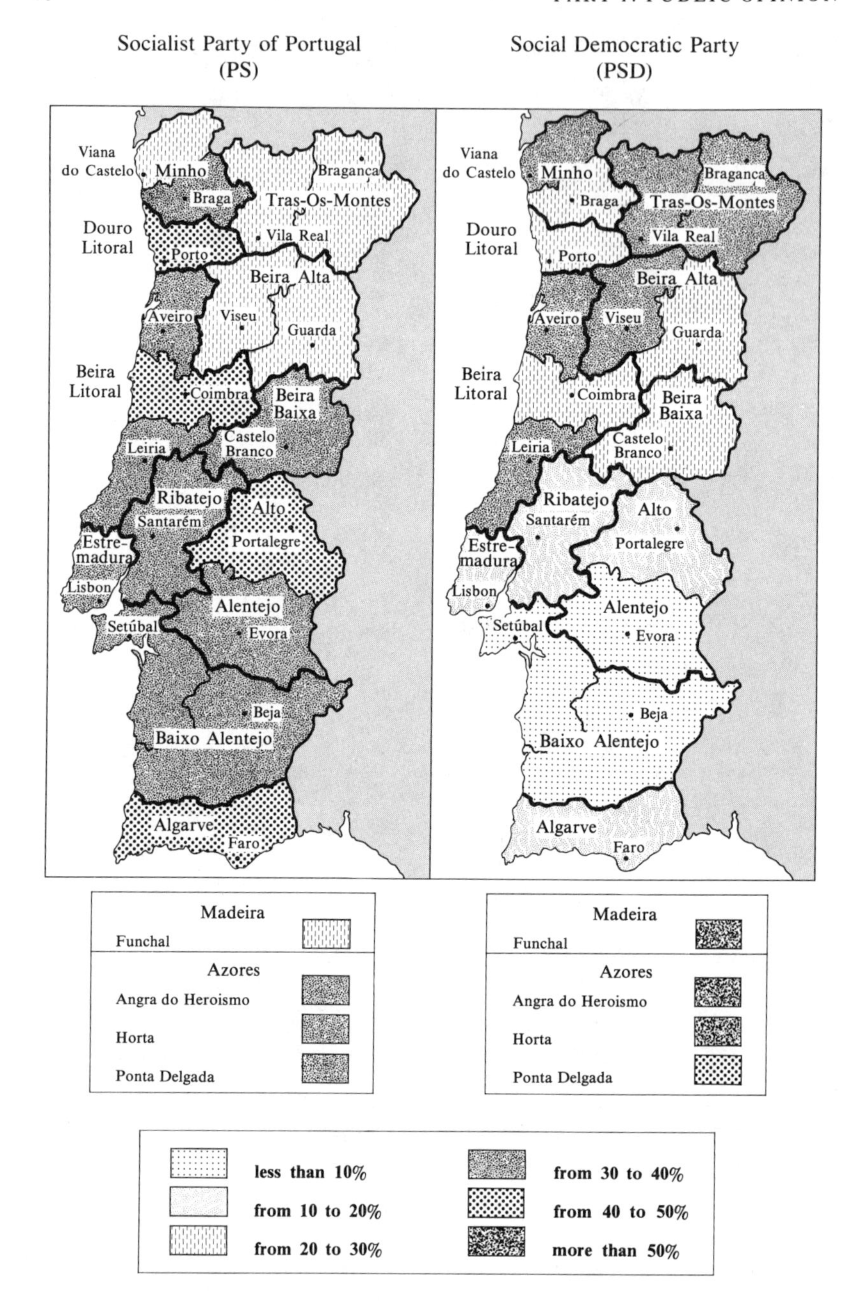

Appendix 1.1 Regional Bases of Party Support in 1976 Elections. From *Le Monde*, 28 April 1976, reprinted in *Portugal Information*, 2d ser., no. 5 (May 1976), pp. 12–13.

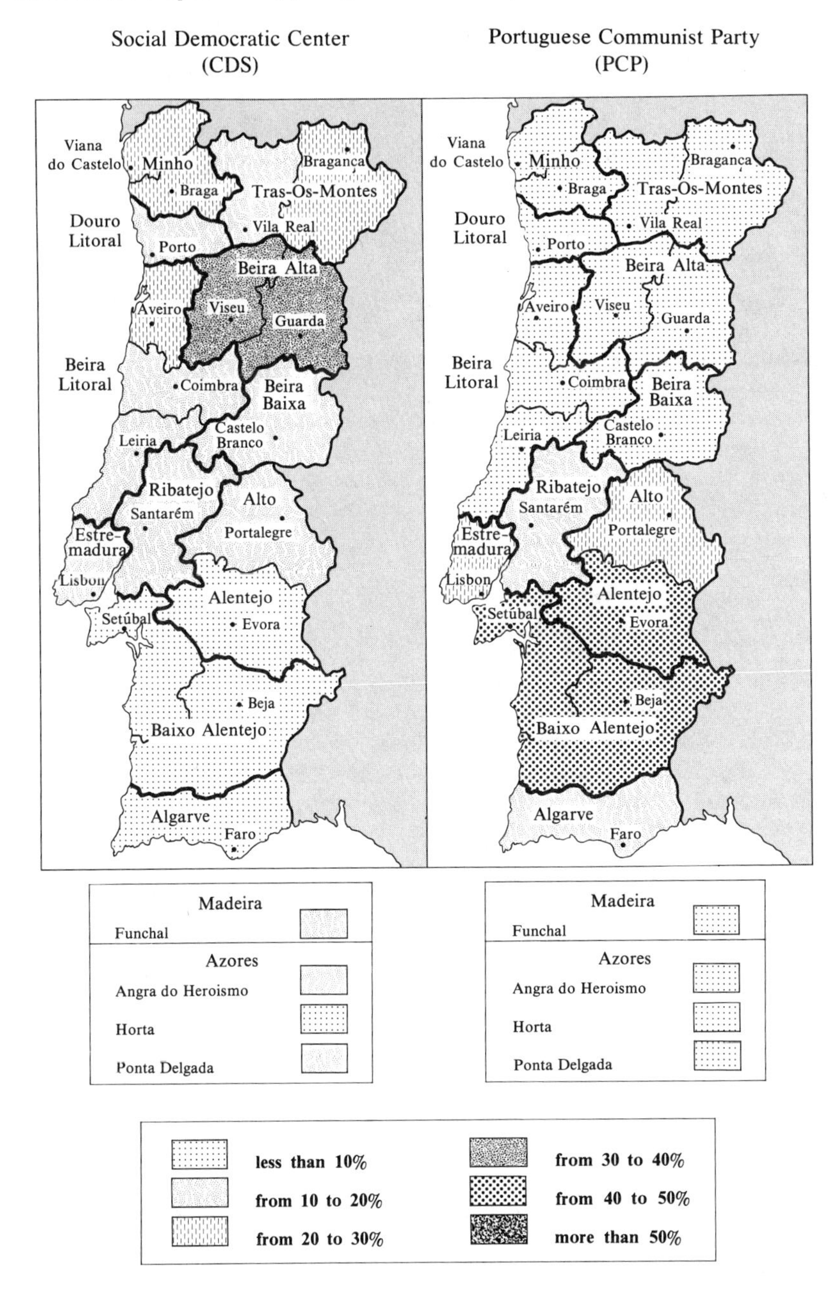

Social Democratic Center
(CDS)
Viana
do Castelo
Minho
Braga
Bragança
Tras-Os-Montes
Vila Real
Douro
Litoral
Porto
Beira Alta
Aveiro
Viseu
Guarda
Beira
Litoral
Coimbra
Beira
Baixa
Castelo
Branco
Leiria
Ribatejo
Santarém
Alto
Portalegre
Estre-
madura
Lisbon
Alentejo
Setúbal
Evora
Beja
Baixo Alentejo
Algarve
Faro
Portuguese Communist Party
(PCP)
Viana
do Castelo
Minho
Braga
Bragança
Tras-Os-Montes
Vila Real
Douro
Litoral
Porto
Beira Alta
Aveiro
Viseu
Guarda
Beira
Litoral
Coimbra
Beira
Baixa
Castelo
Branco
Leiria
Ribatejo
Santarém
Alto
Portalegre
Estre-
madura
Lisbon
Alentejo
Setúbal
Evora
Beja
Baixo Alentejo
Algarve
Faro
Madeira
Funchal
Azores
Angra do Heroismo
Horta
Ponta Delgada
Madeira
Funchal
Azores
Angra do Heroismo
Horta
Ponta Delgada
less than 10%
from 10 to 20%
from 20 to 30%
from 30 to 40%
from 40 to 50%
more than 50%

Notes

1 The sample survey was administered for me in the spring of 1978 by NORMA (Sociedade de Estudos para o Desenvolvimento de Empresas), with support from a Rockefeller Foundation Fellowship in International Relations. I elaborated the questionnaire jointly with Dr. Mário Bacalhau; it was administered to 2,000 individuals in a national representative sample. Some of the results can be found in Thomas Bruneau and Mário Bacalhau, *Os Portugueses e a Política Quatro Anos Depois do 25 de Abril* (Lisbon, 1978). Another survey, carried out by Dr. Bacalhau and NORMA in December 1978, administered 1,000 questionnaires; it has been published under the authorship of Dr. Bacalhau as *Eanes: A Solução?* (Lisbon, 1979).

2 For a more extended discussion of these difficulties, see Thomas C. Bruneau, "Portugal: Problems and Prospects in the Creation of a New Regime," *Naval War College Review*, vol. 29, no. 1 (Summer 1976), pp. 65–83, and the literature cited therein. See also Bruneau, "The Left and the Emergence of Portuguese Liberal Democracy," in Bernard E. Brown, ed., *Eurocommunism & Eurosocialism: The Left Confronts Modernity* (New York, 1979).

3 Two useful, descriptive books on Portuguese political parties are Albertino Antunes et al., *A Opção do Voto* (Lisbon, 1975), and *Partidos e Movimentos Políticos em Portugal* (n.p., 1975). For an analysis of the voting in the 1975 Constituent Assembly election, see Jorge Gaspar and Nuno Vitorino, *As Eleições de 25 de Abril: Geografia e Imagem dos Partidos* (Lisbon, 1976). See also the sensitive analysis of John L. Hammond, "Electoral Behavior and Political Militancy," in Lawrence S. Graham and Harry M. Makler, eds., *Contemporary Portugal: The Revolution and its Antecedents* (Austin, 1979). Also useful is Ben Pimlott, "Parties and Voters in the Portuguese Revolution: The Elections of 1975 and 1976," *Parliamentary Affairs* 30 (Winter 1977), pp. 35–58. For a similar approach to analysis, see Juan Carlos Gonzalez Hernández, "El proceso electoral portugués: Análisis cuantitativo del comportamiento político (1975–1976)," *Revista Española de Opinión Pública*, no. 48 (1977), pp. 205–270.

4 Probably the most comprehensive analysis of the Portuguese economic situation is The World Bank, *Portugal: Current and Prospective Economic Trends* (Washington, D.C., 1978).

5 There are many books that dissect and analyze the Constitution of 1976. Probably the most complete is the 856-page tome by Reinaldo Caldeira and Maria de Céu Silva, *Constituição Política da República Portuguesa, 1976* (Lisbon, 1976).

6 On this point, and for a general report on the survey, see Instituto Português de Opinião Pública e Estudos de Mercado, *Os Portugueses e a Política* (Lisbon, 1973). This information on the table is on p. 59.

7 See Bacalhau, *Eanes: A Solução*, p. 61.

2 *Ben Pimlott and Jean Seaton*

Political Power and the Portuguese Media

Do the media persuade? Or are they merely the tool of the class that controls them, and which can use them for its own purposes? The Belgian sociologist Armand Mattelart suggests that there is a myth of mass communication as an autonomous entity, "a sort of ephiphenomenon transcending the society in which it is inscribed."[1] He sees a tendency to accord to the media the status of a new fetish in Marx's sense of a process or occurrence crystallized "in the form of an object set apart,"[2] abstracted from the real conditions which control its production. Where the media are blamed for problems or crises, "the communications medium is a myth insofar as it elevates a pseudo-cause to the status of actual cause of social occurrences and processes in an undifferentiated way, and thus hides both the identity of the manipulators and the function of the ideas which move in the direction of the social system favoured by the ruling class."[3] Mattelart argues that in this way the communications media have been falsely presented as the dynamizing element in society, and that their true role as the instrument of the ruling class has thereby been effectively disguised.

It is interesting to consider this view in the context of recent Portuguese experience, not least because in Portugal the media have been regarded as playing a politically crucial role for at least a generation, if not since the 1926 military intervention. For many years the media in

Portugal have been the focus of hope and fear, both the arena of political conflict and the prize for which rival parties eagerly contended.

If the media in Portugal have been a fetish, however, they have not been so in Mattelart's (or Marx's) sense of the term. From the earliest days of the dictatorship, and increasingly during its decline, Portuguese of all political persuasions were in no doubt as to the ideological role of the media, or their value to whoever controlled them. More than this, they accorded to the media a persuasive power, and hence a political importance, which did not actually have a basis in reality. In so doing, politicians and political factions created a symbolic significance for the press and broadcasting far beyond the significance of their role as an instrument or tool. Thus, in a paradoxical way, the Portuguese media have had a kind of autonomy: the "myth" has not been without substance.

Repression, Censorship, and the New State

The media and the arts acquired a peculiar significance during the Salazarist dictatorship, which was heightened under the Caetanist oligarchy, because for much of the time the censorship was the most immediate aspect of the repressive nature of the regime. Despite the intermittent brutality and persistent arbitrariness of the regime, Portuguese fascism displayed few of the totalitarian features of the systems it took as models: it was never dynamic or mobilizing in the German or even the Italian sense. Rather, it was (in practice) traditional, paternalist, and conservative, and corporatist institutions were used not to promote but to minimize change and to maximize stability. The regime was far from being nonideological. But the stock of political concepts by which it was guided (characterized by Martins as "Luso-Maurrassism")[4] was more concerned with the preservation of old values than with the inculcation of new ones. Even at its height, the União Nacional was never a mass movement. Popular education was more often regarded as a threat than as a weapon. That the regime should have been so suspicious of innovation and should have considered ignorance the best guarantor of civil order owed much to the dependence of the governing elite on the Church, the army, and the great landowners, and also to the absence, until the 1960s, of any important technologically advanced or modernizing sector.

Consequently government involved restraint far more than direction, and the censorship was an extremely important part of the restraining apparatus of the state. As Martins and others have argued, the highly effective Portuguese strategy was to use terror as economically as possible: something to be brought into play only when other techniques had failed.[5] Salazar was able to rule securely without the bloodbaths of the *caudillo*. The amount of actual violence and physical force employed by the regime in Portugal varied between 1926 and 1974. But there was less official murder, imprisonment, and torture in proportion to population than is usual in countries where basic civil liberties are denied. Increasing urban prosperity from the 1960s, moreover, was accompanied by a decreasing level of physical repression. Some groups (working-class communists in particular) suffered more than others. Nevertheless, a foreign investigation conducted in 1963 found that the total number of people in prison for political offenses amounted to the comparatively low figure of 353,[6] while an estimate made in 1970 (perhaps an unduly optimistic one) gave a total of only 100.[7]

Portuguese authoritarianism functioned on the basis of limits. A degree of freedom from official interference was possible, provided that a threshold of tolerance was not passed. This "negativism" applied most of all to publishing and the media, which (like schools and universities) were seen not so much as means for indoctrination as potential sources of opposition and resistance. The regime did not seek to own or to direct the press (though it was happy when its supporters did so). Instead, it depended on the censor to maintain standards of "dignity" and "decorum" and to act as a bulwark against the forces of chaos and revolution. As Salazar told a journalist shortly before the Second World War, the objective of the government's policy toward journalism and writing was defensive:

> It may seem a paradox, but censorship is to-day the legitimate means of defence that free, independent States have against the prevailing anarchy of thought, against the international confusion of mind. I am not afraid of the criticism of a true journalist provided he is a Portuguese and acts like one. But I am afraid of the minor journalist who, without knowing it, has become denationalised, possibly because his mind is not strong enough to resist the allure of certain facile theories. I must remind you that there is no such thing as Portuguese, French or British Communism, but international Communism, which strives to impair and destroy national independence. Against this ideological imperialism—as dangerous as any other form—the Censorship is surely a lawful means of defence.[8]

The New State was built on memories of the upheavals and disorder of the Republic, and the nightmare of a new collapse, sustained by the reality of a highly organized, clandestine Communist Party (the PCP), haunted the regime until its end—the censor remaining ever sensitive to "the prevailing anarchy of thought," which, if allowed to enter journalism and the arts unchecked, would lead inexorably to revolution in the streets. However, except in the darkest periods, the censorship was not always so rigid, or efficient, as to exclude the possibility of evasion. And, with the introduction of periodic elections, a considerable amount of criticism was allowed for the duration of election campaigns.

These "semi-free" elections, which inevitably resulted in complete victory for government lists, reflected the concern of the regime to assuage international opinion, and also the need for domestic "tension-release mechanisms," which (as Martins has argued) "use up, but do not create or regenerate, the opposition's political capital."[9] Yet on at least two occasions—1949 and 1958—the degree of opposition revealed or created during the campaign was a major embarrassment to the government. Elections were thus rather more than mere exercises in public relations. They were regarded with keen interest even when the opposition decided to withdraw its own lists, and especially when a contest actually took place. For opponents of the regime, the elections were "episodes of latent political communication whereby the opposition seeks to disclose the scale, extent, and intensity of dissent to the effective electors, viz. the armed forces, the Church, and the business oligarchy,"[10] of which only the army was actually capable of effecting changes. As important as the relaxation of prohibitions on freedom of speech and assembly was the partial lifting of the censorship during the campaign period.

There were still major and frustrating limitations. When, in 1969, the censor refused *Diário de Lisboa* permission to publish an interview with Mário Soares, the newspaper, in retaliation, refused to publish a statement by the chairman of the National Union, José Guilherme Melo e Castro; as a result, Soares's statement, in which he declared that the "institutionalization of freedom" was the prerequisite for solving all other problems, was duly printed.[11] However, more subtle methods of checking the voice of the opposition were also employed. Soares himself has recorded the explanation of the governor of a commercial radio station for the latter's refusal to sell time for political broadcasting, despite official assurances: "For a long time I have been trying to get a permit for shortwave broadcasting. Before this statement about election stuff on commercial stations came out, the Government warned me I could say good-bye to it if I let the opposition have any time at all. There is a fortune at stake, you understand."[12]

It was this give-and-take aspect of the regime's relationship with the media that critics found particularly irksome, and which increasingly characterized nonelection periods as well. Where in the past the rules had been clear, in the 1960s and 1970s their operation seemed more arbitrary and unpredictable. Censorship and the regime's developing indecision about the press became central to the controversy between Caetano and his liberal opponents as other aspects of tyranny and the fear of punishment diminished. At the same time, the censorship became sufficiently lax, or unsure, and opponents sufficiently confident and determined, to provide scope through sections of the press for a steady, nagging, half-hidden opposition. By 1974 the media (especially newspapers) were the vehicles for a very muted criticism, and a central cause of resentment directed at the regime as well.

An important essay by José Cardoso Pires,[13] published abroad two years before the coup, is of interest for two reasons: first, because of its description of the bizarre ritualism of the battle involving censor and editor, writer, or publisher—a kind of animal dance in which both sides snapped and pecked with strangely predictable movements, but in which teeth and blood were seldom seen; second, because what Pires actually shows, in spite of himself, is the extent to which the regime was already morally and physically in full retreat. Ostensibly, the author was protesting at the dishonesty or cowardice of the authorities who had reneged on a promise to institute a major liberalization, and was seeking to demonstrate the ennervating effect of the Portuguese form of censorship on serious writing. Thus Pires describes the impact of economic pressures similar to those used against Soares:

> A series of measures frequently put into effect clearly shows, by its gradation, that the final stage is prepared for by creating in the publisher a conditioned doubt and uncertainty. The first move is to alarm him by issuing an unexpected demand that certain books, selected apparently at random from his list, must be submitted to the censor for appraisal. The verdict is then delayed interminably while the book continues to circulate freely. The suspense inevitably leads the publisher to hold up any further activities in relation to the books under scrutiny. Finally, any reference to a particular book ceases to appear in the press. There is no warning and no justification. There is simply a total blank: reviews and advertisements of the doomed book are banned in all newspapers. The book may still be on sale but it is annihilated by the wave of silence imposed by the censor.[14]

Such pressures were frustrating and depressing, but in fact they were scarcely emasculating, and they became less and less effective. There is ample evidence—the writings of Pires himself are an example—that Portuguese literature, so far from being destroyed by censorship, was actually given added purpose by it.

Pires maintains, however, that the effect on journalism was "much more serious" than it was on literature, and it is certainly true that most Portuguese newspapers retained the characteristics of official gazettes by publishing government announcements undigested, avoiding comment, providing no investigative reporting, and using a writing style marked by the worst of bureaucratic clichés and circumlocutions. Under Caetano the main function of the press remained what it had been under Salazar—to communicate official attitudes. Journalism was a semi-clerical subprofession, and it would be absurd to present the pre-1974 press as other than tame and quiescent. Nevertheless, the conflict which Pires describes in Portuguese literature existed on a daily basis in many newspaper offices as well; and precisely because the battle was so constant and repetitive, it came to be seen as the essential political struggle, the trench warfare in the fight against the regime.

In his essay, Pires describes the underground metaphors stimulated by the censorship which had given poignancy to much of Portuguese literature since the 1940s: "dawn" or "daybreak" for socialism; "spring" for revolution; "poppy" for popular victory, and so on.[15] So pervasive were these images that by the 1960s they had formed the basis for a culture that was not so much alternative as dominant. The intellectual revolution, indeed, was largely complete before the political revolution had even begun.

In this process newspaper and periodical journalism had been playing a crucial part. As in poetry and novels, so too in part of the press a whole vocabulary of dissent came into play, a shifting code of hint and innuendo and *double entendre*, designed as much to make the censor look foolish as to engage in oppositional debate, but by its very success reinforcing the increasing contempt that was felt for the authorities, especially among the urban middle classes. There were many devices. The juxtaposing of photographs and copy was a common method; in the last 18 months before the coup, *Expresso* made use of crossword clues, and even included hidden political meanings in children's stories, which the initiated could read as parables.[16] It was an invigorating game, with damaging economic penalties—in terms of presses stopped and issues seized—for arousing the censor's suspicions or disapproval. But the more adventurous dailies, such as *Diário de Lisboa* (with a number of clandestine communists on its staff) as well as the traditionally oppositional *República* and (from 1973) *Expresso*, were continually pushing and testing, as a handful of intellectual journals like *Seara Nova* and *Tempo e Modo* had done for a generation or more. It is certainly no exaggeration to say that the underground language and conventions, created and spread by writers and journalists, fostered the climate of opinion which not only made April 25 possible, but also made quite clear what it was going to be about.

> Grandola vila morena,
> Terra da Fraternidade,
> O povo é quem mais ordena
> Dentro de ti, o cidade.

This old song about the town of Grandola where the people rule, which was used as a signal for the coup, was a code in more senses than one. Other images of the revolution—taking place at dawn, on a spring morning, with a red flower as an emblem—grew out of a long and bitter cultural tradition, given potency by official persecution. It was not by chance that some of the most critical domestic battles of the Caetano period should have been concerned with press and literary freedoms. The failure of the regime to liberalize the press law had precipitated the resignation from the National Assembly of Francisco Sá Carneiro and others on the progressive wing of the ANP (Popular National Action, Caetano's successor organization to Salazar's National Union). This particular event separated the Caetanists from a powerful section of *haut bourgeois* Portuguese society, and dealt a crippling blow to the regime's attempt to present a modernizing image.

A number of literary battles (in particular over the "Three Marias")[17] in the last months of the dying regime served to demonstrate a growing enfeeblement and lack of confidence. Finally, it was a literary event, the publication of Spínola's *Portugal e o Futuro*, which helped to provide the military crisis that gave the MFA (the Armed Forces Movement) its opportunity. In one of the most significant sentences in his published recollections, Caetano stated that two months before the coup he had read Spínola's book and immediately understood "that the military coup, which I could sense had been coming, was now inevitable."[18] There has seldom been a clearer declaration of the political power of the written word. April 25, 1974, was thus in every sense a culmination, an intellectual and cultural event as much as a military and political one. For a long time there had been a growing awareness of a middle-class intelligentsia—expansive, outward-looking, and essentially liberal—steadily gaining confidence in an offensive against an anachronistic and traditional oligarchy whose institutional and corporate supporters were increasingly distracted and unsure, and which was moving toward its last stand.

The Media and the Revolution

The MFA, though initially concerned with the privileges of the officer corps, was already the champion of essentially middle-class, liberal grievances by the time of the coup, as the original MFA program clearly shows. If any doubt remained, the crowds that assembled in Lisbon on April 25 and May 1 determined that, from the start, the coup was to be more than a pretorian revolt. What then was it about? In a word, freedom. The early decisions after April 25 were liberal in nature, of a kind that reflected almost universal desires within the urban bourgeoisie and caused a minimum of offense: the release of political prisoners, the incarceration of the secret police, the legalization of freedom of assembly and of association, the promise of free elections based on universal suffrage, and above all the abolition of censorship and the guarantee of freedom of speech.

The symbolic significance of the ending of the hated censorship was emphasized in a spontaneous move by Socialist party cadres who took over the vacated censor's office in Lisbon, where they established for a time their national headquarters. Indeed, for all the powerful ideological shifts of 1974 and 1975, the Portuguese revolution began as it ended, as essentially a "bourgeois" revolution, asserting the coming of age of a newly expanded and newly prosperous middle class, concerned to establish for itself the freedoms possessed by most of Western Europe. The other major causes of the upheaval, and their manifestations in the former colonies, in factories, in the army, and on the land, threatened but never annihilated the "bourgeois" program.

The strength of the demand for liberal freedoms in the class which (despite shifting labels and alliances) always provided a majority of the ministers and administrators, seemed to ensure a remarkable democratic survival, in spite of continuing predictions of imminent destruction and threats from both left and right. Why were first Spínola and then Gonçalves unable to impose a new authoritarianism, with press controls or restrictions on freedom of expression in a new form? Neither Spínola's Junta of National Salvation nor the Fourth Provisional Government led by Gonçalves were made up of men who had previously shown much interest in liberal democratic principles, and both made some attempts to restrain the activities of the media, or even to direct them. The failure to capitalize on temporary political advantages and silence critical voices may be attributed, in part at least, to a fear of alienating sympathizers inside and outside the government who regarded freedom of expression as a value worth maintaining.

It is not easy to disentangle cause and effect in the rapid evolution of the media after April 1974, and especially between September 1974 and the summer of 1975.[19] Did radicalization of the press, radio, and television lead the revolutionary upheavals, or merely reflect them? The media were certainly swept along by the mood of the times. The "flood-gates" theory, expounded by Caetano as a reason for opposing any sudden relaxation of the censorship, was in one sense vindicated: there was a dramatic increase in the volume of newsprint, and the media responded almost immediately to an unquenchable public demand for discussion of the social and political issues that had previously been taboo. Undoubtedly a kind of competitive political hysteria, in media previously characterized by caution and sobriety, contributed to an urban mood of unrest; and this provided the background to occupations, demonstrations, strikes, and workers' control. Yet the behavior of the media, and of editors, producers, and journalists cannot really be isolated, and should be seen as part of an organic process.

But if the media had a catalytic effect, alongside and not separable from that of parties, groups, unions, and so on, it is important to stress the limitations to any persuasive power over mass opinion which they were generally assumed to exercise. Portuguese newspapers catered to a comparatively small, largely urban, elite. Indeed the press, in contrast to broadcasting, was barely a "mass" medium at all. A poll conducted on behalf of the Ministry of Social Communications at the end of 1976 found that fewer than one Portuguese adult in three claimed to have read or skimmed *any* daily paper during the preceding month; outside of greater Lisbon and greater Porto, the proportion was scarcely one in five.[20] The amount of *regular* newspaper reading in the countryside was much lower, partly because of high rural illiteracy and semi-literacy rates, and partly because of poor distribution. There were no mass circulation newspapers, and no paper was mainly dependent on sales to the poorest people. Indeed, the Portuguese press appears to be among the most elitist in Europe, its readers most commonly young, urban, and skilled workers or members of the middle class.[21]

But in any case, the conventions of the Portuguese press, essentially unchanged since before the revolution, were not geared to a wide or uneducated reading public. There were no Portuguese tabloids. The heavy prose style that had characterized the Salazarist press was maintained, with few concessions to modernity. The subtleties and devices used in some papers to get past the censor had been aimed only at the highly sophisticated. Portuguese journalists had no experience in directing political news and copy toward people who had a low level of political understanding and a limited political vocabulary. As the Lisbon press became increasingly Marxist in its orientation, there was little attempt to make the shades of difference between groups and factions intelligible. Indeed, virtually the whole of the Portuguese press throughout the revolution seemed to be addressed to a readership of *cognoscenti* far smaller even than the number of those who bought and read newspapers. The proportion of people, even among the Lisbon middle class, who were able to follow from the press the rapid movement of events during the spring and summer of 1975 was probably small.

The proportion that depended on newspapers as a source of reliable information about political developments was almost certainly even smaller. In a country with a long history of censorship, there was a universal suspicion of all public media. This suspicion was not diminished in the months that followed April 1974—there was little enough reason to rely on reporting and comment produced by a profession which found it possible to switch from fascist to communist copy with so little difficulty. There is ample evidence—for example, the enormous increase in the audience of the Portuguese section of the BBC—that alternative sources of information became more important, not less, during the period that followed the coup, and most of all during the "hot summer" of 1975. Pires reported a popular Portuguese joke of 1972 vintage: "'What's the latest local news?' asks an immigrant on a visit to Lisbon. 'Haven't the faintest idea,' replies his friend, 'I haven't seen to-day's *Le Monde*.'"[22] In 1975, French, British, and American papers were still being eagerly read—even by politicians—as the most reliable sources on domestic events.

What of radio and television? Radio reached the vast majority of the population. The penetration of television was less complete, and in some rural areas reception was poor and the ownership of sets unusual. However, far more people saw television than saw newspapers. A 1972 poll showed that 67 percent of the population had seen television in the preceding week,[23] and during the revolution the percentage may have been considerably higher. Moreover, television could be understood by illiterates as well as literates (though poorer people may have had access to television sets less often than others). The broadcasting media were thus clearly "mass," and might be expected to have had a much bigger role as political persuaders than newspapers—especially during the months of intense political interest among the general public, when parties could repeatedly attract crowds of a hundred thousand or more to their rallies in the big cities.

Undoubtedly the novelty of open discussion aroused great interest, and political news and discussion were keenly listened to and watched. But the effect that political broadcasting had on the public is not easy to gauge. Politicians tended to assume that television was a weapon of immense power: he who controlled the networks came close to controlling the public response to political events. Such a view—derived in part, as we have seen, from a traditional obsession with media influence and control, and in part from international conventional wisdom about the role of the media everywhere—was clearly quite false. Televised propaganda had no more magical, hypnotic effect on its audience after the coup d'état than before. Indeed, there is strong evidence that control of, or influence over, radio and television did the far left remarkably little good in 1975.

There was never a monopoly of control over the media by any one group after April 1974, but by the time of the April 1975 election the media were certainly dominated by the far left. By the election of April 1976 the situation had been neatly reversed: Lisbon's press and broadcasting had become largely liberal-democratic. If the media, particularly radio and television, had indeed been instruments of persuasive mass propaganda, one might expect there to have been a dramatic falling off of support for the far left between the two elections. In fact, no such trend is visible, and the main contours of the electoral map remained remarkably stable.[24]

The evidence of the elections certainly does not bear out the exaggerated hopes or fears of politicians that control of the media would confer great power to sway mass opinion. It is even arguable that, just as the censorship became the focus of bitter criticism under the old regime—cause for opposition in itself—so the appearance of a left-wing media monopoly in 1975 (and the somewhat crude propagandist uses to which influence over the media was often put) alienated people, creating fears of a new authoritarianism. What is probably true is that the ascendancy of pro-communists in the media—seen by the left as a key to political power—gave an impression of actual power over policies and events where very little power really existed. Consequently, the Portuguese Communist Party was widely blamed (especially in the north) for disruption and economic collapse which it was wholly unable to prevent.

Conclusion

The media may have had little manipulative or persuasive power over public opinion. Nevertheless, they were crucial in the Portuguese revolution in a number of ways.

First, they were a means of communicating instructions or exhortations from leaders to followers, when instant reaction to a new political situation was required. Thus it was through the media that most of the huge demonstrations were announced (though Soares succeeded in holding one of the biggest and most effective demonstrations—over the *República* affair—despite the fact that most of the media were against him).[25] The press became the vehicle for warnings against real or imaginary plots, in order to forestall any possible putschist plans within the officer corps, especially during the anarchic autumn of 1975. Broadcasting was sometimes used to inflame crises by urging militants to participate. The burning of the Spanish embassy was provoked by a television broadcast which urged people to join demonstrators who were protesting against the execution of Spanish anarchists. The media also raised temperatures by bringing the revolution into the family living room; most dramatic of all was the live television coverage of the confusion and discussions among troops participating in the March 11 fiasco. While not persuading or convincing the masses, then, the media had a crucial agitational effect, sustaining or whipping up feelings and militancy among the activist minority.

Second, in the confusing battlefield of an anarchic struggle, the media acquired or built up an important symbolic role. In all coups d'état, broadcasting stations and newspaper offices are early targets; during the critical hours in which those with the power to affect the outcome make up their minds, the media can establish a sense of authority. In Portugal, where legitimacy and authority of a conventional kind disintegrated and virtually disappeared for a period of months, the media were in a strategic position for a very long time, partly because all political actors seemed to believe that people and institutions would be guided by the media in their choice of whom to obey. There is little evidence that this perception was correct—that people did in fact equate the press and broadcasting with a legitimate source of power. What mattered, however, was that a legacy of anxiety and concern about the role and impact of the media had created within the political elite an unshakable faith in their importance. Just as before the revolution many of the most important battles had concerned literary and press freedom, so it was in 1975 as well. The *República* affair was arguably the turning point for the Gonçalvists not because of the actual importance of the paper itself, but because it was seen as a hill that had to be taken. Though Soares lost the skirmish, he won the battle by demonstrating the huge popular anxiety that existed about a far-left media monopoly. In a different way, the radio station Renascença was able to rock the Sixth Provisional Government by symbolizing the uncontrollable features of Lisbon society in the autumn of 1975. Renascença's defiance mattered because of a general acceptance among political and military leaders of the importance of the media. The inability of the government to deal effectively with radio and television appeared for this reason as a symptom of a general lack of control.

Indeed, the rules in 1975 were not so very different from those in 1958 or 1969, when the opposition sought, through the temporary freedoms provided at election time, to convince the army of the strength of dissent. In 1975 political players were still performing before a military audience—Soares seeking to prove the extent of disaffection with the Gonçalves government, and the far left concerned to show the lack of popular backing for Azevedo. As in the past, it was always assumed that the military would be the final arbiter.

In this competition the media played a central part, though less as an instrument than as a prize. The media were seen as a means to an end: decades of struggle against the censorship had invested the media with powers they did not possess. In fact, though the media were sometimes a lubricant, they could not be crudely used as an ideological tool. The media in Portugal obeyed their own laws and were beholden in their influence to nobody. Indeed, there were many features of the Portuguese revolution which could be "blamed on the media" in the sense derided by Mattelart, rather than on the groups or classes that attempted to exploit the press and broadcasting for their own advantage.

Notes

1 Armand Mattelart, "The Nature of Bourgeois and Imperialist Communication," in John Caughie, ed., *Television: Ideology and Exchange*, (London, 1978), pp. 4–5.
2 Karl Marx, *A Contribution to the Critique of Political Economy*, cited in Mattelart, "Nature of Communication," p. 5.
3 Mattelart, "Nature of Communication," p. 6.
4 Herminio Martins, "Opposition in Portugal," *Government and Opposition* (London) 4 (1969), p. 257. Charles Maurras was a political writer and founder of *Action Française*, an extreme right-wing movement that espoused direct action, rejected elections, defended the role of the Church, and made an ideology out of the hereditary principle.
5 Martins, "Opposition in Portugal," p. 263.
6 Lord Russell of Liverpool, *Prisons and Prisoners in Portugal: An Independent Investigation*, cited in Hugh Kay, *Salazar and Modern Portugal* (London, 1970), p. 339.
7 Kay, *Salazar and Modern Portugal*, p. 339.

8 António Ferro, *Salazar—Portugal and Her Leader* (London, 1939), pp. 26–27.
9 Martins, "Opposition in Portugal," p. 253.
10 Ibid., p. 263.
11 L. A. Sobel, ed., *The Portuguese Revolution 1974–76* (New York, 1976), p. 17.
12 Mário Soares, *Portugal's Struggle for Liberty* (London, 1970), p. 247.
13 José Cardoso Pires, "Changing a Nation's Way of Thinking," *Index on Censorship* (London), no. 1 (Spring 1972), pp. 47–63.
14 Pires, "Changing Thinking," p. 103.
15 Ibid., p. 95.
16 Ben Pimlott interview with Marcello de Sousa, Lisbon, July 1978.
17 Maria Velho da Costa, Maria Isabel Barreno, and Maria Teresa Horta, three professional writers, were arrested for offending public morals three weeks after their joint book, *The New Portuguese Letters*, was published in April 1972. Court proceedings began in October, and the trial dragged on for many months. Meanwhile, the cause of the "Three Marias" was taken up by women's organizations and others abroad who protested against a new Portuguese law which made writers, publishers, printers, and distributors legally responsible for the morality of their works. In April 1974, immediately after the coup, the trial ended abruptly and the judge proclaimed the book a work of literary merit.
18 Marcello Caetano, *Depoimento*, cited in António de Figueiredo, *Portugal: Fifty Years of Dictatorship* (London, 1975), p. 232.
19 See Jean Seaton and Ben Pimlott, "The Role of the Media in the Portuguese Revolution" in Anthony Smith, ed., *Newspapers and Democracy: International Essays on a Changing Medium* (Cambridge, Mass., 1980), pp. 176–199.
20 Taking the sample for the nation as a whole, the percentage claiming to have read or skimmed a daily paper in the preceding month was 30. Regional percentages were as follows: greater Lisbon 53, greater Porto 63, Littoral 20, interior north 16, interior south 26 (Source: Ministry of Social Communications [Lisbon, 1976]).
21 See Seaton and Pimlott, "Role of the Media" for a development of these points.
22 Pires, "Changing Thinking," p. 98.
23 Ministry of Social Communications, *Informação popular e turismo*, vol. 1 (Lisbon, 1972).
24 See J. Gaspar and N. Vitorino, *As Eleições de 25 de Abril: Geografia e Imagem dos Partidos* (Lisbon, 1975); Ben Pimlott, "Parties and Voters in the Portuguese Revolution," *Parliamentary Affairs*, vol. 30, no. 1 (Winter 1977), pp. 35–58; and Seaton and Pimlott, "Role of the Media."
25 In the spring of 1975 the workers' committee of the pro-Socialist Party (PS) newspaper *República* demanded the removal of PS members of the editorial staff. The Socialist leader, Mário Soares, succeeded in attracting international attention to what was presented as a further example of the

suppression of press freedoms by the Communists and their allies. Within Portugal, Soares was able to use the *República* affair as a reason for pulling the Socialist Party out of the government, and for holding the biggest demonstration of opposition to the Gonçalves regime that Lisbon had yet seen. Thus Soares adroitly turned a minor, but symbolically important, dispute about editorial control (in which the Communists were probably not involved in any direct way) into a challenge to the whole direction of the revolution. The Fourth Provisional Government fell, and with it disappeared any chance that Portugal would become the Cuba of Western Europe.

PART 2
NEW AND OLD SOCIAL FORCES: THE CHANGING BASES OF POLITICAL POWER

3 *David L. Raby*

Populism and the Portuguese Left: From Delgado to Otelo

The theme of this chapter is the recurrence of populist tendencies in the Portuguese left during the past 30 years. It will be argued that there exists in Portuguese politics a strong populist tendency rooted in the weakness of mass political parties and the traditional strength of personalist charismatic leadership (as in the myth of *Sebastianismo*, and in the historical cases of Dom Miguel, the Duke of Saldanha, Sidónio País, etc.). This tendency was accentuated during the Salazar years by the suppression of normal political activity, by the structural and political weaknesses of the organized opposition to the regime, and by the new pattern of socioeconomic development after World War II. Such latent populism found its most dramatic expression in the election campaign of General Humberto Delgado in 1958 and in his subsequent activities, until his murder in 1965; it re-emerged in 1974–1975, manifesting itself in the "non-party" or anti-party rhetoric of the MFA (Armed Forces Movement), and particularly in the style and doctrine of the MFA's left wing, personified above all by Otelo Saraiva de Carvalho. The author believes that this interpretation is important because without reference to the populist trend it is impossible to understand the nature of the MFA and its political behavior in the revolutionary crisis of 1974–1975—or indeed, to understand the events of that crisis itself.

Populism: A Tentative Definition

Before developing the argument any further, it is necessary to address the question of definition. What do we mean by populism and populist? Few terms have given rise to more controversy among social scientists. They have been applied to the Russian Narodniks, to movements of farmers in the American and Canadian West, to Peronism in Argentina, Varguismo in Brazil, to Egypt under Nasser, to Maoism, and in fact to an endless variety of movements and leaders running the gamut of the political spectrum.[1] Because of this, some writers have wanted to abandon the use of the terms altogether. But despite their apparent imprecision, the terms have an evocative value in describing a certain style or approach to politics: a rhetoric or a discourse, and a pattern of leadership, which differ in important respects from those of conventional party politics or other forms of political domination. A populist movement is one in which charismatic appeal is prominent, in which there is a strong element of personalism and a cult of leadership, in which lack of organizational structure goes hand-in-hand with a heterogeneous social base of support, and in which ideology is ill-defined or even contradictory. Populism is associated with protest and with an anti-status quo ideology and/or rhetoric, but the precise content of this ideology seems almost infinitely variable.

In many discussions of populism the phenomenon is given a pejorative connotation which does little to further its rational analysis. For liberal writers populism is either "abnormal," a deviation from the desirable parliamentary model of development, or primitive—a sign of political and social immaturity;[2] for many Marxists it is a form of bourgeois rule based essentially on demagogic manipulation of the masses, and diverting popular energies from the revolutionary path.[3] In recent years an alternative view has emerged which sees populism, or some of its variants, in a much more favorable light; proponents of this view argue that populism of the left, or of the dominated classes, can be revolutionary, and can even lead to socialism. The most theoretically developed defense of this position is made by Ernesto Laclau,[4] who argues that any socialist movement, to be really successful, must in fact become populist: it is only by the successful articulation of "popular-democratic interpellations" (i.e., of nonclass ideological elements within popular culture) into a "synthetic-antagonistic complex with respect to the dominant ideology"[5] that a socialist movement can become hegemonic.

This is not the place for an extended discussion of Laclau's theory, which concentrates too exclusively on the ideological aspect of populism, and fails to address the problem of the structural and organizational characteristics of populist movements.[6] The value of his approach lies in the attempt at a rigorous exploration of just what it is that such diverse movements have in common: why it is legitimate to describe both fascism and (say) Castroism as populist. Also positive is his emphasis on the progressive potential of some populisms.

For the purposes of this discussion I want to propose a definition of populism which incorporates Laclau's theoretical insights while focusing more closely on populism as movement. My position is that populism is essentially a movement of the petite bourgeoisie, which in a situation of hegemonic crisis attempts to assume control of the political process by mobilizing a mass coalition against the dominant class bloc. Such a coalition is founded on ideological contestation, with a radically anti-establishment discourse synthesized, in the manner described by Laclau, from the most diverse elements; this diversity or inconsistency of ideology corresponds to the heterogeneity of the social base of the movement, often embracing all classes from dissident fractions of the bourgeoisie to workers, peasants, and marginal groups. Social heterogeneity also dictates the organizational weakness and amorphous structure so typical of populist movements, in which charismatic leadership and ideological mystique have to substitute for administrative or bureaucratic bonds, but the same structural weakness gives populism a unique flexibility and dynamism which may enable it to outmaneuver more conventional and solidly based political movements.

For obvious reasons, populism tends to arise more frequently (but not exclusively) in dependent or semideveloped countries, and where the organized left is weak or ineffective. It is possible to distinguish reactionary and progressive populisms; the progressive variety exhibits a strong tendency to radicalize to the left in the course of the political process, polarizing popular sentiment against the dominant bloc and/or against external domination. The process of radicalization leads either to a decisive rupture, with the destruction of the existing power bloc, or to the disintegration of the populist coalition. The clearest example of the former would be Castroism in Cuba from 1959 to 1961;[7] of the latter, the Portuguese MFA in 1974–1975. The MFA was clearly a progressive populism—and so, 16 years earlier, was the Delgado phenomenon; as such, they were each able to initiate a revolutionary process (although neither carried the process to a successful conclusion). Without an analysis of the implications of the populist phenomenon, it is impossible to make sense of the political history of contemporary Portugal.

Delgado's Opposition Career as a Populist Phenomenon

Most readers probably will not require much convincing that the MFA and Delgado movements were, in fact, populist. Both exhibited many of the features commonly associated with populism: ideological vagueness, loose structure, a heterogeneous mass following, charismatic leadership. Both were multi-class, anti-status quo movements led by petit bourgeois elements (significantly, the principal leaders in both cases were army officers); both tended to radicalize under pressure, and both tended to outflank or overwhelm existing parties or organizations of the left. This analysis will concentrate on the Delgado case, with only brief references to the MFA, but the relevance of the argument to the MFA movement should be self-evident.

The impact of Delgado's election campaign in 1958 was truly phenomenal. A career officer in the Portuguese Air Force, General Humberto da Silva Delgado had distinguished himself principally by his boldness and irascibility.[8] He was proud of his participation as a young man in the coup of May 28, 1926, which ushered in the dictatorship, and in the thirties he was an outspoken supporter of the fascist regime, writing pamphlets and radio plays in its defense.[9] Although he later tried to minimize his political role in this period, claiming that his contribution was almost exclusively military,[10] the fact remains that in 1936 he became military adjutant to the General Command of the Portuguese Legion, and assistant commissioner of the Mocidade (the fascist youth movement).[11] When he moved into the opposition camp in the mid-1950s, he was received with understandable distrust by many democrats and socialists.

Those who had followed Delgado's career more closely, however, realized that his ideas had changed substantially as a result of his diplomatic experiences in London, Montreal, and Washington during the 1940s and 1950s.[12] Encouraged by Captain Henrique Galvão (a military comrade who had preceded Delgado in breaking with the regime), a group of prominent opposition intellectuals decided that, as a dynamic personality and a general in active service, Delgado would be their most effective candidate for the 1958 presidential election.[13] The results must have exceeded their wildest expectations: from the very first day of the campaign, Delgado revealed his determination to break free of the (by then) traditional restraints on opposition electioneering under the fascist regime—both the web of legal restrictions and harassment imposed by the authorities, and the self-imposed conventions of respectability and legalism which characterized most of the public activities of the Oposição Democrática. Delgado condemned the 32-year-old dictatorship as a national humiliation, claiming that it had destroyed the hopes of those like himself who had participated in the 28th of May in good faith, expecting national regeneration; and he decided to call what he clearly regarded as the regime's bluff, which was manifest in the climate of fear and intimidation that had developed over the years and which was more effective in demobilizing popular resistance than all of the repressive activities of the PIDE (the secret police) and the GNR (Republican National Guard). "Que o País deixe de ter medo!" ["Let the country cease to be afraid!"] declared Delgado in an interview on May 10,[14] and he showed by his bold and even reckless style of campaigning that he meant business. The famous phrase of his opening press conference in the Chave d'Ouro café, when asked how he would deal with Dr. Salazar if elected President—"Obviamente, demito-o!" ["Obviously, I shall dismiss him!"]—destroyed at one blow the absurd taboo that had been allowed to develop regarding public discussion of the dictator's future.[15]

From this point onward, Delgado's campaign was like a popular explosion. His first campaign stop, in Porto on May 14, turned into a mass rally of unprecedented proportions; despite the censorship's efforts to suppress news of the general's intended visit to the northern capital, he was greeted by a crowd estimated at 200,000 people (about half the total population of the city).[16] On his return to Lisbon two days later, the government used force in an attempt to prevent a similar demonstration, posting large numbers of police and mounted republican guards outside Lisbon's Santa Apolónia station, and whisking Delgado away through the back streets before the multitude had a chance to get near him.[17] The ruse succeeded, but only at the cost of provoking a riot in which considerable police brutality was exercised against the crowds assembled in the Lisbon *Baixa*. The only effect of the incident was to arouse popular anger, and the tone of the campaign became much more bitter. Delgado's agents accused the government of deliberately provoking "a climate of social agitation" as a pretext for cancelling the elections,[18] while the regime's propaganda machine initiated a redbaiting smear campaign against the General (at a time when the Portuguese Communist Party (PCP), in its clandestine publications, was still dismissing Delgado as "General Coca-Cola" and "fascista").[19] The government was rapidly losing control of the situation, as Delgado's campaign turned into a spontaneous mass plebiscite against the regime: throughout the country, huge and enthusiastic crowds continued to turn out to cheer the opposition candidate. There was growing speculation about the attitude of the army if Delgado attempted a coup, and the police appeared increasingly to be the only reliable prop of a tottering regime.

Of course, the New State did not fall in 1958. Salazar hung on until election day, proclaimed Admiral Tomás to be the victor at the polls with 76 percent of the popular vote, and relied on popular demobilization, the ineffectiveness of the opposition, and the self-interest of the officer corps to save the day. His gamble succeeded: the generals failed Delgado (who was relying on them to mount a coup),[20] the opposition did little except voice ineffective protests against the electoral fraud, and the people looked on in disbelief.[21] The regime had weathered what was almost certainly its most severe crisis before 1974.

But the situation was no longer the same; the unprecedented mass mobilization from one end of the country to the other had changed the pattern of Portuguese politics. The myth of Salazarist stability had been destroyed, and another myth had been created: Delgado, deprived of victory, his career ruined, driven into exile in Brazil less than a year later, became a twentieth-century Dom Sebastião for millions of discontented Portuguese. His vocation as popular *caudilho* gave him a unique role in the country's politics, and his ideas, intrigues, and adventures dominated the exile opposition until his murder by the PIDE in February 1965.[22] Always a man of action, Delgado conspired tirelessly. Before leaving Portugal he made three attempts to organize a coup (on June 2, July 27, and December 18, 1958), all of which fell through at the last minute for lack of military support.[23] In exile, his schemes revealed a penchant for the spectacular, an impatience with organizational detail or systematic political work, a naive belief in the efficacy of the deed. More like a nineteenth-century *condottiero* than a mid–twentieth-century politician, he was easy game for opportunists and provocateurs, and the manner of his death is scarcely surprising;[24] we may regard it as the tragic but almost inevitable conclusion of an extraordinary career.

In Brazil, having failed to unite the Portuguese exiles in his Movimento Nacional Independente, Delgado became involved with Henrique Galvão in the famous plan to hijack the cruise liner *Santa Maria* in mid-Atlantic (this was one such scheme which did succeed, at least in the sense that the liner was indeed hijacked in January 1961).[25] His clandestine return to Portugal to participate in the abortive uprising at Beja on New Year's Day 1962 demonstrated once again his courage and his lack of organizational skill.[26] There were many other schemes that never got off the drawing-board, such as the notorious "Plan Laranja" to seize Macau with the assistance of the People's Republic of China and then proclaim a provisional Portuguese government there.[27]

As might be expected, Delgado was an almost impossible man to work with. Stories abound of the personal conflicts in which he became entangled and the difficulties caused in the exile organizations by his intolerance and dictatorial style of work. The PCP, which collaborated with Delgado in the Frente Patriótica de Libertação Nacional (FPLN) from 1962 to 1964, had immense difficulty in persuading him to agree on a fixed plan of action.[28] But what were defects in Delgado's character, from the point of view of systematic organization and consistency, in the eyes of many Portuguese were virtues in terms of the dynamism and prestige of the opposition. Without Delgado, it is doubtful if the PCP would ever have agreed to a program of armed action (except in the abstract), and the predominance of ineffective legalistic methods among the republican and social-democratic opposition would undoubtedly have taken longer to overcome. Although not directly caused by Delgado, the emergence of a combative student movement and of an active Catholic left (both phenomena of the early sixties) were certainly stimulated by his example.

The Populist Character of Delgado's Style and Discourse

The impact of Delgado on the popular consciousness has been alluded to by many contemporaries. Mário Soares relates a telling incident to illustrate this point:

> Luis Roseira, a doctor in Covas do Douro, told me one day about the cult which the poorest strata of the People *[sic]* sustained for Humberto Delgado—considered as a "Messiah," a saviour. As my reaction was a little sceptical, he took me on a tour of the meanest hovels of the Douro region, home of a population living in conditions of indescribable poverty . . . It was true! In many places I found Delgado's portrait, sometimes beside the holy images worshipped by these unfortunate people![29]

Particularly significant was Delgado's popularity among the peasantry and in the most backward and isolated regions of Portugal. These were precisely the regions normally considered most conservative, and peasant smallholders were regarded as the largest source of popular (as opposed to elite) support for the New State. The traditional opposition had notoriously failed to penetrate these areas, being overwhelmingly an urban, educated, middle-class movement dominated by lawyers, doctors, engineers, and café intellectuals; and the Portuguese Communist Party, the main force of the underground working-class resistance, was also extremely weak among the peasantry of the center and north. Yet Delgado's impact in these areas was immediate; it has been suggested that his popularity was even greater in the north than in

Lisbon or the Alentejo. Interestingly, one of the few places where he was actually forbidden from speaking during the election campaign was Braga—traditionally a bastion of conservative clericalism—and this ban led to serious riots by the local population.[30] It seems clear that Delgado's personality—his bold, decisive manner, his contempt for Lisbon bureaucrats and intellectuals, the very fact of his being an officer (indeed, a general)—appealed to the spontaneous instincts of a smallholding peasantry, self-reliant, practical, and suspicious of the *gente de casaca*.

Delgado himself was quite conscious of his charismatic appeal, and as we have seen, false modesty was not one of his faults. In his *Memoirs*, commenting on his clandestine visit to Portugal at the time of the Beja revolt, he wrote:

> Some thirty people spoke to me while I was in Portugal, that is to say, thirty who knew who I really was, and no doubt, in spite of the danger involved, they were unable to resist the temptation to tell others that they had "touched the hand of the saint." . . . This [behavior] is particularly true of Portugal where, three centuries after King Sebastian had been killed in the Battle of Alcacer-Quibir (Morocco), the people still believed that this poor, mad young man would return to save their country . . . Add to this their innate tendency for the mysterious, the rumours spread about my brief stay in the north of Portugal, the announcements by foreign radio stations and in the odd foreign newspaper that found its way in, and the distribution over the years of the stamps bearing my portrait and the motto "I shall return," and you will understand the special excitement in the air, which kindled the very hearts and souls of the people who had sought their salvation in the elections of 1958.[31]

Although Delgado was not responsible for originating the cult of his own personality, which was a spontaneous expression of popular identification with a long-sought-for leadership figure, he did nothing to discourage its development. After July 1958 he regarded himself (not without justification) as the rightfully elected president of Portugal, and conducted himself accordingly. Assuming that he was the natural leader of the opposition-in-exile, he inevitably offended many whose antifascist records were much longer than his own, including some who had been in Salazarist jails when he was an outspoken supporter of the regime. When negotiations were under way to establish the FPLN as a united organization of Portuguese exiles, Delgado wanted its leading body to be called a government-in-exile—with himself, of course, as its president. He was with difficulty persuaded that conditions did not exist for the creation of a government-in-exile, or for even minimal international recognition of such a government.[32]

As president of the Junta Revolucionária Portuguesa (the actual title given to the supreme body of the exile organization in Algiers), he insisted that all delegates should wear suits and ties to its meetings.[33]

If Delgado's style of action tended both consciously and unconsciously to promote his stature as a populist hero, his political discourse was also ideally suited to this purpose. It was a discourse which corresponded perfectly to the model proposed by Laclau, combining the most varied ideological elements from distinct and even contradictory sources. While constantly appealing to patriotism and national traditions (Portugal's eight centuries of nationhood, the glory of the Discoveries and the Empire, etc.) he also frequently disparaged Portuguese behavioral traits—Latin emotionalism, rhetoric, and "empty theorizing"—by contrasting them to "Anglo-Saxon" efficiency and practicality.[34] While calling for social change and reforms, he exalted the "Holy Trinity" of conservative clericalism—"Fatherland, Family, and Religion."[35] He denied any personal ambition: "I do not present myself as a providential individual, a potential 'Fhurer' [*sic*], as a Hitler of shameful memory, but merely as the soldier and citizen who considers himself honoured by your confidence. Gentlemen: I am simply the standard-bearer of your iron will";[36] yet on several occasions he referred to himself as the "fearless" candidate and vaunted his military valor and virility. This is not intended to imply that Delgado's ideology was merely a self-contradictory assortment of disconnected items; on the contrary, it had an inner logic which subsumed all the particular discrete values to which he appealed. It is this unifying theme which is most typically populist.

Two overriding concerns dominated Delgado's speeches during and after the election campaign: unity (the unity of "the people" or of "all Portuguese"), and "independence" (or nonpartisanship). In his opening manifesto he proclaimed himself the "National Independent Candidate": "*Independent* and *apolitical* as he is well known to have been, the candidate, in keeping with his [professional] training, proposes *to rise above partisan movements and concerns* and place himself in a position to understand, support and advance the aspirations of the Portuguese people, regardless of the difference of opinion which may divide them. . . . "[37]

One of his most vigorous accusations against the regime was that it had divided the people of Portugal; his candidacy was intended to constitute a starting point "for the peaceful, orderly, and gradual solution of the burning contradictions which developed in Portugal a long time ago and which are causing more and more irreconcilable division among [*sic*] the hard-working Portuguese family."[38] Indeed, the preoccupation with unity was so emphatic that, while excoriating Salazar and the leading figures of the regime as corrupt, antipatriotic, short-sighted, and reactionary, Delgado appealed for the reconciliation of supporters of both the government and the opposition.

There are in the political sectors of the Democratic Opposition [men of] the most notable moral and spiritual value, whose exclusion has been harmful to the Nation, to its aggrandizement and prestige. There are also within the Situation [i. e., the regime], perhaps more discontented than they seem, good and worthy Portuguese whose sentiments and sincerity have not been corrupted by obscure and mean interests, nor by the orthodoxy of violence. In order to reconcile both groups, many Portuguese, moderates like myself, have joined together in search of an honourable and creative peace . . . [39]

The insistence on unity—on the reconciliation of all members of the nation or at least of all "honorable" members of the nation—is one of the classic themes of populism; and associated with it, the desire to rise above partisan divisions, to transcend "ideological squabbles," is also typical.

Delgado returned to the theme in another key campaign speech on May 18, 1958:

During the memorable and moving session in the Oporto Coliseum, our friend Rolão Preto asserted that monarchists, republicans and socialists, liberals and progressives, these are labels, which they pin on us. Our real family name is only one: PORTUGUESE! I address all of you as a Portuguese who is honoured by your confidence and your loud and stimulating support. I address you independent of ties of party, interest or belief; to all of you, like you a free and fearless man, I address these simple and heartfelt words.[40]

The appeal for unity and reconciliation was also an implied criticism of the different parties and factions of the opposition, condemned by Delgado for their internal divisions—divisions which his campaign, by the sheer force of the popular mobilization it generated, did succeed in overcoming temporarily. Before May 1958 the opposition had been hopelessly divided for almost ten years between right and left wings; this division was still present in the 1958 election and was reflected in the nomination of two opposition candidates. It was only toward the end of the campaign that, faced with Delgado's overwhelming success, the left agreed to withdraw its candidate, Dr. Arlindo Vicente, in Delgado's favor.[41] Unity was thus generated by the movement itself, and it was a unity which only a charismatic leader like Delgado could express, given the absence of any effective hegemonic force within the antifascist resistance. For that very reason, it was a fragile unity which would soon break up under conditions of demobilization or stagnation.

More than the programmatic content of Delgado's platform, it was the style and urgency of his discourse which evoked such instant popular response. Here was a man who spoke directly to the people without mincing his words ("sem papas na língua") and who cut through all the cant and mystification of official propaganda. I have already referred to his famous promise to dismiss Salazar ("Obviamente, demito-o"). Similarly, on several occasions during the campaign, he apostrophized the leading figures of the regime, calling on them in the name of the people to leave—"É tempo de saírem! Cansaram-nos! Cansaram-nos! Reformem-se! Vão-se embora!" ["It's time for you to leave! We are sick of you! We are sick of you! Retire! Get out!"].[42] He had nothing but scorn for the dictator Salazar: the nation was "anxious that the President of the Council should cease to sacrifice himself for its sake—if it is a sacrifice to exchange the life of a little-known Coimbra professor for that of master of a Nation whose virility he has destroyed. . . ."[43] The prime minister was an "obsolete disciple of Hitler and Mussolini . . . who never knew the pleasure, the joy of living and of communicating with the People. . . ."[44]

The symbolism of virility and of military valor was a constant in Delgado's discourse: Salazar was timid and misanthropic, and he lacked virility; the virility of the Portuguese people was denied by a regime which deprived them of their freedom; Delgado himself had proven his valor as a military officer, and in action in 1926; the Mocidade deprived young men of their manhood, branding them like cattle (a reference to the "S" on the belt buckle of their uniforms). This personal, emotional appeal to traditional sentiments of honor and manliness was accompanied by a strong moral tone, condemning the regime as treacherous, corrupt, and decadent. Salazar, Américo Tomás, and Santos Costa (the minister of defense) were not merely repressive and reactionary, they had betrayed their country and besmirched the reputation of its centuries-old culture; Delgado would restore national honor and dignity. "The moralization of public life," or the end of corruption (another classic populist refrain) was point number 3 in his electoral program.[45]

The Social Origins of the Delgado Movement

Delgado's style, program, and rhetoric were typically populist—almost paradigmatically so. But it is necessary to explain the origins of the movement that developed around his campaign, the reasons for the massive and spontaneous popular response to his appeal. What were the objective conditions in Portugal which created a need for a populist *caudilho*, or at least a situation favorable to his emergence?

To begin with, we can refer to history: Portugal was not lacking in precedents for a popular movement focusing on a providential leader. As we have seen, Delgado himself referred to the tradition of *Sebastianismo*, the myth of the boy king who would return to save his country. Mention should also be made of the succession of military commanders with Bonapartist ambitions, from the Duke of Saldanha to Sidónio País.[46] But such a pattern of personalistic leadership does not recur unless conditions remain favorable; and despite the sluggishness of Portuguese social and economic development, by the 1950s conditions had changed substantially in comparison with those of the nineteenth century or even the First Republic. Industrialization and urbanization had created a proletariat, and had also considerably strengthened the urban middle class. These were precisely the forces which were behind the emergence, during the 1940s, of the Portuguese Communist Party and of the Oposicão Democrática as organized movements with mass followings. The predominance of structured, disciplined parties with well-defined political programs is normally inimical to populist politics.

However, it should be emphasized that the development of structured mass parties was still incomplete in the 1950s (and later). Neither the liberal-bourgeois opposition nor the PCP had made much headway among the peasantry, apart from Communist strength among the agricultural laborers of the Alentejo, who were rural proletarians anyway. Also, the quickened pace of capitalist penetration in the countryside after World War II initiated an exodus from rural areas to Lisbon and Porto which had reached significant proportions by the late fifties. There existed, therefore, although on a smaller scale, a mass of recent rural-urban migrants of the type so often referred to in analyses of Latin American populism.[47] Finally, precisely at this stage when their presence was most needed, the main organized forces of the political opposition became dispersed or disoriented. In 1948 and 1949 most members of the liberal-bourgeois opposition lost their nerve and retreated into positions of conciliation with the regime, hoping to win voluntary concessions of democratic rights.[48] Then in 1956 the PCP abandoned its line of popular-democratic revolution and adopted the so-called "strategy of transition," consisting of campaigns to win the peaceful removal of Salazar and one or two of his ministers from power.[49]

When Delgado appeared on the scene, neither of the principal opposition forces was providing a lead in terms of practical antifascist struggle; instead, both were encouraging illusions about the benevolent character of the fascist state and the possibility of a negotiated transition to democracy. The virtue of Delgado was that, despite the ambiguity of his rhetoric about "unity" and "reconciliation," he had no such illusions: he was prepared to use force, and as a general in active service he inspired many people with the belief that he could stage an effective military action where others had failed. But it was not only a question of his military position: he also represented—and this was where his rhetoric and style were so important—the belief in the need for active struggle against the regime, and (although inadequately) the need for mass politics. His bold populist appeal, his desire for immediate results, and his refusal to contemplate defeat all spoke directly to the climate of popular frustration and disorientation arising from the existence of newly mobilized social groups, the general weakness of political organization, and the strategic failure of the organized antifascist opposition. The conjunction of Delgado's personal magnetism with the specific conditions of Portuguese society in the late fifties and carly sixties is well brought out in a recent work by Manuel Sertório, a lawyer and intimate collaborator of the general in his years of exile:

> It is true that, in the period of his candidacy for the Presidency of the Republic and immediately afterwards, Delgado, as a General in active service, was in an ideal situation to create the illusion of being able to bring about the rapid overthrow of the fascist regime by the sheer force of his action. And it is also true that later, in exile . . . the name of Humberto Delgado enjoyed once again the specific conditions to acquire, as indeed happened, a *mythological* dimension. . . .
>
> It is clear, however, that these phenomena would have been insufficient to allow Humberto Delgado to play the role that he did in Portuguese society. They had to be inserted, as was in fact the case, in a highly favourable set of circumstances, which included the real convergence under fascism of different class interests, the weakness of the Portuguese proletariat as a social class *for itself*, the virtual non-existence of organized political parties, the *ideology* of anti-fascism (which concealed the antagonistic contradictions, even under the fascist regime, of the class interests at stake), and the extreme weakness of proletarian theory in our country. . . .[50]

Although in my view Sertório exaggerates the weakness of the Portuguese proletariat as a class-conscious force, this is a convincing analysis of the general situation in which the Delgado phenomenon occurred. There was in many ways an ideal conjuncture for the emergence of a populist coalition: an unpopular and anachronistic regime, slow to adapt to the new demands of capital;[51] a large, subordinate mass, heterogeneous in its class composition; a growing but ill-focused popular discontent; and an ideological and organizational crisis within the working class. The problem was how to translate the populist whirlwind into effective action to overthrow the regime, and this Delgado, with the forces at his disposal, was incapable of doing.

Conclusion: From Delgado to Otelo

In the decade and a half following the explosion of 1958, the conditions which had given rise to that explosion only became more acute: the trend toward European integration and the development of the African liberation wars underlined the incapacity of the regime; accelerated capitalist development in Portugal itself intensified the crisis of the peasant economy and the flood of out-migration from the rural areas, both to the cities and abroad; political mobilization and contestation became increasingly widespread among workers, students, and many petite bourgeois factions; and the slow and painful gestation of new forces on the left only partially overcame the weakness of proletarian political leadership. When the regime fell in 1974, therefore, all of the conditions were present for a repetition of the populist phenomenon of 1958, although in modified form; the only important contrary factor would be the growth during the succeeding months, under the new regime of political liberty, of a multiplicity of organized parties. By 1975 the strength of the parties was indeed one of the factors preventing the victory of the new populism; it did not, however, prevent this populism from having a major impact on the political scene.

First of all, there was the attempted populism of the right personified by Spínola, with his "silent majority" maneuver in September 1974; not surprisingly, given the very recent demise of a dictatorship of the right, this was a pathetic failure. More important, and much more successful in the short run, was the populism of the left of the MFA, particularly in the spring and summer of 1975. Defining itself as "the Liberation Movement of the Portuguese People," the MFA attempted to institutionalize a classic left-populist project. Even the most cursory perusal of the "Documento-Guía para a Aliança Povo–MFA" or the "Plano de Acção Política"[52] reveals the characteristic features: stress on popular unity and on independence from partisan ties, the appeal to a multi-class, heterogeneous mass following, the belief in the efficacy of direct action. But apart from this attempt at populist institutionalization, individual figures within the MFA came to assume a leadership role; the obvious examples are Vasco Gonçalves and Otelo Saraiva de

Carvalho. Vasco Gonçalves failed above all because he lost that most crucial asset of populist leaders, their "independent," non-party status. Becoming identified in practice if not in theory with the line of the PCP, he finally polarized against himself all except this party's regular clientele. Other MFA leaders also played a populist role. Rosa Coutinho, for example, with his jovial, nonchalant manner and distinctive appearance, admired by some and hated by others for his role as high commissioner in Angola,[53] gained notoriety by his off-the-cuff statements in favor of direct democracy and non-party government.

The most successful populist hero, however, was of course Otelo, whose prestige as operational commander of April 25 was reinforced by his transparent honesty and sincere identification with the most oppressed groups in Portuguese society. Otelo's presidential campaign in 1976, although occurring when the peak of the revolutionary crisis had passed, was the purest expression of radical populism anywhere in Europe in the contemporary era. Transcending political divisions among the parties and groups of the revolutionary left, radicalizing popular antagonisms against the state apparatus, and mobilizing a mass popular movement without the support of any of the major organized parties (indeed, faced with their unanimous hostility), his success in polling more than 16 percent of the popular vote was a vivid demonstration of the continuing strength of the populist tendency in Portugal. Had the campaign continued for a few more weeks, and had Otelo enjoyed greater freedom of action, there is no telling how far this movement might have gone. Like Delgado in 1958, Otelo achieved the remarkable feat of winning a large section of the regular supporters of the PCP away from their normal allegiance; it is estimated that about half his total vote came from this source.[54] The potential significance of this achievement can hardly be overstated, since any realignment on the left must involve some breach in the PCP's hegemony over the labor movement—a hegemony which is based on long traditions of militancy and loyalty. Otelo achieved, momentarily at least, what none of the other parties and groups of the radical left had come near to achieving: the winning of a major fraction of the labor movement to a frankly revolutionary perspective. This fact alone is the clearest demonstration of the importance of radical populism in Portugal.

Both Delgado and Otelo (or, in a more general sense, the leadership of the MFA) displayed the typical political behavior associated with populist movements. Both were dynamic, were successful in mass mobilization, and tended to bypass organized political parties; both drew their support from a wide spectrum of classes and groups. Both exhibited the characteristic tendency to radicalize under pressure:

Delgado's rhetoric became more violent by the day as the election campaign proceeded, and later, in exile, he became a partisan of Castro-type guerrilla actions aimed at overthrowing Salazar. Ideologically, Delgado moved from pro-American liberalism to collaboration with the PCP, and from colonialist chauvinism to support for African independence.[55] As for Otelo, his rapid evolution from naive democrat to champion of the revolutionary left is well known. His ideological radicalization went much further than that of Delgado because of his different personal background and the very different political situation in which he operated, but the pattern is essentially the same. In both cases, charismatic leadership coupled with a dynamic of increasing radicalization was able to achieve what established parties and organizations proved incapable of doing, and it is this ability to transcend institutional limitations which is most characteristic of radical populism.

The populist tendency has clearly not disappeared from Portuguese politics, and given the inconclusive character of the resolution of the revolutionary crisis in 1975, it could easily re-emerge to dominate the political scene. To the extent that new forces on the left succeed in channeling popular energies in a radically different way, this latent populism will subside; but any such change is bound to be slow and difficult. A populism of the right could also emerge if the left fails to capitalize on popular discontent, and if the existing state of confusion and division among the parties of the right persists. Mário Soares warned in 1979 of the danger of a new *sidonismo;*[56] and indeed, in the 1981 presidential election the coalescence of the right around General Soares Carneiro, a man widely regarded as an unreconstructed partisan of Salazar, seemed to confirm this prognosis. In the same election Otelo's vote collapsed to a mere 1½ percent, which suggests that left populism has subsided for the time being. But populism is by nature a volatile and unstable phenomenon, and it would be a rash observer who would predict that it will not recur in Portugal in the medium term. In this writer's opinion, the only thing which could prevent it would be the emergence of a new hegemonic force within the working class and popular movement.

Notes

1 See, for example, Ghiţa Ionescu and Ernest Gellner, eds., *Populism: Its Meaning and National Characteristics* (London, 1969); Ernesto Laclau, *Politics and Ideology in Marxist Theory* (London, 1977); Nicos Mouzelis, "Ideology and Class Politics: A Critique of Ernesto Laclau," *New Left Review,* no. 112 (Nov.–Dec. 1978), pp. 45–61.

2 Examples of the liberal approach are David Apter, *The Politics of Modernization* (London, 1969); Gino Germani, *Política y sociedad en una época de transición* (Buenos Aires, 1965); Kenneth Minogue, "Populism as a Political Movement," in Ionescu and Gellner, eds., *Populism*, pp. 197–211.

3 This approach is derived essentially from Marx's treatment of Bonapartism in *The Eighteenth Brumaire of Louis Bonaparte*. Also relevant is Gramsci's treatment of "Cæsarism"; see Quintin Hoare and G. Nowell Smith, eds., *Selections from the Prison Notebooks of António Gramsci* (London, 1971), pp. 210–226.

4 Laclau, *Politics and Ideology*, pp. 194–198.

5 Ibid., p. 173

6 This point is well made in the article by Mouzelis, "Ideology and Class Politics," although I believe the critique needs to be developed even further in view of the startling implications of Laclau's theory.

7 For a good study of Castroism as radical populism, see Nelson P. Valdés, *Ideological Roots of the Cuban Revolutionary Movement*, University of Glasgow Institute of Latin American Studies, Occasional Papers, no. 15 (Glasgow, 1975). It should be emphasized, as Valdés observes, that radical populism does not in and of itself lead to socialism.

8 In his *Memoirs*, Delgado boasted of how in 1926 he personally sought out a sergeant who had wounded him during a minor revolt the previous year, and gave him a beating-up. He mentions several other instances that illustrate his vanity and short temper (Humberto da Silva Delgado, *The Memoirs of General Delgado* [London, 1964], pp. 44–45).

9 Humberto Delgado, *A Marcha para as Índias*, a historical play in two acts broadcast on July 8, 1940, by the Emissora Nacional, on the 443d anniversary of Vasco da Gama's first departure for India; 2d ed. published by the magazine *Defesa Nacional* (Lisbon, 1954). Also, Humberto Delgado, *28 de Maio*, a play in three acts broadcast on May 28, 1939, by Rádio Club Português, Parede, Portugal; published by Casa Portuguesa (Lisbon, 1939). Most notorious was Delgado's book *Da Pulhice do "Homo Sapiens"* (Lisbon, 1933), a scurrilous attack on leading republican politicians.

10 Interview with Delgado in the Lisbon newspaper *República*, May 10, 1958.

11 "Elementos biográficos do Sr. General Humberto Delgado," in Victor Dimas, *Humberto Delgado—o homem e três épocas* (Lisbon, 1977) pp. 11–13.

12 Delgado helped to negotiate the secret agreement with Britain for the use of the Azores bases during the Second World War. From 1947 to 1950 he was Portuguese representative with the International Civil Aviation Organization in Montreal, and from 1952 to 1957 he was military attaché in Washington. See Dimas, *Humberto Delgado*, pp. 11–13, and Delgado's *Memoirs*.

13 The original impetus for Delgado's candidacy apparently came from Henrique Galvão. See Dimas, *Humberto Delgado*, pp. 179–181.
14 *República*, May 10, 1958.
15 *República*, May 10, 1958.
16 See reports in the Lisbon newspapers *República, O Século*, and *Diário Ilustrado* for May 15, 1958; Dimas, *Humberto Delgado*, p. 232 (photograph); and Delgado, *Memoirs*, pp. 105–106.
17 *Diário Ilustrado* and *O Século*, May 17, 1958.
18 Communique from Delgado's campaign headquarters, from an article cut by the censor from *O Século*, May 18, 1958, in *O Século* archive, Lisbon.
19 Mário Soares, *Portugal Amordaçado* (Lisbon, 1974), pp. 205–207.
20 See Delgado's famous letter to the Four Generals, July 27, 1958, in Delgado, *Memoirs*, pp. 131–141.
21 There were, in fact, spontaneous strikes and demonstrations of protest in the industrial belt around Lisbon; see the Communist party's clandestine newspaper *Avante!* nos. 257 (June 16–30, 1958), 258 (July 1–15, 1958).
22 On Delgado's murder, see Manuel García and Lourdes Maurício, *O Caso Delgado* (Lisbon, 1977); Pedro Ramos de Almeida, *O Assassínio do General Humberto Delgado* (Lisbon, 1978); and Valério Ochetto, *Em Prol da Verdade* (Lisbon, 1978).
23 Delgado, *Memoirs*, pp. 113, 131–141, 162.
24 Manuel Sertório, *Humberto Delgado: 70 Cartas Inéditas (A Luta contra o Fascismo no Exílio)* (Lisbon, 1970), pp. 53–54.
25 However, according to some reports Delgado's participation in the *Santa Maria* episode was minimal. See Soares, *Portugal Amordaçado* p. 296; Delgado, *Memoirs*, pp. 186–199.
26 Soares, *Portugal Amordaçado*, and Delgado, *Memoirs*.
27 Author's interview with Dr. Fernando Piteira Santos, Feb. 28, 1977, Lisbon.
28 Alvaro Cunhal, *Relatório da Actividade do Comité Central ao VI Congresso do PCP* (Lisbon, 1975), pp. 134–136; Sertório, *70 Cartas*, pp. 48–53.
29 Soares, *Portugal Amordaçado*, p. 260. All translations in this chapter are the author's, unless otherwise indicated.
30 *República*, June 3, 1958; *O Século*, June 2 and 3, 1958.
31 Delgado, *Memoirs*, pp. 222–223.
32 Author's interview with Dr. Fernando Piteira Santos, Feb. 28, 1977, Lisbon.
33 Author's interview with Dr. Manuel Sertório, April 1977, Lisbon.
34 From the beginning Delgado exhibited admiration for "Anglo-Saxon" or "Nordic" virtues. Thus in his 1933 book, *Da Pulhice do "Homo Sapiens,"* Delgado ridiculed verbose Portuguese republicans and compared them with English statesmen, who were monarchists and yet "much more liberal, democratic and *honourable*, which is the *main thing*. . . ." (pp. 242–243; Delgado's emphasis). In a newspaper article in the *Diário de*

Notícias Nov. 23, 1943, he praised English women for their contribution to the war effort, which might serve as an example for the "weeping peoples" (*povos-chorões*) like the Portuguese. Similar references can be found in his later writings.

35 *Proclamação do General Humberto Delgado, Candidato à Presidência da República*, published by the Porto Campaign Committee (Porto, 1958), p. 20.

36 Delgado's speech in Porto, reported in *República*, May 15, 1958.

37 *Proclamação*, p. 19; emphasis is the author's.

38 *Proclamação*, p. 15.

39 *Proclamação*, p. 23.

40 Dimas, *Humberto Delgado*, pp. 184–185, n. 15.

41 The unification of the two candidacies took place through the so-called "Cacilhas Pact"; see *República*, May 30 and 31, 1958.

42 Delgado's speech in Porto, reported in *República*, May 15, 1958); and his speech in the Liceu Camões, Lisbon, quoted in Dimas, *Humberto Delgado*, pp. 184–194, note 15.

43 Interview with Delgado in *Diário Ilustrado*, May 10, 1958.

44 Speech in Liceu Camões, in Dimas, *Humberto Delgado*, pp. 184–194, note 15.

45 *Proclamação*, p. 26. See also his speech in Porto, in *República*, May 15, 1958.

46 The Duke of Saldanha: liberal *caudilho* of the mid-nineteenth century. Sidónio País: military president, December 1917 to December 1918. See A. H. de Oliveira Marques, *Historia de Portugal* (Lisbon, 1976), pp. 94–103, 273–276.

47 Germani, *Política y sociedad*; Torcuato di Tella, "Populism and Reform in Latin America," in Claudio Véliz, ed., *Obstacles to Change in Latin America* (London, 1970), pp. 47–74; Octávio Ianni, *La formación del estado populista en América Latina* (Mexico City, 1975).

48 A detailed discussion of this subject is found in José Silva, *Memórias de um Operário* 2 (Porto, 1971).

49 Alvaro Cunhal [Duarte], *O Desvio de Direita no Partido Comunista Português* (clandestine pamphlet, 1961); [Francisco Martins Rodrigues?] *Elementos para a História do Movimento Operário e do Partido Comunista em Portugal* (Lisbon, n.d.), pp. 52–60.

50 Sertório, *70 Cartas*, pp. 13–14; emphases in the original.

51 This factor, which cannot be analyzed in detail here, was fundamental: by the 1950s the Estado Novo was not only repressive and unpopular, it was also revealing its incapacity to reconcile the needs of small and medium capital with the increased domination of the monopoly sector. See Francisco Rafael, Jorge B. Preto, et al., *Portugal: Capitalismo e Estado Novo* (Porto, 1976).

52 The documents are available in José Pedro Gonçalves, ed., *Dossier 2a. República* 2 (Lisbon, 1977), pp. 748–758, 773–780.

53 For an unfavorable view of Rosa Coutinho, see Douglas Porch, *The Portuguese Armed Forces and the Revolution* (London and Stanford, 1977), pp. 116–119.

54 On Otelo's campaign, see António Tavares Teles, *Otelo* (Lisbon, 1976); and [Otelo Saraiva da Carvalho], *Otelo: O Povo É Quem Mais Ordena* (Lisbon, 1977), a collection of Otelo's campaign speeches.

55 On Delgado's ideological evolution, see Sertório, *70 Cartas*, pp. 40–45.

56 *O Jornal* (Lisbon), Mar. 15, 1979. By a new *Sidonismo* Soares presumably means authoritarian rule by a charismatic, right-wing military leader.

4 *Tom Gallagher*

From Hegemony to Opposition: The Ultra Right before and after 1974

Over the past 150 years governments in Lisbon have tended to be less conservative than their equivalents elsewhere in Europe, although Portugal experienced Europe's longest noncommunist authoritarian regime during the second and third quarters of the twentieth century. During the greater part of the nineteenth century Portugal witnessed a long liberal ascendancy, which survived into the interwar years of the twentieth century. Perhaps the seminal event determining the course of domestic politics during this era was the 1832–1834 civil war waged between absolutist and liberal elite groups.[1] Victory could have gone either way, so finely balanced were the competing forces. Ultimately, the advance of liberalism elsewhere in Europe during the early 1830s may have just tipped the balance against the traditionalist *miguelistas*.[2]

Seen in retrospect, this progressive victory is perhaps the most striking breakthrough that forces to the left of the classical right have engineered to date in Portugal—the revolutions of 1910 and 1974 not excepted.[3] For the next three generations, the Portuguese right would find itself in a position of weakness, isolation, and general marginality: the power of the church, the aristocracy, and the absolutist monarchy was being fundamentally curtailed, and the time had not arrived when the professional military, the middle class, and other cornerstones of the newer liberal elite would begin to adopt a counterrevolutionary perspective. In 1910, it was perhaps largely a result of the weakness of the Portuguese right that republicanism was able to triumph with such apparent ease. Lacking resources and influential group commitment to its cause after long years in the political wilderness, the doctrinaire right was in no position to forestall this last, and at first glance most spectacular, "radical-jacobin" upheaval.[4] If there had been a strong reactionary lobby in politics before 1910 it is debatable whether the republicans could have engineered such a painless succession on or after October 5; conceivably, political polarization along monarchist-republican, left-right, or civil-military lines could have led to confrontation and perhaps to a situation of the kind that existed in Spain before 1936, or to a modified, twentieth century version of the 1832–1834 conflict.

However remote the possibility may have appeared in 1910, republican politicians were determined to prevent the restoration of the old order. The first year of the Republic witnessed the creation of a multiparty democracy. Yet right-wing traditionalists refused to get involved in electoral politics for the greater part of the 16-year Republic's lifetime. Their preference for abstention can be explained in several ways. First of all, anti-republicans were most reluctant, for a long while after 1910, to recognize nonmonarchist institutions. Second, the active arch-conservative constituency was a narrow one through at least the initial third of the parliamentary Republic. In 1910 traditionally conservative sectors, such as the business world and the landed classes, had not been noticeably alarmed by the advent of the Republic.[5] Until republican failures began to socialize these elements in an authoritarian direction, the traditional right could only derive ongoing support from the *haute bourgeoisie*, lay Catholic elements in the middle class, the clergy, and the most patrician elements in the military. Later the Portuguese right's national constituency would be substantially broadened by middle-class defectors disillusioned with the Democratic party, which was the main political force between 1911 and 1926. The stranglehold this party of the center maintained on elections effectively prevented the rise of a reform movement on either the right or the left of the political scene. Instead, lonely *ultras* on the far right employed force to subvert the post-1910 status quo, but with little tangible success.

It was a coalition of conservative republican officers and opposition republican parties that eventually mounted the first successful uprising against an incumbent Republican administration.[6] These moderate right-wingers always posed a greater danger to constitutional republican government than the monarchists or members of the *integralista* movement—the first real manifestation of the radical right in Portugal.[7] Integralism was always an extremely diffuse political creed, perhaps best summed up by what it opposed: liberalism, individualism, socialism, and any doctrine thought to deny religion, the family, and traditional values. It had only one theorist of note—António Sardinha (1889–1925)—and even when he was alive the right-wing jacobins who made up the integralist movement were particularly dependent on political ideas emanating from the French right.

Late in 1917 Major Sidónio País (1872–1918), an increasingly conservative republican leader, seized power at the head of a right-wing, civil-military alliance. The brief duration of his rule has helped to obscure the fact that the *Sidonista* regime was Europe's first twentieth century republican dictatorship. Sidónio País, like Napoleon III, can be characterized as a political dictator somewhat ahead of his time. In 1918, Portugal briefly acquired the military *caudilho* for whom a replacement would be so difficult to find eight years later.

Lisbon became during the brief *Sidonista* period a laboratory for the kind of politics that would follow after 1926. Right-wingers of various hues collaborated in government and worked to prevent a doctrinaire republican recovery. Had the *Sidonista* experiment endured for a longer period, it could conceivably have encouraged the rise of a strong right-wing party with a personalist, Luso-fascist, traditional Catholic, or nationalist perspective. But it did not endure, and even now, following 48 years of dictatorship, Portugal has yet to witness the emergence of a major party based on any of these political precepts. Until comparatively recently, interest groups such as business and the professions and institutions such as the church and the military were able to dominate the Portuguese right. Any chance the *Sidonista* regime had of being the seedbed for a secular party of the right, of the type that was shortly to become a feature of politics elsewhere in the Hispanic and Mediterranean world, was destroyed by conflict within the right-wing camp.

The monarchist question continued to divide traditionalists, exacerbating tensions which in 1918 led to the collapse of the *Sidonista* dictatorship. This issue produced a cleavage in the right-wing camp that lasted throughout the greater part of the parliamentary Republic, and it undoubtedly helps to explain why the storm-tossed Republican regime was able to last as long as it did. Eventually, during the 1920s, a serious rethinking of tactics seems to have led to the conclusion that dogged adherence to the monarchy was hampering the anti-liberal cause by making it too particularist. Thereafter many doctrinaire rightists quietly abandoned monarchist restoration as a public objective. This move made the traditional right acceptable to many middle-class urban elements who were foresaking liberal political values out of political frustration, or as a result of a decline in their living standards.

The monarchist bogey also provided the military with an excuse for defending beleaguered republican ministries.[8] By emphasizing less contentious issues, right-wing activists were able to clear the ground for a counterrevolutionary movement that enjoyed massive army support.

The 1926 Revolution and its Consequences

Like Portugal's two other modern political watersheds, the revolutions of 1910 and 1974, the 1926 revolution was a relatively bloodless armed revolt which triumphed over little or no opposition, thanks to the existence of a political vacuum at the heart of the state. For the second time in Portugal, a broad-based coalition transcending ideology, social class, and previous political allegiances carried out the initial seizure of power. However, one political tendency was destined to supplant the rest: in 1926 it was the authoritarian right that emerged triumphant, and Portugal fell to an undemocratic regime far more oppressive than anything this Iberian state had experienced in modern times.

A *ditadura militar* (military dictatorship) marked the first stage in the authoritarian process.[9] Yet for Portugal, where pretorianism has been a traditional vice, military rule was then as it is now a relatively uncommon form of government. Indeed, if one were to compare a typology of Portuguese government with a typology of government in Spain or in some of the Latin American states one would find that despite the military preponderance in nineteenth- and twentieth-century Portuguese politics, no military figure has yet to enjoy a successful period of extended governmental tenure in Lisbon. Portugal's three major dictators of the past 250 years, Pombal, Salazar, and Caetano, have each been civilians. As an institution the Portuguese military has evidently lacked the determination to exercise power in its own right, independent of civilian political forces. Usually soldiers in government have ruled on a caretaker basis, often in collaboration with civilian helpers. This pattern would assert itself again after 1926.

At no point was the *ditadura militar* exclusively military, even though politically-minded officers were deeply hostile to civilian rule per se during the 1920s.[10] Possessed of a strong corporate identity, the Portuguese military then as later tended to mirror and be influenced by prevailing civilian political attitudes. During the predominantly military phase of the 48-year dictatorship, ruling officers created no new political structures. Non-party rule, the authoritarian creed, and a written constitution would have to await the full civilianization of the *ditadura*.

Perhaps the most interesting feature of the *ditadura militar* was the ascendancy that junior-ranking officers briefly exercised over President Óscar Carmona and his government. In 1926 and 1927, according to one distinguished source,[11] *integralista* officers were able to determine the composition of the cabinet and the timing of government reshuffles—a state of affairs described as "barracks-room parliamentarism" by António Sérgio.[12] George Guyomard, the author of the only full-length contemporary study of the *ditadura militar*, also talks of the "Lieutenants Soviets" of this period.[13] However, their marked inability to set out politically defined aims doomed the military young turks to a transitory political role. Although many were self-styled integralists, few of the younger military activists appear to have treated integralism as a serious political doctrine that could have provided the ideological basis of a new authoritarian state. Instead, the inability of politicized officers to offer a coherent alternative to democracy, in tandem with the triumph of extremist views within the military establishment, facilitated the emergence of an authoritarian polity dominated by civilians.

It is generally acknowledged that Dr. António de Oliveira Salazar's appointment as minister of finance in 1928 was the main stage in the demilitarization of the regime. However, one could take issue with the commonly held view that the professor from Coimbra was a *deus ex machina* who emerged from nowhere to rescue the Portuguese nation at one of its most difficult moments. As well as being one of the best-known Portuguese economists of his day, Salazar was already a leading figure of the Portuguese right by 1928. The competition was hardly fierce: until the closing years of liberalism, doctrinaire rightists had refused to take part in normal political life and were loathe to organize orthodox parties. Accordingly, the reactionary right had produced few, if any, nationally known personalities able to rival Portugal's future prime minister. Salazar did not have to eclipse any Portuguese figures of the stature of Spain's Calvo Sotelo or Gil Robles. Nevertheless, in his attempt to create a personalist autocracy (and the writer believes that he did not just drift into this situation), the Portuguese leader faced bitter opposition from certain quarters on the right.

As the finance minister's preference for a traditionalist regime of order and hierarchy became increasingly apparent in the 1930s, discontent grew in radical sectors. For integralists and fascists the União Nacional, an official movement staffed from the outset by loyal Salazarist retainers, offered few allurements.[14] More to their taste was the "blueshirt" movement that emerged in 1932 under the leadership of Francisco Rolão Preto (1893–1977), one of the founders of Portuguese integralism. "National syndicalism" was the movement's alternative title, and it derived much of its program from its near-namesake in Germany.

However, national syndicalism emerged after the political succession had been worked out, probably to the satisfaction of most Portuguese rightists. Salazar's financial measures and the decisive defeat of the progressive republican left enabled him to amass strong support for his new political structures from within the spectrum presented by Portuguese right-wing politics.[15] A reactionary and nonrevolutionary brand of ultraconservatism was in the ascendant. Traditional authoritarianism had won out over more radical and secular brands. The lower middle class, which to a certain degree provided the focal point of Preto's support, was not collectively in the mood for revolutionary adventure; the chaos of the republican era was too fresh in bourgeois minds. Order came to be preferred to political experimentation, for years of disorder had blunted the social radicalism of petit bourgeois groups—at least for the time being.

The political ascendancy that Salazar and his supporters acquired in the early years of the counterrevolution enabled them to subordinate other right-wing groups that did not owe their existence to the New State.[16] Salazar's own "party" affiliation, the Academic Center for Christian Democracy (CADC), along with the integralist movement, the Liberal Republican Union, the Union of Economic Interests (UIE), and the blueshirts were dissolved in the early 1930s.[17] The abrupt manner in which Salazar sought to decapitate rival poles of right-wing authority angered some conservatives. As a result, Francisco Cunha Leal (1888–1970), the Liberal Republican *chefe*, re-entered the republican family. But on the whole the creation of a monopoly on the Portuguese right was treated with relative equanimity by disinvested conservatives. Quite a large number were co-opted into Salazarist cabinets.

Another route of vertical mobility was provided by quasi-political state organizations such as the União Nacional, the Mocidade Portuguesa, the Legião Portuguesa, and the Secretariado Nacional de Informação; these were structures specifically created to channel support for the regime and to execute other rudimentary political tasks.[18] Without exception, they were weak organizations which atrophied as time elapsed. None were allowed to develop any independent traits. Beyond the confines of the cabinet and the government bureaucracy, conservative political influence was reflected in such major national institutions as the military, the church, the business world, the security apparatus, and corporatist structures. Given the absence of strong rightist parties, most of these institutions acted as conservative, anti-radical strongholds. This was true above all of the corporatist structures. Created in the early years of the New State, these sprawling bureaucratic agencies enrolled many of the middle- and lower-ranking counterrevolutionary activists who had emerged in Portugal before and after 1926. Their time and energy was channeled into building a largely fictitious corporate state in which labor, capital, and the state supposedly worked in harmony for the benefit of producers, consumers, and the nation. With the passage of time, honest right-wingers came to view this image of interclass solidarity as a sham which did not bear any relation to social and economic conditions as they really existed in Salazar's Portugal. However, during the 1930s many sectors of the Portuguese right (except the business world) greeted the emerging corporatist edifice as a great experiment in social engineering. Its luster diverted attention from more overtly political issues for a long period and, accordingly, helped to stabilize the New State regime in its formative stages.

Radical right-wingers would have been appeased by the fact that the regime used much of the integralist vocabulary in formulating its corporatist program. Salazar's realization of the threadbare quality of Catholic conservative propaganda, in a country whose secular traditions stretched back to the mid-eighteenth century and the Marquês de Pombal, may have prompted him to espouse the institutional hallmarks and messianic rhetoric of corporatism. By latching on to what was then a still-novel political creed, the Portuguese leader was able to forge a clear identity for his political system during its formative years. Corporatism made the New State appear as different as possible from the pre-1926 regime. More important, it enabled Salazar to argue that he was not just a pocket-sized emulator of Hitler. Until the veneer began to crack after World War II, his governing system was able to acquire the reputation of being a significant political innovation and not just another offbeat Latin *régime personnel.*[19] Above all, Salazar was able to make use of the social justice aspects of corporatism to cloak anti-working class economic measures in idealistic garb.

Ultimately the two primary elements that corporatists often claimed to be the basis of their political philosophy were absent from the Portuguese scene. Decisional authority was not devolved to self-governing corporations; nor was there created "a natural organic harmony" based on voluntary mutual consent between capital and labor.[20] Several factors may have caused Salazar to be outwardly loyal to the style of corporatism while surreptitiously foresaking its substance. Quite plausibly, Salazar may have feared a reduction in his own authority if an inordinate amount of power was devolved to "unknown institutions."[21] It could also be argued that he was afraid that unbridled corporatism might throw the national economy into a state of dangerous flux. Perhaps the systematic propagation of corporatism never occurred in Portugal because the traditionalist nature of society made a developed right-wing ideology unnecessary. Portugal had experienced neither reformation nor industrial revolution, and no major parties of the left emerged until the 1970s. With more than half of the population illiterate in 1930, traditional society had remained substantially intact in Portugal, unlike Italy and Germany, where the social and political order had largely broken down before the emergence of fascism and nazism.

Salazar's regime of traditional order and hierarchy gave the wealthier classes unbounded opportunities for exploitation and enrichment. This state of affairs effectively dampened intra-elite unrest for a relatively long historical period.[22] However, as the dictator-premier aged and the New State became an increasingly centralized one-man autocracy, opposition to his rule developed within the right-wing power structure. Admiral Manuel Quintão Meireles, Captain Herique Galvão (1895–1970), General Humberto da Silva Delgado (1906–1965), Colonel (later General) Francisco da Costa Gomes (b. 1914), General Júlio Botelho Moniz (1900–1970), Marshal Óscar Carmona (1869–1951), and Marshal Higínio Craveiro Lopes (1894–1964) were the main New State luminaries who either became lapsed *situacionistas*[23] or turned into active opponents of the *ditadura* in the 15-year period between 1946 and 1961.[24] The one loyalist institution from which the important oppositionists emerged was the military. Significantly, very few civilian cabinet ministers appear to have defected to the opposition camp during Salazar's twilight years, or indeed at any point in the post-1933 period.[25]

Some of the more cautious rebels would have preferred to replace the New State with a façade of democracy, or with a strong presidential state along the lines of Gaullist France. However, pluralism remained anathema to Salazar, even after the fall of European fascism. To liberalize the country was at best to suffer the return of squabbling politicians or, at worst, to allow communists to slip in. Nevertheless, civilian opposition remained weak in Portugal, and it became increasingly apparent that the regime had more to fear from supposed supporters within the power structure than from manifest opponents outside. The most daunting threats to the regime's existence during its 48-year history emanated from within the state's apparatus.[26]

If Salazar had not made dependence upon a single individual such a key feature of the regime that regime might have developed more flexibility and cohesion. A less insular ruler might have drawn lessons from a state such as Mexico, where an authoritarian, depersonalized polity has derived enormous long-range benefit by subsuming political individualism within a collective bureaucratic framework. However, by the 1950s the New State under Salazar was already demonstrating a singular incapacity for making rational long-term policy decisions.

In 1961 the aging dictator was almost overthrown in a revolt planned by a group of officers that included almost the whole top echelon of Portugal's defense staff. Salazar's intransigence over Portuguese Africa, and military fears that the army would be unable to control a deteriorating situation in Angola, were important factors that lay behind the plotting. The regime actually faced more opposition from senior officers in the spring of 1961 than it did 13 years later. However, overconfidence, last-minute timidity, and failure to estimate Salazar's resolve to stay in power combined to defeat the conspirators. They belonged to a politically active military organism that had not produced a successful coup in 35 years.

Gradual realization that war in Africa was not going to lead to imminent catastrophe on the Congolese model further weakened the resolve of groups opposed to the regime. No modernization of political life occurred, even when Salazar delegated increasing power to much younger men. After his retirement in 1968, Portugal remained an immobile still polity.

The Caetano years have not yet been thoroughly explored, and the failure of the new prime minister to liberalize the regime still remains a puzzle to some. Several factors helped to ensure that there would be no major break with the past: the underground strength of the Portuguese Communist Party (PCP) and the absence of strong moderate opposition foci; the manner of Salazar's departure in 1968, which was far more precipitate than Franco's; the ultra rightist fear that collapse in Africa would be a corollary of liberalization in the metropolis; and the slow pace of societal change, which was not accompanied by the rise of liberal technocratic groups such as those that were emerging in Spain.[27] Beyond a few cosmetic measures, no major steps were taken to democratize Portugal. Most elements in the regime did not think that the right could remain intact in a post-authoritarian state, let alone hold on to power in an alliance with centrists, as had happened in post–1976 Spain. Under Caetano politics remained taboo. The Popular National

Action and SEDES[28] were essentially stillborn agencies that failed to make an impact on political life in the early 1970s. By then Salazarism without Salazar had become an increasingly impossible undertaking; Salazarism had been difficult enough to sustain during the dictator's twilight years.

The Old Right Disinherited

Following the *golpe de estado*[29] of April 25, 1974, the institutions from which the right derived its strength were either revamped (the military, the business world) or dismantled (the state corporations, the Legião Portuguesa, the PIDE).[30] Deprived overnight of much institutional backing, archconservatives were forced to rebuild their shattered movement from scratch. Some of the first parties to be formed in the wake of the dictatorship's collapse were those of the ultra right: the Liberal Party, the Progress Party, and the Portuguese Nationalist Party (the last dedicated to "renewing the struggle interrupted by April 25").[31]

During the summer of 1974, few people were aware that Portugal would shortly be traveling down the path of social revolution, perhaps further than any other Western European country has gone in the last 100 years. Uncertain about their own strength, the architects of the coup, the Armed Forces Movement (MFA), had agreed to a relatively conservative high officer becoming postdictatorial Portugal's first head of state. General António Ribeiro de Spínola (b. 1910), with his goal of a strong presidential democracy,[32] may have represented for much of the right their one remaining hope that something of traditional Portugal could be salvaged from the wreckage of the old order. However, by October 1974 General Spínola was no longer president of Portugal. His appeal for help from the *maioria silenciosa*—silent majority—evoked a much more lukewarm response for him in 1974 than it would for others in 1975. Unreconstructed right-wingers were unable to agree among themselves, for blame was still being apportioned for the collapse of the *ditadura*. Shortly afterward, ultra-conservative parties were banned by the radical military authorities and their leaders placed in custody.

By late 1974, the genuine right had shrunk to a handful of parties. Some, like the Portuguese Monarchists, tried to swim with the left-wing tide by calling for "communes with a king," but a Portuguese Sihanouk had not yet appeared on the horizon. Francisco Sá Carneiro (1934–1980), the leader of the Popular Democratic Party (PSD/PPD)[33] also used extravagant left-wing language in 1974–1975. His party—based on the church, small landowning members of the peasantry, and the urban middle class—has been compared with the Mouvement Republicain Populaire, originally a liberal Catholic force that emerged in France during the last days of the Vichy regime, and which later drifted so far to the right that its leaders even backed the French settlers in Algeria against De Gaulle.[34] Since 1975, the PSD/PPD has moved steadily rightwards; by the late 1970s some observers were describing the party as the most right-wing force with parliamentary representation in Portugal. Previously this accolade had been reserved for the Social Democratic Center (CDS), "a potent alliance of high intellectuals and Catholic squirearchy"[35] deriving support from the conservative, Catholic Opus Dei and (before March 1975) from the leading monopolies. Branded by the left as a refuge for former fascists, the CDS only narrowly escaped being proscribed in 1974–1975. Latifundists, bankers, and industrialists—three of its key support groups—fell victim to the revolution during or after March 1975.

Catholic northern Portugal, the most tradition-minded area of the country, was left untouched by much of the ferment. Most of the revolutionary action was confined to Lisbon, Porto, and the south. On the first anniversary of the 1974 coup an opportunity to gauge the national mood was provided by elections for the constituent assembly. The results revealed that 48 years of authoritarian rule had produced one of the most radical electorates in Western Europe, with almost 60 percent of the total vote going to parties espousing different shades of Marxian leftism. Perhaps just as significantly, the elections demonstrated a strong antipathy to authoritarian political solutions, with the rhetorically Marxist Socialist Party (PS) receiving three times as many seats as the Portuguese Communist Party.

Re-emergence of the right after April 1974 first took the form of separatism. For the greater part of 1975, the threat to political pluralism appeared to come mainly from the militant left, especially from the PCP. The first organized resistance to the encroachments of this party flared up on the Atlantic islands during June 1975.[36] A full month before law and order began to deteriorate on the mainland, major anticommunist agitation was reported from the Azores and Madeira, and rioting and bombing continued on the islands long after violence in the rural areas of the metropolis had subsided. The Atlantic islands were witnessing the first strong manifestations of separatism—an atavistic sentiment generated by archconservative notables, previously staunch defenders of Portugal's imperial patrimony.[37] In the end a break did not occur, not so much because of the strength of ties with the mainland, but because would-be secessionists feared that the islands might be taken over by major North American crime syndicates.[38]

During 1975 centrifugal tendencies also surfaced in north central

Portugal when it appeared likely to some that Lisbon and the south were doomed to a "red," collectivist future. However, no soldier, party politician, or faction leader was able to cement his authority; instead, with a kaleidoscopic collection of military and civilian institutions jostling for supremacy, it became increasingly difficult to see where real authority lay in revolutionary Portugal. Such utter confusion encouraged the noncommunist parties, the Church, and men of affairs in the north to launch a strong counterattack against the left-MFA coalition in general and the PCP in particular. Half a century of Salazarism had never produced as much anticommunism as north central Portugal witnessed in 1975. More than 200 PCP offices were burned in a rural *jacquerie* coordinated mainly by two right-wing underground movements, the Portuguese Liberation Army (ELP) and the Democratic Movement for the Liberation of Portugal (MDLP).

Kulak elements, along with ordinary rural dwellers under the influence of village notables and local clergy, proved combustible material for these *maquis* groups. In the peasant north, according to one enthusiastic British observer, the MDLP was able to set up "an impressive infrastructure supplying the logistical base for a future attempt at a counter-coup."[39] Likening the situation in the north to "a Vietnam-style people's war," this commentator reported that many villages were under the de facto control of vigilante committees. Such reports may have played a major role in causing radical officers of the MFA to bow out in favor of those moderate MFA elements who were strong enough, by the end of 1975, to end the procommunist phase in government. As a consequence of these developments, Portugal is no longer able to count herself among the select group of Western European countries untroubled by regional or separatist unrest.

The New Right

The rural revolt that occurred in 1975 has no obvious precedent in Portuguese history, except perhaps the inchoate Maria da Fonte peasant uprising of the 1840s. While nineteenth-century rural Spain was convulsed by a series of Carlist wars, the Portuguese countryside remained politically dormant during most of that time, as it did during the republican and Salazarist eras. Before 1975 there is no record of major antagonism between the central government and provincial society, although suspicion, ignorance, neglect, and exploitation definitely underlay the relationship between the urban center and the rural periphery.[40]

Accordingly, the 1975 explosion came as a shock to Portugal's revolutionary but still urban-oriented rulers. Only in retrospect is it possible for outsiders to understand the depth of the shock, for the north's resistance to change has been as decisive for contemporary Portugal, if not more so, as the past forays of Carlism have been for modern Spain. Like the Paris students of May 1968, Portugal's rural dwellers were a traditionally weak sector that overnight virtually brought the national rulers to their knees. And like the *évènements* of 1968, the Portuguese rural upheaval of 1975 subsided almost as quickly as it had come. After 1975 rural Portugal returned to the quiescence it had known during most of its recent history. Despite the strength of anticommunist feeling demonstrated in 1975, it has not become a stronghold for the new right. The Confederation of Portuguese Farmers—the organization that successfully mobilized many agriculturists in 1975—has failed to preserve the hegemonic role that it briefly exercised north of the river Tagus. This is as surprising as the fact that the PCP has made several small, but perhaps significant, comebacks in areas of rural Portugal previously regarded as hostile to it.

Besides commercial farmers and unsophisticated peasants, the *retornado*[41] community was another group that failed to fulfill its militant right-wing potential during the 1970s. During 1974–1975, almost a million returning white European colonials crowded into the restricted dimensions of metropolitan Portugal. To some observers they appeared as a rootless, combustible force of the kind that had provided the springboard for the radical fascism of interwar Europe. In France after 1958, the ratio of white colonial refugees to members of the settled community was six times less than that in Portugal in the mid-1970s, and in France they had been a major force for political instability. However, if bitter in mood and extreme in viewpoint, the Portuguese *retornados* have remained extraordinarily passive so far. Looked at from a slightly longer perspective, their passivity may not seem so astonishing, for recent history has shown that Portuguese settlers in Africa possessed little proclivity for political activism. During the New State era white separatism in Portuguese Africa was conspicuous by its absence, even though the Portuguese in Africa had major grievances against the government.[42] The fact that whites in Angola and Mozambique did not rebel in 1974 when the new regime in Lisbon issued a swift timetable for Portuguese withdrawal from Africa provides another clue to their subsequent passivity.

Besides the absence of a mobilized right-wing base in Portugal, a permanent party of the extreme right has also been conspicuous by its absence. Throughout the 1970s, the ultra right continued to embrace those Portuguese upholding elitist and antidemocratic principles similar to the principles enunciated during the Salazar era. It was not until 1977 that a party specifically harking back to the old order became a permanent part of the Portuguese scene. There are at least three reasons which explain the delayed appearance of a counterrevolutionary party. First, with their conservative policies after 1975, the CDS and the PSD/PPD have "stolen the clothes" of many ultra-right leaders and appeased their followers. If in the 1970s, as in the liberal-republican era, there had been a vacuum on the constitutional right, more extreme variants might have made themselves felt much sooner. Second, the revolution and the loss of empire had a traumatic effect on right-wingers, who had no history of party building behind them. With their institutional strongholds demolished or revamped by the left, the cadres of the Portuguese right needed time to take stock and reset their bearings. Third, the right needed time to establish a new set of leaders in the grey dawn of postdictatorial Portugal. This has not been easy, as several personalities, mainly in the military, have been battling for the succession. Generals Spínola, Galvão de Melo, Soares Carneiro, Pires Veloso, and Kaúlza de Arriaga are the most prominent potential *caudilhos*. Major Sanches Osório, Admiral José Pinheiro de Azevedo, Major Jaime Neves, and Captain Alpoim Calvão are pretenders of the second rank. These figures are by no means relics from the old order. Undoubtedly, the events of the 19-month revolution served to socialize a number of prominent personalities, as well as more ordinary Portuguese, in the direction of mass mobilization. Today, ex-communist activist Vera Lagoa and antifascist Admiral José Pinheiro de Azevedo are among the stalwarts of the new right.[43]

Nevertheless, it was a veteran conservative luminary who established the first important far-right party. The Movement for Independent National Reconstruction (MIRN) first emerged into the limelight during 1977, the brainchild of General Kaúlza de Arriaga; in October 1978 it was renamed the Party of the Portuguese Right (PDP)—a novel reversal in view of the worldwide tendency of conservative parties today to give themselves nonideological or even fairly progressive titles. Kaúlza's declared aim was "to bring about a convergence of all the non-marxist forces . . . and . . . to see the replacement of incompetent ministers with statesmen."[44] In several respects the outlook of this new right party differs from that identified with the fallen regime. The PDP calls for a strong presidential democracy rather than outright dictatorship,[45] although Kaúlza has added the proviso that it "may well be that democracy will be abandoned . . . if statesmen do not emerge."[46] Corporatism is another tenet of the old order that is not unduly stressed by the new right. However, in two important respects—its virulent anticommunism and its rampant pro-imperialism—the new right is a faithful mirror of older forms.

Kaúlza de Arriaga had intended to stand in the presidential elections that took place in December 1980.[47] Support for a far-right candidate was expected to come from groups like the *retornados*, commercial farmers, businessmen, senior public sector workers, managers, and nonworking-class youth. Support from nonworking-class youth is evidence that the revolution has radicalized at least one important new element in a conservative direction. After backing the revolutionary left in 1975, many upper-class and middle-class adolescents apparently began to shift to the extreme right. For example, in 1977 the Portuguese press began to publish articles about Lisbon high schools which were virtually in the grip of militant right-wing pupils, among whom Salazar and Hitler cults were flourishing.[48] "Democracy is a state of affairs where the dog is equal to his master and where any lad can beat up his father" was the sobering comment of one bitter adolescent.[49]

Economic depression and the rise of middle-class unemployment has undoubtedly sharpened the militancy of young bourgeois adults facing the prospect of unemployment or of work far below their class expectations. The growth of what amounts to a fascist youth culture in Portugal has also been encouraged by the proliferation of right-wing propaganda, which ranges from lampooning assaults on democratic politicians to nostalgic biographies of Salazar.[50] Radicals, undoubtedly preoccupied with putting their abortive socialist revolution under the microscope, have produced amazingly few damning critiques of dictatorial Portugal. Not surprisingly in this situation, right-wing polemicists have been able to claim success in a concerted attempt to portray the New State as an era of progress, stability, and unparalleled statesmanship. Manuel Alegre, a Socialist Party politician has even written that "a veritable counterrevolution has taken over in ideological circles. The press, schools, and the churches have either fallen victim to the reactionary offensive or have become its instruments."[51] The rehabilitation of Salazar and Caetano in the minds of certain sectors of the Portuguese public is probably the new right's greatest achievement.

Nevertheless, factionalism, personality clashes, and the fact that a larger segment of the public still remembers the pre-April 25, 1974, period with fear and loathing continued to limit the appeal of ultraconservatism throughout the 1970s. During these years right-wing activists worked in a narrow political ghetto, unable to manipulate or derive help from the major institutions that were once the supporting pillars of the ruling authoritarian right in Portugal. Since 1974, forces on the opposite end of the political spectrum have sought to institutionalize their rule by creating, or taking over, a whole set of institutions and state structures. The Ministry of Education, the 1976 constitution, the nationalized industries, the Council of the Revolution, and the collective farm complex in the Alentejo have in significant ways prolonged the influence of the left beyond the collapse of the revolution in 1975. But with the far right still in the political wilderness on the fifth anniversary of the April 25 coup, it is not without irony that these legacies of the revolution appear likely to suffer the same fate as the corporations and other old-regime institutions, if they have not done so already.

Conclusion

In the late 1970s Europe found itself without an authoritarian regime of the right for the first time in more than 50 years. This situation is unlikely to continue for long if countries are wracked with the kind of difficulties that Portugal has been grappling with since 1975. If democracy fails to provide solutions for Portugal's grave socioeconomic problems, a militant right-wing recovery is more likely than another revolution. A reversion to the Salazarist era or to something even worse is not beyond the bounds of possibility; unlike the fascist regimes of Germany or Italy, the fallen regime in Portugal was not sufficiently outlandish to make its re-emergence completely out of the question.

Salazar's New State was in several respects a relatively bland tyranny. This was hardly because the dictator-premier was a mild-mannered professor (which he was not); it had more to do with the fact that Portuguese society was still relatively immune from the economic and class tensions that had produced much more violent backlashes in Spain and Germany. In 1926, the army-backed counterrevolution brought the curtain down on 16 years of middle- and upper-class political infighting; it was not a pre-emptive strike against an encroaching "red" revolution. However, long years of dictatorship followed by traumatic revolution have decisively radicalized the working class, and would-be *golpistas* are likely to find it much more difficult to take and hold power in the 1980s than was the case in the 1920s.

The odds are that if Portugal is going to experience another bout of noncommunist authoritarian dictatorship, the style and methods of the regime will owe more to the experiences of Germany, Indonesia, and Chile than to the blander authoritarian regimes of Italy, Vichy France, Greece, and New State Portugal. With the exception of Germany, the counterrevolutions in these states were brought about by military fiat.

The fact that in the mid-1970s Portugal's army toppled Europe's oldest noncommunist dictatorship does not rule out the occurrence of such a steep regression in Lisbon. At least one serving officer—General Pires Veloso, who was actually promoted during the most radical stage of the 1975 revolution,—has openly emerged as a partisan of the militant right. Many reactionary activists see an increasingly conservative armed force as a surrogate for a dynamic political movement.

The seventies have come to an end with various conservative urban and rural sectors in Portuguese society still to be mobilized. In Portugal there is no equivalent to the combative Fuerza Nueva led by Blas Pinar in Spain after Franco's death. Violence by the extreme right has been conspicuous by its absence.[52] The extreme right is divided over ideology, tactics, and personalities, as it was during the first decade or so of the parliamentary Republic. Now, as then, it remains a lingering threat to democracy in a region where pluralism has had an awesome failure rate. Iberian reaction has always capitalized upon liberal-democratic misrule, and there is no reason to suppose that things will be any different if the Second Republic (1974–) in Lisbon begins to take after its predecessor.[53]

Although the civilian right received little attention between 1974 and 1979, it should not be completely disregarded. A growing Salazar cult is evident. Reactionaries today passionately revere the figure who, more than anybody else, prevented the rise of a developed right-wing party in Portugal. If a dynamic, participatory right had been encouraged during the Salazar era, the 1974 coup would not have been as painless as it was, and it is likely that its architects would have encountered far greater resistance. It was the habit of the authoritarian regime to regard the existence of parties (even if ideologically congenial) as an unacceptable compromise with "demo-liberalism." Nevertheless, a relatively long period of constitutional civilian rule may yet give rise to a far-right party with firm roots among certain sectors of the public. Alternatively the military, or even the PSD/PPD or the CDS, may emerge as the standard bearer of the far right. This suggestion is highly speculative, but one thing is certain: the time is still far off when the Portuguese ultra right will be as irrelevant as authoritarian rightist movements are currently in most liberal democracies.

Notes

The author wishes to thank the British Academy for kindly making available a grant which enabled him to deliver this paper at the Second International Conference on Modern Portugal at the University of New Hampshire, Durham, on June 23, 1979.

1 It was a rather elitist form of liberalism that dominated Portuguese politics after 1834. Nevertheless, the authorities pioneered some important economic and social reforms and permitted opposition to the left of the main parties. Under a more traditionalist and regulatory political system, the Portuguese Republican Party could not have functioned so openly, and the types of opposition generated would probably have been quite different.

2 *Miguelistas* were partisans of King João VI's younger son, Prince Miguel (1802–1866).

3 Ben Pimlott, co-author of chapter 2, for example downgrades the importance of the 1974 revolution, once it is placed in historical perspective. He claims that "many of the most important changes that are apparent today were, in fact, well advanced in 1974," and that (with the exception of the agrarian reforms) the coup d'etat of April 25, 1974, "set the seal on socio-economic developments that had already occurred" (Ben Pimlott, "Socialism in Portugal: Was it a Revolution?" *Government and Opposition* [Summer 1977], pp. 332–333.

4 João Franco, briefly dictator in 1907–1908, received no enduring backing from the increasingly isolated monarchist elite.

5 The Portuguese Republican Party had more in common with the post-1820 Iberian jacobin parties than with the socially radical republican parties that emerged in Spain after 1930. The landed classes were rendered quiescent by the fact that land reform was not on the republican agenda before 1910. Approaching change in the rural power structure might have been the one thing that would have lead to a reactionary mobilization during the last years of the monarchy. Young scions of the provincial rural oligarchy would play a prominent role in the rebirth of the extreme right after 1914. However, after 1910 the republican parties did not seriously consider even minimal agrarian reform until the twilight years of the parliamentary Republic.

6 I do not consider the "Movement of Swords" of January 1915 to have been republican Portugal's first successful rising, since the emergence of General Joaquim Pimenta de Castro's controversial four-month government owed more to the maneuvering of Portugal's civilian head of state, Manuel de Arriaga (1840–1917).

The terms used here to distinguish between the moderate right (moderates) and the far right (*ultras*) are important, and their meanings are not readily apparent outside Portugal. Generally speaking, the moderates are conservatives who favor the use of republican forms of government, including regularly held elections, while the *ultras* are those in Portugal comprising the radical or counterrevolutionary right who support or have supported the recourse to authoritarianism. In contrast to Spain, Portuguese *ultras* for the most part ceased to be promonarchist during the 1920s and became strong supporters of the regime Salazar created in the 1930s (ed.).

7 The Lusitanian Integralist movement, which emerged in 1914, is the subject of a Ph.D. dissertation being prepared by Miguel Esteves Cardoso in the Government Department of Manchester University, England.

8 Although the Portuguese military grew increasingly conservative after 1914–1915, most full-time officers rapidly came to accept the durability of republican forms and showed little nostalgia for monarchists ideas or symbols. A partial explanation for the military's acceptance of the new institutions can be found in the fact that the armed forces had already become strongly republican in a passive way before the 1910 revolution, something which King Carlos I (1863–1908) ruefully commented upon toward the end of his reign.

9 The evolution of the military regime is explored in Tom Gallagher, "'The Mystery Train': Portugal's Military Dictatorship 1926–32," *European Studies Review*, vol. 11, no. 3 (July 1981), pp. 325–54.

10 It was this hostility which thwarted Francisco Cunha Leal, a politician much respected on the orthodox right before 1926, in his bids to direct the course of the new authoritarian regime during and after 1926.

11 António Sérgio, "Cartas de António Sérgio ao Capitão Sarmento Pimental," *Diário Popular*, Mar. 24, 1977.

12 Ibid.

13 George Guyomard, *La Dictature Militaire au Portugal: Impressions d'un Retour de Lisbonne* (Paris, 1927), p. 93.

14 The União Nacional (National Union) name was borrowed by Egypt's President Nasser for his movement in the 1950s in the direct light of Portuguese experience. In pre-1959 Quebec, a Union National government was in power for more than 20 years under the leadership of Maurice Duplessis, a right-wing traditionalist influenced by Salazar. See Brian Crozier, "Lusitania," *Spectator* (London) (Oct. 24, 1970), p. 476.

15 It would be wrong to assume however, that Salazar's regime enjoyed general acclaim during the preliminary years of the authoritarian regime. This is a view advanced in the writings of most foreign observers who commented upon Salazar's Portugal before World War II. A very different impression is given by the British embassy reports from Lisbon to the London Foreign Office during the 1930s.

16 The New State was the regime's official title between 1930 and 1969.

17 The CADC had been founded in 1912; much valuable light is shed on its elite Catholic outlook in Manuel Braga da Cruz, "As Origens da Democracia Cristã e o Salazarismo," *Análise Social* (Lisbon), no. 54 (Apr.–June 1978), pp. 265–279, and no. 55 (June–Sept. 1978). pp. 525–609. The UIE and the Liberal Republican Union were founded in 1925 and early 1926, respectively; integralism dates from 1914, as we have seen. None of these groups were in public existence by the tenth anniversary of the 1926 coup.

18 The Mocidade Portuguesa, the regime's official youth movement, experienced an increasingly fitful existence from 1936 to 1974; see Lopes Arriaga, *Mocidade Portuguesa: Breve História de uma Organização Salazarista* (Lisbon, 1976). The Legião Portuguesa, an elite militia also founded in 1936, was always more visible than the Mocidade and perhaps even the União Nacional; see Josué da Silva, *Legião Portuguese: Força Repressiva do Fascismo* (Lisbon, 1975).

19 In the years before World War II, Salazar was eulogized by western

antiradicals in much the same way Alexander Solzhenitsyn was feted in the West during the 1970s.

20 Phillippe C. Schmitter, *Corporatism and Public Policy in Authoritarian Portugal* (Beverly Hills and London, 1975), pp. 24–25.

21 Howard J. Wiarda, *Corporatism and Development: the Portuguese Experience* (Amherst, Mass., 1977), p. 115.

22 In the mid-1950s, Mary McCarthy's "Letter from Lisbon," *New Yorker*, Feb. 5, 1955, pp. 83–101, revealed some of the appalling poverty behind the social justice veneer.

23 *Situacionistas* were devotees of the status quo in authoritarian Portugal. Richard Robinson defines the "situation" as "the prevailing regime or government"; see his *Contemporary Portugal: A History* (London, 1979), p. 33.

24 Franco Nogueira, Portugal's foreign minister from 1961 to 1969, and author of a major biography of Salazar, has discounted the claim that President Carmona became hostile to Salazar after 1945. In a wide-ranging interview I had with Franco Nogueira (London, October 6, 1979), he asserted that the only time Carmona might seriously have considered replacing Salazar was during the closing years of World War II. Great Britain was then putting pressure on Lisbon to cut off exports of wolfram to Nazi Germany, and through the British ambassador, Sir Ronald Campbell, seeds of doubt were sown in the president's mind about the wisdom of Salazar's policies. Several times Carmona pressed the prime minister about exports of wolfram to Germany, but in the end a major breach was avoided.

25 A useful profile of Salazar's cabinets can be found in Paul H. Lewis, "Salazar's Ministerial Elite," *The Journal of Politics* vol. 40, no. 3 (Aug. 1978), pp. 622–647.

26 In a revealing and controversial book, one oppositionist purports to show how bitterly divided anti-Salazarist forces were in the 1962–1965 period. This was a time when Ben Bella, the leader of newly independent Algeria, made welcome many left-wing Portuguese exiles. See Patricia McGowan (Pinheiro), *O Bando de Argêl* (Lisbon, 1979).

27 Caetano came to the premiership after a period of semi-opposition in the early 1960s. Paradoxically, if a *serving* minister with some reformist intentions (and there were a few) had succeeded Salazar, he might have been able to force the pace of change with greater success than Caetano could. Having been out of government for 10 years, the new premier appeared to be on probation for much of the 1968–1974 period. The absence of a Spanish-style alliance between the head of state and the head of government was, of course, another factor which stymied major institutional change.

28 Popular National Action was the name given to the União Nacional when it was reorganized by Caetano in 1969. SEDES stands for the Sociedade para o Desenvolvimento Económico e Social (Society for Economic and Social Development); for an appraisal of this pressure group, see Norman

Blume, "SEDES: An Example of Opposition in a Conservative Authoritarian State," *Government and Opposition* (Summer 1977), pp. 351–366.

29 A *golpe de estado* is a broad-based military coup which turns out the existing political rulers. To explore the background to the coup in this chapter would be to duplicate what has been done in many articles and monographs already. Suffice it to say that the coup occurred mainly because of the prolongation of a colonial war, which turned the military from a supine instrument of state will into a politically aware force whose thoughts were increasingly at variance with the antiquated ideas of its political masters in Lisbon.

30 The PIDE was the secret police. Its role and influence are analyzed in Tom Gallagher, "Controlled Repression in Salazar's Portugal," *Journal of Contemporary History*, vol. 14, no. 3 (July 1979), pp. 385–403.

31 The Insight Team of The Sunday Times, *Insight on Portugal: The Year of the Captains* (London, 1975), p. 165.

32 The West German journalist Gunter Wallraf has amassed evidence to show that Spínola was not wholly committed to the democratic path in 1974–1975. See his *A Descoberta de uma Conspiração: A Acção Spínola* (Lisbon, 1976).

33 In the autumn of 1976, Sá Carneiro's party was renamed the Social Democratic Party. While many people prefer to use the label PSD/PPD to clarify the fact that this is the same party, today it is called the PSD. This is the form the editors' have adopted for use throughout this volume.

34 Ben Pimlott traced the social composition and platforms of the major parties in a perceptive article written not long after the close of the revolution. See Ben Pimlott, "Parties andVoters in the Portuguese Revolution: The Elections of 1975 and 1976," *Parliamentary Affairs* 30 (Winter 1977), pp. 35–59.

35 Ben Pimlott, "Right Turn in Portugal," *Spectator* (London), Jan. 28, 1978, p. 10.

36 The nature of the ongoing unrest in the Azores is discussed in Tom Gallagher, "Portugal's Atlantic Territories: The Separatist Challenge," *The World Today*, Sept. 1979, pp. 353–360.

37 José de Almeida, the leader of the separatist Azores Liberation Front (FLA), sat in the National Assembly as a government deputy for a northern mainland constituency before April 25, 1974. João Bosco Mota Amarel, who became the first president of a regional government on the Azores in 1976, was a reformist deputy in the National Assembly during the early 1970s.

38 For information tending to corroborate this admittedly bizarre claim, see *Expresso (Secção Revista)*, Nov. 4, 1978, pp. 1–4, the long investigative article entitled "1975: Americanos, O.A.S. e Almeida reunem-se em Paris para negociar a independência dos Açores." Reports in the Lisbon press during the summer of 1979 claimed that the FLA had been close to proclaiming a unilateral declaration of independence on the islands in August 1978.

39 Robert Moss, "Portugal, the Conservative Alternative," *Spectator* (London), Sept. 13, 1975, p. 338.

40 Maybe this is not wholly true. In 1968 the town of Chaves in Trás-os-Montes was seized by its inhabitants in an uprising which saw the local gendarmerie disarmed and reinforcements from Porto compelled to retreat in some disorder. The cause of the townspeople's anger was the fact that an important football match involving the local team had been rigged in favor of the opposition. Civic peace was restored only when the authorities agreed to a replay. This incident constitutes a little-known backdrop to the hot summer of 1975, and provides an indication that the regime's well-known backing of football as a tool of depoliticization was a double-edged sword.

41 *Retornados* means literally the "returned ones."

42 Nevertheless, it ought to be recalled that Angola was one of the places where opposition presidential candidate General Humberto Delgado made a particulary strong showing in the 1958 elections.

43 Between 1975 and 1979 very few political figures moved from right-wing to left-wing parties. Perhaps if any public figure can be described as having travelled leftward during this time it is President Eanes. However, he was fairly progressive to begin with; many observers made a mistake in characterizing him as a Portuguese Pinochet during the 1976 presidential elections.

44 Pimlott, "Right Turn in Portugal," p. 10.

45 During Portugal's first experiment with democracy before 1926, Salazar's party, the Centro Católico, formally backed pluralism, and the future dictator even described democracy as an irrestible phenomenon in a speech he made at Porto in May 1914. See Hugh Kay, *Salazar and Modern Portugal* (London, 1970), p. 24.

46 Pimlott, "Right Turn in Portugal," p. 10.

47 Franco Nogueira had been urged to stand as a candidate in the 1980 presidential elections. In 1979 a petition containing thousands of signatures was drawn up, urging him to return to Portuguese politics from his London exile. In the event, no candidate stood on an explicitly far right platform, although two officers, generals Galvão de Melo and Pires Veloso (previously associated with the far right) tried unsuccessfully to appeal to center-right opinion; both men received little more than 1 percent of the vote. More successful was General António Soares Carneiro, the presidential choice of the ruling Democratic Alliance, who came in second to President Eanes in 1980, with 40 percent of the vote.

48 See, for instance, "Liceu Dona Leonor, Chocadeira Fascista," *Diário de Lisboa*, Mar. 28, 1977, pp. 10–11. Since then reports of militant right-wing movements in Portugal's schools have multiplied.

49 Quoted in Fernando da Costa, "Porque se Refugiam os Adolescentes," *Expresso*, Dec. 22, 1978, pp. 6–7.

50 A lampoon of President Eanes by right-wing satirist Augusto Cid was seized by the authorities in July 1979. According to the *Manchester Guar-*

dian, more than 10,000 copies of a sequel entitled *Eanes El Estático* [*Eanes, the Unmoveable*] were sold on the first day of publication. See Jill Jolliffe, "Brisk Black Market in Book that Lampoons Portugal's President," *Manchester Guardian*, Nov. 26, 1979.

51 *Le Monde* (Paris), Apr. 27, 1978.

52 With the exception of the murder of General Humberto Delgado in 1965, no major political figure has been assassinated in Portugal since 1921. Despite its grave socioeconomic problems, Portugal was one of the few West European countries to be spared major bombings, assassinations, kidnappings, and other forms of political violence during the latter half of the 1970s.

53 The fact has to be faced that no democratic leader (or political party) has ever emerged in Portugal who, for a sustained period of time, has been able to capture the imagination of the Portuguese electorate. This was perhaps just as true of the 1976–1979 period as it was of the 1910–1926 era. In Portugal during this century, periods of democratic civilian rule have been associated with austerity, chaos, and depressed living standards. The New State and monarchist eras were associated with fierce exploitation of lower income groups. However, in the medium and short term, the 1910 and 1974 revolutions did not lead to dramatic and irreversible improvements in working-class living standards. By Christmas 1977, the real wages of Lisbon transport and industrial workers were down to 1970 levels, thanks to the austerity policies of the Soares government.

5 *Bill Lomax*

Ideology and Illusion In the Portuguese Revolution: The Role of the Left

Its gladiators found the ideals and the forms, the means of self-deception they needed, that they might hide from themselves the bourgeois limitations of the struggle in which they were engaged.
—Karl Marx, *The Eighteenth Brumaire*

Many observers of Portuguese events in the heady days of 1974 and 1975 believed that they were witnessing one of the most revolutionary socialist developments to have occurred in Western Europe since the Second World War. Five years later, however, not only had the socialist-inclined officers of the Armed Forces Movement (MFA), as well as the Communists and members of other professedly revolutionary parties, fallen from power and influence, but even the democratic socialism of Mário Soares and the Socialist Party of Portugal had taken a back seat to the more conservative forces of the military and the Portuguese bourgeoisie. Most remarkable of all, all this happened without any large-scale and violent repression of the working class and the popular movement comparable to the bloody counterrevolutions that brought an end to other twentieth-century revolutionary movements, from Germany in 1919 to Chile in 1973. The Portuguese revolution has died out "not with a bang but a whimper," and the foreign visitor to Portugal today can be hard put to credit that the revolution of April 25 ever took place.

The purpose of this essay is to analyze some of the myths and illusions that prevailed during the "hot summer" of 1975, and to try to discover just what was the social reality that lay behind the political rhetoric of the Portuguese revolution. Perhaps the most prominent of such myths was that which saw at the center of the "Portuguese revolution" a left-wing movement oriented around the MFA, which, in close collaboration with the Portuguese Communist Party (PCP) and other sections of the left, was credited with the responsibility for bringing about the overthrow of the fascist regime on April 25, 1974. This collaboration was seen as subsequently developing into a much broader-based popular movement that aimed at the establishment of socialism of either an East European or a Third World orientation—a movement that was finally defeated with the failure of its alleged attempt to seize power in a coup on November 25, 1975.

Central to this thesis is the notion that it was forces external to Portuguese society that were responsible for the downfall of fascism: but for the colonial wars and the development of opposition to them among the armed forces in the colonies, but for the determined action of the radicalized officers of the MFA, the Portuguese fascist regime would have remained intact. Moreover, this argument contends that, following the downfall of the regime on April 25, it was again the deliberate action of the left-wing officers of the MFA that launched Portugal in the direction of "a genuine revolution" and "a transition toward socialism."[1]

This is a thesis with which I wish to take issue. It is one which greatly exaggerates the autonomy and impact of both political institutions and political ideologies in periods of revolutionary conflict and social change; which accepts the commonest of all illusions about revolutions—namely, that they are made by revolutionaries—confusing the subjective intentions of leaders and participants in a revolutionary process with the actual social changes in which they are involved. In opposition to this approach, I hold that the function of political ideologies and political institutions is rarely that which their expressed aims imply, and that they are not autonomous and creative movements in their own right, but forces whose roles and effects are limited and conditioned by the wider social context of which they are a part. Thus I shall argue that, in the Portuguese case it was economic and social conflict within the society, and not political or ideological intervention, that was responsible for the course of events that have paradoxically been described as constituting "the Portuguese revolution."

Portuguese Fascism and the Opposition before April 25

In assessing just how true it is to assert that the MFA was necessary for the overthrow of fascism, let alone for the social changes that ensued, it has to be conceded that there was no other oppositional force on the left that had any direct impact on the development of Portuguese society in the early 1970s, or posed any real threat to the continuance of the fascist state. It is also interesting to observe the considerable extent to which the entire spectrum of the opposition—including the Portuguese Communist Party, though in a way peculiarly its own—mirrored the nature of that Portuguese regime.

The Portuguese fascist regime, albeit a police state exercising arbitrary powers of arrest, imprisonment, and torture, was never in the full sense of the word a totalitarian regime. It never really sought to extend its power down through the whole society, but remained content to control society from above in the interests of a ruling elite that strictly confined and circumscribed itself. Portuguese fascism did not seek to mobilize society, but rather to impose stasis, if not stagnation, upon it; thus the political elite had neither any mass base nor any organized linkages with the population at large.[2] The abnormally low levels of literacy and education made this gap between the elite and the masses even greater, and perhaps for this reason the democratic and socialist opposition also recruited itself largely from the educated and professional classes—and therefore, in its social composition and cultural outlook, had more in common with the proregime intelligentsia than with the illiterate and uneducated workers and peasant masses.

"The traditional opposition," we are told, was "overwhelmingly an urban, educated, middle-class movement, dominated by lawyers, doctors, engineers, and café intellectuals."[3] Thus two left-wing visitors to Portugal in the early sixties had felt forced to comment, after meeting a prominent opposition figure, on the incongruity of his condemnation of the regime as a system of exploitation and repression while being dutifully served mid-afternoon tea by his house servants; and they had gone on to remark of the opposition that "they always speak with emotion of 'the people'—but with few exceptions they are totally uninterested in the political organization of workers and peasants."[4] This elitism characterized even the most radical elements of the noncommunist opposition, and went hand in hand with a putschist strategy for the seizure of power that occasionally resulted in spectacular and dramatic actions—such as Captain Henrique Galvão's seizure of the liner *Santa Maria* in 1961, Palma Inácio's hijacking of a Portuguese airliner to drop leaflets over Lisbon, Beja, and Faro later the same year, and the attempted Beja rising of January 1962—but rarely, if ever, resulted in mobilizing large-scale mass opposition to the dictatorship.

The ideology of the republican, democratic, and socialist opposition was thus directed more toward the intelligentsia than toward the masses. Seeing themselves as the spokesmen of westernization, of the incorporation of Portugal into the industrial and parliamentary world of modern Europe, opposition members seemed more like the Russian Cadets at the beginning of the twentieth century than like representatives of contemporary opposition (let alone revolutionary) movements. This Portuguese opposition had more than once expressed its willingness to cooperate with the regime in the interests of liberalization; as a recent commentator suggests, for the opposition the real crime of fascism "was not the perpetuation of intolerable social inequalities, nor even the repression that it imposed, but the improper way in which it monopolized the entire political game in the hands of its own faithful followers."[5] Moreover, the emergence of the "liberal wing" of the National Assembly around Sá Carneiro and of SEDES (the pressure group of liberal Catholics and progressive-minded professionals and technocrats) as an oppositional force at the beginning of the seventies showed the extent to which significant sections of the opposition gave expression not to the exploited masses of Portuguese society, but to the business and technological intelligentsia that aspired to a more modern and efficient capitalist socioeconomic order.[6]

To the extent that there had ever been a more mass-based political movement of the left in Portugal, this was represented by the strongly anarcho-syndicalist workers movement of the first decades of the twentieth century—a movement that was gradually replaced by the hegemony of the Communist party, which was formed in 1921 and came to dominate the working-class movement after 1934, at the same time substituting for the earlier revolutionary syndicalism a far more reformist political practice. However, even the Communist party, in terms of its social composition, was not so different from the other sectors of the opposition, its most active membership being drawn largely from doctors, lawyers, and small businessmen in the countryside, and from intellectuals, students, members of the professions, and shop and office workers in the towns. According to the recently published memoirs of a former clandestine party functionary in the 1960s, the Portuguese Communist Party was "a party of the city," it "never attained any real implantation among the peasantry," and "the direction of the proletarian and communist political struggle in the country was always in the hands of a certain radical petty-bourgeoisie."[7]

By the mid sixties the PCP had become "fundamentally a party of cadres"[8] and, with its ideology of a "national and democratic revolution," seemed more interested in establishing itself as an organized and entrenched force that would have to be reckoned with in any postfascist state than in articulating, let alone practicing, any actual strategy for the overthrow of the regime.[9] It too was prepared to collude to a considerable degree with the existing regime, in order to be able to build up its apparatus and widen its base, by working through certain quasi-legal front organizations like the Democratic Electoral Commissions, established in 1969, and the general trade union confederation Intersindical, founded in 1970. (In fact, ever since the mid thirties the official party line had favored working within the fascist "national unions" to any attempt to maintain antifascist union activities in clandestinity.) In this way the PCP was able to build up a nationwide organization of cadres with bases in certain sectors of the industrial working class and among the southern agricultural labor force of the Alentejo, as well as among office workers in the urban centers.[10]

The Stalinist reformism of the PCP inevitably engendered breakaways by more radical elements, particularly under the influence of the worldwide wave of student radicalism of the 1960s. The first Maoist, or Marxist-Leninist, group broke away from the PCP in 1964, following the development of the Sino-Soviet conflict; in 1969 another group broke away to form the Revolutionary Brigades (favoring armed struggle and insurrection), which later (1973) set up the Revolutionary Party of the Proletariat (PRP). Another left-wing group favoring armed struggle was the League of Union and Revolutionary Action, formed in 1967 around the flamboyant figure of Palma Inácio. By 1974 the largest and strongest, and certainly the noisiest, Maoist group was the Movement to Reorganize the Party of the Proletariat (MRPP), formed in 1970. These developments saw the PCP being increasingly overtaken on its left, to the extent that a former senior official of the fascist secret police (the PIDE) could subsequently remark of the Communists that "in the last years before April 25, it was they who gave us the least work."[11] None of these far-left groups, however, gained any sizeable implantation in the working class, nor any significant support outside the urban centers of Lisbon and Porto, where their support came mainly from students and left-wing intellectuals.

Thus even in the years of *marcellismo* there were no oppositional forces on the left that appeared to be potential mobilizers of a movement capable of overthrowing the fascist regime. At the same time, major social changes were in progress that were increasingly undermining the viability of the regime—changes that did not have to be activated by any forces of political opposition.

The Real Crisis of Portuguese Society

If one were to judge the viability of Portuguese fascism simply by its ability to contain forces of purely political opposition there would be considerable grounds for believing that, except for the development of the MFA, the Caetano regime could have remained solidly in control, as the previous section shows. The point that was missed by many commentators at the time, however, is that the institutional structure of Portuguese fascism that Caetano inherited from Salazar had been created not only to resist forces of overt political change, but, more significantly, the development of the more progressive and competitive forces of a modern industrial economy.[12]

Unlike fascism in Germany and Italy in the 1920s and 1930s, which embodied a certain developmental dynamic, the Salazar regime had created a police state not in order to regiment and mobilize society in the interests of the more advanced sectors of capital, but to freeze the social structure in a way that maintained the hegemony of a backward and neofeudal ruling class.[13] The ruling class of Portuguese fascism benefitted from a backward agriculture, dominated by large latifundia in the south and fragmented family smallholdings in the north, and from an equal dichotomy in industry and commerce between a small number of conglomerates dominated by a handful of powerful families and a mass of small businessmen and entrepreneurs, all based on a colonial empire that provided both a source of cheap raw materials and secure and protected markets. In a word, it was an archaic social system that provided considerable economic benefits for a few at the cost of low overall productivity, and that resulted in the lowest per capita income in Western Europe, together with the highest rates of illiteracy, infant mortality, and infectious diseases.[14]

When Salazar's deck chair collapsed under him in September 1968, causing a cerebral hemorrhage from which he was never to recover, the system that he had personified for more than forty years had also reached the end of its road. That it could have survived so long into the twentieth century is a phenomenon perhaps explainable only by Portugal's cultural and physical isolation from the rest of Europe. It was certainly a system that could not continue much longer in a Europe that was becoming ever more integrated economically, culturally, and socially. This reality had been recognized even by Caetano, but though he had at first favored change he had proved powerless to implement it against the vested interests in the power structure of the fascist regime, and the obstinate refusal of the Salazarist ultra-right to concede the superstructural changes necessitated by the development of more modern and progressive capitalist forces.

It would be wrong, however, to see the last years of the *Estado Novo* (New State) in terms of a conflict between the political elite of fascism and the ascendant bourgeoisie, or in terms of a model of bourgeois revolution drawn from the French experience of 1789. If "the Salazarist mentality always revealed itself profoundly anti-capitalist,'' as the young Portuguese historian José António Saraiva has written,[15] there is little to show that the mentality of the Portuguese capitalist class was ever particularly ''anti-Salazarist.'' If the institutions of Portuguese fascism ''had been created to resist capitalism as much as liberalism,'' as Kenneth Maxwell has put it,[16] there is little evidence that Portuguese capitalism ever displayed any particular resistance to the institutions of fascism.

Nor is it valid, as some recent commentators have suggested, to explain events in terms of a conflict between different sections of the bourgeoisie, between finance-capital closely associated with small business, latifundia, and colonial interests on the one hand, and productive capital invested in the more modern sectors of Portuguese industry on the other.[17] The fact is that large capital in Portugal was highly concentrated in a very few hands, and it was the same few giant corporations that controlled the banks and had financial interests both in Portuguese agriculture and in the colonies that also invested in the more modern industrial developments.[18] Thus the impasse at which Portugal stood at the beginning of the 1970s was the impasse not only of the fascist regime, but also of its economic base. The contradictions that characterized Portuguese development were contradictions at the heart not only of Portuguese society, but also of Portuguese capital. They were contradictions that not only could not be resolved within the political structure of the regime that Caetano inherited from Salazar, but which the Portuguese bourgeoisie, by reason of its very nature, was incapable of resolving by its own efforts.[19]

The late 1960s had already seen significant shifts within the internal balance of capital, with more capital-intensive constructions being formed in conjunction with foreign capital, the most prominent of which was perhaps the Lisnave shipbuilding and repair complex. Multinational corporations like Ford, General Motors, Timex, ITT, and Plessey also set up firms in Portugal. These shifts led in turn to a reorientation of trade away from the colonies and toward Europe, until in 1973 almost half of Portugal's foreign trade was with the EEC (European Economic Community) and less than a sixth was with the colonies. Such changes had unavoidable domestic consequences for the development of both Portuguese capital and the Portuguese working class.

For capital, they made less viable the small family enterprises that had not only prospered and been protected under Salazar, but that also provided the central ethos of the cultural hegemony of the fascist regime, mirroring and reproducing at the social base the paternalism of the regime itself. At the same time, the requirements of the new industrial developments came increasingly into conflict with the continuing reluctance of the state to finance industrial development, the restrictive credit policies of the banks, the highly unproductive state of Portuguese agriculture (both in the north and in the south), and with the drain imposed upon the economy by the colonial wars. However, it was not only the rigid and entrenched political institutions of fascism and the forces of the ultra-right that blocked the development of the more modern productive forces, but also the vested interests of the Portuguese bourgeoisie themselves in the more archaic sectors of the economy that held them back from any fully determined commitment to industrial progress. Not only the fascist regime, but also Portuguese capital itself lacked a fully developed capitalist consciousness, and thus what so many commentators have overlooked is that the April 25 revolution was necessary not only to overthrow the political regime of fascism, but to transform the entire social and economic structure of Portuguese capitalism.

For labor, the expansion of the urban concentrations of Lisbon, Setúbal, and Porto around the new industries of electronics and technology, the large complexes of car assembly plants and shipyards, and the expansion of the textile industry led to the rapid growth of a new working class, often uprooted from the countryside and entering a work situation in the large factories that favored its radicalization and the development of class consciousness in a way that had never been possible in the smaller and older businesses. The containment of such forces, as well as the maintenance of the dynamic of modernization, called for more liberal and flexible labor controls than those of a rigid and authoritarian police state. Yet instead of allowing for the freer articulation and conciliation of interests through the development of free trade unions and genuine forms of collective bargaining (as had at first been expected of Caetano's short-lived "opening to the unions" of 1969), the 1970s were to see Portuguese capitalism increasing its repression against the working class and thus tightening the lid on an ever more explosive situation.

July 1968 had seen a successful strike by Lisbon's transport workers, followed later in the year by strikes on the railways and in the Lisnave shipyards. In January 1969 striking workers occupied the factories of Ford and General Motors, and in the following weeks a strike wave involving more than 70,000 workers developed which continued throughout the year and culminated in November in a workers' occupation of Lisnave; the strikes were only brought to an end by savage police repression. In the following years rising inflation served to stoke working class discontent, while the increasing shortage of manual labor that resulted from conscription for the wars and massive emigration had in turn raised the workers' bargaining strength. Though a strike at the Portuguese airlines TAP in July 1973 had been severely repressed, it was followed by growing demands for higher wages and a strike wave in the textile and electronics industries in October and November. January 1974 saw a strike at the Sorefame engineering works, and in February it was the turn of the workers of the Lisbon Metro to take strike action. In April the electronics industries erupted again, with strikes at Siemens, Phillips, Plessey, Standard Electric, and Applied Magnetics; one estimate puts the total number of workers involved that month in strike action, in a country where strikes were legally forbidden, at more than 100,000. Nearly all of these strikes developed outside of the official unions, and in many cases were led by workers' commissions formed spontaneously at plant level.[20]

On the eve of April 25, 1974, Caetano's regime stood at an impasse, facing economic difficulties—in his own words, "the most serious ever known in Portugal."[21] A few days after the coup the MFA captain Salgueiro Maia, who had played quite a prominent role in the events, explained that the army officers decided to act because "we came to the conclusion that . . . if we did not act it would be the population that would do so," and the country could fall "into a civil war in which the people might take up arms." It was precisely to offset such an eventuality that the MFA officers chose General Spínola to head the new regime, because he appeared to be the person most able to ensure that power would not "fall into the street."[22]

As for the leaders of the old regime, by 1974 the political elite was so demoralized as to have completely lost its will to resist. The Armed Forces Movement was probably the most unsecret conspiracy in revolutionary history, and, as long as two months before the coup, Caetano had already come to accept its inevitability.[23] Indeed, the failure of a premature uprising by the Caldas de Rainha garrison on March 17, far from serving to put the regime on its guard, seems to have increased its sense of powerlessness, while in the final event, on the morning of April 25, none of the armed forces still at the disposal of the regime were deployed to resist the coup.

One might even go so far as to contend that if the MFA had not existed, it would have been necessary to invent it. Certainly the function of the coup was not to instigate social change, as many commentators of both left and right have implied, and as many members of the MFA themselves came to believe; its function was, rather, as one of the more discerning observers was to recognize, "a rationalization or consolidation of tendencies which had merely been held back by the institutional and ideological inflexibility of the old regime."[24]

At the same time, the coup served to do more than set a seal on developments that had already occurred. It released a whole range of social forces that had been held back under the fascist regime—forces that, far from being inspired by either the MFA or any other oppositional movements, had been almost completely unforeseen by them. This spontaneous and revolutionary social movement that surged forth from the Portuguese people following the collapse of fascism was not the product of any form of political agitation or mobilization, but of social tensions and pressures already existent within Portuguese society. Indeed, most of the actors on the political stage, including the Portuguese Communist Party which has often been portrayed in the Western media as the main force behind the revolutionary process, "seriously underestimated the revolutionary potential in the situation," as Kenneth Maxwell has since remarked.[25]

The Communist Party and the Working Class

When Alvaro Cunhal returned to Portugal a few days after the coup, many commentators compared his reception at Lisbon airport with Lenin's arrival at the Finland Station in October 1917. Alvaro Cunhal, however, was no Lenin, and, far from placing himself at the head of the popular movement of opposition to the provisional government after April 25 (as the Bolsheviks had in Russia in 1917), he led his party immediately into the government, where it took up positions often less radical than those of the Socialist party. Condemning "unrealistic" and "irresponsible" strikes and "unauthorized" occupations and seizures of private property as playing into the hands of reaction, the Communist party was to show itself as more interested in establishing for itself positions of power and influence within the existing social order than in leading any revolutionary offensive against it. The result was that for almost the first year of the revolution the Communist party was to direct all its energies into restraining and repressing the rising workers' movement, and even today it prides itself on having been "the first to advance the idea of a politics of austerity."[26]

The Portuguese working class was little disposed to heed such calls for moderation, order, and discipline. Freed from repression and able to meet and organize for the first time in a lifetime, the workers expressed their long-standing grievances in immediate demands for the purging or *saneamento* of management officials associated with the previous regime, for better working conditions and shorter working hours, for paid holidays, and, most strongly of all, for higher wages (frequently the demand was for a minimum salary of 6,000 escudos per month). In the wave of strikes that developed in the immediate aftermath of the fall of fascism, it was primarily the younger workers in the newer industries (steel, shipyards, electronics, etc.) and in the newly expanded divisions of older industries (textiles, construction, etc.) who played the most militant and important roles. In many of these industries the Communist party had little previous implantation, and at general meetings of the shop floor workers were able to express their demands in a direct and unmediated way, often launching strikes that were opposed not only by local Communist party cells, but also by the official union leaderships. In the majority of such cases the strikes were led and directed by workers' commissions elected directly by general assemblies of workers, and in the more radical instances strikes culminated in factory occupations and work-ins, like those at the Timex (watch manufacturing), Messa (typewriters), and Sogantal (textile) plants.[27]

According to one far from complete estimate, the number of such conflicts escalated from 17 in the first week after April 25 to 31 in the second week, 87 in the third, and 97 in the fourth, while by the end of May the number of workers who had gone on strike has been put as high as 200,000.[28] On May 25 the government finally conceded a national minimum wage of 3,300 escudos a month, but this was far from enough to halt the strike wave, which was now joined by transport and postal workers, fishermen, and bakers. To counter the growing strength of this workers' movement, the Communist party and union leaders joined with right-wing generals like Spínola and Galvão de Melo in charging that the workers' actions were threatening the democratic conquests of April 25 and playing into the hands of "reactionaries and counter-revolutionaries." The Communist party organized demonstrations against the bakers' strike, which it described as "the most serious moment of the reactionary offensive . . . opening the way to the counter-revolution,"[29] and on June 1 the Communist-dominated Intersindical even called a demonstration against "strikes for strikes' sake."[30]

These measures served to check the first wave of strikes, but not for long. Before the end of June discontent flared up again with new struggles in the post office and other public services, among newspaper workers and fishermen, in the new factories of Mabor, Toyota, and Efacec-Inel, and at TAP, the Portuguese airline. The Communist party denounced the 35,000-strong postal workers' strike in June as playing into the hands of reaction and once again organized public demonstrations against the strikers, while the government prepared to call in the armed forces to end the dispute. In the face of these threats the strikers returned to work on June 20.[31]

The First Provisional Government of Palma Carlos fell on July 9, to be replaced by one in which the MFA was more directly represented and which was headed by the procommunist General Vasco Gonçalves. The new government, far from marking a shift to the left, inaugurated a much sterner and more authoritarian approach toward labor unrest. While Spínola denounced the prevailing "climate of anarchy," his new prime minister Vasco Gonçalves declared that the time had now come for a "true period of austerity," and demanded "hard work by all the Portuguese at all levels."[32] A new state security force—COPCON (Continental Operations Command)—was created, which at first had none of the left-wing character it was later to assume; it was employed essentially as an antistrike force, and was seen by many on the left as little more than an attempt to resurrect the fascist PIDE. On August 17 the government passed a law which, while formally legalizing strikes for the first time in fifty years, in fact greatly restricted the right to strike, and was generally regarded as an "anti-strike law."[33]

These measures were used to repress the strike movement by breaking the most militant strikes in August and September 1974—at Sogantal, *Jornal de Comércio*, TAP, and Lisnave. The conflict at TAP had been developing since April 25 around the issues of *saneamento*, wage rises, and contracts, but had been held back by the unions. When a general assembly of workers rejected union appeals for moderation and called an all-out strike for August 26, its action was denounced in advance by the PCP cell at TAP as "an act of sabotage of the ongoing process of democratization."[34] The next day military forces under the command of COPCON and personally directed by Otelo Saraiva de Carvalho occupied the airport, whose personnel were placed under military command.[35] On the same day COPCON troops were also sent to break up the workers' occupations at Sogantal and *Jornal de Comércio*. When a general strike of the press was called in solidarity with the strikers at *Jornal de Comércio*, on September 4, it was supported by all other newspapers except the communist-controlled *Diário de Lisboa* and *O Século*.[36] When the Lisnave shipyard workers decided to march into the city center on September 12 to demonstrate publicly for the implementation of their long-standing demands, their action was opposed by the PCP cell at Lisnave as one from which "only the reactionaries could profit" and which would "open the road for the reinstauration of fascism"; the minister of labor declared the demonstration illegal, and the government sent paratroopers in an attempt to prevent the march—though they were forced to withdraw in the face of some four to five thousand determined shipyard workers.[37]

In all of these actions against the workers the government was firmly supported by the Communist party, whose leader declared that "today . . . whoever struggles against the government is the counter-revolution."[38] Indeed, as one far from ultra-left American report concludes, "Communists and Socialists in the Cabinet had cooperated with governmental moderates, helping to curb strikes, contain wage demands and even to restrict the press."[39]

The supposedly leftward shifts of the government, following the further rightist fiascos of September 28, 1974, and March 11, 1975, which saw respectively the resignation and flight from Portugal of Spínola, and the increasing weight of the Communist party within each successive provisional government, gave birth to little change in the government's attitude toward the workers' grievances. The Fourth Provisional Government, appointed on March 25, 1975, was also under the premiership of Vasco Gonçalves, but with the Communist party and its military allies holding the key economic and planning posts. It speedily decreed the nationalization of the banks and other key sectors of the economy, and introduced measures to encourage agrarian reform in the Alentejo; but it also brought forth a new austerity program in the name of "the battle of production," calling upon workers to forego "unreasonable" wage demands for the sake of the national interest.[40]

Gonçalves' minister of labor, Captain Costa Martins, outspokenly attacked the continuing strike movement as the product of "political agitation," even declaring that "strikes, in general, can be considered as counter-revolutionary," while the Communist party itself denounced striking workers for "paralyzing the revolutionary process."[41] When the Lisbon telephone workers struck for higher wages on June 19, the government sent in troops to occupy the central telephone exchange. After the withdrawal of the troops, however, the strikers reoccupied the building, and eventually the government conceded to their demands.

At this point both the government and the Communist party, while stepping up their verbal assaults against the workers' movement, were beginning to lose the loyalty of the soldiers, as troops sent against demonstrating and striking workers either refused to intervene or directly fraternized with the workers. At the same time political groups to the left of the Communist party, like the Movement of the Socialist Left (MES) and the Revolutionary Party of the Proletariat, as well as the Maoist Movement to Reorganize the Party of the Proletariat and the Union for Popular Democracy (UDP), began to gain an increasing influence among more militant sectors of workers, and, more significantly perhaps, among certain sections of the armed forces, in particular the military police and COPCON. Also at this point General Otelo Saraiva de Carvalho, the commander of COPCON, became increasingly sympathetic to the ideas of the PRP. When COPCON refused to remove occupying workers from the broadcasting station Rádio Renascença, and when it allowed the newspaper *República*, previously closed down by the government, to reopen under workers' control, it became increasingly clear that the Communist party no longer had the means at its disposal to discipline and control the working class. (In this respect it is perhaps not without significance that the government was most heavily criticized by the Socialist and Popular Democratic parties not for those situations in which the Communist party was firmly in control of the workers' movement, but for disputes like Rádio Renascença and *República* in which the PCP was clearly in a minority.)[42]

In the middle of July 1975 the Fourth Provisional Government finally collapsed as the Socialists and Popular Democrats withdrew their support, leaving the Communists and their allies in the MFA so isolated that they could find no other means of governing the country than through the military triumvirate of Costa Gomes, Vasco Gonçalves and Otelo de Carvalho. The triumvirate, which was formed on July 27, appointed the Fifth Provisional Government of procommunist military officers and civilian technocrats that was to maintain a highly tenuous existence until its replacement by the Sixth Provisional Government, under Admiral Pinheiro de Azevedo, on September 19, 1975. The Fifth Provisional Government was in reality a government in little but name, marking not the height of Communist party strength, but its total impotence, even though it was apparently in the seat of power. Hence the absurdity of claims by so-called moderates on the Council of the Revolution, who boycotted the swearing-in ceremony of the Fifth Government on August 8 on the grounds that it was imposing on Portugal an "Eastern European" style of "bureaucratic dictatorship."[43]

On the contrary, as Otelo Saraiva de Carvalho was subsequently to observe, "In truth, on no other occasion after April 25 was the Communist Party in so real a situation of weakness as in the hot summer of '75."[44] Thus the continuing momentum of the revolutionary process in Portugal as it developed during the summer of 1975 was not a product of communist agitation, of any form of conscious political mobilization either from above or from below, but a product of conflicts within society which had been unleashed and given free rein by the collapse of the entire structure of institutional and ideological control of the old regime, and which the Communist party, despite all its efforts, had been unable to reimpose.

Popular Power and the Revolutionary Left

To point out the conservative and even counterrevolutionary role of the Communist party is not to deny the revolutionary and popular nature of the social movement which it sought to restrain. There was most certainly an authentic and revolutionary movement of the popular masses in Portugal at that time, which led many sections of the Western left to see in those spontaneous initiatives at the social base that gave birth to a proliferation of workers' commissions and other institutions of "popular power" the potential for a socialist regime that would be more revolutionary than the parliamentary socialism of West European social democracy and more democratic than the bureaucratic dictatorships of East European communism.[45] A closer analysis of this movement, however, suggests that the reality behind it was often less radical than either the desires or fears of many observers and participants at times made it appear.

The creation of workers' commissions to lead and coordinate strikes, during the strike wave of May to July 1974, was as often a negative response to the absence of union structures through which to struggle for better wages as it was to any positive desire for direct democracy. Once wage rises were conceded, workers' interest in the commissions began to recede; many of the commissions turned into union-style bureaucracies or fell into the hands of unrepresentative political activists—either event only reducing popular support and participation even more. This appears to have been the fate of the inter-enterprise commissions founded in the aftermath of the TAP strike in 1974, which had tried to unite different factory commissions on a class-wide basis, but which, though successful in calling several large public demonstrations in February and March 1975, seemed unable to organize any coordinated workers' actions in the factories.[46]

Similarly, when the workers' movement took on an apparently more radical form after the events of September 1974 and March 1975, many factories were occupied and taken into "self-management" by their workforces out of a desire to keep the factories open and maintain employment and wages (at a time when their former bosses, unable or unwilling to pay the higher wages agreed to by the government, were either going bankrupt or seeking to close down their firms), rather than out of any conscious attempt to transform social relationships in the factories. Indeed, the more radical experiments in self-management and workers' control tended to occur in the smaller businesses and firms exactly because this was the sector that the state was not prepared to invest in. Factory occupations often took place only after earlier demands for nationalization had been refused, or the owners had sought to close down their firms and leave with their capital. Moreover, in the vast majority of factories it seems to have been the more skilled, specialized, and educated workers—often office workers or even members of the former management—who were elected to the commissions; the rank and file workers felt a need to delegate the powers of management to such "superiors." Experiments in more direct and egalitarian forms of industrial democracy, however significant, were few and far between.[47]

Similar criticisms can be made of the much-vaunted agrarian reform in which many commentators have seen a genuine revolution from below, or even the most significant transformation and permanent achievement of the Portuguese revolution. While too large a subject to cover in detail here, it can be said that perhaps the most remarkable aspect of the agrarian reform was just how long it took to get under way. In the first year of the revolution the rural workers' demands were primarily for the formation of union organizations, wage rises, and security of employment—demands largely directed toward the state and the landowners themselves. It was only in August and September 1974 that a series of strikes broke out to enforce these demands, after it became clear that the majority of landowners were not willing to concede them.[48]

The first land occupations did not occur until January 1975, and in most cases those involved seizures of land left uncultivated by their owners. Though the formation of cooperatives spread after March 1975, when many former landowners fled the country and the Fourth Provisional Government gave official encouragement and legal sanction to the movement, that movement took on its most large-scale aspect only toward the end of September 1975, when the Ministry of Agriculture agreed to state funds being made available to pay salaries in the cooperatives. Within little more than a month more than three times as much land was occupied as had been in the previous year and a half. Even then, the majority of cooperatives came under the centralized control and bureaucratic management of the Communist-dominated unions. More radical attempts at autonomous forms of organization and the establishment of more egalitarian work relationships were rare, and they were the first to be repressed by the state after November 25, 1975.[49]

Some commentators have seen the housing struggles and the occupations of empty properties that broke out spontaneously in the shantytowns and the poor and overcrowded neighborhoods of Porto, Lisbon, and Setúbal in the immediate aftermath of April 25 as among the most autonomous and revolutionary aspects of the social movement in Portugal; they have seen in these actions "a new type of social organization" with characteristics of a radically "anti-capitalist" and "anti-private property" nature.[50] In the first two weeks following April 25 some 2,000 properties were occupied, often on the spontaneous initiative of general assemblies in working-class districts. However, these actions were sternly denounced by the government as "serious infringements of the established order," and even most of the residents' commissions formed during the struggle later came to oppose such "lawless occupations."[51] Though some of the residents' commissions were undoubtedly among the most spontaneous and autonomous forms of popular power, and even succeeded in organizing on a wider basis in inter-commissions in the larger urban centers, the government and the Communist party put all of their efforts into emasculating them and subordinating them to the organs of local administration.[52]

It could also be an illusion to see even the most radical occupations as representing some anticapitalist collective consciousness when, to the contrary, they were often inspired by long-standing aspirations toward private ownership. Indeed, the more radical demands for the provision of collective services (day nurseries, clinics, schools, etc.) often were raised not in the poorest, but in the more prosperous workers' districts. The residents' commissions soon attracted the attentions of the far-left parties, and often became forums for their ideological combats. There were even places where each party had its own commission, while the workers themselves became less and less involved.[53]

These considerations can perhaps help to explain the paradox resulting from the prominence attained by certain sections of the revolutionary left and the left wing of the MFA as advocates of popular power in the summer of 1975 and the rapidity with which the same movement evaporated when faced with the right-wing offensive of late November. Exactly because the Communist party had placed itself at the head of the government, rather than at the head of the workers' movement, a political vacuum existed into which the political groups of the far left were able to enter. The far left was thus able to move in step with the popular movement, creating the illusion—among the leftists themselves as well as among observers—that it was either leading or representing the popular movement. It was able to impute its aims and its ideologies to the wider movement, whose actual ambitions were generally much more basic, much less radical. It was even able to call into being structures and organizations which for a time appeared to represent and institutionalize a nationwide popular movement, but which were to find themselves, when the crunch came, completely devoid of any substantial social base.[54]

Typical of the organizations that blossomed in the spring and summer of 1975 were the Revolutionary Workers' Councils called into being by the left-wing Revolutionary Party of the Proletariat, which tried to raise the slogan of "All Power to the Workers' Councils" and to set on foot a national movement of revolutionary workers', soldiers', and sailors' councils. The whole enterprise of creating these councils, however, came from outside the actual struggles of the workers and despite all the efforts of the revolutionaries, the councils never found any firm foothold in the factories. Therefore when the Second National Congress of Revolutionary Councils was staged in Lisbon on August 2 and 3, though it attracted many leftist students and intellectuals, not to mention a coterie of young tourist revolutionaries, actual workers were few and hard to find.[55]

The idea of a council system of popular power appealed, if not to the workers, at least to the left wing of the military, and at the beginning of July 1975 a guide-document on the People-MFA Alliance was adopted by the General Assembly of the MFA. It proposed a nationwide political structure of popular power, based on popular assemblies in workplaces and neighborhoods, as a revolutionary alternative to the bourgeois structure of parliamentary representation.[56] Such popular assemblies came to be created only in neighborhoods in which military units dominated by the left of the MFA were stationed; such units took upon themselves the responsibility of calling the assemblies into existence. The most well known popular assemblies were those of Pontinha, Olivais, and Marvilha in the zones of the regiments RE-1 and RALIS. The movement to create popular assemblies failed to become general in working-class districts outside the influence of the military, and those popular assemblies that were formed had only a transient and short-lived existence.[57]

Despite these setbacks, the idea of popular power was raised again and again: in the COPCON document of August 13, in the Manifesto of the Revolutionary Unity Front of August 25, and following these proclamations, in the initiatives taken to establish more esoteric versions of popular power—the National Secretariat of Workers' Commissions called into being by the MRPP; the Workers' United Will Win (TUV) set up by the MES; and the Provisional Secretariat of Organs of Popular Will promoted by the UDP. None of these movements, however, were ever more than paper tigers, acts of political theater, or attempts to intervene from above; they were not direct expressions of the broad popular movement itself.[58]

In the end, the increasing prominence and triumphalism of the left in 1975, while further nourishing its self-delusions, may not have served to mobilize the masses, and may well have worked in the opposite direction, deepening the gap between the ideological posturings of the leftists and the direct economic struggles of the workers, who came to feel themselves increasingly distanced and alienated from their aspiring political and revolutionary leaders. The almost surrealistic nature of so many of the political spectacles, the variety of leftist organizations claiming to represent the true interests of the proletariat, as well as the dogmatic and sectarian bickerings within and between leftist groups, may well have served to speed up the alienation of the masses. As two observers at the time commented, "One could say that each political group had its own workers' commissions, that each union organization served the political group that had come to win control of its leading organs. This struggle for power within their organizations had as its result the withdrawal and demobilization of the workers."[59] In this way, as another commentator remarked, in Portugal the revolutionaries proved to be "part of the problem, not part of the solution."[60]

The high point of leftist politicizing in Portugal thus proved to be the low point of the revolutionary movement. How else can one explain the complete rout of the left and the popular movement in the face of the right-wing coup of November 25, and in particular the total evaporation of SUV (Soldiers United Will Win)—an attempt well past the eleventh hour to create a rank and file soldiers' movement to resist the growing rightward trend within the ruling bodies of the MFA and the military high command, that proved even more transient than any of the previous creations of the left?[61]

Transition Toward Socialism . . . or the Reconstruction of Capitalism?

If the MFA was not the "motor of the Portuguese revolution" driving it forward to socialism that many of its supporters considered it to be;[62] if the Communist party was not the mobilizer of the working class against the established order of capitalist society; and if the creations of popular power of the revolutionary left embodied more rhetoric than reality, then what exactly was the Portuguese revolution of 1974–1975? If the ideologies of these different left-wing military and political movements are recognized as political myths that served to mobilize the masses, but with far different results than their aims suggested, then what was the social reality behind the political rhetoric? What interests, in the final analysis, did these ideologies and movements really serve? What social changes were actually taking place behind the camouflage of strident calls to socialist revolution?

One of the first commentators to come to grips with these problems was Nicos Poulantzas, who in his *Crisis of the Dictatorships* clearly recognized that Portugal did not see even "the beginning of a transition towards socialism," and that "socialism was never really on the agenda."[63] For Poulantzas, what was at issue in the Portuguese events was the rise of a modern and European-oriented domestic bourgeoisie that was in conflict with both the older agrarian and financial interests and the *comprador* bourgeoisie who were tied to foreign capital. This domestic bourgeoisie demanded not only more progressive financial and agrarian policies, but also greater freedom of expression, more democratic forms of representation, and the conciliation of interests—in other words, a "democratic break" with the dictatorship. The domestic bourgeoisie, however, was too weak to bring about such a radical change by its own efforts; the overthrow of the dictatorship and its replacement by a democratic regime necessitated a temporary alliance with the working class and the popular masses. Hence the paradoxical phenomenon of a revolutionary movement with a socialist ideology and a proletarian social base that was objectively limited to the attainment of bourgeois democratization.

While Poulantzas' thesis is remarkable for its lack of illusions about the course of the Portuguese revolution, it remains too schematic and ideological. Not only are there no real grounds for alleging a conscious conflict of interests between Portuguese capitalism and the fascist regime, but it is even less valid to postulate an autonomous domestic bourgeoisie in conflict with banking, agrarian, and colonial interests. To the extent that one could speak of a distinct domestic bourgeoisie in Portugal, it would not have been found in the more progressive sectors of capital, but among the small and medium sized firms that were protected by fascist legislation and were resolutely opposed both to modernization and to any opening toward Europe. The capitalist interests that invested in the newer industrial developments were the same giant corporations that controlled banking, and that had both interests in the colonies and links with foreign capital. If there was a conflict over Portuguese development, it was a conflict that became explicit only at the ideological and political levels.[64]

The political conflict found expression, after the 1969 elections, in the reformist project launched by Marcello Caetano and the so-called "Marcellist technocrats." Its aim was to bring about a controlled program of "liberalization-modernization" involving a liberalization of the regime, the expansion of education and other social services, and an opening toward the unions. At the time a number of Portuguese leftist commentators, such as the emigré group that published the journal *Cadernos de Circunstância* in Paris in the late 1960s and the writer João Martins Perreira in his book *Pensar Portugal Hoje* (published in Portugal in 1971), considered that this technocratic project represented the interests of the most advanced sectors of Portuguese capital, which would almost inevitably win out over the older financial, agrarian, and colonial interests that were allied with the die-hard "ultras" who sought to maintain intact the orthodoxy and rigidity of the fascist regime.[65]

In reality, no significant sectors of capital in Portugal—neither domestic capital nor foreign multinational interests—were prepared to dissociate themselves from the fascist regime and the privileges it bore them. As another emigré commentator subsequently sought to explain, it was not that such "liberal and neo-liberal measures were not compatible with or favorable toward capitalism—they certainly were so, but not in Portugal at that time. . . . Certain advanced groups tried to promote a 'neo-liberal capitalism' and modern methods of management, but there did not exist any social forces of sufficient strength to put such projects into practice."[66] The technocratic project, incapable of finding any social base, was thus stillborn from the start, and Caetano's "Estado Social" "died even before it had been born."[67]

With the removal of the Marcellist technocrats from the direction of economic affairs in the governmental changes of August 1972, and the resignation from the National Assembly of the liberal wing around Sá Carneiro in February 1973, the prospects for Caetano's "renovation in continuity" were finally exhausted. From then on Caetano was to be little more than "a mere spectator of events which succeeded each other at an ever increasing speed."[68] The regime he had inherited from Salazar had now reached a dead end: it could not continue without change, but it was strong enough to prevent change from being brought about gradually and peacefully. Revolution became a necessity for development. The victory of "the Captains of April" was inevitable.

The overthrow of the established institutions and social structures of pre-1974 Portugal necessitated a revolutionary mobilization far out of proportion to the social changes it was finally to bring about. The liberation of the productive forces of a more modern capitalist development was only to be possible under the impetus of a radical socialist ideology that could serve to mobilize the popular masses against the rigid and ultra-conservative structures of the Portuguese regime, and against the vested interests opposing changes in the existing system of Portuguese capitalism. Hence the paradox of the Portuguese revolution: the contrast between its expression at the level of political ideology and its achievements at the level of socioeconomic transformation.

The Social Movement and the Role of the Left

The Portuguese revolution was not all mere illusion. The collapse of the institutional structure of fascism and the destruction of established authority gave birth to a situation in which civil society was almost completely freed from the institutional and ideological constraints of a sovereign state power. The social movement that developed directly out of the immediate struggles at the social base was undoubtedly an authentic and popular force. The workers' commissions in the factories, the housing occupations and residents' commissions in workers' neighborhoods, the land seizures and the agricultural cooperatives—all of these, whatever their shortcomings, were indisputably autonomous developments arising from the direct and spontaneous initiatives of the workers themselves, often in the face of direct and determined opposition from the MFA, COPCON, the Communist party, and the unions.[69]

The extent to which this movement carried within itself the potential for a revolutionary transformation of the social order; the extent to which it was condemned to inevitable defeat at the hands of the state and the reconsolidation of domestic and foreign capital; and the extent to which it was an "impossible revolution," as some of its most committed supporters have implied, are questions that will continue to be debated for years to come.[70] In retrospect the one fact that has to be recognized is just how slowly this movement radicalized itself in the course of its struggle and development, compared with other twentieth-century revolutionary situations.

From the start the Portuguese workers proved themselves able to act firmly and decisively in defense of their immediate class interests—seeking above all to preserve their employment, to obtain secure contracts and higher wages—but almost always they acted within the existing structure of capitalist relationships. Attempts to radically transform social relationships, whether in the towns or in the countryside, emerged only spasmodically, and often in a fragmented and defensive way. The workers looked first to their employers, secondly to the state, and only in the last resort to themselves as the means of transforming their social situation. The social movement in Portugal was thus never able to present an effective challenge to the power and authority of the capitalist state.[71]

Traditional Leninists would no doubt explain the failure of the social movement in Portugal in terms of its "economism"—i.e., the pursuit of immediate economic goals, with indifference to the wider political struggle. The Portuguese working class, it could be said, failed to pass from a "class-in-itself" to a "class-for-itself," and so proved incapable of carrying through a revolutionary transformation of society. However, the political leadership offered to the workers by the Portuguese left suffered equally from the opposite weakness—"voluntarism," or the pursuit of political aims with little regard for objective socioeconomic realities. Almost all of the groups of the Portuguese left acted throughout in a particularly voluntarist fashion, appearing to believe that if only they presented the workers with the correct ideological line, the right political leadership, and the appropriate organizational forms, the road would immediately be opened to the socialist revolution.

The revolutionary movement in Portugal was thus characterized by both economism and voluntarism, which resulted in a vast gap between its economic and its political aspects. In their everyday struggles the workers confined themselves to predominantly economic demands, only rarely recognizing the need to raise their struggle to the broader political level, and almost never succeeding in doing so. This weakness of the social movement was only strengthened by the predominant Leninism of the Portuguese left, which encouraged the view that politics was the reserve of professional leaders, of the Portuguese "political class," of the "doctors" of the different political parties, the revolutionary "majors" of the MFA, and the various vanguards of the revolutionary left. The Jacobinism so characteristic of the Portuguese left found a perverse echo in the traditional *sebastianismo* of the popular masses, and the prevalence of illusions in the MFA, the Communist party, and the revolutionary left did much to retard the development of an active class consciousness and autonomous political practices among the workers themselves.

The left in Portugal therefore did as much to retard as to advance the course of the social movement, while its role in the actual development of the revolution was largely illusory and epiphenomenal. The left was able to rise to a certain political prominence, but only by default—a result of the inability of the Portuguese bourgeoisie, at either the political or the economic levels, to play a progressive and dynamic role in modernizing the economic and social structures of Portuguese capitalism. The collapse of fascism created a political vacuum into which the military and political left were able to step, but the role they played was in essence merely a surrogate one. It was not a case of their aims, ideologies, and institutional forms shaping and directing economic and social change, but rather that they played a certain integrating and stabilizing role, championing but also restraining and channelling the explosion of popular forces that followed April 25, until such a time as the more conservative forces of the state and the bourgeoisie were able to reestablish their authority over civil society.

Even if the left had been more successful, there is no reason to assume that its continuance in power would have heralded any radical transformation of the social order, or represented any real alternative for the lives of the masses. The different left-wing projects represented little more than different means for reconsolidating state power and reimposing social order and discipline over civil society. If the Communist party had proved more successful in controlling the workers' movement, it is possible that its order would have been at least as preferable among the technocrats and administrators of modern capitalism as the more liberal approach of the democratic parties. Even the popular power concepts of the revolutionary left could have provided a fairly effective means of controlling the labor force and disciplining society at large.

What, then, remains of value in the Portuguese revolutionary experience of 1974–1975? If the abolition of capitalism was never the order of the day, were the hopes and aspirations of those years, the conflicts and struggles, all in vain? Or did they carry within themselves the germs, the future possibilities, for a freer and more egalitarian society? Certainly there was an authentic revolutionary movement of the popular masses in those years, a movement that arose directly out of the struggles at the social base and independently of the political forces that sought to intervene in, manipulate, and dominate that movement. Although the movement proved too weak to take full advantage of the opportunities presented to it, it contained the potential for a future transformation of society. Perhaps more than those of any other revolutionary conflict of the twentieth century, the events of 1974–1975 in Portugal reconfirm the validity of Marx's assertion that "the emancipation of the working classes must be conquered by the working classes themselves."[72]

Notes

The present essay is a considerably revised version of a paper presented to the Second Meeting of the International Conference Group on Modern Portugal at the University of New Hampshire in June 1979. It has been prepared as part of a wider research project on the revolutionary process in Portugal in 1974–1976, financed by the Ford Foundation, for the generous support of which I am particularly grateful. I would also like to express my thanks to Gerard Vignola and Edgar Rocha, who provided most useful comments and criticisms in discussions of earlier versions of this paper.

1 John L. Hammond, "Portugal: Two Steps Forward, One Step Back," mimeographed (City University of New York, 1978), p. 27.
2 On the nature of the Portuguese political elite before April 1974, see Hermínio Martins, "Portugal," in M. S. Archer and S. Giner, eds., *Contemporary Europe* (London, 1971), pp. 63–65.
3 David L. Raby, "Populism and the Portuguese Left: From Delgado to Otelo," in this volume, chapter 3. For a similar assessment, see also Hermínio Martins, "Opposition in Portugal," *Government and Opposition* (London), vol. 4, no. 2 (Spring 1969), p. 263.
4 Peter Fryer and Patricia McGowan Pinheiro, *Oldest Ally* (London, 1961), pp. 200–208.
5 Eduardo Lourenço, *O Fascismo Nunca Existiu* (Lisbon, 1976), p. 182.
6 On SEDES, see Norman Blume, "SEDES: An Example of Opposition in a Conservative Authoritarian State," *Government and Opposition* (London), vol. 12, no. 3 (Summer 1977), pp. 351–366; and Emílio Rui Vilar and António Sousa Gomes, *SEDES: Dossier 70/72* (Lisbon, 1973).
7 J. A. Silva Marques, *Relatórias da Clandestinidade: O PCP Visto por Dentro* (Lisbon, 1977), pp. 73, 59, 321.
8 Ibid., p. 359.
9 "National and democratic revolution" had been the central slogan of the PCP program for many years. First advocated by Alvaro Cunhal in 1943, it became the basis of the program adopted by the Sixth PCP Congress in 1965 ("Programa do PCP," in *Partido Comunista Portugues, Programa e Estatutos do PCP*, 3d. ed. [Lisbon, 1974], p. 17).
10 For one of the few analyses in English of the PCP, see Manuel Villaverde Cabral, "The Portuguese Communist Party: An Interpretation of Fifty Years of History," in Howard Machin, ed., *The End of Eurocommunism?* (London: Methuen, forthcoming).
11 Fernando Gouveia, *Memórias de um Inspector da P. I. D. E.* (Lisbon, 1979), p. 439.
12 This argument has been presented most precisely in Kenneth Maxwell, "Portugal: A Neat Revolution," *New York Review of Books,* June 13, 1974, pp. 18–19.
13 On the specificity of Portuguese fascism, see José António Saraiva, *Do Estado Novo à Segunda República* (Lisbon, 1974), pp. 58–68.
14 Maxwell, "A Neat Revolution," p. 17; Martins, "Portugal," p. 66.
15 Saraiva, *Do Estado Novo,* p. 63.
16 Maxwell, "A Neat Revolution," p. 18.
17 This view has been expressed by Maxwell, "A Neat Revolution," p. 19, while other variants of it (discussed later in this essay) have been put forward by João Martins Perreira, *Pensar Portugal Hoje* (Lisbon, 1971), pp. 98–99; and Nicos Poulantzas, *The Crisis of the Dictatorships* (London, 1976).

18 On this point, see Francisco Rafael et al., *Portugal: Capitalismo e Estado Novo* (Porto, 1976), p. 141, where it is argued that "the economic interests were plainly the same." For fuller details on the nature of the industrial corporations, see Maria Belmira Martins, *Sociedades e Grupos em Portugal* (Lisbon, 1973, reissued 1975).

19 The inability of the Portuguese bourgeoisie to carry through a neocapitalist transformation was pointed out by Carlos Almeida and António Barreto, *Capitalismo e Emigração em Portugal* (Lisbon, 1970); see also 3d ed. (Lisbon, 1976), p. 76, where Almeida and Barreto analyze the factors that in their view "objectively prevent the bourgeoisie from democratizing its national revolution."

20 On the strike movements before April 25, see Maria de Lurdes Lima Santos, Marinus Pires de Lima, and Vitor Matias Ferreira, *O 25 de Abril e as Lutas Sociais nas Empressas* 1 (Porto, 1976), pp. 21–31; José Pires, *Greves e o 25 de Abril* (Lisbon, 1976), pp. 23–54; and F. Avila et al., *Portugal: l'Autre Combat—Classes et Conflits dans la Société* (Paris, 1975), pp. 40–49.

21 Marcello Caetano, cited in *O Jornal* (Lisbon), Apr. 20, 1977.

22 Captain Salgueiro Maia, interviewed in *Fatos e Fotos* (Lisbon), May 1974; and reprinted in Henrique Barrilaro Ruas, ed., *A Revolução das Flores* 1 (Lisbon, 1974), pp. 62–63.

23 Marcello Caetano, *Depoimento* (Rio de Janeiro, 1974), p. 196.

24 Ben Pimlott, "Were the Soldiers Revolutionary? The Armed Forces Movement in Portugal: 1973–1976," *Iberian Studies* (Keele, England), vol. 7, no. 1 (Spring 1978), p. 15.

25 Kenneth Maxwell, "The Thorns of the Portuguese Revolution," *Foreign Affairs* (London) vol. 54, no. 2, (Jan. 1976), p. 263.

26 Alvaro Cunhal, interviewed in *Diário de Notícias* (Lisbon), Nov. 6, 1979.

27 For fuller details of this strike wave, see Orlando Neves, ed., *Mil Dias: Diário de uma Revolução* (Lisbon, 1978), pp. 191–196; F. Avila et al., *l'Autre Combat,* pp. 49–58; and Santos, Lima, and Ferreira, *O 25 de Abril* 1:31–55.

28 Neves, ed., *Mil Dias,* pp. 193–196; Robert Harvey, *Portugal: Birth of a Democracy* (London, 1978), p. 53.

29 *Avante!* (Lisbon), June 7, 1974.

30 Neves, ed., *Mil Dias,* p. 204; see also F. Avila et al., *l'Autre Combat,* pp. 58–68.

31 F. Avila et al., *l'Autre Combat,* pp. 63–68; Neves, ed., *Mil Dias,* pp. 199–201; and Santos, Lima, and Ferreira, *O 25 de Abril* 2:9–33.

32 Vasco Gonçalves, *Citações de Vasco Gonçalves,* ed. Serafim Ferreira (Lisbon, 1976), p. 17.

33 Decree Law no. 392/74 (Aug. 27, 1974); see the chapter "A Lei da Greve ou a Lei Anti-Greve," in Pires, *Greves,* pp. 243–275.

34 Appeal by PCP cell at TAP, Aug. 25, 1974, cited in F. Avila et al., *l'Autre Combat,* p. 147.

35 Neves, ed., *Mil Dias,* pp. 222–228; Pires, *Greves,* pp. 186–241; and Santos, Lima, and Ferreira, *O 25 de Abril* 3 (1977): 41–156.
36 Neves, ed., *Mil Dias,* pp. 228–231; F. Avila et al., *l'Autre Combat,* p. 68.
37 Neves, ed., *Mil Dias,* pp. 231–233. For a detailed account of the demonstration and the events leading up to it, see Maria de Fátima Patriarca, "Operários da Lisnave de 12 Set. 1974," *Análise Social* (Lisbon), no. 56 (1978).
38 Alvaro Cunhal, speech in Braga, Nov. 30, 1974, reprinted in Alvaro Cunhal, *A Revolução Portuguesa* (Lisbon, 1975), p. 352.
39 Lester A. Sobel, ed., *Portuguese Revolution: 1974–1976* (New York, 1976), p. 78.
40 Gonçalves, *Citações,* pp. 21–22.
41 Captain Costa Martins, Apr. 29, 1975, cited in Judith Balso, ed., *O M.R.P.P.* (Lisbon, 1977), p. 35.
42 For a more objective account of the *República* and Rádio Renascença affairs than that which was generally presented in the Western media, see Phil Mailer, *Portugal: The Impossible Revolution?* (London, 1977), pp. 227–236. On *República,* see also Fernando Dil and Carlos Pina, *Operação República* (Lisbon, 1975).
43 Extracts from the "Document of the Nine," reprinted in Fernando Ribeiro de Mello, ed., *Dossier 2ª República* 2 (Lisbon, 1977), pp. 796–803.
44 Otelo Saraiva de Carvalho, interviewed in *Voz de Povo* (Lisbon), Nov. 23, 1979.
45 See, for example, Steven Lukes, "Dual Power in Portugal," *New Statesman* (London), Sept. 19, 1975.
46 Mailer, *Impossible Revolution?,* pp. 150, 152, 248–252. For a similar interpretation, see also M. Vieira and D. Oliveira, *O Poder Popular em Portugal* (Coimbra, 1976), pp. 29–31.
47 For further details and discussion of the movement of self-management, see F. Avila et al., *l'Autre Combat,* pp. 67–68, 115–116; José Barreto, "Empressas Industriais Geridas pelos Trabalhadores," *Análise Social* (Lisbon), no. 51 (1977); and Manuel Villaverde Cabral, "The Movement for Self-Management in Portugal," in *The Future of Socialism in Europe* (Montreal: Inter-University Centre for European Studies, forthcoming).
48 Neves, ed., *Mil Dias,* pp. 239–244. For fuller accounts of the movement of agrarian reform, see A. de Vale Estrela, "A Reforma Agrária Portuguesa," *Análise Social* (Lisbon), no. 54 (1978); and Fernando Oliveira Baptista, *Portugal 1975—Os Campos* (Porto, 1978).
49 See Manuel Villaverde Cabral, "Agrarian Structures and Recent Rural Movements in Portugal," *Journal of Peasant Studies* (London), vol. 5, no. 4 (July 1978), pp. 411–445; Claude Collin, "Enquete sur les cooperatives agricoles au Portugal," *Les Temps Modernes* (Paris), (Nov. 1976); and Ch. [Charles] Reeve, "Après le 25 novembre portugais: répression et résistance dans le milieu ouvrier," *Spartacus* (Paris) (Mar.-Apr. 1976).
50 Chip [Charles] Downs et al., *Os Moradores à Conquista da Cidade* (Lis-

bon, 1978), p. 61; Vitor Matias Ferreira, *Movimentos Sociais Urbanos e Intervenção Política* (Porto, 1975), p. 62.

51 Neves, ed., *Mil Dias,* p. 250; Luis Leitão et al., "Mouvements urbains et commissions de moradores au Portugal: 1974–1976," *Les Temps Modernes* (Paris) (Nov. 1978), p. 672.

52 On the housing struggles, see Downs et al., *Os Moradores;* V. M. Ferreira, *Movimentos Sociais*; and "Movimentos de Moradores: Luta Pela Habitação," *Intervenção Social* (Lisbon), no. 2 (Sept. 1979).

53 For a more critical viewpoint, see Leitão et al., "Mouvements urbains."
While Lomax discounts much of the spontaneity of the movement to establish residents' commissions, see chapter 7 of this volume, by Charles Downs, for a contradictory point of view (ed.).

54 A similar view of the revolutionary left can be found in José António Saraiva and Vicente Jorge Silva, *O 25 de Abril Visto da História* (Lisbon, 1976), pp. 155–160.

55 On the program of the Revolutionary Workers' Councils, see Partido Revolucionário do Proletariado, *Projecto Povo-MFA: Conselhos Revolucionários* (Lisbon, 1975). For a critical view of their second congress, see "Dossier on Portugal," in *Solidarity* (London), vol. 8, no. 3 (1975), pp. 20–21.

56 "Aliança Povo-MFA," July 8, 1975, in Mello, ed. *Dossier 2ª República,* pp. 773–780.

57 See Vieira and Oliveira, *O Poder Popular,* pp. 53–64.

58 A highly critical account of the revolutionary left in the summer of 1975 can be found in Mailer, *Impossible Revolution?* pp. 241–262, 271–278. For a more sympathetic view, and for most of the documents of this period, see Jean Pierre Faye, *Portugal: The Revolution in the Labyrinth* (Nottingham, England, 1976).

59 J. M. and G. V. [pseuds.], "De l'Incertitude a la Fin des Illusions," *Spartacus* (Paris), (Nov.–Dec. 1975), p. 12.

60 Mailer, *Impossible Revolution?* p. 355.

61 On the role of the SUV, see *Os SUV em Luta* (Lisbon, 1975); and, from a highly critical viewpoint, Charles Reeve, *L'Expérience Portugaise: La Conception Putschiste de la Revolution Sociale* (Paris, 1976).

62 Serafim Ferreira in his Introduction to Serafim Ferreira, ed., *MFA: Motor da Revolução Portuguesa* (Lisbon, 1975), p. 10.

63 Nicos Poulantzas, *The Crisis of the Dictatorships* (London, 1976), pp. 135–136, 144.

64 See Rafael et al., *Capitalismo,* p. 141, where it is argued that "the hypothetical opposition remained simply at the level of ideology."

65 See *Cadernos da Circunstancia: 67–70* (Porto, 1975); and Perreira, *Pensar Portugal Hoje* (1971, 1979).

66 A. B., "O Estado e o Desenvolvimento," *Polémica* (Rome), no. 4 (1973), p. 52.

67 Saraiva, *Do Estado Novo,* p. 105.

68 Ibid., p. 106.

69 The significance of the revolutionary movement at the social base, as distinct from that of the self-styled political revolutionaries, was recognized by João Martins Perreira in *O Socialismo, a Transição e o Caso Português* (Lisbon, 1976); the fullest account of it so far has been provided in Mailer, *Impossible Revolution?*

70 For a particularly interesting and perceptive discussion of these questions, see "A Impossível Revolução Portuguesa," *Subversão Internacional* (Lisbon), no. 5 (1979), pp. 18–22.

71 A similar view of the nature of the social movement is expressed in Saraiva and Silva, *O 25 de Abril Visto da História,* pp. 150 and 186, where the authors discuss the constant estrangement of the social movement from the struggles taking place at the level of state power.

72 Karl Marx, "General Rules of the International Working Men's Association" (1864), in Karl Marx and Friedrich Engels, *Selected Works in Two Volumes,* vol. 1 (Moscow, 1962), p. 386.

6 *John R. Logan*

Worker Mobilization and Party Politics: Revolutionary Portugal in Perspective

The aim of this essay is to document and to account for the subordination of worker mobilization to party politics following the overthrow of the corporatist regime in Portugal in 1974. The sudden limitation imposed on the state's direct repressive capacity at that time (symbolized by the abolition of the PIDE, or secret police) unleashed a wave of spontaneous mobilization among workers—strikes, factory occupations, and the emergence of ad hoc workers commissions and assemblies. These events threatened the fragile balance of power among conservative and progressive elements of the new provisional government, provoking a predictable effort by the state to contain workers' activities. But more interesting is the fact that they also disrupted a relatively stable pattern of state-class relations which had developed during the early 1970s.

While the Caetano regime had repressed class conflict, it had also tolerated a limited autonomy of the official trade unions that enabled opposition parties—particularly the Portuguese Communist Party (PCP)—to organize. From the regime's point of view this appears to have been a strategy of co-opting the opposition, channeling it into an arena in which it could be controlled, and seeking valid representatives of the working class with whom to negotiate wages and working conditions. In short, the strategy reflected the "liberal" current in an authoritarian system. From the viewpoint of the Communist party, that strategy offered the possibility of developing an organizational base from which the party could hope to gain control of an emerging labor movement.

This de facto arrangement was upset by the revolutionary situation of mid-1974. The dominant theme in the history of the labor movement since that time has been the effort of the Communist party to consolidate its unexpected opportunity to have organizational control of the working class, defending this base first from the spontaneous mobilization of workers and attempts by far-left groups to radicalize the government, and subsequently from the efforts of the socialists and social democrats to translate their electoral strength into effective influence in the labor movement. Other issues—wage bargaining, the purging of persons who collaborated with the former regime, the nationalization of industry, worker control, union structure—have arisen since 1974; but these have been secondary to, because they became instruments of, party politics. How this phenomenon originated in the class structure of a country which was at the same time a colonial power and on the periphery of the Common Market will be discussed in the next section of this chapter. I will then describe the limited reforms in labor law that were instituted by Caetano, and the conditions under which the communist-dominated union confederation Intersindical was created. Finally, I will outline the two main phases of labor history since 1974, the period of attack from the left (1974–1975), and the period of attack from the right (1976–1979).

Dependent Development and Class Structure

A principal reason for the success of Salazar's corporatism was the heterogeneity, geographic dispersal, and small size of the working class which it was intended to contain. The fiscal policies that balanced the national budget tended to limit the growth of this class by discouraging investment in the domestic economy, and the economic elites who supported Salazar (especially the financial consortiums in control of the modern sector of the economy) were willing to accept limited development as the price for political and economic control. Beyond this, however, Salazar expanded the possibilities for the growth of mercantile capitalism through the exploitation of the African colonies. Such expansion had two important effects with respect to domestic politics: it allowed for a steady flow of profits to the groups that dominated trade, and it created a new working class which was located disproportionately in white collar and service sector employment, rather than in industry.

After the first guerrilla activity in Angola in 1961 and the revolts in Guinea in 1963 and Mozambique in 1964, it was colonial struggle and not domestic class conflict which became the main threat to Portuguese corporatism. Already under pressure from the United Nations for his colonial policy, Salazar was forced to seek diplomatic support among his NATO allies, and especially the United States, which avoided criticism of Portuguese colonialism. Like Spain a decade before, Salazar submitted to the pressure of the industrial countries to allow foreign investment and expanded trade—in effect, to facilitate Portugal's integration as a dependent state in the capitalist world system as the means of preserving its empire. The share of foreign capital in current investment in Portugal was allowed to rise from less than 1 percent in 1959 to 21 percent in 1969. Foreign capital reached 52.2 percent of Portugal's total manufacturing investment in 1968, and the country's trade deficit exploded from 7.7 billion escudos in 1961 to 21.8 billion escudos in 1971.

Dependent development in Portugal during the 1960s, stimulated by closer links to international capitalism, generated a growth in the GNP at the rate of 7 to 8 percent in the later years of the Salazar period. Agriculture's share of production declined from 20 percent of the GNP in 1963 to 14.6 percent in 1969. In the same years manufacturing output grew at a rate of about 12 percent annually in constant prices, rising from 27 percent to 33.3 percent of the GNP. The value of production in modern industries such as chemicals, metalwork, and auto manufacturing nearly doubled, while growth in the traditional food, textiles, and clothing sectors was somewhat slower.

As the foreign share of investment grew, particularly in the modern industries, it also became more capital intensive; by 1971 the average foreign-controlled firm had eight times the capital investment of domestic firms.[1] Foreign investors (principally from West Germany, Great Britain, and the United States) controlled 100 percent of the petroleum refining industry, 81 percent of electrical machinery production, 72 percent of tire manufacturing, 62 percent of the auto and truck industry, and 48 percent of the chemical sector.

The selectivity and capital intensive nature of these investments accounted for the fact that while they had a great impact on the structure of the economy and on the distribution of production by sector, their effect on the occupational structure of Portugal was minimal. The dominant trends in the work force of the 1960s were the acceleration of emigration and the depopulation of the countryside, since rural poverty and traditional agriculture had been largely untouched by public or private investment.

Emigration caused a major shift in the sectoral distribution of the active work force: the number of persons in the agricultural work force and fishing declined from 1,337,000 in 1960 to 847,000 in 1973, corresponding to a drop from 42 percent to 28 percent of the active work force. Yet the number of workers in manufacturing increased only by about 8 percent in that 13-year period, from 669,000 to 728,000. A large part of the increase, 38,000 workers, was accounted for by the textile industry, while employment in one of the most dynamic sectors from the point of view of investment—chemicals—actually declined slightly.[2] Rather than concluding that, with respect to the occupational structure, Portugal industrialized in the post-1960 period, it is more accurate to say that the agricultural sector became depopulated, with its work force moving primarily out of Portugal. Most of the movement into the nonagricultural work force within Portugal was directed toward transportation (+27 percent), construction (+34 percent), and especially banking, insurance, and real estate, in which the number of workers more than tripled during the period. In part this growth was a result of increased tourism, but a greater part resulted from the expansion of trade and the flow of capital through the country.

What growth there was in the labor force was heavily concentrated in the five provinces which in 1960 had less than half of their labor force in agriculture: Lisbon, Porto, Setúbal, Aveiro, and Braga. Setúbal, located on the coast adjacent to Lisbon, experienced a substantial industrial expansion, particularly in modern sectors such as chemicals, petroleum products, and auto manufacturing. The northern provinces of Porto, Aveiro, and Braga, which have historically been the manufacturing centers of the country, expanded their traditional industries, particularly textiles. Lisbon, the capital and largest city, consolidated its position as the commercial and financial center of both Portugal and the colonies. Its expansion in the 1960s was almost entirely a result of the growth of the female labor force, and was disproportionately concentrated in the commercial and white collar sectors. The number of office workers in Lisbon grew by 52 percent during the decade, and by 1970 accounted for 44 percent of the national total; the number of professionals in Lisbon increased by 45 percent, constituting 39 percent of the national total by 1970.

In summary, Portugal's development in the 1960s was determined first by the expansion of links with its colonies, and second by its integration into the world economy as a market, a source of manpower, and a site for tourism and investment. The occupational structure generated by this pattern was disproportionately mercantilistic (commercial-financial white collar), and the industrial working class was divided between traditional industries in the north and newer capital-intensive industries in the south. The Portuguese working class was therefore a composite of workers in quite varied positions. Their main common bond was not their relation to capital, but their link to an authoritarian state which had repressed any autonomous organization of workers since the early 1930s.

State-Class Relations in the 1970s

Marcello Caetano became president of the Council of Ministers in 1968. It was a time when there was growing evidence of combativeness in some working-class sectors, with scattered conflicts among bank and office workers and in many of the new industries concentrated in the industrial suburb of Barreiro. Among the most visible conflicts was the one between Lisbon transport workers and the British-owned Carris transit firm, which involved a series of mass meetings (some broken up by police) and a four-day period in July 1968 during which workers refused to collect fares. Within the first three months of Caetano's government, extending into early 1969, there was a wave of strikes which, though quickly repressed, helped to make labor relations a significant issue of public policy.

Portugal at that time was fully enmeshed in two contradictory trends. First, the domestic economy was growing at a fast pace under the influence of rapidly expanding foreign investment and trade, with additional stimulus from emigrant remittances and tourism. This development pattern, however, was reaching its limits because of a shortage of skilled (literate) workers, the weak participation of domestic capital, and the low level of state investment in infrastructure, education, and services (the state share of capital formation, for example, declined steadily through the 1960s). Second, the resources of the state were becoming increasingly tied up in colonial wars from which traditional elites—entrenched in the ministries and corporatist bureaucracy, and continuing to profit from their control of trade with the colonies—refused to withdraw.

Caetano's policy in this situation was to promote a federalist solution to the colonial problem (seeking in part to require the colonies to accept a greater share of the costs of the wars) and to support the Europeanization of the domestic economy.[3] That choice implied bringing a new cadre of technocrats into the government, as well as the development of public support for the regime as a counterweight to the traditional elites on whom he was forced to rely for support in 1968–1970. In my view this is the meaning of the "political spring" of 1969, during which Caetano announced parliamentary elections for the following fall, lifted some press censorship, and made cosmetic changes in the name and structure of the secret police and the corporatist party organization. It was his hope to co-opt dissent within the system, converting it from a liability to a political resource.

His policy with respect to labor is best understood as an effort to remove the state from its direct role in wage bargaining and the management of conflict, to deflect international pressure for labor reform, and to enlarge the regime's social base. The bases for implementing the policy were decree laws (*decreto-leis*) 49058 and 49212, announced in the summer of 1969. The first of these ended the requirement for ministerial confirmation of union election results (the requirement had been used to void the bankworker elections of 1969, among others), substituting instead a system in which the eligibility of candidates was confirmed before elections by worker commissions within the local union. In addition, the right of the government to suspend union officials for cause was made subject to judicial review. The second decree strengthened the position of unions in wage bargaining by imposing maximum time limits for the successive stages of initial negotiation, conciliation, and arbitration.

These changes allowed opposition groups to organize more effectively within the existing union structure in those sectors which had developed an informal leadership in struggles in the 1960s; other sectors were unaffected. These groups took advantage of the less repressive atmosphere during the 1969 parliamentary election period, and drew upon the political network established by the opposition during that campaign to organize opposition slates in many union elections in 1970. Such slates were successful in several key unions, including those of the metalworkers in both Lisbon and Porto, wool-workers, and various white collar workers (in banking, offices, cashiering, and insurance) in the Lisbon district.

The new union leaderships were on the whole highly politicized, and sought to use their formal positions not only for aggressive wage bargaining, but also to raise the level of class consciousness and the potential for conflict at the factory level and to develop links among unions for political lobbying. They recognized that most industrial conflicts had been spontaneous, reactions to specific conditions or incidents within the workplace, and easily channeled through bureaucratic structures of the state or union system. They attempted to create a closer link between the union leadership and workers through frequent general assemblies and the selection of factory delegates as intermediaries. In addition, by October 1970 they had established Intersindical, a confederation of more than 20 individual unions.

From the point of view of worker militants, the Caetano reforms offered an opportunity for far greater accessibility to workers, public visibility, and to some extent protection from repression, as long as they worked within the margins of the law. Yet because both labor legislation and the court system remained in the control of the regime and subject to its manipulation, for union militants there was constant tension arising from their use of union positions to solidify opposition to the regime and the potential for bureaucratic entrapment. In fact, no sooner had labor activists begun their work within the union structure than the regime began to limit their opportunities. In October 1970, two more decree laws concerning labor were promulgated. The first (no. 492/70) affected the composition of arbitration panels: rather than having the third member of such panels chosen by agreement between the management and labor representatives, he would be selected by the Ministry of Corporations, which subsumed both the employer and worker associations in the corporatist structure. This change had the immediate practical impact of limiting awards gained through arbitration. The second decree law (no. 502/70) allowed the minister of corporations to suspend union officials and to close union offices before, and pending the outcome of, judicial review of the substance of allegations; this law was invoked in the case of the metalworkers union of Lisbon in November. In addition, the regime began routinely to prohibit union assemblies and to prevent public meetings of Intersindical, forcing it into semiclandestinity by 1972.

The case of the Lisbon metalworkers union is indicative of how the regime opened up and then abruptly limited the possibility of using the unions as a base for political opposition.[4] The officials of this union, who were elected in June 1970 and were all drawn from the Portuguese airline TAP, immediately pressed for rejection of the wage pact that had been concluded by the outgoing leadership. In general assemblies and in leaflets directed to union members, they argued that TAP and the government had connived to complete the wage negotiations before they could be affected by the new labor law, and that the reforms themselves were simply an effort "to control the union movement from the outside" and to "set salary level and working conditions always within the limits established by the dominant class." They attempted to improve communication with the workers by establishing factory commissions, and diverted funds previously used for subsidizing the cost of schoolbooks for members' children to support a professional negotiating staff. Following the prohibition of a public meeting called for October, and in solidarity with the other unions of the Intersindical confederation, they refused any longer to request authorization for such meetings. Clearly the union officials were making full use of their formal positions. In November they were suspended from their positions by the government on the grounds that they had begun "to move at the margins of the law, assuming even towards the legitimate authorities positions of truly illicit confrontation, imperiling the spirit of collaboration and social peace which, as corporatist leaders, with authority and responsibilities expressly defined by law, they were bound to respect and promote."[5] The government's action was ultimately upheld by the courts, and a new slate of officers imposed by the Caetano government held office until early 1974, when new elections were held just before the April coup.

Labor Politics after 1974

Whereas the Caetano years were characterized by intermittent reform and repression, and state-class relations were kept within the bounds of the official union structure and legislative and court action, the first three months after the April revolution were marked by unbounded labor conflict. The overthrow of Caetano, the abolition of the secret police network, and the first steps toward democratic freedoms created a semirevolutionary atmosphere for working-class action. Scores of spontaneous strikes were organized by worker assemblies in every economic sector, some quite brief and others lasting for a month or more. These conflicts were directed primarily at the achievement of wage demands, but they were also oriented toward structural changes in class relations. In many cases workers demanded the purging of managers and directors identified with the old regime, and called for the control of production or work organization to pass to worker assemblies. Even wage demands involved structural changes, often calling for wage freezes or ceilings at the top of the scale and disproportionate increases for the least paid.

This wave of conflict was successful primarily in larger firms and sectors in which workers had a tradition of organization and militancy. In many other cases, however, it was met with intransigence by employers using all of the weapons available for resistance. These included layoffs, lockouts, refusal to implement national contract terms, selective attacks on activists, freezing investment or production, and in extreme cases flight abroad with all of the firm's liquid assets.

The new government was drawn into the conflicts in two ways. Increasingly, it assumed the role of mediator, using military force to impose settlements on both sides, with the result that industrial conflict became highly politicized. At the same time, the government itself as a major employer sought (through administrators who had retained their positions since the coup) to limit wage demands, to regain normal hierarchical control, and to put an end to purges by worker assemblies. This use of state power was partly related to the fact that the conservative General Spínola had a major role in policy making at least until July of 1974, but such an explanation does not account for the continuation of the containment policy well after Spínola's fall from power. In general terms, the state was fulfilling its normal function of maintaining production and promoting capital accumulation, a function equally important to regimes of the right and the left.

The main formal expression of the containment policy was the anti-strike decree law no. 392/74, promulgated in August 1974. This legislation, which purported to guarantee the right to strike that had been prohibited by corporatist legislation, was in the context of the period a tool for the suppression of conflict, following the general lines urged by the employers association. Most significantly, it legalized the lockout as a "defensive" weapon of employers in cases where conflicts exceeded the bounds of the strike law—which included most cases through the year 1974. The law prohibited strikes motivated by political or religious goals, solidarity strikes, and strikes aimed at changing the terms of existing union contracts before their expiration; it left unclear the status of strikes by public employees (articles 4–6). The law also outlawed work stoppages by isolated groups of workers in strategic sectors of an enterprise, as well as factory occupations (article 7); it guaranteed access to work by employees who chose not to join a strike (article 14). In addition, it attempted to incorporate strikes into a formal bureaucratic process of contract negotiation, requiring a conciliation period of 30 days after the presentation of written demands before the commencement of a strike; authorized only strikes called by the union involved or by a majority vote of the entire workforce; and required a minimum 7 to 10 day advance notice of the calling of a strike (articles 8–11). Finally, the law authorized the government, at its discretion, to suspend a strike, to determine whether a strike conformed to legal requirements, and to impose fines on the responsible parties (articles 27–28).

The Collaboration of Worker Organizations with the MFA

The most difficult issue to evaluate, in the first year of the Portuguese revolution, and the most central to an understanding of the labor movement in Portugal, is the part played by the Portuguese Communist Party and Intersindical. In the early 1970s the opposition parties worked as a coalition in labor activity. The dominant force, however, was the Communist party, which effectively controlled Intersindical, while parties of the far left—whose initial base was the student movement of the 1960s—had only scattered grassroots support before 1974. This fact became critical to post-1974 dynamics, as the Communist party used Intersindical to assume the leadership of most unions and emerged as the single representative of labor in dealing with the state. PCP control of labor through grassroots support, cadres of activists, and the union bureaucracy was further reinforced by the selection of party member Avelino Gonçalves as the minister of labor in the First Provisional Government.

The policy of Intersindical, which made it a useful ally of the military and cemented its position within the government, was to collaborate with the effort to contain labor militancy. In instructions to its militants, in public rallies, in the press, and through pronouncements of the Ministry of Labor the party labeled the surge of industrial conflicts reactionary, "playing into the hands of the fascists." In the key metal sector, the union leadership agreed to a wage settlement of 4,500 escudos, well below their original demand of 6,000 (which had long been the Intersindical demand for a national minimum wage). This settlement provoked numerous wildcat strikes, including the occupation of the Berliet division of Metalúrgica Duarte in May of 1974, but the union leadership remained in general control. A mark of the degree of constraint exercised by the party is the fact that despite the mobilization of workers in spontaneous conflicts throughout the country, most conflicts were again channeled through the formal union structure by the end of 1974.

The strategy of collaboration with the government had multiple motivations. Intersindical's justification for suppressing conflicts was based on its reading of the new political situation:

> Opportunistic elements of both the right and the far left, exploiting the natural impatience of workers for the satisfaction of their just demands, are drawing them into a type of action which, objectively, serves the reactionary forces, who are interested in taking advantage of anarchy and economic chaos to break the unity of the working class and its alliance with the Armed Forces Movement [the MFA]. Given the nature of the present moment of class struggle, it seems evident that the strike is one weapon to use to resolve conflicts in the workplace, but it is a weapon which should be used as an ultimate recourse, after exhausting all other means, in order to prevent the advantages which all the enemies of the People, of Democracy, and of the workers, would reap from an indiscriminate and unnecessary use of the strike.[6]

Intersindical's strategy should also be understood in terms of the Communist party's desire to strengthen its links to the MFA, to protect its base of support in the many small or poorly organized firms where strikes could lead to financial collapse or effective retaliation, and to prevent worker mobilization outside the union structure.

Containment was something of a gamble for the Communist party. By opposing the wave of strikes in 1974 the PCP risked the loss of grassroots support and opened itself to electoral challenges in future union elections. Workers involved in many strikes severely attacked the party's role in the labor movement.[7] The party, however, attained organizational control over the major part of the labor movement: Intersindical expanded from a confederation of 22 unions before the coup to more than 200 by August 1974, when it held its first union congress with the support of the MFA. While responsibility for the Ministry of Labor implied a loss of popularity and prestige within the working class, it was also critical in maintaining or assuming control of major unions. In the office workers union, for example, party militants were allowed by the ministry to occupy the administrative offices and to install a provisional leadership,[8] which undercut potential opposition by securing the approval of plans for new elections within one month and requiring candidates to obtain a minimum of 500 petition signatures to run for office.[9] More overtly, Ministry of Labor and military intervention were major elements in the sequence of events in the chemicals union. In this case, militants affiliated with Intersindical were able to replace the previous independent leadership in March 1975 in special elections (won by a small margin), following a series of conflicts within the union during which the former officials were temporarily jailed.[10]

The main feature of this first year of the revolution from the perspective of the working class was the relative ease with which repression by a corporatist state, in which workers were not represented, was replaced by the subordination of workers' perceived needs to the requirements of the organization that purported to represent them. During this period, class relations were heavily marked by bureaucratic manipulation of the labor movement through means not dissimilar in substance (though of course quite different in ideological content) from those used by Caetano's state. As early as June 1974, the transportation union leadership had complained that "Intersindical shows itself in its true character as manipulators [*sic*] of processes which were so dear to the former deposed regime."[11] This complaint reflected the general theme of attacks from the far left on the "social fascist" nature of the Communist party—a theme that became a major issue in the period following formation of the Fourth Provisional Government in March 1975. But the main point is that the Portuguese working class had neither the tradition of militancy, the factory-level organization, nor the independent leadership to enable it to resist domination from above.

Challenges to Intersindical Control

The second phase of the postrevolutionary period coincided with a major shift in national politics. After August of 1975, the Gonçalves government with which the Communist party had allied itself was replaced by a series of governments in which the Socialist party (PS) was the main force. Even before this time Intersindical had come under attack in a number of key unions from a coalition of anticommunist parties. As early as December 1974, the Intersindical-affiliated leadership was replaced by an opposition slate in elections of the merchant marine and fishermen's union; the new leadership advocated a 35-hour week and 6,000 escudos in monthly wages. Opposition slates also won elections in January 1975 in the transportation and Porto bankworkers' unions by margins of 2 to 1 or better.

In June and early July of 1975, the Communists lost control of two unions of professionals (the doctors and lawyers unions) to conservatives, marking the formal transition within those unions from the corporatist period, in which the Communists had assumed leadership of the strong antifascist forces in the unions, to a new period in which professional interests and prerogatives became predominant. At the same time, Intersindical suffered a much more substantial loss in the large and influential bankworkers' union of Lisbon, one of the strongest early proponents of Intersindical in the Caetano period. In similar elections in August and September, slates supported by Intersindical were defeated repeatedly by noncommunist coalitions in unions of banking, insurance, journalism, and office workers.

Such losses, concentrated in the large and financially strong white collar unions (which had been in the vanguard of class mobilization before 1974), created the possibility of a serious struggle for control of Intersindical in 1976. Like the losses in professional unions, they marked the end of a long period during which labor activists of the PCP had successfully claimed leadership of workers' opposition to the corporatist structure on a nonpartisan basis. By the end of the summer of 1975, the majority of workers in the white collar sector were seeking a more aggressive leadership, given Intersindical's reluctance to press wage demands for a relatively affluent sector; they preferred the moderate socialism of the Socialist party to the disciplined bureaucratic structure of the Communists. Such a position, of course, was consistent with their near middle-class status, and reflected the anti-Communist mobilization in national politics at the time.

There was a period, therefore, when Communist party control of the labor movement was in doubt. In early 1976 an opposition coalition of the far left, the Socialists, and the social democrats launched a drive to obtain control of Intersindical, calling for a union congress to reorganize the labor movement. This attempt failed for two major reasons. First, the coalition could not be maintained when the Socialist party became the nation's main governing party. The radicals made aggressive use of their union positions to bring the white collar unions into a "secretariat of union struggles" to oppose government policy. Unable to tolerate this tactic, the Socialists allowed the leadership of the key Lisbon office workers union to fall to the Communists rather than remain in the hands of their erstwhile partners. The Socialist-majority leaderships of several other unions lost effective control to general assemblies dominated by Communist militants. Second, as the PS in power continued to press for austerity measures, wage limits, and other unpopular measures, it lost its potential for leadership of the major unions. By late 1977 it had lost control of the Lisbon commerce workers union, as well as its only blue collar unions, the northern metalworkers and mineworkers unions.

Having failed to win control of Intersindical, the Socialists chose to build an alternative union structure, the União Geral de Trabalhadores (UGT). Their strategy clearly was to translate their electoral strength into a claim to represent the working class, even in the absence of organizational strength. Thus workers were allowed to enroll as individuals in the UGT, and in some sectors the UGT fostered the creation of new trade unions to compete with unions affiliated with Intersindical. The Socialists and Social Democrats also attempted to use their strength in the legislature to change the structure of existing unions: to require that elections be held in workplaces (to cut abstentions and presumably to improve their standing), and to replace the union general assembly with an indirectly representative union congress as the ultimate source of power in unions (to compensate for their lack of grassroots militants). However, it was only as an opposition party that the PS was able to build a real union presence, and the future development of the UGT depends on the UGT's ability to maintain autonomy from the parties in power.

Intersindical, meanwhile, was forced to become more representative of the working class, and herein may lie the one positive note in my account of worker mobilization and party politics. For once out of power at the national level, and as a result of its competition with the other parties, the Communist party chose to develop closer links with other factions in the union structure, settling for coalitions rather than direct control of local unions, and bringing in new leadership. It was also put in a position to lobby strongly to protect gains made in the first two years of the revolution—gains in worker control, nationalization of industries and financial institutions, and employment security.

One possible reading of the situation in 1979 was that after five years of formal democratic processes, the political situation may have given the Portuguese working class greater influence over its own union organizations. But given the composition of that class, the very real limits to its power in the workplace, the limits to democratization of the national government, the relative independence of political parties from their popular bases, and the political and economic constraints imposed by other countries, the Portuguese working class had a difficult road ahead.

Notes

1 Luis Salgado de Matos, *Investimentos estrangeiros em Portugal* (Lisbon, 1973).
2 Statistics taken from Instituto Nacional de Estadística de Portugal, *Estatísticas de Trabalho* (Lisbon, 1974), p. 12, table 5.
3 Lawrence S. Graham, *Portugal: The Decline and Collapse of an Authoritarian Order* (Beverly Hills, 1975).
4 Summarized in detail in Francisco Marcelo Curto and Victor Wengorovius, *Uma questão sindical: o processo dos Metalúrgicos de Lisboa* (Porto, 1972).
5 Curto and Wengorovius, *Uma questão sindical*, p. 44.
6 Taken from Intersindical, *Documentos Sindicais 1970–1974* (Lisbon, 1974), p. 39.
7 Detailed accounts of these conflicts are provided in Maria de Lourdes Lima dos Santos, et al., *O 25 de abril e as lutas sociais nas empresas* (Porto, 1976).
8 *Diário de Lisboa,* Apr. 28, 1974.
9 *Diário de Lisboa,* May 3, 1974.
10 *Expresso,* Jan. 17, 1976.
11 *Diário de Lisboa,* June 19, 1974.

PART 3
ALTERING THE STRUCTURES OF THE STATE: THE PROBLEMS OF INSTITUTIONALIZING CHANGE

7 Charles Downs

Residents' Commissions and Urban Struggles in Revolutionary Portugal

On April 29, 1974—four days after the military coup—more than 100 families living in shantytowns occupied a new government housing project on the outskirts of Lisbon. In the next two weeks more than 2,000 houses were occupied around the country. On April 30 the residents of a municipal housing project in Porto met in general assembly and elected a *comissão de moradores* (residents' commission, or CM). The next day they marched together in the May 1 celebrations and presented the government with a list of demands calling for the elimination of repressive housing regulations and the improvement of physical conditions in housing. They called upon the residents of other housing projects to organize themselves; many soon followed. On May 11, 300 residents, representing 230 families living in a group of 50-year-old "temporary housing" shanties (*barracas*) in Lisbon met in assembly. They drew up a list of demands for "streets, water, and a new *bairro*" (neighborhood), and elected a CM. They too called upon other *bairros de barracas* (shantytowns) to follow suit; and others did.

These are but three examples of the beginnings of the popular movement unleashed by the April 25 coup. The following revolutionary period, 1974–1975, was rich in the creation and activity of autonomous local popular organizations. There were hundreds of companies operating under forms of worker control or *auto-gestão* (self-management), with factory assemblies and workers' commissions as the highest authorities. Groups of agricultural workers occupied land to "bring it under the control of those who till it," and formed more than 500 cooperative and collective forms. Junior officers and especially soldiers began organizing themselves to improve conditions and eliminate status differences within the armed forces, as well as to guarantee that they would be "always, always on the side of the people."[1] In the neighborhoods, commissions were elected to represent local interests, demanding (and sometimes making) changes in the physical and social conditions of housing and neighborhood life. Together these grass roots organizations were to be the basis for a revolutionary transformation of the state and society, according to the projects for popular power held by the revolutionary left and the Portuguese Communist Party (PCP).

This chapter will focus on one of these forms of organization, the *comissão de moradores*, and the urban struggles in which it was involved. The CM experience is not well known outside Portugal. Because is was important and yet remains poorly understood, the highlights of its history will be recounted.[2] Thus we will be able to examine the concrete development of the autonomous movements of people from many different classes, organized around real problems encountered in their daily lives, acting within the context of changes in the political conjuncture—i.e., the relationships of class political forces in qualitatively different periods.

The discussion centers on urban struggles in the main coastal cities of Lisbon, Porto, and Setúbal—the three largest cities in Portugal.[3] While urban organizing and struggles were not limited to these cities, it was there that they were concentrated. In each of the cities the struggles involved different problems and political forces, and evolved differently. Although the discussion refers to these differences and draws on the events of the struggles in all three cities, it is obviously colored by the experiences of the author as a resident of Lisbon during the second half of the period considered, and by the research and interviews conducted for a joint study of the CM and the urban social movement in Setúbal.[4]

We will first look at the material and political conditions in which the CMs arose and developed. Then we will examine the experiences of the CMs as individual units—their formation, demands, and accomplishments. After that we will turn to the main common struggles waged by the CMs, and to the experiences of different coordinating bodies. We will conclude with a short summary of two of the themes highlighted by the Portuguese experience: the multiclass nature of the urban movement, and its relation to the state.

The Context of the Urban Struggle

Nearly 30 percent of all Portuguese families lacked minimally decent housing in 1974.[5] That alone is sufficient to indicate that the housing question was critical and involved large segments of the society. But it is worth looking quickly at the development of the Portuguese economy and society in the years preceding 1974 to understand the specific nature of the housing crisis and how widespread it was.

Until about 1960, Salazar pursued a policy of trying to keep out foreign influences, be they cultural or economic. In 1961 armed struggle for the liberation of Angola began; it was followed by similar movements in Guinea-Bissau (1963) and Mozambique (1964). To overcome opposition to the war by western countries, Salazar made concessions by opening Portugal to foreign investment. As the need for political and military support grew and the hope to modernize the Portuguese industrial structure developed, the government took further steps to favor foreign investment. From 1965 on, foreign capital began investing in auto assembly plants and in light industries (especially textiles and electronic assembly). By the beginning of the 1970s, heavy industry was expanding greatly (particularly in machinery, shipbuilding, and petrochemicals) either under the control of or in partnership with foreign capital.[6] At the same time, small-scale Portuguese agriculture was in a severe crisis: the number of agricultural employers declined from 136,541 in 1950 to 17,100 in 1970.[7]

These two factors caused an intensive migration to the main cities. Setúbal, the most extreme case, grew 15 percent from 1960 to 1970, and 34 percent from 1970 to 1975.[8] Migration brought to the cities a lot of people looking for housing that did not exist, or for which they could not pay; and they had to make do as best they could—in shacks, in rooms, crowding together. Further complicating the lack of housing were the rapid development of tourism and a 1969 law which, for the first time, allowed banks to make medium-term loans (one to five years) to finance housing. These circumstances combined to produce a situation in which only the most profitable housing was built.

To summarize the housing situation in early 1974, 30 percent of the population lived in substandard housing. There were many old houses left empty for speculation and future rebuilding. Significant numbers of better paid workers and professionals gave 25 to 40 percent of their incomes for housing that frequently was insufficient in terms of basic infrastructures (roads, sewers, etc.). And there was also a hidden aspect of the crisis—new housing so expensive that it was unsaleable.[9] It was to change these concrete conditions that people organized themselves into *comissões de moradores*.

However, bad housing conditions alone do not explain why CMs were formed when they were. Neither do they explain why people occupied housing at some times and not at others, nor why ordinary people went from concern with their individual lives to concern with changing their housing conditions to concern with changing the government and society. Although we may account for these changes in various ways, the most important cause involved alterations in the political conjuncture—that is to say, in the political relationships among various classes and fractions of classes. To understand this situation it is helpful to divide the two years in which the CMs engaged in their greatest activity (1974–1975) into four periods which correspond to developments in the national conjuncture; each reflects changes in the unity and hegemony of the state, the autonomy and role of the armed forces in repressing or tolerating the popular movement, and government support or opposition to popular organization.[10]

April 25, 1974, to October 1974 (First and Second Provisional governments)

The coup of April 25 undid the coalition which had ruled under fascism and eliminated one of its main tools for social control—the secret police. There followed an explosion of struggles for certain minimum conditions in both the factory and the neighborhood. This period was marked by two dramatic efforts to re-form a modernized version of the ousted ruling bloc: the attempted presidentialist coup of Palma Carlos in early July, and the Spinolist "march of the silent majority" on September 28.

October 1974 to March 1975 (Third Provisional Government)

September 28 was the second strong warning of the need to make structural changes in the economy and the society in order to avoid a return to the old order. In the second period the political organizations clarified an antimonopolist political position. At the same time, the armed forces passed from a position of repressive force to positions of neutrality and/or support for the population's demands. The period ended with the suppression of the right wing within the military, in the aftermath of the attempted military coup of March 11, 1975.

March 1975 to November 25, 1975 (Fourth, Fifth, and Early Sixth Provisional governments)

During this period the popular organizations gained much more strength and radicalized their positions. The open struggle for political power became the center of attention for all. In part because of this struggle the distance between the leadership and the base of the urban movement began increasing toward the end of the period. While this period included three provisional governments, it can be considered as one because the state was of continually decreasing importance in terms of daily or practical activities; it was increasingly weak, neutralized, and ignored. Both a cause and effect of the state's weakness was the fact that its most basic structure, the armed forces, became not only less reliable, but began to actively question orders to side with the popular movement, thus threatening the very existence of the government.[11] The local political conjuncture varied widely from city to city during this period. Local organizations became much more highly coordinated, and situations of dual power developed at the city level. The period ended with the rightist military coup of November 25, and the strengthening of the repressive power of the bourgeois state.[12]

November 25, 1975, to June 1976 (Sixth Provisional Government)

The November 25 coup eliminated any possibility of the left and popular forces achieving power. Repressive forces returned to their traditional role of opposing the occupation of houses and factories and other demonstrations of popular will. For workers and their organizations, the period was one of defensive struggles. They tried to defend their recent conquests against attacks from the government as well as from the growing fascist offensive, which was directed against both their achievements and the coalition that had staged the coup on November 25. The legislative elections of April 25, 1976, showed continued support for those parties nominally on the left. Popular organizations began to remobilize around the presidential elections scheduled for June 27, 1976.

Creation of the *Comissões de Moradores*

With an idea of the material and political conditions in which CMs arose, and of the circumstances that gave them political significance and practical effectiveness, we can turn to their creation and functions. CMs developed in the post-April 1974 political situation. There had been very little urban struggle under fascism,[13] but within a matter of weeks there were dozens of CMs. They began almost exclusively either in those neighborhoods which had struggled during fascism, or in other poor neighborhoods that followed the earlier examples.

CMs usually started when an "organizing committee" convoked a general assembly of the *bairro* to discuss the problems of the *bairro*—e.g., housing, infrastructures, repressive government regulations—or problems resulting from the occupations of the first two weeks after April 25, 1974. During the assembly a list of demands and grievances was drawn up and a CM was elected. The latter frequently consisted of the organizing committee plus a few more people. The CM then formulated demands and proposed forms of action, all to be further discussed with and ratified by the neighborhood assembly.

We can distinguish four phases in the formation of CMs, corresponding to the four periods in the national political conjuncture outlined earlier. The first two months after April 25 saw the formation of CMs in most of the shantytowns, as well as in Porto's *bairros camarários* (municipal housing districts). Few other CMs were formed until mid-August, when some shantytowns began forming CMs in response to demands of the Serviço Ambulatório de Apoio Local (SAAL, the Mobile Local Support Service).[14] At this point local government institutions also became important in the creation of CMs. The MDP/CDE began promoting meetings to form commissions at the level of the *freguesia*, to cooperate with it in controlling local governments.[15] There were occasions when local officials consciously and explicitly refused to hear the complaints of individual residents unless they could show that they were representatives of a CM. Although such instances were more frequent in Lisbon than elsewhere,[16] they served to spread the idea of organizing to other *bairros* besides the poorest.

The second phase began about November 1974 and extended to March 1975. The "cultural dynamization campaign" organized by the Armed Forces Movement (MFA) pushed the idea of people organizing themselves to determine and solve local problems. For example, in early 1975 the municipal government of Setúbal began to encourage those *bairros* still without a CM to elect one, to enable them to take part in the general assembly of the *concelho* of Setúbal in early March.[17] Elsewhere CMs emerged in shantytowns still lacking such organizations in order to take part in the SAAL process. Finally, another type of spontaneous local organization appeared—"occupant commissions"—as a consequence of the housing occupations that had begun in February. These commissions were frequently formed (especially in Lisbon) in opposition to those CMs linked with neighborhood local government councils (*juntas de freguesia*, or JFs) which had denounced the occupations and occupants as "opportunist" and "wildcat" (*selvagem*). From this point on the principle of "autonomy in relation to all levels of government" became an important aspect of the CM movement.[18]

By April 1975 there were 38 occupant commissions and 21 CMs in Lisbon, as well as the government's 54 formally constituted JFs. During the third phase (March to November 1975) additional CMs were formed, especially after the MFA in July adopted a document calling for the eventual creation of a socialist state, based on direct democracy through CMs and worker commissions (*comissões de trabalhadores*, or CTs). This period also saw the renovation of many already existing CMs. By November Setúbal had 30 CMs representing more than three-quarters of its population. Approximately one-quarter of this population was located in shantytowns, another one-third in poor neighborhoods, and a little less than one-half in neighborhoods composed principally of the petite bourgeoisie and better paid workers. The percentage of CMs in the latter type of neighborhood was higher in Setúbal than in Lisbon and Porto.

After November 25, few new CMs were created. Those that were reflected little organizing work, and were more likely the result of partisan political or specifically electoral acts. The conditions for creating CMs had passed.

CM Functioning and Accomplishments

In talking with members of a CM, or reading their statutes, one nearly always encountered the phrase, "The CM is a unitary, nonpartisan grass roots organization which represents the interests of the dwellers of this area," or some similar equivalent.[19] The CM was based on an effort to solve local problems, in which the interests of all residents theoretically would be the same and in which party politics should not enter. The idea that it was a political but nonpartisan organization was a hard-fought-for and staunchly defended position. Thus militants or sympathizers of different parties—left, right, or center—and the majority without party allegiance could work together, united by their acts instead of being divided by their words. While there were undoubtedly times when a party manipulated a CM, the divisiveness of sectarian struggle was greatly reduced.

Once elected, the first tasks of the CM normally were to formalize a list of demands and to draw up statutes. The statutes normally defined the *bairro* assembly (composed of all district people of more than 16 or 18 years of age) as the highest level of power (or the base of power). The assembly elected the CM, and the CM was responsible to it. Generally speaking, the need for new elections arose for one of three basic reasons: when some members resigned because of a lack of interest, tiredness, or internal conflicts in the CM; when the population, because of conflicts, decided to recall a CM; or when the CM had served out its mandate (normally one year).

In practice the CM met weekly, or sometimes fortnightly, and the assembly was convoked occasionally as special issues arose. Within the CM there might be various working groups, and a coordinating committee that met by itself once each week. The statutes of one CM called for nine working groups: housing, infancy and old age, culture and sports, health and aid, price control, fund raising, *associativismo* (cooperation for mutual aid), urbanism, and public relations. Each working group made an analysis of the pertinent situation in the *bairro*, and proposed demands or looked for other ways to solve the problems encountered.

The demands finally made by a CM were attempts to resolve basic local problems. Those *bairros* with especially bad housing conditions demanded housing; those with deficient physical infrastructures or without such services demanded sewers, electricity, and street repairs; those lacking basic public facilities and services demanded schools, child-care centers, public transportation, trash collection, telephone booths, and social centers; those with higher income and consumption levels and better services demanded such nonessentials as parking lots and heating for swimming pools. Other *bairros* demanded pharmacies or clinics with free services for all. Finally, *bairros* with special problems (e.g., *bairros camarários*) demanded their resolution. Although no general study has been made of such demands, data from Setúbal suggest how common the different demands were: one-third of Setúbal's 30 CMs demanded housing; more than five-sixths demanded physical infrastructures and basic equipment of one kind or another; two demanded nonessential equipment; and three demanded pharmacies.

In considering the objective accomplishments of the CMs, two other kinds of CM action must be added to the list. CMs frequently developed programs of cultural activities (films, debates, sports, literacy courses, *festas*); and some CMs took part in the direct sale of agricultural products.[20] While an "accomplishment" did not necessarily fulfill a corresponding "demand," it is clear that much was achieved. For example, in Setúbal all housing problems were in some stage of resolution and basic physical and social conditions had been improved by the end of 1975. Three-quarters of the *bairros* had improved physical infrastructures, and two-thirds had improved social facilities.[21] Two free pharmacies had been created, and cultural activities and the sale of agricultural products were each important for one-half of Setúbal's CMs. It is interesting to note that the demands for "non-essential equipment" were the only ones not met in some way.

The CMs attempted not only to improve the material conditions of the *bairros*, but also to increase the participation of people in the control of their daily lives. There are both quantitative and qualitative problems in evaluating such participation. Qualitatively, there is no objective way of knowing what "good" and "poor" levels of participation (80 percent? 10 percent?) would be after the complete lack of local participation and power that characterized fascist society. On one hand, there was a far higher proportion of people taking part in the CMs than normally participates in local politics in western countries; on the other hand, those involved in the CMs nearly always felt that there was not enough participation. We cannot quantify the participation because rarely did the CMs keep more than occasional, haphazard records of the number of people involved in various activities, and because many different kinds of participation were possible.

Recognizing these limitations, we can distinguish four types of activities in which people of the *bairros* participated: specific projects of subgroups within the CMs, meetings of the CMs as a whole, *bairro* assemblies, and demonstrations related either to specific urban issues (such as housing) or more general political issues. Several general observations can be made:

—People generally participated more when issues had great local import
—They were more willing to give moral support than to work actively
—The people who were most active were not the young; rather, they were people from 30 to 50+ years of age, from the *bairro*, who were strongly committed to what they were doing
—There were comparatively more younger people (in their 20s) active in the newer *bairros* than in the older ones
—All age groups went to demonstrations
—Those active in the *bairro* were often the same persons who were active in the work place (unions, workers' committees)
—There were many more women than men active in the basic work of the CMs
—Many more men than women had seats on the CMs
—Participation of all types was consistently much greater in the shantytowns than in other *bairros*
—In other *bairros*, there might occasionally be an assembly of 200 or more people, but normally 100 people was considered a good turnout
—The type and degree of participation was sensitive to the overall political conjuncture

Sensitivity to the political situation was particularly important in Portugal. The rapid spread and the growth in influence of the CMs reflected changes in the political conjuncture (up to November 25,

1975) more than they did the practical work of the CMs. The huge turnouts for demonstrations called by the CMs in the summer of 1975 were signs of support for the projects of the CMs (and workers' commissions) rather than signs of their organizational strength. This weakness was clearly shown in the general demobilization after November 25.

But demobilization was not the end of CMs, although some did come to an end at that time or shortly afterward.[22] Those that maintained the strongest activity were, first, CMs in shantytowns linked to the SAAL process, and, second, those CMs which had done more active local organizing and had advanced such concrete projects as the operation of day-care centers. The activities of some CMs became limited to particular projects.

The right-wing coup of November 25 radically altered the concrete possibilities for change—a situation that was reflected in people's consciousness. In 1975 people insisted that the housing problem was a social one and the struggle for decent housing a collective one: "I won't leave my shack until everyone in this *bairro* can go together. We won't be divided." Such collective action was objectively possible—through struggle—and was happening. In 1976 the same people, as individuals, were building a house, or trying to get a priority on a social housing waiting list because "there is no longer any other way."

Finally, the period of general demobilization saw a growth in partisan influence and manipulation in many CMs, both by the PCP and the revolutionary left. This development occurred especially in CMs with weak followings and tended to further reduce those followings. No matter how democratic the formal structure of an organization, it could not remain de facto democratic without active popular participation.

Common Struggles

"Houses Yes, Shacks No."

"Houses for All—Against Capitalism."

"Decent Hosuing for All."

"Not One House without People as Long as There are People without Houses!"[23]

These are the slogans which set the tone for the two longest-lasting common urban struggles. Such struggles were an important part of the CM movement, and warrant attention in evaluating the activities of the residents' commissions. Both mass movements were struggles for housing: the first was aimed at replacing the shantytowns with new *bairros* and reconstructing old housing; the second aimed at the occupation and habitation of vacant housing.

In the weeks immediately following April 25, 1974, most of the CMs formed were in the shantytowns of Lisbon and Setúbal, and in the rundown areas and *ilhas* of Porto.[24] The basic demands were for the state to intervene to provide infrastructures in the old *bairros* and, eventually, new housing. At the end of July 1974, SAAL was created as part of the national Housing Development Fund to support local "initiatives of poorly housed population to cooperate in the transformation of the *bairros*, investing their own latent—and eventually monetary—resources."[25] The program required that the population of a participating *bairro* be organized in an association or cooperative. SAAL offered technical help and a basic investment fund; the population would either borrow the rest of the money, or use its own labor to build the housing. SAAL was a nationwide program that grew to include almost all shantytowns and severely rundown areas in all major urban areas. However, it is important to note that since the success of SAAL generally involved a large amount of organizing and political mobilization, it was not simply a technical solution to the housing problem. Its technical (and especially bureaucratic) steps required pressure from the CMs to move forward, and in turn frequently produced political effects that went beyond the SAAL program.

The CMs soon found themselves involved in political disputes. They disputed with local government authorities who had to approve all operations, had to expropriate the necessary land for housing, and were the channel for project money. They disputed with the central government, which determined the ground rules for participation in projects and rates of interest, as well as with the state bureaucracy that furnished technical help and was at the other end of the channel of funds. Accordingly, the list of demands drawn up on February 15, 1975, by the Coordinating Commission of Lisbon Area Shantytowns and Poor *Bairros* entered into all of these areas of dispute. It included demands to have new *bairros* built in the same places as the old ones, to have a date set for the beginning of construction, to limit the maximum rate of interest to 2 percent, to insure that representatives of the poorly housed would control the distribution of all public housing, and to guarantee that until such housing was available all vacant housing could be occupied by those in greatest need. The commission rejected self-help construction and the rehabilitation of existing shantytowns, as well as proposed regulations for the formation of cooperatives.

While many shantytown residents were acting through CMs to resolve their housing needs, others in substandard housing took a more aggressive line of action, occupying vacant dwellings outright. The first of these occupations was that of April 29, 1974, at the new government housing project in Lisbon, already noted.[26] Over the next two weeks another 1,500 to 2,000 occupations took place in Lisbon, and others around the rest of the country. On May 11 the government published a decree to legalize the occupations made up to that time.

One and one-half years later there had been three waves of housing occupations. Closely related to developments in the national political conjuncture, they showed a progression, radicalization, and generalization of consciousness on the part of the occupants which were reflected not only in occupants' organizations, but also in the targets they selected.

The first wave of occupations took place at vacant government-owned housing, much of which was new and some of which was not even finished. It developed as a consequence of the need for housing by large numbers of people; popular reactions to the corrupt and thoroughly discredited system for assigning government housing, whereby thousands of undistributed units were on hand; and the popular perception that the regular police force would not be sent in to intervene, since the MFA's program had called for its purging and reorganization. Essentially the sum total of numerous individual acts, it ended within two weeks when there was no more government housing to occupy.

Even though only government housing was occupied, during the first wave both large and small property owners felt insecure. Their insecurity was increased by a few scattered occupations of old private homes during the summer of 1974. As a response to this and other problems in the housing market, the government published *decreto-lei* (decree-law) 445/74 on September 12. This law allowed a landlord 120 days to rent his housing, once it was "habitable"; if, after 120 days, housing was not rented, it had to be reported to the *junta de freguesia*, which would rent it in the name of the landlord. The law also prohibited nearly all demolitions until adequate legislations should be drawn up.[27] Not surprisingly, very few landlords cooperated: many did not report housing, and many owners of newly built housing refused to "complete" it by leaving off a light switch or some other minor finishing detail. As the end of the waiting period drew near, there was much discussion among political and mass organizations of how the landlords could be made to obey the law, and of having the CMs work with the JFs in vigilance groups. In fact, committees were formed to locate uninhabited housing, but frequently worked independently of the JFs.

On February 18, 1975, the 120-day limit on vacant property expired.

That night the second big wave of occupations began, with private housing as the target. The law which was intended to prevent the attack on private property had helped to create the conditions that legitimated the attack. It is estimated that some 2,500 apartments were occupied in Lisbon in the ensuing days.[28]

These occupations were considerably more organized than the first wave had been; since the first wave had set an example, it was known when the 120-day waiting period would run out, and committees had been formed to coordinate the action. Once a house was occupied, a meeting was held to decide who would live there; two criteria were followed: "being in need, and not being afraid, because there were many who needed housing who wouldn't take the risk."[29] This time there was police repression, and it forced the occupants to organize themselves further. There were some evictions, but the occupation of other private housing continued, though at a slower rate. With the change in political relations that came in the wake of the attempted rightist military coup on March 11, 1975, occupations increased once more.

The second wave continued into April. The vast majority of the occupations were for the benefit of individual families in need, and they were much more organized than those of the first wave, with the occupiers remaining organized once they were in their new housing. Many buildings were occupied to provide day-care centers, clinics, and other facilities, as well as party headquarters.

Four examples taken from the second wave period might help to clarify some of the conflicts and responses that developed around the occupations. A special problem arose when an occupied house belonged to an emigrant worker, or was the main source of income for an elderly person; in such cases occupiers were sometimes evicted, and it became accepted practice not to touch the house. This practice was made easier when COPCON[30] began to keep a list of such houses: when someone wanted to occupy a house, he checked the list; if the house was unlisted, the occupation took place and was registered. In at least one case—in Setúbal—a housing project builder managed to turn those working for him against the occupiers. When the builder threatened to close down the project and leave the workers unemployed if the occupiers stayed, the workers evicted the occupiers. A third conflict is exemplified by popular reaction to disputed local government action. The *câmara* (local government) of Setúbal and the local military held a public meeting in which they condemned the wave of occupations, set a date for the houses to be vacated, and explained that the houses would then be given to those who needed them most. One shantytown resident expressed the general reaction with these words: "The Housing Development Fund and the *câmara* promise a lot but don't do anything; you can't have a revolution by legal means."[31] Most stayed in the houses they had occupied. In yet another case, when utility companies refused to give contracts to occupants who did not have rent receipts, company workers began hooking up water, electricity, and gas at the order of the CM, without contracts.

The first wave of occupations involved several thousand units of government housing; the second involved several thousand units more of private housing. But only rarely was *new* private housing occupied. The basic reason seems to have been an awareness on the part of potential occupants of what was possible. Occupiers never doubted that they would have to pay rent—and the rent on a new apartment, even without the increases resulting from speculation, would be beyond the means of someone living in a shantytown. As one occupant put it: "We want to pay; we aren't here to rob anyone." Housing was seen as a basic right for all, and adjusting rent according to income had already been proposed by groups of occupants, political parties, and even some local governments. However, neither the general conditions nor the necessary level of organization existed to put in question the right of a landlord to rent private property and the traditional bases for determining the amount of that rent.

In the summer of 1975 the general political mood shifted leftward, and a third wave of occupations took place. In September and October 1975, various CMs announced that "in order to avoid occupation by opportunists" they would proceed with the systematic occupation of all remaining vacant housing, which would then be distributed to those most in need. Although these proposals were never fully implemented, the occupation of new private apartment buildings did begin at this time. This third wave was less intense than the previous two had been, but it was a qualitatively new phase. Occupations were well organized. They were frequently motivated by groups from the revolutionary left, and sometimes by groups of refugees who had returned from Africa during the decolonization process. While the occupations were normally made with some expectation of eventually paying a rent related to income, there was no guarantee of such rent. Most of the occupiers in this phase were not people from shantytowns, but they were people who needed housing.

To whatever degree they were organized, supported, and repressed, all of these occupations were illegal according to the laws of the day. They were the result of autonomous movements by lightly organized masses of people going beyond the law, who argued that if the workers did not fight to defend their own interests, no one else would. But the problem of regularizing each situation by legalizing the occupations was immediately posed. This problem became identified with people of two different political orientations: those who, despite different ideologies, were united by the possibility of social change based on the activation of a popular movement, and those with different specific class interests who were united in their opposition to the development of a popular movement. The issue of legalization brought these groups into confrontation and served to show not only their respective weaknesses and strengths, but also those of the state.

After the first wave of occupations, the government published a decree which essentially recognized the rights of the occupants. But it stated clearly that each case was to be carefully reviewed, and that no further occupations would be tolerated. No review ever took place, and the occupants remained in their new homes.

Following the second wave of occupations (which involved older private housing), the CMs responded in one of two ways to landlords who refused to come to agreement with occupants. Those CMs that were linked to *juntas de freguesia* legalized occupations, when possible, with the *câmara* acting in the place of the landlord (according to *decreto-lei* 445/74). In contrast, autonomous CMs argued that the only possible "legalization" was through the "struggle of the masses." They pointed out that bureaucratic legalization was practically impossible in cases in which, as a result of political differences, the CM and the JF refused to cooperate. They also called attention to the general lack of concern with the future arising from the favorable political conjuncture at that time, including specifically, COPCON's support of the *comissões de moradores*.

Recognizing these inconsistencies, many people—especially those involved in the state and in COPCON—continued to express concern about the legalization of the occupations. In early April 1975, the press began speaking of a forthcoming "revolutionary law" on housing that would complete the work of and be a substitute for *decreto-lei* 445/74. In fact, there were two proposals: both began by referring to the housing crisis, and both said that it was not acceptable to have "houses without people as long as there are people without houses"; both wanted to provide justice and began by legalizing the occupations made up to that time. But there the similarities ended, for they were concerned with very different kinds of justice.

The COPCON proposal focused on those who desperately needed housing, at a time when there was good vacant housing available. It defined housing subject to occupation or distribution as "all uninhabited housing that does not endanger human life.'' It effectively legalized all occupations, with only a few exceptions.

In contrast, the law adopted was concerned with justice for the landlords and private property. It started out by legalizing the occupations, and then provided exceptions that effectively made 80 percent or more of the occupations that had taken place illegal. This law was immediately dubbed the ''anti-occupation decree,'' and a number of buildings were occupied in protest. Public protest reached its high point with simultaneous demonstrations of some 30,000 people each in Lisbon and Porto on May 17, 1975. These had been jointly called by the coordinating bodies of the CMs in the shantytowns and the occupants of Lisbon housing, and of the *bairros camarários* and *subalugas* of Porto.[32] The main demands of the demonstrators were the repeal of the anti-occupations decree, the legalization of all occupations, a response to the lists of demands already presented by the *bairros* involved in SAAL, government recognition of the CMs, and the purging of the administrative commission of the Porto *câmara*.

The first two demands were basically ignored by the government, although evictions were suspended and the Porto administrative commission was removed shortly afterward. In the ensuing months there were only a few scattered occupations, but the issue of occupations continued to be discussed. The right used the occupations as both an example of and a scapegoat for the general political and economic crisis, and blamed occupations for the crisis in the construction industry. A member of the national commission of the Socialist party (PS) said on television, ''How can one ask the builders to build homes if they are going to be occupied?'' And in mid-September 1975 the PS and the PPD[33] made the de-occupation of occupied housing a condition for their participation in the Sixth Provisional Government. The third wave of occupations developed in the weeks following this demand.

Two months later, the government tried to reinstitute trials to evict occupants, but found it was unable to carry out its will. At the first such trial in six months, on November 4, the local CM rather than the occupant appeared as the defendant, and the judge refused to hear the case. Then the 400 occupants in attendance invaded the court and held a popular judgment, absolving the defendant. The same scene was repeated many more times.

By the fall of 1975, it was clear that the overall political conjuncture would soon change again: the working class and the popular movements could not continue organizing and taking increasing amounts of effective power in the economy and society while ignoring the decisions of the government at a time when the bourgeoisie was reestablishing control over the state and the forces of repression. A more stable relationship of forces would have to be achieved by the clear dominance of one bloc of classes or the other.

Following the November 1975 rightist military coup general disorganization and waiting characterized the housing movement. The police and the military raided some occupied housing, factories, agricultural cooperatives, and unions. Then, in January 1976, eviction trials began again. Occupants and those involved in self-imposed rent reductions organized to resist the evictions. But even though evictions were carried out, two years later (in February 1978) most occupants were still in their houses, with their situations unresolved. In Setúbal a few more occupations occurred, which were slightly different than those carried out earlier. These were the actions of construction workers in government-guaranteed projects, who then called the shantytown CMs to discuss the distribution of housing. Nevertheless, the political conjuncture had changed drastically, and the movement of occupations had come to an end.

Localized Struggles

While the fight to replace the shantytowns and the occupations were the main nationwide housing struggles, there were other important common struggles that had a strong local impact. We will look at two of them: the struggle for the autoreduction of rents in Setúbal, and the struggle of the *bairros camarários* (municipal housing districts) in Porto.

The housing crisis was not only a problem for the poor who lacked decent housing. It also affected many others from all classes who, while they had decent housing, had to pay 25 to 40 percent or more of their incomes for it. Given this problem, there were two possible demands that could be made: a flat ceiling on rent, or rent established at a set fraction of income. Both proposals were made in Portugal. The first, as a political project, required considerable effort focused on the indignation likely to be felt by those struggling to pay a higher than average rent. Its disadvantage was that potential active participation was limited to that 10 or 15 percent of the population who had far more expensive housing than the average—and, normally, more than average income. For everyone else this proposal seemed to lead to an irrelevant struggle, or worse, a struggle of the privileged few. The second proposal—rent as a fraction of income—potentially included shantytown dwellers as well as better paid workers and professionals, but posed problems of control and the need for organization at a higher level.

In Setúbal residents of three newer *bairros*, meeting at the end of May 1975, defined their position by saying that "rent should be 10 percent of family income," but "due to the lack of conditions to carry out this proposal . . . we approve the payment of 500 escudos per room, and 300 escudos if it is in the basement, as a first step."[34] In the first month some 600 families reduced their rent to these levels. Eventually there were about 1,500 families in the struggle, representing three-quarters of the less than 2,000 apartments with rents of more than 500 escudos per room.

Those who began the struggle for the reduction of rents did not see the 500 escudos as the principal objective. On the one hand, rent reduction was a way to attack urban speculation, hopefully leading to a new housing policy and "challenging the reformist CMs and local governments"; on the other, it was a way to reach "large numbers of people who had not yet been motivated by a revolutionary process which directly affected them, by bringing them together around one problem—housing—in which they could have a large and objective effect."[35]

Reactions to the struggle were varied. In some *bairros* many said they supported it even though it had little to do with them. Others said that it was a struggle of privileged *bairros*—and classes. A member of a shantytown CM said that "it is a struggle of those who demand swimming pools. If they want swimming pools they can come here [to the shanties] in the winter."[36] After a long debate the coordinating body for local CMs, the residents' council, gave its support to the families engaged in rent reduction. But the struggle was criticized as "reformist," and there were votes against it in the council. Local government did not take a position, saying the problem transcended its authority, while the central government said that the struggle was "illegal and subject to penalities."[37] But the first attempt to bring a participant to trial ended with expressions of solidarity on the part of the court's workers and the judge. Legal processes were suspended, and the movement for rent reduction spread. With the third wave of occupations that began in September, many occupants entered directly into the struggle, paying 500 escudos per room in rent.

In the new conjuncture of political forces created by the rightist coup of November 25, the government resumed its attack on the rent reduction movement. Many dropped out of the struggle, but many others continued out of necessity. Only for this point in time are there data showing that those in the struggle were not "privileged": a survey carried out in March 1976, when the minimum wage was 3,300 escudos per month, revealed that while the average family income of those in the rent struggle was 7,000 escudos per month, the average monthly rent was 3,000 escudos—43 percent. In May 1976 there were still 600 families involved in that struggle.

In Porto, in contrast, the local struggle centered around poorly constructed and poorly served public housing. According to Porto's municipal housing regulations, permanent residence in such housing was dependent on "good moral and civil conduct." Before April 25, public housing was policed by informers who checked everyone's private lives and made sure that no one had a pet, painted a room, installed a lamp, or made any other "esthetic" alteration without written permission. Those who violated regulations could be evicted, or they could be sent to a special part of one project which was known to the residents as "Tarrafal"—the name of a fascist concentration camp in Cape Verde.

By 1974, there were some 50,000 people living in *bairros camarários* in Porto. These projects were the result of an urban renewal program begun in 1956, the purpose of which was to remove rundown *ilhas* (slums) from the center of the city, expelling their populations to the outskirts of town, and allowing more profitable use of the land. People were carefully screened before being put into the housing projects, and care was taken that people from the same *ilha* would go to different projects—the consequences of a policy of "mixing the diverse elements of society."[38] The *bairros camarários* quickly became known as "*ilhas ao alto*" (islands in the air) because of their poor construction, partial lack of infrastructures, and total lack of public facilities. They had the added disadvantage of being far from the center of town and very poorly served by public transport.

There was already a long history of strong conflict between these *bairros'* inhabitants and city hall. This was where the first CMs in Portugal were formed: on April 30, 1974, the inhabitants of "Tarrafal" met in assembly, elected a CM, and drew up a list of demands. The Porto *bairro camarário* of Pastcleira immediately followed their example, and the two CMs marched in the May 1 celebrations. They then called upon the other *bairros camarários* to follow suit; within a short time, most had.

In July and August, 1974, the CMs formed a coordinating body, the *Plenário*, which included all CM members in Porto's municipal housing districts. Its first task was to draw up a list of demands focused on eliminating the draconian public housing regulations and the purging of the chief administrator and informers who enforced them. They also demanded better transport and public facilities, and recognition of the CMs as the legitimate representatives of the inhabitants of the *bairros*.

Later on, the *Plenário* elected a central commission composed of one member from each CM.

Though the regulations were suspended de facto, the Porto city government tried to ignore the demands of the CMs. Later on local authorities began to speak of an "experimental" recognition for a period of one year, in the clear hope that the situation would have returned to normal by then. The situation finally was altered when the administrative commission of the Porto *câmara* was removed in May 1975, and was replaced by a military administrative commission (CAM). This came about as a result of conflicts between the old administrative commission and many groups, including the municipal workers, *bairro* residents involved in SAAL, and those living in municipal housing and in *subalugas*. The new military administrative commission accepted the principal demands of these groups and their organizations, and a "municipal council" was created to represent them. Representatives of the central commission of the *bairros camarários* were appointed to a section of the *câmara* to exercise popular control over the relevant municipal services.

Coordinating Bodies

During the urban struggles of 1974–1975 many different coordinating organs were created. They can be separated into three different types: coordinating organs based on CMs involved in the same struggles, those based on all CMs of a region, and those based on uniting the CMs with other types of organizations.

The first problems of coordination to be posed were always those of the immediate organization of a particular struggle—whether for SAAL, for occupations, or for regulation changes; this was coordination among groups with the same specific problem. The coordinating body in this case was basically a defensive structure created to give mutual support, to share information, and to plan tactics. An additional function was to spread the struggle to *bairros* not yet involved, but which had the same problem. Coordinating bodies of this type existed in all three main cities for each of the struggles we have discussed. While such bodies would normally support other struggles, their main concern was with their own particular problem. Because they were so homogeneous, they were not subject to many internal structural conflicts arising from differences over defining problems or class base.

Later on attempts were made to form a more general type of coordinating body representing all the residents of a city, and capable of dealing with many problems. Two such residents' councils were formed in June 1975—one in Setúbal and one in Porto. Both were formed "in order to have an organized struggle for the resolution of the problems of the city's *bairros*,"[39] and to further the organization of the *bairros*. But in neither city was this project alone enough to sustain the councils.

The Revolutionary Council of Porto Residents (CRMP) was created to coordinate the participation of CM delegates in the municipal council, which had been formed by the recently installed military administrative commission of the *câmara*. The CRMP included representatives from most of the CMs in the city; they came primarily from *bairros* SAAL, and *camarários*. When the military administrative commission left in September 1975, the *câmara* returned to its practice of ignoring the CMs. The CRMP then took a strong position against the *câmara*, and the *bairros camarários* representatives left the CRMP to maintain what they had won—local control over certain municipal services. Linked now mainly to SAAL, the CRMP continued its operations and focused its attention primarily on problems of general political mobilization.

In Setúbal, the residents' council was formed more because it seemed like a "good idea" than in response to a concrete need. In the beginning the council was well received and included almost all of the CMs in the city. In practice, however, this particular mix of CMs with different problems and different social bases immediately ran into difficulties. The CM for SAAL continued meeting separately to decide its strategy, in spite of the fact that other CMs objected and declared that "decent housing is a problem for all." The Setúbal council did set up work groups on different urban problems, which made some progress; but the council was cut short when the opportunity arose for CMs to join a broader coordinating body.

The idea of creating a third type of coordinating organization arose from recognition of the fact that, in order to solve their problems, the CMs needed to intervene directly in political and social life. CMs throughout Portugal discovered that they would gain the power and authority to do this by working with other organizations facing the same kinds of problems—e.g., workers' commissions, unions, and similar groups. In practice, this type of coordination arose in two ways: as a general project for creating a structure more representative of poor and working people (and eventually a structure of government based on these organizations), and as an immediate response to local situations. Facilitating the creation of coordinating organizations was the MFA assembly's document of July 8, 1975, calling for a "system of popular organization . . . fundamentally based on the Commissions of

Workers and *Comissões de Moradores*," with the "final and ultimate objective of the construction of socialist society. . . ."[40]

In Setúbal in late July 1975, the Committee of Popular Organisms of Setúbal (COPS) was created. Like other organizations of its kind around the country, it did not get past the point of drawing up a proposal for popular coordination, based on the ideas of popular assemblies and armed vigilance. Afterward a participant commented: "Many sessions were used up discussing statutes. Who has a right to vote? Who doesn't? Do the trade unions vote? Sporting clubs? Who has more votes? How many? Who has fewer? Meetings were used up that way on the objectives also: for a popular democratic revolution; for a socialist revolution; to defend democratic liberties. . . . No one ever reached agreement on anything. The problems were so theoretical, and at the same time so bureaucratic."[41] People wanted to coordinate their struggles; they even believed it was necessary, but needed something specific to work around.

Nevertheless, in two cases it was possible to set up effective coordinating organizations of the third type; these were the Porto Municipal Council and the Setúbal Comité de Luta (Committee of Struggle). In May 1975, after many months of ineffectual work, the administrative commission of the *câmara* of Porto found itself the target of attacks from many sides. Municipal workers were on strike; they had purged the president of the *câmara* and a section head, and garbage was mounting in the streets. When some 30,000 *moradores* demonstrated on May 17, one of their demands was the purging of the municipal president. As we have seen, the administrative commission resigned and was replaced by a military administrative commission (CAM) on May 28. In a service order dated May 31, the latter "recognize[d] the CMs of the *bairros camarários* and other CMs as organs of effective collaboration and participation in the decisions within the power of the President of the Câmara Municipal of Porto." The order also stated that "within 30 days these commissions should present a proposal for their organization, procedures, and functions."[42] On June 17, the CAM announced that "as of today the Administrative Commission will meet weekly . . . with the true representatives of the workers of this city."[43] This order was the basis of authority for the Porto Municipal Council. With the goal of eventually creating a final structure, a temporary consultative commission was set up composed of six CM representatives (three each for the *bairros camarários* and other CMs), three from the *juntas de freguesia*, and three from the municipal workers. By the time of its last meeting (September 5, 1975) representatives from the trade union confederation and volunteer firemen were included, and plans existed to include soldier and police representatives.

The Porto Municipal Council came to an end with the demission of the CAM (September 13) in response to both military and civilian objections to its activities, and with the change of political conjuncture that led to the formation of the Sixth Provisional Government. There was a short struggle to defend the CAM and the Municipal Council, but they were soon lost in other events.

In Setúbal the creation of a general coordinating council representing various groups was triggered by a specific political event. On the morning of September 29, 1975, the government sent in troops to occupy the radio and television stations in Lisbon, in order to control the news—especially news of military matters. In response to this action, a meeting was called by some CMs of the Setúbal residents' council, some workers' commissions, and some soldiers. The Setúbal Comité de Luta was formed by the meeting to coordinate activities in case there were further rightward moves on the part of the national government, as well as to coordinate individual local struggles and to initiate more general struggles. A few days later its general structure was formalized; its secretariat had six delegates from the workers' commissions, four from the CMs, and five from the soldiers' commission in the local barracks.

From COPS and other experiences, those involved in the *comité* had learned that unifying people around problems faced in the *bairros* and factories was far more important than long theoretical discussions. In the beginning they explicitly agreed not to theorize and not to define statutes or objectives. The *comité* was to be a group to develop (*dinamizar*) popular organization, whose members would discuss the concrete problems of the city and its workers; only after work groups were formed and functioning to deal with these problems would they discuss issues of structure.

Various work groups were immediately formed to deal with housing, health, infancy, city-country links, and organizing activities (*dinamização*). In its regular weekly meetings with several hundred people in attendance, the *comité* decided on and directed a number of particular projects: the occupation of necessary land and the beginning of construction for a long-stalled public housing project; the loan of workers by construction companies to SAAL; support for the occupation of the local newspaper by its workers; and the promotion of city-country links. It proposed—although it was never able to put into effect—the occupation of all vacant housing and its distribution according to need, with rents set according to family income. It also initiated discussions about converting factories that were in crisis to other lines of production. Finally, it tried to organize local defense against the right-wing coup of November 25, 1975.

Clearly the *comité* was created in response to a specific national political crisis, as well as to the need local CMs felt for a more powerful body to move ahead with such projects as construction under SAAL auspices and the occupation of houses. While the *comité* was created independently of the *câmara*, they were not hostile to each other. The *câmara* was close to the PCP, and tried to reorient municipal services to popular needs. The *câmara* was left to run the city, but the *comité* functioned as a real center of power in matters that were beyond the competence of the *câmara*. By early November 1975, the *comité* was criticizing itself for becoming isolated from its base. Before remedies could be effected the November 25 coup took place. For the *comité* there followed a short period of clandestinity, and significant demobilization.

The changed political situation meant that it was no longer possible to maintain a single, united center as a base for popular political struggles, but it did not bring an end to all activities of the *comité*. The practical work of the *comité* had often focused on urban issues, which were of more direct interest to the CMs, and it was these organizations that suffered greater demobilization after November 25. In mid-January 1976, separate secretariats were formed for the workers' and residents' commissions on the grounds that each would be able to concentrate on the issues that concerned it most; the secretariats would meet together whenever necessary. In addition, the PCP preferred keeping the workers' commissions, in which it had more influence, free of the CMs and free of any association with the name "Comité de Luta." The *comité* name was eliminated at the end of March 1976.

Conclusion

Throughout the urban struggles of 1974–1975 two common themes were present: the multiclass nature of the different movements, and their sensitivity to changing political forces at the national level. The series of urban movements involved large numbers of people from different classes and social groups, and organized them around common concrete problems. This was the basis for the creation of an ill-defined but clearly extant popular movement—a movement that was much larger than any which could have been created by focusing on the workplace alone. It included unemployed men and women, youths, office employees and production workers from small and large factories, professionals, and small shopkeepers.

Nevertheless, the composition of the multiclass urban movements varied from one place to another. In Porto and Lisbon they were composed basically of the poor, including especially low-paid skilled and unskilled workers, office employees, street vendors, and small shopkeepers. Only in Setúbal did the urban movements include large percentages of workers from modern industries, and service and professional employees of the new petite bourgeoisie.

Because they were multiclass movements, there were internal tensions that easily became conflicts when differences over concrete problems arose (CM–SAAL and the *bairros camarários* in Porto) or differences in class composition were involved (shantytowns and the struggle for rent reductions in Setúbal). Tensions also surfaced not only between individual CMs, but also between CMs and the workers' organizations. The divisiveness of such conflicts was sometimes increased by sectarian fighting. Yet one of the most important factors in reducing divisiveness was mutual belief in the same general progressive movement. In fact, none of the conflicts that occurred proved to be based on antagonistic class interests.

The urban movements (like the popular movement generally) were dependent on the state, and yet, at the same time, conceived of themselves collectively as an alternative to the old state. To understand this point we must keep in mind the political conditions under which the movements developed. While the April 25 coup had destroyed the unity and hegemony of the dominant bloc of classes, the apparatus of the state remained intact even though it was divided and immobilized. Furthermore, one sector of the state—the armed forces—increasingly legitimated the creation and actions of the popular movement, rather than repressing it. It was the crisis of the ruling bloc—and thus of the state—that created the general conditions under which the urban movements developed and conceived of the necessity of an alternative to the existing state. In their concrete struggles those who joined the movements usually found themselves up against the state in its role as a regulator or as a bureaucracy that blocked solutions. They found that the traditional state apparatus was not responsive, and they were at times forced—and able—to carry out its functions.

Eventually necessity began to be converted into a virtue. The urban movements came to see themselves collectively as part of an alternative to the traditional state, and the state legitimated that viewpoint. Earlier the MFA had supported the principle that local organizations should determine and participate in the solution of local problems; later the MFA spoke of direct action on the part of the CMs in determining goals, solving problems, and controlling the state.

The two most developed practical examples of the potential role of grass roots organizations occurred during a political conjuncture that was characterized in part by an intensification of the crisis of the ruling bloc and the nearly complete immobilization of the traditional state apparatus. The Porto Municipal Council was legitimated by and worked closely with a part of the state, doing what the latter should have done but was incapable of doing. The Setúbal Comité de Luta worked parallel to the state, imposing political decisions on problems which were normally outside the competence of the state. Both examples showed that there were practical alternatives to the traditional state apparatus—alternatives in terms of the organization of the state structure, and in terms of the classes that the state would serve.

Notes

An earlier version of this chapter was published in *International Journal of Urban and Regional Research*, vol. 4, no. 2 (June 1980), under the title "Comissoes de Moradores and Urban Struggles in Revolutionary Portugal."

1 Slogan of agricultural workers' organizations and agrarian reformers; slogan of the popular movement in general and of soldiers' organizations in particular.

2 For more detailed history and discussion of urban struggles in Portugal, consult A. Botelho and M. Pinheiro, *O Conselho Municipal do Porto* (Porto, 1976); Charles Downs, "Community Organization, Political Change and Urban Policy: Portugal 1974–1976" (Ph.D. diss., University of California at Berkeley, 1980); Charles Downs et al., *Os Moradores à Conquista da Cidade* (Lisbon, 1978); F. Dubus, G. Lamarzelle, and A. Osmont, "Urbanisme et Transition: Les Luttes Urbaines au Portugal," manuscript (L'École des Hautes Études en Sciences Sociales, Paris, 1977); Victor Matias Ferreira, *Movimentos Sociais e Intervenção Política* (Porto, 1975): and Francesco Marconi and Paula Oliveira, *L'Architectura come pratica politica: Portogallo: il Saal* (Milan, 1977). The best general history of this period is Avelino Rodrigues, Cesário Borga, and Mário Cardoso, *Portugal Depois de Abril* (Lisbon, 1976).

3 The respective populations were: Lisbon, 830,000 (1970); Porto, 325,000 (1970); Setúbal, 65,000 (1974).

4 See Downs et al., *Os Moradores*, and Downs, "Community Organization." Unless otherwise specified, all information on the urban struggle in Setúbal comes from these studies.

5 Instituto Nacional de Estatística, *O Recensamento da População*, 1970 (Lisbon, 1970).

6 Luis Felipe Salgado Matos, *Investimentos Estrangeiros em Portugal* (Lisbon, 1973).

7 Instituto Nacional de Estatística, *O Recensamento da População, 1950* (Lisbon, 1950) and *O Recensamento da População 1970* (Lisbon, 1970).

8 Gabinete de Planeamento de Setúbal, *Plano de Estrutura do Concelho de Setúbal* (Setúbal, 1977).

9 Setúbal was a little better off than Lisbon or Porto. According to the local planning office, at the end of 1974 there were slightly more than 20,000 units of housing in the city, and some 3,600 families who needed to be rehoused; there were some 450 empty old houses, and 3,500 new houses about to be finished; and some 2,000 working-class and petty bourgeois families who were paying 25 to 40 percent of their incomes for rents that were as high as the minimum wage. See Downs, "Community Organization," chapter 4.

10 For further discussion of these periods and the other political struggles at that time, see the references listed in note 2, especially Rodrigues, Borga, and Cardoso, *Depois de Abril*.

11 The government got to the point of using terrorist tactics—e.g., bombing an occupied radio station—when it was otherwise unable to enforce its decisions.

12 November 25 is the critical date marking the end of this period, but its events should be analyzed in terms of the political processes preceding them. Furthermore, while their effects were immediate in the Lisbon area, they were only felt in Porto (for example) a month later.

13 There had been ad hoc struggles in some poor neighborhoods around such issues as water, urban renewal, and evictions.

14 For more information on SAAL, see the section "Common Struggles" later in this chapter, and the references cited in note 2.

15 The MDP, the Movimento Democrático Português (Portuguese Democratic Movement), was an organization close to the Portuguese Communist Party (PCP). Created as an electoral front before April 25, it provided many of the people who staffed local government institutions after that date. The CDEs (Comissões Democráticas Eleitorais) were municipal organizations formed by the MDP before 1974. In late 1974 they fused to form one political party, the MDP/CDE.

The *freguesia* is the smallest administrative unit in Portuguese government, and is governed by a *junta da freguesia*. Normally each *freguesia* is composed of many *bairros*. In 1978 in the city of Setúbal there were 4 *freguesias*, in Lisbon, 54.

16 As a result a CM in Lisbon generally represented a larger area and population than those in Setúbal or Porto.

17 The *concelho* is an administrative unit composed of several *freguesias*; its jurisdiction is roughly equivalent to that of a city. It is governed by the *câmara* (a town council) and an administrative commission (a kind of plural executive, charged with administrative responsibilities, the head of which has the title of president). For a more detailed discussion of local government structures and how they were made more representative under the 1976 constitution without changing labels, see Walter Opello's discussion in chapter 9 of this volume (ed.).

18 Estatutos, Comissões Revolucionárias Autónomos de Moradores e Occupantes, adopted in May 1975.

19 "A CM é uma organização de base, unitária e apartidária representativa dos interesses dos moradores da respectiva área de inserção" (Article no. 1, Statutes of the Comissão de Moradores, Bairro do Liceu, Setúbal). This section is strongly based on the experiences of CMs in Lisbon and Setúbal; the process in Porto was somewhat different.

20 The direct sale of agricultural products, known as the "city-country link" (*ligação cidade-campo*), was an attempt to sell directly from agricultural cooperatives to consumers. It was seen both as a political attack on the intermediaries and as a means of providing better economic conditions for the cooperatives and the consumers. Some saw it as an aspect of an alternative organization of society; others, primarily as a defense against inflation. While such sales took place all around the country, they were relatively more widespread in Setúbal than elsewhere.

21 It is worth noting that this action included the creation of five popular day-care centers between July and November 1975—a direct outcome of the autonomous efforts of the CMs. Four were the results of occupations staged for that purpose, and one was formed in the community center being built as part of a SAAL project.

22 There were cases in 1976 in which a CM was unable to replace people who resigned or to resigned itself because no one showed up at assemblies called for those purposes.

23 "Casas Sim, Barracas Não." "Casas para todos, Contra Capitalismo." "Habitação Condigna para Todos." "Nem uma casa sem pessoas enquanto há pessoas sem casa!" Slogans used at the May 17, 1975, (and other) demonstrations called by the *comissões de moradores*.

24 *Ilhas* means "islands," literally. Nineteenth-century Portuguese houses usually had a thin garden in back where it was common to put up many small shacks and to rent them as housing. Such shacks became the permanent housing for several families; there might be groups of 70 to 150 people in an *ilha*. There were cases of more than 200 families in one *ilha*, where the interior of an entire block was exploited as a unit. Frequently the only sanitary services and water would be next to the main house, under the control of the landlord.

25 Nuno Portas, Secretary of State for Housing and Urbanism in the Second and Third Provisional governments, in an interview in the newspaper *República*, Aug. 30, 1974.

26 This discussion of housing occupations is based primarily on the processes that occurred in Lisbon and Setúbal. In Porto, where different conditions prevailed both politically and in the housing stock, the process developed differently (e.g., there was little vacant government housing to occupy; systematic occupation of old private housing began in April 1975 under the control of the CMs [mostly linked to SAAL]; and the next wave of occupations was for collective services, in October).

27 Early demolition was one response of landlords to the controls placed on their right to rent their housing as they wished.

28 Elvira Simóes et al., "Um Contributo para a Análise do Processo de Ocupações em Lisboa e Arredores," manuscript (Instituto Superior de Serviço Social, 1976).

29 Downs, "Community Organization," p. 153.

30 COPCON (Comando Operacional do Continente) was the military force created on July 12, 1974, to "intervene directly to maintain and establish order, in support of and at the request of the civilian authorities," rather than having to depend on the unreliable and disliked police and national guard inherited from fascism. Over time it began giving more support to the popular movement; in a press conference on April 28, 1975, its commander said, "The Comissões of Moradores are small cells intensely living the Revolution; thus, I give them my full support in as much as they can be the real advisors for the resolution of the housing problem."

31 *O Setubalense*, Mar. 23, 1975.

32 The *subaluga* system entailed subletting a house room by room, which created very crowded conditions and provided five to ten times the normal rent. There were more than twice as many people living in sublet housing as there were in shantytowns. But Porto, where this system was furthest developed, was the only city with a significant movement against it. After court battles, the physical blocking of evictions, and several demonstrations, the central government passed a law to regulate the *subalugas*. The law, which only applied to Porto, limited the total rent that could be charged to 125 percent of the legal rent.

33 The PPD (Partido Popular Democrático) changed its name to the PSD (Partido Social Democrático) a year later. For this reason it is frequently referred to as the PPD/PSD.

34 Downs, "Community Organization," p. 159. In the newer *bairros* rents averaged more than 700 escudos per room, while in the rest of the city the average was less than 200 escudos per room (500 escudos = 20 U.S. dollars in 1975).

35 Ibid., p. 160.

36 Ibid., p. 282.

37 Ibid., p. 160.

38 Sergio Lopes, "État et 'Moradores'" (Master's thesis, L'École des Hautes Etudes en Sciences Sociales, Paris, 1977), p. 23.

39 Statutes of the Residents' Council of Setúbal, in Downs, "Community Organization," p. 677.

40 "Guidelines to the Alliance between the People and the MFA," in Downs, "Community Organization," p. 684.

41 Downs, "Community Organization," p. 314.

42 Botelho and Pinheiro, *O Conselho Municipal*, p. 27.

43 Ibid., p. 28.

8 *Nancy Bermeo*

Worker Management in Industry: Reconciling Representative Government and Industrial Democracy in a Polarized Society

The essential problem of . . . democratic socialism [is] how is it possible to radically transform the state in such a manner that the extension and deepening of political freedoms and the institutions of representative democracy are combined with the unfurling of forms of direct democracy and the mushrooming of self-management bodies?
—Nicos Poulantzas, "Towards a Democratic Socialism" [*New Left Review* 109, p. 79]

How might representative democracy and self-management be combined? This is indeed "the essential problem" of democratic socialism. It is also a problem that loomed large in the minds of many Portuguese on April 25, 1976, when the Socialist party (PS) won control of the nation's first freely elected government in fifty years. The institutions of representative democracy would now confront the many self-management bodies which had mushroomed throughout the nation during the revolutionary period.

This chapter describes the emergence of a particular group of self-managed structures—worker-run industrial firms—and analyzes how these structures have fared in their confrontation with the postrevolutionary Portuguese state.[1]

According to the national constitution of April 1976, worker management was to be the dominant form of industrial organization in the newly liberated Portuguese state.[2] Owned collectively and governed by freely elected managers, worker-run enterprises seemed to be the very embodiment of democratic socialism. Yet, despite nearly unanimous endorsement by the democratically elected constitutional assembly, worker management has never assumed the proportions foreseen. Worker management has encompassed fewer than 3 percent of all industrial firms, and involved fewer than 6 percent of all industrial workers.[3] Ironically, worker-managed industrial firms warrant attention not because they are numerous, but because they are not numerous. They are a critical part of that "transition to socialism" that was never made.

Worker Management during the Revolutionary Period

Worker management is a system of organization which allows workers the right to exclusive use of enterprise facilities and income, and the right to elect all enterprise decision makers. In revolutionary Portugal, worker management assumed two forms: self-managed firms and cooperatives. Self-managed firms, or *empresas em autogestão*, were those firms which became worker-run but not worker-owned. Credentials from government ministries entitled workers to the use of the enterprise and its products, but legal ownership—that is, the title of the firm—remained in the hands of the original proprietor. The private owner's title yielded no material benefits whatever, but it implied that the transfer of property was not final and that legal procedures might eventually force restoration.

Workers opted for the self-management alternative when they were content with the day-to-day control of an enterprise. When workers sought to control *and* to own an enterprise, they formed cooperatives. In some cases, workers were able to do this by purchasing a firm whose premises they had occupied, or by integrating the former owners into the new management system. In other cases, workers voted to form a cooperative (and in fact established a new legal entity), but were unable to gain control of the firm's title; these cooperatives, like self-managed firms, remained in a state of *indefinição patrimonial*, or undefined ownership. The existence of this ambiguity was to prove increasingly problematic as the postrevolutionary state took shape.

It is difficult to assess how many self-managed firms actually emerged in the revolutionary period.[4] Some firms were self-managed only briefly before the return of a private owner or the onset of bankruptcy; other firms became self-managed in fact, but never reported their changed status to legal authorities. Table 8.1 excludes both sorts of firms, but gives the best information available on self-management during the provisional governments. The data (derived from a 1976 Ministry of Labor survey) indicate that more than 280 firms entered into self-management, and that these were located in nearly all branches of economic activity and in all but two of Portugal's 18 districts.

Table 8.2 describes the scope of the cooperative sector during the period of the provisional governments. Like self-managed firms, coop-

TABLE 8.1
Self-Managed Firms by District and Industrial Sector

District	Commerce/ Tourism	Construction	Extractive Industries	Services	Manufacturing Industries	Transportation/ Communication	Total for District	% of Total
Aveiro	—	—	—	—	13	—	13	4.6
Beja	—	—	—	—	3	—	3	1.0
Braga	—	—	—	—	22	1	23	8.2
Bragança	—	—	—	—	—	—	—	—
C. Branco	—	—	—	—	3	—	3	1.0
Coimbra	3	—	—	1	6	—	10	3.5
Évora	2	—	1	1	2	—	6	2.1
Faro	3	—	—	2	—	—	5	1.8
Guarda	—	—	—	—	—	—	—	—
Leiria	1	—	—	1	2	—	4	1.4
Lisboa	27	4	—	9	51	2	93	33.3
Portalegre	1	—	—	—	3	—	4	1.4
Porto	9	1	1	4	70[a]	—	85	30.1
Santarém	1	—	—	—	7	—	8	2.8
Setúbal	1	2	—	2	9	—	14	5.0
V.do Castelo	1	—	—	—	—	—	1	.3
Vila Real	—	—	—	—	2	—	2	.7
Viseu	—	—	—	—	1	—	1	.3
Continent Subtotal	*49*	*7*	*2*	*20*	*194*	*3*	*275*	*97.5*
Funchal[b]	4	—	—	—	3	—	7	2.5
Total	53	7	2	20	197	3	282	100.0

SOURCE: Ministério do Trabalho, Ministério do Planeamento e Coordenação, Instituto de Apoio das Pequenas e Medias Empresas Industriais.

NOTE: Figures are for February 1976.

[a]Three textile firms were given one governmental credential as a single self-managed unit. The figure recorded here includes the three firms as separate entities.

[b]For the city of Funchal only; figures for the island of Madeira were not recorded. Figures for the Azores are not available.

TABLE 8.2
Cooperative Firms by District and Industrial Sector

District	Auto Repair	Construction	Fishing	Manufacturing Industries	Extractive Industries	Total for District
Aveiro	—	—	—	14	—	14
Beja	5	1	—	11	—	17
Braga	1	3	—	11	—	15
Bragança	2	—	—	3	—	5
C. Branco	—	—	—	4	—	4
Coimbra	1	2	1	10	—	14
Évora	—	6	—	4	5	15
Faro	—	15	4	4	—	23
Guarda	1	1	—	2	1	5
Leiria	1	7	20	8	—	36
Lisboa	12	28	7	216	2	265
Portalegre	—	2	—	3	—	5
Porto	2	4	1	87	—	94
Santarém	3	18	—	16	—	37
Setúbal	3	14	7	48	—	72
V. do Castelo	1	3	2	—	—	6
Vila Real	—	1	—	—	—	1
Viseu	2	3	—	2	—	7
Continent Subtotal	*34*	*108*	*42*	*443*	*8*	*635*
Islands[a]	—	2	12	10	—	24
Total	34	110	54	453	8	659

SOURCE: *Ex-Comissão de Apoio às Cooperativas* (unpublished records).
NOTE: Figures are for December 1976.
[a] Azores and Madeira.

eratives emerged throughout the nation and throughout the economy. More than 600 were accredited in less than two years, while scores of others awaited accreditation. The enterprises described in these two tables were neither the smallest nor the largest firms in the nation. Cooperatives averaged 45 workers while self-managed firms averaged 61.[5] Few worker-run firms involved less than 10 workers and less than 10 percent involved more than 100 workers.

How did worker-managed firms come into being? The firms had complex histories but generally they fell into one of two categories. Some were *new firms* initiated by unemployed workers in activities such as construction and domestic services which did not require large capital investments in the start-up phase. Others were *transformed firms* involving establishments which were privately owned and managed before the 25th of April. This group encompasses nearly all firms in the manufacturing and mining industries, and most enterprises involved in commerce and tourism. It has been argued that most of the transformed firms merely "fell" into thc hands of workers "like rotten fruit from an old tree."[6] The simile is not unreasonable. Many firms became worker-managed simply because private managers refused to run them. These were typically older, smaller firms whose very existence depended on low labor costs and stable markets. When the 25th of April brought a break in market stability and wage increases of more than 30 percent, such firms underwent a period of crisis. Their owners simply could not, or would not, meet the new costs of doing business. The European recession exacerbated the situation even further.

Many owners responded by trying to dismiss workers. Others, believing that their firms were permanently ruined, attempted to minimize losses by selling off plant equipment or by pocketing what capital their firms still held. Viewing these actions as direct challenges to their own livelihood, many workers moved to occupy firms; others took over only after owners had abandoned enterprises altogether. In both cases, workers assumed control of what crises and confusion had left behind. But workers who acted aggressively in occupying firms were often better off than their more passive counterparts. Aggressive workers took possession of property which was still productive enough to warrant the attention of a private owner. Passive workers—those who waited longest—usually inherited ruined firms.

There has been much debate about the relative incidence of aggressive and passive firm transformations. The author's interviews with businessmen and business lobbies revealed a clear consensus that aggressive transformations were far more numerous. From the business perspective, the emergence of worker management was merely the product of a radical and indiscriminate assault on private property.[7]

Systematic research into enterprise histories suggest that this view is exaggerated. A 1976 Ministry of Labor survey of self-managed firms reveals that passive transformations were far more numerous than aggressive transformations. In answer to the question "why did your firm become worker managed?", worker representatives offered the six responses in table 8.3. Responses in the first two categories reflect a passive transformation process. Waiting for bankruptcy or abandonment, workers in these firms did not assume the managerial task until they had no other choice. Responses in the four other categories imply aggressive worker initiatives. When workers took control of an enterprise because of fraud, contract violation, unlawful firings, or managerial incompetence, they illustrated that they were willing to assess managerial policies and to act aggressively on the basis of their assessments.

In table 8.4, the incidents of passive and aggressive transformations are compared. In every geographic region, reasons reflecting a passive transformation process outnumbered reasons reflecting an aggressive take-over. Even in the Lisbon area, where the workers were and remain most radical, workers were more likely to assume control because of bankruptcy and abandonment than for any other reason. Indeed, Ministry of Labor figures indicate that approximately 60 percent of all transformed firms were abandoned before the institution of workers' control.[8]

The crisis conditions surrounding their origin made the transformed firms of the revolutionary period heavily dependent on state assistance. From the outset, these firms needed technical aid, financial aid, and legal support. The future of the sector was thus very much dependent on the policy of the governing political party. How did the first postrevolutionary governments respond?

Policy Initiatives during the First and Second Constitutional Governments

There was reason to believe that a Socialist party majority in government would enhance the future of worker management in Portugal. The Socialists had been the only major party to consistently champion workers' control in its programs and public statements.[9] Embracing the idea of "self-managing socialism," the party program of 1974 envisioned a society wherein the means of production would "naturally be social property," managed "democratically" by collectivities of

TABLE 8.3
Reasons for Establishing Workers' Control
(percentage of responses)

Reason Cited	Lisbon	Porto	Other Areas[a]	Total
Bankruptcy	7.7	9.5	9.5	8.7
Abandonment	44.3	52.4	52.4	48.7
Fraud	9.6	4.8	14.3	8.7
Contract violation	15.4	19.0	19.0	17.4
Managerial incompetence	11.5	11.9	0.0	9.6
Unlawful firings	11.5	2.4	4.8	6.9

SOURCE: Ministry of Labor.
NOTE: These data are extracted from a Ministry of Labor questionnaire survey of all transformed firms existing in 1976. The results were never published.
[a]The category "Other Areas" includes the responses from all the firms located outside the districts of Lisbon and Porto.

TABLE 8.4
Reasons for Transformations
(in percentages)

Region	Aggressive	Passive
Lisbon	48.0	52.0
Porto	38.1	61.9
Other areas	38.1	61.9
Continent total	42.6	57.4

SOURCE: Ministry of Labor.

workers.[10] Party spokesmen gave a most explicit endorsement of worker management during the constitutional assembly in 1975. Speaking on behalf of the PS, deputy Carlos Lage proposed,

> the progressive transfer of the property and management of all enterprises to collectives of workers . . . We want to make very clear that collective appropriation of the means of production is not, for us, nationalization. . . . The favored form of collective appropriation is self-management, or, direct management by workers.[11]

Stressing "social" rather than "nationalized" property and "worker" rather than "state" management, the PS made a concerted effort to distinguish its philosophy from that of the Communist party (PCP), and to be the most vocal advocate of self-management and cooperativism in the party system.

These early statements of support for worker management proved somewhat misleading. Worker-managed industrial firms were not the target of an all-out offensive, but they were not the beneficiaries of continuous support either; they were, instead, the victims of a somewhat benign neglect. A review of the highlights of relevant Socialist party policy during the First and Second Constitutional governments will illustrate this point.

The first major piece of legislation affecting worker management during the First Constitutional Government was law 821/76. Known as the Suspensão de Acções, or Suspension of Suits, this law protected self-managed enterprises from certain forms of legal difficulties. Specifically, it suspended any repossession suits filed by ex-owners, and prevented the future filing of any similar suits. It also prevented landlords from evicting any self-managed firm from rental property for any reasons other than the nonpayment of rent.

As its text states, the *Suspensão de Acções* was intended to temporarily "safeguard the existence of self-managed firms" while the government drew up legislation "to clarify and define" the legal status of the sector. The law went into effect on November 12, 1976, for a period of 90 days, but was continuously renewed until nearly two years later when the Second Constitutional Government finally defined the status of the sector.

It is evident that law 821/76 provided important legal protection for self-managed firms. Accordingly, Socialist leaders deserve some credit for trying to make good on their promises of support. But the law was late in coming, and once passed did not provide as much protection as it might have. For example, it protected only those firms that were "accredited" by government ministries; this meant that cooperatives, which by law were not accredited, were left totally unprotected. But even self-managed firms were not protected completely. The most serious legal problems that worker-managed firms faced were suits related to the payment of debts. These were not filed by ex-owners but by material and equipment suppliers. Such suits often resulted in the auctioning or repossession of enterprise assets, and sometimes brought production to a complete halt. Law 821/76 provided no protection from these suits, despite the fact that such protection had been requested.[12]

Thus the Suspensão de Acções law assisted the worker-managed sector, but did not provide the degree of support desired by many. The same can be said of the second major Socialist initiative on behalf of worker management—the establishment of the Instituto António Sérgio do Sector Cooperativo (INSCOOP). INSCOOP was created in December 1976 to support "the establishment, strengthening and expansion of all cooperative initiatives which respect the cooperative principles evoked in the national constitution."[13] Though a planning commission for the institute was established as early as August of 1976, INSCOOP did not formally begin to function until after June 1977.

By that time there were nearly 1,000 industrial and service cooperatives in existence. The institute was given the weighty task of providing these and more than 1,600 other cooperatives with both studious attention and a vast array of services. The services fell into four main categories: (1) the institute staff was to study at least nine principal issues related to cooperatives (ranging from fiscal legislation to accounting procedures), and to use the studies as the bases for sectoral planning; (2) the staff was to inform the public about cooperatives through national and international publications; (3) the staff was to train cooperative members and specialists; and (4) the staff was to coordinate a broad range of government activities related to the sector—activities involving the proposal and review of finance credit and property legislation, social security and tax regulations, and much more.

The immense scope of the institute's responsibilities suggested that the organization might indeed be a powerful asset for all cooperatives. This was no doubt the intention of certain Socialist party leaders, such as the widely respected Henrique de Barros, who had conceived of the institute. But high expectations were not easily fulfilled. The institute was soon criticized for not serving its functions, and the Socialist party (closely identified with INSCOOP) was widely criticized for not complying with its constitutional commitment to worker management.

The basis for this criticism was not what the institute did, but what it failed to do. Representatives of cooperatives (e.g., on World Cooperative Day) criticized INSCOOP for not drafting fiscal legislation, for not drafting credit legislation, and for not elaborating a cooperative legal code to update the current code, which had been written in 1888. It is true that the institute failed to produce any final products in these fields during more than a year of operation, and some critics speculated that this failure was actually a veiled attempt at political sabotage. But one need not resort to speculations about the motivations of the INSCOOP staff to account for its shortcomings. The institute's structural position within the Portuguese bureaucracy is sufficient to account for most of its failures.

The role of INSCOOP vis-à-vis other departments of government was extremely precarious. The institute was to work jointly with several other ministries in the elaboration of policies, but had no checks whatever on ministerial activities. If ministries chose to ignore IN-

SCOOP, they could, and did. For example, the institute designed an interministerial council which was to meet regularly to resolve the problems of cooperatives; members of cooperative support groups, operating in each ministry, were supposed to attend, but in fact ministerial response was extremely uneven. The Ministry of Transportation maintained a support group of two individuals and did send a representative to council meetings. The Ministry of Labor designated an ad hoc support group, but did not oblige its representative to attend meetings (and he did not). The Ministry of Industry went a step further and abolished its support group altogether several months after it began working. Thus, in the industrial and service sectors at least, the institute had to rely almost exclusively on its own resources.

If these resources had been ample, the interests of cooperatives might still have been well served, but INSCOOP's resources were not in keeping with its responsibilities. Consider the important issue of staffing: the funds that the institute received from the national budget were only sufficient to pay for sixteen professional staff members (two in Porto and fourteen in Lisbon). Of these, most were under 30, none had a graduate degree, and many had not completed undergraduate work; fewer than half had ever had any practical experience with cooperatives.

Dedicated individuals might have overcome these disadvantages had it not been for other budget-related programs. As it was unable to finance its own education programs, the institute solicited support from the United Nations. Two renowned United Nations experts set up an extensive education program, but were forced to enlist six of INSCOOP's most experienced staff members to do so. This left only eight staff members to perform all other functions of the institute. The Department of Study and Planning was eventually reduced to two professionals, one of whom was not even paid by the institute. The department of coordination was eventually reduced to only one individual, and the post of legal counsellor was left vacant altogether. As one might predict, the institute's training function was well served, but other functions faltered. INSCOOP continued to suffer from a lack of credibility, though it initiated formal attempts to meet the demands of cooperatives.

When these structural weaknesses were combined with the political in-fighting common to most postrevolutionary organizations and with an alleged association with the increasingly unpopular Socialist party, it was almost inevitable that the institute failed to be the powerful agent that cooperatives desired. But even if INSCOOP had been powerful, the worker-managed sector as a whole would not have been helped, for the institute had no authority to deal with self-managed firms.

The third major Socialist initiative that proved disappointing to worker-managed firms was the self-management legislation which was passed during the Second Constitutional Government. The legislation consisted of two parts. The first, *decreto-lei* 66/78, created the National Institute of Self-Managed Enterprises (INEA); the second, *decreto-lei* 68/78, spelled out internal regulations for self-managed firms and the means by which relevant title disputes would be resolved.

Marcelo Curto, Socialist minister of labor from July 1976 until March 1977, had called for legislation to address these issues even before he was named minister. He drew up legislative proposals soon after the national assembly convened in 1976, but the assembly's Commission of Labor continually postponed their discussion. It was not until March, 1978 when the Socialists had formed a coalition with the Christian Democrats, that the bills were finally brought to a vote. Meanwhile, hundreds of firms continued to operate with no permanently designated owner. This legal ambiguity virtually eliminated any possibilities such firms had of obtaining bank loans and functioned as a strong disincentive to reinvestment.

The Socialist party's bills passed the first of two required rounds of voting shortly after being submitted to the national assembly. Their passage was assured by the votes of the Center Democrats (CDS), the PS coalition partner, but all other parties opposed them.

Communist opposition proved most problematic for it was associated with demands from the self-managed sector itself. The PCP had sponsored its own self-management bills after conferring with a group called the Secretariat of Self-Managed Enterprises (SEA). The SEA was composed of representatives of several self-managed firms and though it was criticized by some as being merely an arm of the PCP, no one could deny that it was the only organization which even claimed to represent the self-managed sector. The SEA led opposition to the PS bills before they passed the first vote and continued to criticize them afterward.

Representatives from 75 enterprises issued a harsh public critique. The critique focused first on the structuring of INEA: the proposed legislation stated that the institute was to be run by a president (nominated by the prime minister), and by several ministerial representatives (nominated by cabinet ministers). Critics thought this unjust for it implied that self-managed enterprises themselves would have no representative on the institute's executive body.

Criticism also focused on the scope of INEA powers. The PS bill gave INEA considerable control over enterprise administration. INEA could rule on the validity of any enterprise election, dismiss elected officials, and replace them with its own appointees until new elections were held. INEA could also determine the ideal size of enterprise commissions, force modifications in size after elections had taken place, and dismiss any elected workers or even an entire workers' commission on the grounds of "incompetence" or "negligence."[14] Most important, INEA had the power to control the profits of any firm which was involved in an ownership dispute. Such powers, and others, were thought excessive by the self-managing firms.

But self-managing firms, and other proponents of worker management in general, were most perturbed by the advantages the proposed legislation would bring to former owners. The Socialists' proposals allowed for the complete restitution of firms to ex-owners if it could be proven that these owners or their representatives had committed no acts "deleterious to the firm or the national economy," and that these individuals had not manifested a "disinterest equivalent to abandonment" before the initiation of worker management. Once the proposals became law, former owners had a period of two years within which to initiate restitution procedures. Workers could be jailed if they resisted restitution "through any means" after the court had ruled.

Faced with strong and elaborate criticism from self-managed firms, the Socialist party might well have altered its proposals dramatically before they were signed into law, but it proved unable or unwilling to do so. In the final version of the legislation, INEA was restructured to include seven elected representatives of worker-managed firms, but no other major demands were met. Thus, though the laws sponsored by the Socialists were welcomed by some as providing a much-needed legal framework for self-managed firms, most of the firms themselves had wanted more—more power within the state apparatus, more power to control their own affairs, and more protection from ex-owners.

Neither the self-management laws, nor the *Suspensão de Acções*, nor the operation of INSCOOP proved wholly satisfactory to worker-managed firms. Each of the Socialist initiatives during the First and Second Constitutional governments were criticized as either half-measures or deliberate attempts to sabotage worker management.

Explaining the Socialist Party Response

Why was the Socialist party unable to meet the needs of the worker-managed sector? Why did the discrepancy between verbal support and concrete policy emerge? Stating that the discrepancy was a result of pressures from the bourgeoisie is accurate, but not particularly useful. Few, even within the party itself, would deny that owners' interest groups exerted strong pressures on the Socialist governments. But what made these pressures viable? Tactically, this is the critical issue.

One factor which worked to the advantage of owners was the political division within the Socialist party. Party leaders were not uniformly enthusiastic about the viability of worker management. The two Socialist ministers of labor provide examples of contrasting perspectives and policies: Marcelo Curto was a highly vocal advocate of self-management before, during, and after assuming his ministerial post;[15] Maldonado Gonelha rarely, if ever, took a public position on either self-management or cooperatives, and did not initiate any legislative proposals in the field. The contrast between Curto and Gonelha alone suggests a potential for policy discrepancies within the party.

Another factor which worked to the advantage of owners was the party's numerical weakness in the national assembly. Holding only 102 of the 264 seats in the legislature, the party could not pass bills without the support of another parliamentary group. Since the enmity between Socialists and Communists rendered PS-PCP cooperation unlikely, the Socialists typically turned to the PSD (Social Democrats) and the CDS for supporting votes. This meant making concessions, and such tactical concessions usually favored private business interests. For example, the original version of the *Suspensão de Acções* legislation contained a provision which would have protected self-managed firms from all forms of lawsuits; but this was removed from the final version in order to assure passage of the law.

Concessions affected the final version of the 1978 self-management legislation as well. Law 68/78 provided much less protection for worker-managed firms than the proposal from which it had been derived. The original proposal (bill 60/1) stated explicitly (article 41:2:b) that owners' repossession suits would not be heard if it were proven that worker management was initiated when the enterprise was in a state of bankruptcy, or when the enterprise did not manifest "economic viability." This last clause applied to a majority of worker-managed firms, and might have provided an acceptable degree of protection had it not been stricken from the final version of the law.

A third factor which made owners' pressures more effective was the miserable state of the Portuguese economy. Faced with crises in agriculture, in public industries, and in intervened firms,[16] the Socialist government gave worker management in industry a relatively low priority. While proposals for support languished in committee, the difficulties of worker-managed firms increased and arguments concerning the "greater efficiency" of private management gained wider appeal.

The credit restrictions associated with the International Monetary Fund loan negotiations[17] probably did not make pressures from ex-owners more effective but definitely did force contradictions in Socialist party policy toward worker management. Since the time of the earliest transformations, worker-managed firms had great difficulty securing credit from commercial banks, and the nationalization of the banking sector did not alter this situation. Then as now, private owners—even owners of firms in difficulty—could use personal property as loan collateral, but worker-owners generally owned little or no property and thus could not use this form of guarantee. Nor could they use their collectively held enterprise as collateral, because its ownership was, more often than not, in dispute. Recognizing that their position was not competitive, and desperate for credit assistance, worker-managed firms had sought special arrangements long before negotiations for IMF assistance. What they wanted specifically was a bank for cooperatives—an institution in which they would not have to compete with private firms for financing. They also sought special loan guarantees when dealing with commercial banks.

These demands probably constituted the most urgent appeals that worker-managed firms made to the government. Prominent Socialists such as Henrique de Barros lobbied consistently for the establishment of a *banco cooperativo* and for the concession of special guarantees. But the restrictions involved in the IMF agreement impaired such efforts: "tight money" and a deliberate governmental move away from assistance to small-scale enterprises implied even greater credit problems for worker management in the future, and also implied strong constraints for any Socialist efforts to affect credit policy.

This list of factors that might explain the discrepancy between Socialist promises and policies is no doubt incomplete. But it does illustrate why structures of direct democracy in industry were not easily articulated with the representative democracy that emerged in Portugal's postrevolutionary period. The democratic institutions which brought the Socialist party to power constrained the party in its policy making role. Important constraints emanated from the parliament. The competitive electoral system nurtured parties which gave expression to the interests of private business elites. These groups capitalized on divisions between the Socialist and Communist parties and easily forced the former into legislative compromise.

The institutions of the nation's mixed economy created further constraints. The freely elected constitutional and national assemblies had chosen to preserve a market economy in which worker-managed firms were at a competitive disadvantage. Emerging so often from the "rotten fruit" of the prerevolutionary capitalist system, worker-run firms commanded relatively few material resources. Suits and boycotts from the private sector made a bad situation even worse. But most serious was the competition for bank loans: burdened with ownership disputes and possessing little collateral, worker-managed firms were seriously hampered in the race for scarce financing. In the economic sector and in the legislature, the by-products of representative democracy compromised the interests of direct democracy.

The Lasting Importance of the Worker-Managed Sector

Despite all of these constraints, worker-managed firms have survived and even prospered in some cases. The importance of the sector has not diminished over time. Though more than a handful of firms have gone bankrupt, industrial and service cooperatives are continuously increasing in number: there are at least 400 more such cooperatives today than there were at the end of 1975, and cooperatives have more than 50 federations. INSCOOP and INEA remain in operation and have a vested interest in the survival of the sector. Most important, the hostility that worker-managed enterprises encountered has fostered a certain militant solidarity among firms. Many workers who were not radicalized before their firms were transformed have become radicalized in the process of defending their new experiment. The words of a middle-aged, devoutly religious member of a textile cooperative exemplify the process:

> "The Communists, the Socialists, all the people of the Left used to scare me. Now I know they're not so bad. Our little firm needs them. . . . My neighbors say I'm a communist now—who knows, maybe I am?"[18]

The 1979 electoral triumph of the center-right coalition threatens, but does not doom, the worker-managed sector. Its continued growth, its links with government agencies, and its increased internal solidarity suggest that the sector may not be easy to liquidate. The parties of the left may well play a more supportive role than they have in the past. The Communist party has drawn up a variety of bills to assist the sector, and PS leaders have begun a wide range of new support initiatives.[19] Worker-managed firms thus remain both an important vestige of the revolutionary period and a surprisingly durable option for the organization of property.

Notes

1 To my knowledge there are only three academic publications that deal with worker-managed firms in the industrial and service sectors. These are: João Carlos Pereira Bastos, *Cooperativas Depois de Abril* (Coimbra, 1977); José Barreto, "Empresas industriais geridas pelos trabalhadores," *Análise Social* 13 (1977) 51; and Luís Calado, "Empresas em autogestão: que futuro?" *Economia e Socialismo*, nos. 23 and 24 (1978). Works on worker management in agriculture are too numerous to cite here, but some of the best publications include Fernando Oliveira Baptista, *Portugal 1975—Os Campos* (Porto, 1978) and Afonso de Barros, *A Reforma Agraria em Portugal: Das Ocupações de Terras à Formação das Novas Unidades de Produção* (Lisbon, 1979).

2 See articles 55, 56, 61, 84, 89, and 90 of the 1976 constitution. Article 90 states that the social property sector (which is composed of worker-managed firms) "will become predominant" in the national economy.

3 The reference is to all firms employing more than five workers and located in either the manufacturing, mining, construction, or service industries. Figures are from the time of the author's research in 1978 and are from files in the Ministry of Labor and the Instituto António Sérgio do Sector Cooperativo (INSCOOP).

4 Officially, the revolutionary period ended when the Socialist party won control of the First Constitutional Government in July 1976. In fact, the revolutionary period began to draw to a close with the emergence of the Sixth Provisional Government in September 1975, when the Socialist party first gained the ascendency in the state apparatus.

5 The average number of workers per cooperative was calculated by the Comissão de Apoio as Cooperativas (CAC) in December 1976, based on a sample of 41 percent. The comparable figure for self-managed firms was calculated by the author from unpublished Ministry of Labor data.

6 Calado, "Empresas em autogestão," p. 10.

7 The generalizations made here are based on open-ended interviews with former owners, lawyers of former owners, staff members of the Confederation of Portuguese Industries (CIP), and staff members of the Association of Portuguese Industries (AIP).

8 Ministry of Labor, Office of Self-Managed Enterprises, unpublished survey, 1977.

9 Concentrating its attention on a push for nationalization and for the expropriation of latifundia, the Communist party distanced itself from the issue of worker management in industry. Though industrial cooperatives received the party's endorsement, militants cautioned workers against "group capitalism."

10 *Declarações de Princípios e Estatutos do Partido Socialista*, pamphlet (Lisbon, 1974), p. 16.

11 *Diário da Assembleia Constituinte* (1975), no. 70, pp. 2218, 2225.

12 As early as January 1976, the CAC had proposed legislation which would have protected firms from any legal actions related to debts contracted under private management. The proposal was modeled on legislation which already protected certain government-run firms.
13 See law 902/76.
14 See bill 100/1, article 22.
15 Curto wrote on self-management before and after becoming minister, maintained personal contacts with workers in many self-managed firms, and sponsored each of the bills that eventually became self-management law.
16 Intervened firms were enterprises that experienced severe managerial crises during the revolutionary period and were, as a result, taken over temporarily by government-appointed management teams.
17 On August 25, 1977, the Socialist government initiated an austerity program involving stringent credit restrictions. The program was a condition for the receipt of a 50 million dollar IMF loan and some 750 million dollars in loans from individual nations.
18 Interview conducted in Guimàraes, July 1978.
19 Socialist party leaders began to take stronger initiatives on behalf of the worker-managed sector as soon as the party entered the opposition in July 1978. The party sponsored an international conference on self-management in October 1978, and a similar initiative on behalf of cooperatives less than one month later in Braga. Additionally, party notables such as Marcelo Curto, Delmiro Carreira, and João Cravinho established the Center for the Study and Support of Self-Managed Firms, to provide legal, technical, and financial assistance to *empresas em autogestão*. Stronger actions were accompanied by stronger statements of verbal support. During the party's Third National Congress, for example, self-managed firms were officially endorsed as the "concretization of the democratic socialist project," and the development of cooperatives was described as a "fundamental objective for the decade of the 80's." The duration and effect of these measures and statements remains to be seen.

9 *Walter C. Opello, Jr.*

The Continuing Impact of the Old Regime on Portuguese Political Culture

In recent years the political culture of Portugal has been characterized as "corporatist"; that is, as elitist, authoritarian, bureaucratic, Catholic, and patrimonial.[1] This view of Portuguese political culture derives from a school of Latin American scholars who find that corporatism is a unique and distinctive feature of Ibero-American political systems.[2] Among scholars who apply this framework to Portugal, there is disagreement on the characteristics they are defining. One position, that of the culturalist, stresses attitudinal variables, individual orientations, and a comprehensive view of Portuguese society, politics, and history.[3] The other position, that of the structuralist, views corporatism solely in institutional terms as a specific political response to a set of socioeconomic problems.[4]

It is now evident, however, that corporatist institutions were neither well entrenched nor very significant in the policy-formation process during the Salazar-Caetano dictatorship. The best evidence for the wrongheadedness of this assumption was the rapid disintegration of Portugal's putative corporatist system, without significant resistance, on April 25, 1974.

Nevertheless, despite the weakness of corporatist perspectives as an explanatory device, there are important continuities in political behavior between the old and the new regimes. It is my contention that the Portuguese case can be better understood by employing an organizational approach to the study of political structure and culture. In taking such an approach, the content of Portugal's political culture will not be inferred from the ideology of elites or from formal-legal arrangements; nor will political structure and the policy-formation process be inferred from the plans of institution builders or elite ideology. Instead, political culture will be conceived as complementary to but not a substitute for other explanations. Although structure and culture will be seen as establishing limits for one another, political culture will be viewed largely as a response to a particular type of regime that has a specific organizational format. The Portuguese case will be approached in terms of the interaction between the actual political structure of the regime and the political culture, thus avoiding the pitfalls of uniqueness and determinism as well as the tendency to assert that structure alone is the decisive factor in the policy-formation process.[5]

For reasons of economy, this cultural and structural analysis of Portugal's political system is focused at the local level.[6] It is divided into three parts: the first examines the actual political structure and policy process at the local level during both the dictatorship and the present democratic regime; the second presents the findings of a political culture survey of the same locale; the third and concluding part brings the findings of the previous sections together and shows that while Portugal is not a unique case and needs no special corporatist framework in order to be understood, it does shed light on the more general problem of how state structures are altered once particular patterns of behavior have become institutionalized.

Local Political Structure

Before examining the present structure of local government and the actual policy-making process at that level of government, a brief look at local structures during the Salazar-Caetano dictatorship is in order. This will provide a perspective on the changes and continuities in local political structure since April 25, 1974.

Under the dictatorship, Portugal was organized into a three-tiered hierarchical system of geographical units. The smallest of these was the parish (*freguesia*), which was governed by a board (*junta de freguesia*).[7] The board consisted of three members (*vogais*): a president, a secretary, and a treasurer, who were required to hold regular meetings to carry out their responsibilities. At this level there was also a justice of the peace (*regedor*) who represented the police and the central administration. A number of parishes formed a county (*concelho*), which was governed by a mayor (*presidente da câmara municipal*), appointed by the central government, and by a municipal council (*câmara municipal*). The counties were combined into eighteen districts (*distritos*) on the mainland and four on the adjacent islands of Madeira and the Azores.[8]

Although the formal powers of the parishes were extensive (e.g., they could tax, expropriate land, pass local ordinances, and the like), they were in fact restricted to serving as administrative agents of the national government in four areas: (1) registering voters (*recenseamento*) (2) administering various legal papers (*atestados*) (3) certifying and providing welfare for the poor, and (4) establishing medical posts.[9] Moreover, each parish was financially dependent upon the municipal council, which itself was financially dependent upon the central government. Under the law, 25 percent of the total income received by the municipality (most of which was in the form of a central government subsidy) was to be spent on public works projects within the parishes. Of the money given to the parishes, 10 percent was to be distributed equally to all. Although the remaining 90 percent was to go to those parishes most in need, no single parish was to receive, over time, a sum greater than that of the others.[10]

The policy-making process was highly centralized and the decisional flow was from the top down. Most communication took the form of directives and administrative decrees, which preempted local initiatives and which the municipalities and parishes were obliged to carry out and enforce. Moreover, the dictatorship discouraged political activity even within the structure of the system. The only political association that was allowed to organize was the National Union (União Nacional), which later became known as the Popular National Action (Acção Nacional Popular). The National Union was organizationally very weak at the local level, functioning only at election time to approve lists of candidates. Furthermore, there was an almost complete lack of economic, social, and religious associations to act as aggregators and articulators of individual or group interests. Thus local level political life during the dictatorship was "characterized by minimal and trivial politics . . . [c]onstraints on local-level political activity in the Portuguese state emanated from the governmental administrative process and the manner in which decrees were enforced at the local level. Although the *junta* was ideally a 'political' body and the *regedor* an 'administrative' position, they were both, in effect, administrative agencies. Power and decisionmaking within the parish were inconsequential, while the administrative bureaucracy was of utmost importance. . . ."[11] Although Portugal's new democratic elite has retained the dictatorship's three-tiered system of local government, elected legislative and executive components have been grafted onto previously existing structures.[12] The parish remains the primary unit of local government, but it now has a unicameral assembly (*assembleia de freguesia*) which is elected directly by the people living in the parish; its members serve for three years.[13] While the executive branch of the parish is still the parish board, the president, treasurer, and secretary are elected by the assembly from its own membership.[14] As before, the president of the board is the key official in the parish and as such coordinates the board's activities, convokes its meetings, and represents the parish before governmental units at higher levels.

The second tier of local government still consists of municipalities (*municípios*), which conform to the boundaries of the pre-1974 counties. However, there are now three elective organs of local government: (1) the municipal assembly (*assembleia municipal*), composed of the presidents of the county's parish boards as well as an equal number (plus one) of members elected directly;[15] (2) the municipal chamber (*câmara municipal*), the executive branch of the municipality, composed of a mayor and six directly elected aldermen (*vereadores*);[16] and (3) the county council (*conselho*), a consultative body composed of representatives from the county's economic, social, cultural, and professional organizations. The mayor, no longer appointed, is the person who receives the most votes among those running for the chamber. The mayor is the only salaried elected official, and like the board presidents at the parish level he is the key governmental official at the county level; as such he convokes meetings of the chamber (usually every two weeks), executes directives, and supervises municipal employees.

As in the pre-1974 period, both levels of local government—the municipality and its parishes—have been granted extensive powers. Both theoretically can impose taxes, pass local ordinances, expropriate lands, grant licenses, and set the number and salaries of municipal employees. In an effort to decentralize local government and involve the citizenry more directly in the decision-making process, the municipal chamber and the parish boards are now required to submit to their respective assemblies for approval a yearly plan of activities and a budget, as well as yearly reports on management and accounts.

It would appear from this formalistic description of Portugal's new governmental structures at the local level that the citizenry of the county is well integrated into the decision-making process and that effective participation has been achieved. After all, in the county of Porto de Mós where research for this paper was carried out local authorities have been granted power over a wide range of governmental activities; local assemblies are now directly elected; the executives of the parishes and of the county are theoretically responsible to local assemblies, and have been granted control over local administration; and both the parishes and the municipality have the power to finance activities in their own locales.[17]

However, despite these changes, the reality is altogether different. Most powers are still preempted by the national state, and the actual structure and policy-formation process of local government in Porto de Mós is little different from that of the previous regime. An analysis of the minutes of the meetings of the municipal chamber and interviews with local elected officials reveal that the chamber and the parish boards in Porto de Mós are actually little involved in local policy making because of administrative and financial constraints on their ability to make independent decisions on local priorities—constraints similar to those that existed during the dictatorship.

The parish boards and the municipal chamber remain, for the most part, administrative arms of the state, and as such are required by the administrative code (Código Administrativo) to attend to a wide range of local services. Thus the plan of activities and the budget for the municipal chamber is not really a policy document setting forth concrete goals and priorities for the county. Instead, it is a "shopping list" of unprioritized projects and needs within the municipality's public works responsibilities. Moreover, the yearly report of activities is simply a detailed accounting of the administrative, technical, and financial activities of the chamber.[18]

As for the parish boards, their function is still primarily that of an administrative conduit between the parish and the municipality. The plan of activities shows that each parish board submits to the municipal chamber its public works needs, which are simply listed in the plan unaltered and without priority. While there may be efforts by the presidents of the various parish boards to influence decisions of the chamber, the general approach, as during the dictatorship, is to avoid making choices and to spread the municipality's meager resources as evenly as possible among the parishes.

Minutes of the meetings of the Porto de Mós municipal chamber show that there is no significant difference between meetings held after April 25, 1974, and those held before.[19] The meetings are not policy-making sessions. The chamber continues to function much like an administrative committee routinely considering building permits, granting licenses for markets and fairs, and approving the disbursement of petty sums of money to pay personnel and purchase equipment.

As before, the state must ultimately approve all activities of the municipal chamber and may veto any decisions considered illegal under the administrative code. Like the French system upon which it is modeled, local government and the national state are linked together by the administrative tutelage (*tutela administrativa*) exercised by the civil governor of the district. The governor, who is appointed by the Ministry of Internal Administration, has overall responsibility for the proper functioning of local government in the district. Governors see to it that local governments carry out national laws, and can conduct inquiries and investigations into their activities. The governor has the power to dismiss local officials if it has been demonstrated that they have behaved illegally, failed to fulfill their administrative tasks, or refused to carry out decisions made at higher levels.[20] This means that although they are now elected, mayors as well as presidents of parish boards are still the administrative representatives of the state at the local level. As agents of the state they are ultimately responsible to the civil governor and not to their respective municipal and parish assemblies. Moreover, the presidents of the parish boards still spend between 80 and 90 percent of their time doing routine legal chores (*atestados*), and the mayor spends the bulk of his time carrying out administrative duties connected with the management of the county.

The second constraint on the ability of the municipality and its parishes to make independent decisions on local priorities is financial. As they had during the dictatorship, local governments have two sources of revenue. One source is "ordinary" revenue derived from small fines and from direct taxes on agricultural and industrial production and on business within the municipalities, as well as from taxes on building permits, markets and fairs, public advertising, and hunting, dog, and bicycle licenses. This revenue is used to pay for routine maintenance on local roads, sewers, and water supplies, as well as the salaries of local functionaries. The other source is "extraordinary" revenue granted by the central government for specific projects beyond the financial capability of the municipality, such as the electrification of a village or the building of a school.[21]

Table 9.1 shows the revenue of the county of Porto de Mós by source. It can be readily seen that about 34 percent of the county's total revenue comes in the form of extraordinary grants from the national state for specific public works projects. Such financial dependence is compounded by the fact that some 11 million escudos of ordinary revenue, or about 46 percent, is composed of grants from the state, about one-half of which are earmarked for road maintenance and municipal employees' salaries; the remaining 5 million escudos is a free

TABLE 9.1
Revenues of Porto de Mós, by Source, 1977
(in millions of escudos)

Source	Amount	Percentage of Ordinary	Percentage of Total
Ordinary			
Locally derived	13,958,276	54	
State grants	11,776,000	46	
Ordinary subtotal	*25,734,276*	*100*	*66*
Extraordinary	13,762,306		34
Total revenue	39,496,682		100

SOURCE: Câmara Municipal de Porto de Mós, "Relatório de Actividades e Contas de Gerência de 1977," mimeographed, p. 9.

grant to be used as the chamber sees fit. This means that a total of 25,538,306 escudos, or about 65 percent, of the municipality's income is in the form of subsidies from the state. Without these grants the chamber would not have sufficient revenues from ordinary sources to pay the wages of its employees and to meet its debt service obligations.

Administrative and financial dependence on the central government suggests that whatever independence and policy-making power the municipality has gained theoretically since April 25, 1974, much of it has been nullified in practice. These constraints limit the municipal chamber to making decisions only on routine administrative matters and to the maintenance and improvement of municipal services. While some projects and parishes receive more attention from the chamber than others because of perceived need from a public works point of view, the chamber is not really free to make political choices and decisions on local priorities. Such decisions are effectively made for the chamber at the highest reaches of the state's administrative apparatus where all projects, even the most petty, must be approved and financed.

Interviews with the mayor, three aldermen, and five parish board presidents of Porto de Mós revealed that the constraints imposed by the state have had a strong effect on their attitudes and behavior. First, all of the officials interviewed thought of themselves as administrators and viewed the running of local government as a matter of efficient management, teamwork, and impartiality. Some perceived holding office as an onerous administrative duty that had to be performed conscientiously and impartially because no one else was willing to do it. The interviews suggest that nonpartisan attitudes and behavior are fairly widespread. In only one case did an elected official conceive of himself as representing a particular party and set of interests. Generally, party labels have much less meaning at the local level than they do at the national level, and divergencies among the local elected officials interviewed are nonideological and concerned almost exclusively with differing views on administrative matters.

Second, the submerging of individual and partisan interests suggests that local officials tend to view the county as a harmonious unit encompassing a uniform local interest which is constantly being exploited by the national state. Not unlike the perception of France's basic administrative unit, the commune, by the French, the Portuguese county is perceived as a *fortaleza* besieged by the administrative apparatus of the state, and the mayor and his "team" of aldermen are perceived as its defenders.[22] The mayor is clearly viewed in paternalistic terms as the head (*patrão*) of a large family whose primary responsibility is to defend the county and use his influence to "bring home the bacon" from the central government.

Finally, all officials interviewed in Porto de Mós expressed considerable frustration with the administrative and financial constraints imposed by the central government, which prevent them from representing their constituents and playing a more direct role in local policy formation. Because of their frustration and the fact that they receive no salary for their work, none of the elected officials interviewed evidenced any political ambitions. None hoped to stand again for the same office or seek higher office. Thus local office holding does not foster the development of political skills, nor does it commit people to new democratic structures.

In conclusion, it can be said that the actual political structure of government at the county and parish levels in Portugal is still very much an integral part of the administrative apparatus of the central government, despite attempts by the new elite to democratize and decentralize local political structures. Local officials, although now elected, are still essentially bureaucrats, and policy formation for the county still takes place at the highest levels of the administrative system.

It is important to understand that this state of Portuguese affairs has been produced neither by a deep, underlying corporatist political culture nor by some corporatist ideology and master plan of the previous regime's elite. Recent historical evidence suggests that Salazar had actually come to power in 1928 without a clear ideology or master plan, and that it was not until the early 1930s that the organizational base was laid for what was to be called the New State (Estado Novo).[23] Furthermore, Portuguese corporatism, as it emerged as the central tenet of Salazar's New State ideology, was not purely an aspect of any inherently distinctive, natural Ibero-Latin cultural tradition. Although there was some hint of corporatist ideas present in the political ideologies that emerged at the beginning of the twentieth century, corporatism as it appeared in Salazar's version was a variant of a modern political ideology that was emerging in the 1930s in Central Europe, and that was carried into Portugal from France and Germany by an elite which was attempting to legitimize new political institutions and policies.[24]

Moreover, from the inception of the New State with the ratification of the Constitution of 1933, which described Portugal as a "unitary, corporative Republic," there had been only a few periods during which corporations were established, and no sustained commitment to the task. Throughout the dictatorship Salazar concentrated his energies on reinforcing the administrative apparatus of the state rather than on building the corporations, which were theoretically intended to be quasi-autonomous structures for the channeling of demands and support from the citizenry below to the regime at the top. Despite Marcello Caetano's efforts to revitalize and implement the system after Salazar's death on July 27, 1970, in the early 1970s Portugal's corporatist structures remained at best legalistic and only partly complete.[25]

Salazar's New State survived for nearly 50 years primarily through the activity of its bureaucracy. Behind the corporatist façade, the actual policy-formation process had become dominated by a technocratic elite which made decisions at the top, with little or no input from the citizenry below. During the dictatorship, the locus of policy formation was Salazar and his cabinet. Gradually, government ministers became less important as politicians and more important as administrators and technicians.[26]

While ostensibly corporatist, the reality of the Salazar-Caetano dictatorship was that of the demobilized, depoliticized, administrative state in which the making and implementing of public policy were dominated by the technocracy and political conflict was consciously limited to the bureaucratic arena. In both law and practice, "the dominant attitude present throughout Portuguese territory was one that conceived of the roles of central authorities as administrators of public services to a quiescent population, as defenders of public order against the enemies of the state, as agents of a ruling class committed to policies designed to insure the survival of greater Portugal."[27]

Thus the hallmark of Salazar's New State was not its corporate structures. It was, instead, the "overinstitutionalized" administrative apparatus with its preponderance of technocrats in the policy-formation process.[28] The emphasis on administration and depoliticization reinforced a tendency of the public bureaucracy to play an increasing role in Portuguese society and to act as a source of continuity and stability over time. Ever since the time of the absolutist Marquês de Pombal, (1750–1777), administrative reforms had been made in response to changing socioeconomic circumstances and to political upheavals; these reforms led to a gradual merging of the social, economic, and political sectors of society that has obscured distinctions between political and administrative structures.[29] The dictatorship's concentration on the bureaucracy and its success in controlling policy formation has left democratic Portugal with a legacy of a deeply entrenched, autonomous, and inmovable national administration which continues to overwhelm local political structures, and which still controls the local policy-formation process.

Local Political Culture

It has been demonstrated that the organization of the political structure and policy process at the local level in Portugal are the result of bureaucratic overinstitutionalization and not of corporatism. Attention can now be devoted to questions of political culture, which is conceived here as the pattern of individual attitudes and orientations among the members of a political system.[30] Individual orientations can be broken down into two basic components: orientations toward the political system, and orientations toward the self as a political actor. Orientations toward the political system includc knowledge of the political system (cognition), feelings of attachment to the political system (affectation), and judgments about the political system (evaluation). Orientations toward the self as a political actor include the individual's sense of how one should participate in politics (obligations), and one's feeling of political influence (competence).[31]

One of the primary tools for measuring political culture is attitudinal

TABLE 9.2
Citizen Level of Political Awareness, Porto de Mós
(N = 193)

Level	No. of Respondents	Percentage
Low	111	57.5
Medium	33	17.1
High	49	25.4

TABLE 9.3
Citizen Level of Political Knowledge, Porto de Mós
(N = 193)

Level	No. of Respondents	Percentage
Low	66	34.2
Medium	81	42.0
High	46	23.8

surveys.[32] The data that follow are based on such a survey, carried out during the summer of 1978. The personal interviews averaged 30 minutes in length and were designed to elicit a citizen's orientations to the local political system and to the self as an actor in that system.[33] The interviews were conducted by a team of students recruited from the local secondary school (*liceu*) and trained by the author. Respondents were selected from voter registration lists by a method that gave every individual of voting age living within the county of Porto de Mós an equal chance of being selected. Within each of the county's 13 parishes a sample was selected proportionate to the voters registered in that parish; by this process 309 individuals were chosen. However, only 193 of those selected were actually interviewed because many people were absent from home or had emigrated since the registration lists had been prepared. A much smaller number were ill or refused to be interviewed. Of those interviewed, 97 were men and 96 were women; they ranged in age from 18 years to more than 80—although 34 individuals refused to give their age.[34]

The first orientation to be examined in the light of survey responses is knowledge of the local political system. This orientation has two aspects: awareness of local political affairs, and knowledge about how local government works. An index of levels of awareness was compiled from responses to the following three questions: Do you understand the political problems of the county? Are you interested in news about local politics? Do you talk about local politics with your family? The data, given in table 9.2, suggest that the level of awareness of local politics among the citizenry is rather low. Only 30.6 percent of the respondents said that they understood the county's political problems; only 30.1 percent had more than an occasional interest in local political news; and only 21.2 percent talked about local politics with their families.

An index of political knowledge about the workings of local government was compiled from responses to the following two questions: Who makes the decisions in your parish and in the county? Do you know the names of any of the county's officials? The data given in table 9.3 suggest that the level of political knowledge about the operation of local government in the county is medium. Of those respondents who had an opinion about the first question, 50.3 percent named either the president of their parish board, the mayor of the county, or the board or chamber itself. Only 3.1 percent thought some other political entity, such as one of the political parties or the municipal or parish assembly, made political decisions. A large number of the respondents (69.9 percent) could not name a local official; of those respondents who could, 90 percent mentioned either the mayor or the president of their parish board.

The picture of political knowledge that emerges from these data suggests that the citizens of the county are oriented toward the "downward" side of the local political system—that is, the administrative apparatus. The respondents seemed to be reasonably knowledgeable as to who or what entity makes local political decisions. However, they were less knowledgeable about what individuals made those decisions. On the other hand, these data suggest that the respondents had little awareness or interest in the "upward" side of the local political system—that is, its political policy-making structures. Only about one-third of the respondents claimed to understand the county's political problems, had an interest in local political news, or talked about politics at home. The great bulk of the citizenry of the county appears not to be oriented toward input structures, and is generally disinterested in and ignorant of the county's political problems.

With respect to feelings of attachment to the local political system, the respondents were asked, When you give your point of view to an official of the parish board or the municipal chamber, do you feel that your opinion is taken into consideration? It was assumed that the attitude people have toward local government is influenced by the treatment they receive at the hands of functionaries. It can be safely assumed that if fair and considerate treatment is expected, citizens will be favorably disposed toward the local political system.

Table 9.4 shows that the expectations of fair treatment were quite high among the respondents. Nearly one-half (46.6 percent) of the respondents expected to be treated fairly by local officials, while 32.7 percent did not expect such treatment or expected it only some of the time. These findings suggest that not only are the citizens of the county oriented toward the administrative side of the local political system, but that they are favorably inclined toward those structures as well. Positive feelings toward local government are also reflected in the citizenry's evaluation of the local political system.

TABLE 9.4

Citizen Expectation of Fair Treatment, Porto de Mós
(N = 193)

Expectation	No. of Respondents	Percentage
Yes	90	46.6
Sometimes	27	14.0
No	36	18.7
Don't Know	40	20.7

TABLE 9.5

Citizen Level of Evaluation
of Local Political System, Porto de Mós
(N = 193)

Level	No. of Respondents	Percentage
Low	19	9.8
Medium	47	24.4
High	127	65.3

To determine the respondents' judgment about the local political system, an index was compiled from answers to two questions: Do you think that the activities of the parish boards and the municipal chamber tend to make conditions better in the county? Do you think that the people would be better off without the parish boards and municipal chamber? Table 9.5 reveals that well over one-half (65.8 percent) of the respondents had a high evaluation of the activities of local government, and that a huge majority (90.2 percent) had a medium to high evaluation. These results indicate that not only are the citizens of the county oriented toward the administrative side of the local political system, but that they also evaluate positively the impact of these bureaucratic structures on living conditions within the county. Only a small minority of citizens (9.8 percent) rated local government low and believed that conditions within the county would improve if local government would disappear. The findings suggest that the citizens of the county are strongly allegiant to the administrative structures of local government.

But what of their feelings about local political structures? How does the citizenry of the county evaluate the parish and municipal assemblies: To find out, the respondents were asked, What do you think of the activities of your parish assembly or the municipal assembly? Table 9.6 shows that nearly one-half of the respondents had no opinion about the activities of the local elected assemblies; of those who expressed an opinion, only 26.9 percent viewed the assemblies in a favorable light,

TABLE 9.6
Citizen Evaluation of Local Assemblies, Porto de Mós
(N = 193)

Opinion	No. of Respondents	Percentage
Valuable	52	26.9
Sometimes valuable	20	10.4
Not valuable	25	13.0
Don't know	96	49.7

while 23.4 percent perceived them as not or only sometimes valuable. These findings are quite consistent with those that show the citizenry of the county to be oriented toward and favorably disposed to administrative structures, and not oriented toward and generally disinterested in and ignorant of the county's new political policy-making structures.

Further evidence for this conclusion is provided by the respondents' answers to two questions designed to measure the saliency of political policy-making structures: Do you have contact with any political group or organization? With which political party do you identify?[35] The index compiled from these questions is presented in table 9.7. It shows that the salience level of input structures is generally low. This finding reinforces other data indicating that political structures are only vaguely perceived by the citizens of the county, at least as far as local government is concerned.

It can be concluded from the data given above that Portugal's new political policy-making structures are not viewed with feelings of attachment, and that they do not receive high evaluations for their effectiveness. These attitudes are in sharp contrast to the strong attachments to and positive evaluations of the administrative side of the local political system.

It is now appropriate to discuss the way the respondents viewed themselves as political actors, and their feelings of competence as such actors. To find out how they conceived of themselves as political actors, they were asked, What role should people like yourself play in local political affairs? The results, given in table 9.8, indicate that nearly 60 percent of the respondents had either a passive conception of their role or had no conception of themselves as political actors. Typical answers of those classified as passive respondents were: be content with what one has; cooperate; work harder; be humble; and cooperate with the authorities. Among those classified as active respondents, typical answers were: speak to the parish board and municipal chamber; discuss the issues and problems; and look at the alternatives.

Only three respondents mentioned participating in the parish or municipal assemblies, attending party meetings, or voting in one's own interest. These data suggest, then, that few citizens in the county conceive of themselves as active participants in politics.

How did the county's citizens view their competence as political actors? A competency index was compiled from responses to the following four questions: What would you do if your parish board or the municipal chamber was debating a regulation or a project that you considered unjust? If such a situation were to occur in the future, would you try to do something to change it? If you tried to influence your board or the municipal chamber, do you think your efforts would be successful? How would you proceed if you wanted to get something done by your parish board or the municipal chamber? The data in table 9.9 show a tendency toward a high level of competence among the respondents, which is quite surprising in the light of other findings which show that they do not perceive of themselves as active political participants. How can this contradiction be reconciled?

The answer lies in the distinction that can be made between political and administrative competence.[36] It appears that the respondents do not perceive of themselves as able to influence local government by organizing groups or threatening to withdraw their support. Rather, they perceive of themselves as being able to influence local government by individually attending meetings of the parish board or the municipal chamber, and by appealing to a set of rules of proper and moral administrative conduct. As the data has shown, a large propor-

TABLE 9.7
Level of Salience of Input Structures, Porto de Mós
(N = 193)

Level	No. of Respondents	Percentage
Low	87	45.1
Medium	76	39.4
High	30	15.5

TABLE 9.8
Citizen Political Role Perception, Porto de Mós
(N = 193)

Role	No. of Respondents	Percentage
Active	81	42.0
Passive	59	30.5
Don't know	53	27.5

tion of the respondents expect fair treatment from local officials at least some of the time, believe that their point of view is given consideration, and seem willing to protest what they consider to be an unjust project or regulation.

This sense of administrative competence does not derive from the respondents' active attempts to influence government, but rather from their belief that local government officials should be controlled by rules of moral conduct that curb the arbitrary exercise of power. Their belief in a moral code can be seen in their replies to the following question: In your opinion, what are the most important qualities for a local elected official to have? As table 9.10 shows, only a little less than one-third (27.9 percent) of the respondents had no idea of what qualities they expected in elected officials. Of the 72.1 percent who did express an opinion, nearly one-half (32.6 percent) said that they expected local elected officials to be honest above all. After honesty, the qualities most frequently mentioned were "hardworking" and "impartial."

Additional evidence of the belief in a set of rules of moral conduct

TABLE 9.9

Citizen Level of Competence as Political Actors, Porto de Mós (N = 193)

Level	No. of Respondents	Percentage
Low	59	30.6
Medium	43	22.3
High	91	47.1

TABLE 9.10

Qualities of Local Elected Officials, Porto de Mós

Quality	No. of Respondents	Percentage
Honest	63	32.6
Hardworking	22	11.4
Impartial	11	5.7
Good	9	4.7
Just	8	4.1
Serious	6	3.1
Sincere	5	2.6
Attentive	4	2.1
Active	3	1.6
Competent	3	1.6
Good politician	3	1.6
Knowledgeable	2	1.0
Don't know	54	27.9

TABLE 9.11
Citizen Attitudes toward Bribes, Porto de Mós

Attitude	No. of Respondents	Percentage
Don't know	26	13.5
Do nothing	42	21.7
Protest, denounce	125	64.8

can be seen in the responses to the question, What would you do if you knew that an elected official of the county had accepted bribes? The data given in table 9.11 show that the great majority of the respondents would denounce and protest such behavior. This suggests that the respondents not only expect local officials to abide by a code of moral conduct, but also expect them to behave according to a set of proper administrative procedures. It also suggests that ordinary citizens conceive of elected officials as administrators, and the running of local government as essentially a question of good management, impartiality, and conscientiousness.

The data gleaned by the survey suggest that the political culture of Porto de Mós is still a "subject" one. That is, the administrative side of the local political system is generally more salient than the political policy-making side, and evaluations of the self as a political participant are quite low. The respondents seemed to be well aware of the various local administrative political structures; they were affectively oriented toward them; and they generally evaluated the activities of local government favorably. Although the respondents did demonstrate a measure of administrative competence, they did not conceive of themselves as active and competent political participants capable of influencing the local decision-making process through involvement in policy-making structures.[37]

It should be emphasized that this political culture is not corporatist per se, and does not derive from an underlying corporatist tradition. It is, instead, a political culture composed of the kinds of attitudes and orientations that would be expected in a depoliticized political system dominated by the administrative apparatus of the state. The actual structure of local government has been and still is very much an integral aspect of the central administrative system. Local elected officials have been and still are essentially bureaucrats. And the decision-making process still takes place at the higher reaches of the state's bureaucracy. It would be very unusual for a local political structure of this sort to foster anything other than subject attitudes, orientations, and behaviors toward the political system.

Conclusions: The Asymmetrical Polity

Recently the Portuguese political system has been analyzed by employing cultural and structural variants of the corporatist framework. This chapter has taken issue with such analyses and has suggested that Portugal can be better comprehended by utilizing an organizationl approach which draws attention to the interaction between the actual political structure and the political culture. Looked at this way, it has been shown that the real underlying structural links and policy process were, during the "corporatist" New State, and still are in today's democratic system, administrative and technocratic. It has been also demonstrated that Portugal's political culture is not "corporatist," or deterministic of political structure. Indeed, it has been made clear that Portuguese political culture is a set of subjective and passive attitudinal and behavioral responses to the overwhelming power and control exercised by the administrative apparatus of the state.

None of this is particularly unique to Portugal. The administrative state, as exemplified by the Portuguese case, has numerous historical and modern variants not limited to Ibero-Latin geographical regions.[38] Like many other less-developed countries with long histories of absolutism, empire, and dictatorship, Portugal's political system gradually evolved into a bureaucratic polity as various elites sought to modernize the society by consolidating power and authority over the national territory, and by seeking to rationalize the political process. Because of the early emergence of and the overwhelming control exercised by the administrative system, Portugal, not unlike other less-developed countries with similar histories, has only recently (April 25, 1974) been able to take the major step of creating a specialized political infrastructure of political parties and interest groups independent of the administrative apparatus of the state, and capable of aggregating and articulating the demands and support of the citizenry.

Thus there is today a severe imbalance between the salience, power, and legitimacy of Portugal's local political policy-making structures and its bureaucratic policy-implementing structures.[39] The deliberate efforts by previous elites, especially during the dictatorship, to demobilize and depoliticize the system and to increase the efficiency and rationality of the administrative apparatus has brought about a fusion of bureaucratic and political roles and structures in the minds of the citizenry. Politics and politicians are seen in essentially bureaucratic terms. The local elected officials who were interviewed tended to think of their roles in administrative terms, and perceived the running of local government as an exercise in good management. There is no clear-cut distinction between the role of politician and the role of bureaucrat in the public consciousness.

The local decision-making process, therefore, operates largely without the benefit of autonomous "political brokers." Despite the fact that local officials are now elected and must gain "approval" for their "policies" from elected assemblies, there still are no institutionalized structures and roles for clarifying, delineating, accommodating, and channeling the demands and support of the citizens in ways consistent with the democratic process. The absence of such structures and roles means that the citizenry is still cut off from any meaningful voice in policy decisions.

These structural and role deficiencies are compounded by Portugal's local political culture. The problem is not the presence of Portugal's putative corporatist tradition but, rather, the persistence of adaptive orientations and behavioral patterns that have emerged in response to the overinstitutionalized administrative apparatus of the state. The orientations toward the administrative side of the political system, and the passive conception of the self as a political actor, only serve to reinforce administrative structures and roles and to inhibit the development of autonomous political structures and roles. At the local level citizens do not yet have a set of appropriate orientations and attitudes concerning the role of politicians and autonomous policy-making structures.

Portugal's local subject political culture is, in turn, reinforced by the extant political system because the actual policy-making structures and roles remain fundamentally congruent with the orientations and behavior patterns of the citizenry. The citizenry's cognitions of the local political system are accurate, and its evaluations of that system are favorable. This means that for the few citizens for whom the policy-making aspect of the political system is generally more salient and who conceive of themselves as politically active there will be great difficulty in becoming competent, self-confident, and experienced political actors.

If this cycle is ever to be broken, independent, autonomous policy-making structures and differentiated political roles must emerge at the local level. It is through the efforts of political parties and politicians that the state's overinstitutionalized administrative apparatus can be reformed and controlled in a way more consistent with the democratic process. If local government is to become something more than a mere administrative arm of the state, and if local elected officials are to become something more than bureaucrats, the state must be decentralized and local elected officials must become directly accountable to local elected assemblies and the citizenry. Policy formation must become a matter of local priorities and must reflect goals that the citizenry has chosen and is willing to pay for. Only then will Portuguese voters and politicians learn the full meaning of political choice and democracy.

Although this chapter reports the results of research carried out in only one rural county, its findings can in all probability be extrapolated to most of rural Portugal. Since the structure of government and the policy-formation process are the same throughout the country, there is no reason to assume that the political culture of other rural areas would be radically different than that of Porto de Mós. The only exception to this generalization about rural political culture might be found in certain zones of the Alentejo where the Communist party is well implanted, and where, as a consequence, the political mobilization of the citizenry is much higher than in other rural areas. It may also be unsafe to extend the conclusions from Porto de Mós to municipalities and parishes which are heavily urbanized. In large metropolitan areas, such as Lisbon and Porto, the financial resources of local government are likely to be greater and the population more diverse and politicized. It is possible that in these areas local government has a much greater political dimension, that elected officials perceive themselves as and behave as politicians, that the citizenry is more politically active, and that the policy process is more democratic. These questions can only be definitively answered by further research of sites representative of Portugal's contrasting socioeconomic ecologies.

Notes

Support for field work in Portugal from May to July 1978 was provided by the Calouste Gulbenkian Foundation, Lisbon, and the Committee on Faculty Research, the University of Mississippi. I wish to thank João António de Sousa Domingues and Mário José Vieira de Cruz for excellent and enthusiastic research assistance. I also wish to thank James R. Scarritt, Gary H. Brooks, and Ronn J. Hy for their advice on an earlier draft of this chapter.

This chapter presents a revised version of data published in *Análise Social* (Lisbon) 15 (1979), pp. 655–672; and in *Comparative Politics* 13 (Apr. 1981), pp. 271–289.

1 The leading spokesman for this view is Howard J. Wiarda. See his *Corporatism and Development: The Portuguese Experience* (Amherst, Mass., 1977).

2 Major theoretical statements of this school can be found in Howard J. Wiarda, "Toward a Framework for the Study of Political Change in the Iberic-Latin Tradition: The Corporate Model," *World Politics* 25 (Jan.

1973), pp. 206–235; Howard J. Wiarda, ed., *Politics and Social Change in Latin America: The Distinctive Tradition* (Amherst, Mass., 1974); and Frederick B. Pike and Thomas Stritch, eds., *The New Corporatism* (South Bend, Ind., 1974).

3 This is the position of Wiarda. See in particular his *Corporatism and Development*.

4 The leading spokesman for this position is Philippe C. Schmitter. See his *Corporatism and Public Policy in Authoritarian Portugal* (Beverly Hills and London, 1975).

5 On this approach, see Kenneth Jowitt, "An Organizational Approach to the Study of Political Culture in Marxist-Leninist Systems," *American Political Science Review* 58 (Sept. 1974), pp. 1171–1191.

6 The research was conducted in a mountainous county (*concelho*) of 20,290 inhabitants within the district of Leiria. Although the bulk of the population of the county consists of poor farmers and rural workers who cultivate apples, the region's primary agricultural produce, there is some light industry, especially ceramics and textiles. For the most part the inhabitants reside in small population concentrations (*povoações*) scattered throughout the county. There are, however, two fairly large villages. One is Porto de Mós, from which the county takes its name, and which is the seat of local government. The other is Mire de Aire, which is the focus of the county's industry and is in close proximity to a set of spectacular caverns, a major tourist attraction. Although the county has experienced some emigration, the population is fairly well balanced between the sexes; there are 97 men for every 100 women. All references to Porto de Mós in the text are to the county, not the village, unless otherwise noted.

7 In chapter 7 by Charles Downs, the *juntas de freguesia* are called "neighbor units of government." This is because in urban Portugal the original designation "parish" has ceased to have much meaning. In the same way "marginal government" is a more accurate English language analogy for urban *concelhos* than "county," which captures here the character of rural *concelhos*. Nevertheless, the reader should be aware that the actual *município* setting is complex, as subsequent pages in this chapter show, and was simplified in Down's chapter to fit the cases of Lisbon, Porto, and Setúbal (ed.).

8 Joyce Firstenberg Riegelhaupt, "Peasants and Politics in Salazar's Portugal: The Corporate State and Village 'Nonpolitics,'" in Lawrence S. Graham and Harry M. Makler, eds., *Contemporary Portugal: The Revolution and its Antecedents* (Austin, 1979), pp. 163–173. See also José Cutileiro, *A Portuguese Rural Society* (Oxford, 1971).

9 Norman Blume, "Neighborhood Administration in Lisbon: The Juntas de Freguesia," *National Civic Review* 64 (May 1975), p. 250.

10 Riegelhaupt, "Peasants and Politics," p. 171.

11 Ibid., p. 172.

12 The 1976 constitution authorizes two basic units of local government subordinate to the parliament, the cabinet, and the prime minister: the auton-

omous regions of the Azores and Madeira; and the territorial politico-administrative subdivisions on the mainland—the parish (*freguesia*), the municipality (*município*, whose boundaries conform to those of the *concelho*, or county), and the district (*distrito*). These territorial subdivisions include both rural and urban areas in one governmental unit; there are no unincorporated rural areas in Portugal (as one finds in the United States). The structure of government is basically the same for all units, urban and rural, at the same level. The differences are only in the elaborateness of the functions performed and the size of elected bodies. Although the constitution has retained the dictatorship's tripartite geographical subdivision of the country, it calls for the substitution of administrative regions for the districts. For more details on the new organization of local government, see Walter C. Opello, Jr., "The Second Portuguese Republic: Politico-Administrative Decentralization since April 25, 1974," *Iberian Studies* 7 (Autumn 1978), pp. 43–48.

13 The county of Porto de Mós has 13 parishes ranging in size from Alcaria, the smallest with about 300 citizens, to Mire de Aire, the largest with about 3,000. The size of parish assemblies depends on the voting-age population of the parish. Parishes having less than 1,000 registered voters have 9 assembly members. The number of members increases with population size, reaching 27 in parishes with more than 20,000 registered voters. In parishes of more than 30,000 voters, representation is increased by one seat for every 5,000 registered voters. In parishes of less than 301 registered voters, the assembly is replaced by a "town meeting"; all registered voters in the parish are entitled to attend and take part.

14 Parishes with less than 5,000 registered voters have two board members; those with between 5,000 and 10,000 registered voters have two additional board members; in those of more than 20,000 voters there are four additional members.

15 The size of the municipal assemblies depends upon the number of parishes found within the county. The municipal assembly of Porto de Mós had 27 members, 13 of whom were the presidents of the parish boards and 14 of whom were elected directly.

16 The number of aldermen varies with the number of registered voters in the county. Counties of more than 100,000 registered voters have ten aldermen; those having between 10,000 and 50,000 voters have six; and those with less than 10,000 voters have four. Porto de Mós has six aldermen.

17 These characteristics of effective decentralization and citizen involvement in local policy formation are from Gordon Smith, *Politics in Western Europe* (New York, 1973), pp. 256–257.

18 Câmara Municipal de Porto de Mós, "Plano de Actividades e Orçamento para 1977," mimeographed (Porto de Mós, 1977, 1978).

19 Câmara Municipal do Concelho de Porto de Mós, "Actas das Reuniões da Câmara Municipal," Livro de Actas, nos. 63–67.

20 To insure that the governor does not act arbitrarily, the dissolution of any

local unit requires the approval of the district assembly (*assembleia distrital*), which is composed of the mayors of the district's counties and two members of each municipal assembly found in the district.

21 This dependency has not been significantly alleviated even though a new local finance law, passed in 1978, instituted a system of revenue sharing which returns about 18 percent of all taxes collected by the central government to the municipalities, according to a taxes-paid formula.

22 Mark Kesselman, *The Ambiguous Consensus: A Study of Local Government in France* (New York, 1967).

23 Douglas L. Wheeler, *Republican Portugal: A Political History 1910–1926* (Madison, 1978), chapter 14.

24 See Manuel de Lucena, *A Evolução do Sistema Corporativo Português* (Lisbon, 1975).

25 Thomas C. Bruneau, "The Portuguese Coup: Causes and Probable Consequences," *The World Today* 30 (July 1974), pp. 278–279. Further evidence for the hollowness of Portugal's corporations is provided in Harry M. Makler, "The Portuguese Industrial Elite and Its Corporative Relations: A Study of Compartmentalization in an Authoritarian Regime," *Economic Development and Change* 24 (1976), pp. 495–526.

26 Paul H. Lewis, "Salazar's Ministerial Elite, 1932–1968," *Journal of Politics* 40 (Aug. 1978), pp. 622–647.

27 Lawrence S. Graham, *Portugal: The Decline and Collapse of an Authoritarian Order* (Beverly Hills and London, 1975), p. 17.

28 On the concept of "overinstitutionalization," see Mark Kesselman, "Overinstitutionalization and Political Constraint: The Case of France," *Comparative Politics* 3 (Oct. 1970), pp. 21–44.

29 Graham, *Collapse of an Authoritarian Order*, p. 17.

30 On this conceptualization of political culture, see Gabriel A. Almond and Sidney Verba, *The Civic Culture* (Princeton, 1963); and Lucian Pye and Sidney, Verba, eds., *Political Culture and Political Development* (Princeton, 1965).

31 It should be noted that the strictly "nonpolitical" orientations of the individual to social relations and civic cooperation are not included in this study.

32 See, for example, Almond and Verba *The Civic Culture*; Donald J. Devine, *The Political Culture of the United States* (Boston, 1972); and Bradley M. Richardson, *The Political Culture of Japan* (Berkely and Los Angeles, 1974). Some work on political culture has been done using in-depth interviewing and emotive techniques. See Edward C. Banfield, *The Moral Basis of a Backward Society* (New York, 1958); Richard H. Solomon, *Mao's Revolution and the Chinese Political Culture* (Berkeley and Los Angels, 1971); and David D. Laitin, *Politics, Language, and Thought: The Somali Experience* (Chicago, 1977).

33 The questionnaire was based on that of Almond and Verba; see *The Civic Culture*, Appendix.

34 Although no test-retest procedures or reliability coefficients were em-

ployed, there is no reason to expect that the questionnaire would be unreliable over time. The validity of the items were ensured, first, by asking colleagues if they thought the items measured what they were intended to measure, and second, by asking Portuguese colleagues if the items had been rendered into the Portuguese in a form that the ordinary citizen would understand. For an example of this approach to reliability and validity, see Fred N. Kerlinger, *Behavioral Research: A Conceptual Approach* (New York, 1979), pp. 132–141.

35 For a discussion of Portuguese political parties and Portugal's first two elections, see Ben Pimlott, "Parties and Voters in the Portuguese Revolution: The Elections of 1975 and 1976," *Parliamentary Affairs* 30 (Winter 1977), pp. 35–38.

36 The politically competent citizen is one who plays an influential role in the decision-making process and participates through the use of implied or stated threats if demands are not complied with. On the other hand, the administratively competent citizen is the individual who does not participate in the decision-making process, but is aware of rights and duties under the rules to which he appeals (he does not demand) to guard against arbitrary action by government officials. See Almond and Verba, *The Civic Culture*, pp. 214–216.

37 See Almond and Verba, *The Civic Culture*, pp. 17–21, for the characteristics of a "subject" political culture.

38 See S. N. Eisenstadt, *The Political System of Empire* (New York, 1963).

39 This political-administrative dichotomy is discussed by Fred W. Riggs, *Administration in Developing Countries: The Theory of Prismatic Society* (Boston, 1964). See also Fred W. Riggs, "Bureaucrats and Political Development," in Joseph La Palombara, ed., *Bureaucracy and Political Development* (Princeton, 1963); Riggs, "The Structures of Governmental and Administrative Reform," in Ralph Braibanti, ed., *Political and Administrative Development* (Durham, N.C., 1969), pp. 200–324; and Riggs, "Bureaucratic Politics in Comparative Perspective," *Journal of Comparative Administration* 1 (May 1969), pp. 5–38.

10 *Lawrence S. Graham*

Bureaucratic Politics and the Problem of Reform in the State Apparatus

Discussion of administrative reform is no newcomer to Portugal; nor is the observation that politics and bureaucracy are inextricably mixed. Eras of major transition there as elsewhere usually have involved transformation in state organizations responsible for carrying out the policies of those in command. Similarly, when changes in political direction have taken place, either revolutionary or reformist in nature, they have been linked to attempts to alter the performance of governmental bureaucrats. In such settings policymakers concerned with practical politics rarely assume that agents of the state—its civil servants—will automatically carry out their dictates unless persons sympathetic to their wishes are located in positions of responsibility and mechanisms for attaining compliance enter into force.

Any discussion of public administration in Portugal since April 1974, be it an analysis of current practices or recommendations as to how best to tackle the issue of reforming the public bureaucracy, must begin with an awareness of this reality. Since no administrative system is self-contained or entirely the product of current governmental choices, it is important in dealing with the Portuguese case to establish first what the legacies of the past are, and how they have shaped present-day public organizations, attitudes toward government, and perceptions of bureaucratic roles.[1] Once we have been able to determine what public bureaucracy is and is not in Portugal, we will then be in a better position to review the impact of the changes since 1974 on the administrative system and their implication for administrative reform.

Portugal's Bureaucratic Legacy

Portugal's administrative system as we know it today is the consequence of nearly a half century of authoritarian rule, in which one man —Dr. António Salazar—shaped the state and its institutions to fit his policy choices. Frequently called a corporate state, from a comparative perspective both cross-nationally and diachronically (contrasting one Portuguese regime type with another—constitutional monarchy, parliamentary republic, dictatorship, and semi-presidentialism), the most apt term is bureaucratic-authoritarian. Jorge Campinos has made it clear that the New State was above all else a presidential regime dominated by Salazar, in which the chief executive ceased to be the president of the Republic and the prime minister became the focal point for the system.[2] Never given to extensive consultation, Salazar ruled the country from his offices in São Bento from 1932 to 1968 through a hierarchical set of controls. Over time these offices became institutionalized in the form of a single complex staff organization known as the Presidency of the Council of Ministers. A distinct ministry, or supraministry, it contained a core group of reliable officials, civilian and military—personally accountable to Salazar—charged with the responsibility of reporting on, controlling, and regulating various aspects of Portuguese life. In this setting the Council of Minister as a collective body constituted really only a formality, for Salazar preferred to deal with his ministers individually or in small numbers, according to the issue at hand. Not until Caetano assumed the premiership did the focus of power shift toward the Council of Ministers and did policy making become a more collective responsibility.[3]

As the supreme head of government and with powers concentrated in his person, Salazar extended his rule over Portugal and maintained it through the development of an effective set of hierarchical organizations—effective in the sense that they served his regime well as instruments of control and regulation. At the apex stood Salazar and the Presidency of the Council of Ministers. Under his jurisdiction and subject to his wishes served individual ministers; under them, directors-general and directors of administrative services within the ministries.

Throughout the Salazar era, ministerial turnovers were frequent. Of the 143 ministers appointed between 1926 and 1969, 49 percent served for 2 years or less. The pattern of unequal tenure in different ministries gives further insight into how Salazar used bureaucratic politics to his advantage within ministries critical to his survival. In Interior, Education, Overseas, and Foreign Affairs the average tenure was less than 3 years; in Justice, 3 years; in Finance and Agriculture, 4.3 and 4.7 years, respectively.[4] In Finance, Defense, and Foreign Affairs Salazar took an immediate and direct interest, and frequently assumed the ministerial responsibilities himself. This contrast between the stability of the regime and the instability of its ministers is to be explained in terms of the concentration of power in the hands of one man (Salazar), his reliance on advisors and men of personal confidence in his own ministry (the Presidency of the Council of Ministers), and the stability of appointments at the level of the directors-general and directors of administrative services, where the principle of lifetime appointments (*cargos vitalícios*) received legal sanctioning.

At the regional and local levels the same hierarchical principles of rule applied. Civil governors represented the government in each district, answering directly to the minister of the Interior. Within the municipalities (local government units combining urban and rural areas), municipal presidents filled this function. Named from above and selected from within the locality, these men presided over local administrative councils (a kind of plural executive called *câmaras*) and representative bodies (termed *concelhos*).[5]

Prolonged authoritarian rule (1926–1974), when joined to the traditions of a unitary state extending back over centuries, has given tremendous institutional weight to the practice of referring virtually all administrative matters arising in the provinces to Lisbon. Examples abound of routine operations in Portugal in which citizens and bureaucrats outside the capital have readily concluded that successful resolution could be obtained only through action by a central ministry, and in many cases by no one else but the minister himself. The requirement of all sorts of legal documentation has accompanied the institutionalization of these practices. Such patterns of administration, sanctioned by long-standing tradition and reinforced by the New State's hierarchical controls, are and will continue to be tremendously difficult to reverse. To paraphrase the words of a former minister of agriculture, one of the great evils in Portuguese public life is the excessive centralization from Lisbon, which is centuries old and which everyone engages in whether they are identified with the center, the right, or the left. Compounding this situation—one that involves extensive delays, much paper work, and timidity on the part of lower-level bureaucrats who will not act without approval from above—has been the development of a parallel trade specializing in the preparation of illegal documentation. Ranging from inscription on the social security rolls (*previdência social*) to certificates of various sorts, such documentation provides a way to bypass the red tape one so frequently encounters in going through normal channels.

A corollary to this sort of administrative system is frequently an excessive division of responsibility below the top and the fragmentation of the public bureaucracy into a series of competing public organizations, within which there is substantial rivalry among bureaus for scarce resources, power, and prestige. During the New State era (1930–1974) the primary bureaucratic power domains were those belonging to the directors-general and the directors of administrative services. At this level turnover in personnel was restricted. Whereas ministers came and went with frequency, the directors stayed on and in practice were responsible for the great majority of the work carried out by the government. Not uncommon were situations in which a three-way jousting for power and influence occurred within the bureaucratic arena provided by the ministries: between the ministers or secretaries of state and their directors, and among the directors themselves.

Such was the situation I encountered in 1971 in the then Ministry of Corporations, where I was conducting in-depth interviews of civil servants charged with managerial responsibilities; the interviews were part of a single-organization case study within the wider context of a general study of the Caetano government. While there was a clear-cut pattern of authority established in accord with a formal hierarchical model, administrative reality pointed in the direction of substantial bureau autonomy. The minister of corporations and social security and the secretary and undersecretary of state for labor and social security headed all operations in this state sector. Operating from below, but in secure positions with a strategic advantage derived from their control of programs and services key to the ministry's operations, were the director-general of labor and corporations and the director-general of social security and housing. As men with lifelong appointments these directors were extremely powerful figures, jealously guarding their bureaucratic domains. Only in the instance of the National Employment Service (Serviço Nacional de Emprego) was it possible to talk in terms of autonomy of action on the part of a subordinate. It was headed at the time by a man much younger than the directors who appeared to be far more capable than his immediate superiors. This administrator was charged with the important responsibility of keeping records on official and unofficial internal and external worker migration. What made possible his freedom of action and successful working relationship with the management team at the head of the ministry was the fact that this service had its own autonomous financial basis (the Fundo de Desenvolvimento da Mão-de-Obra), and did not have to negotiate its primary budgetary allocations through the director-general.

There are two reasons for giving these capsules of administrative history: first, to establish through example the fragmentation already existing within the central ministries before 1974, and, second, to suggest that actual internal bureaucratic power relations before April 25 of that year did not necessarily follow hierarchical lines. Another and perhaps more important factor undercutting the government's formal hierarchical organization charts was the uneven pattern followed in distributing financial resources. It was quite common in the New State to discover all sorts of corners and safe areas of operation, funded by separate accounts and taxes reserved for a particular administrative unit, as was the case in the employment service referred to above. The distribution of field services was also highly uneven, with some ministries—such as Education and Corporations (Labor)—maintaining extensive networks of provincial inspectorates, and others—such as the State Secretariat for Agriculture—having minimal provincial representation. Where field services did exist, they served to enhance the power and prestige of directors in Lisbon. Further insight into this fragmentation of authority and competing jurisdictions is to be gained from awareness of the presence of parallel structures—a term used by Portuguese government personnel to refer to the duplication of services, arising from the jurisdiction of one ministry being jealously defended by its management team and necessitating the creation of a similar service in another ministry in order to get actual programs executed.

The Impact of Revolution on Administration

Following the collapse of the Caetano government, reaction against the old bureaucratic controls moved in two directions: toward dismantling the Presidency of the Council of Ministers as a supraministry overseeing and regulating the administrative system as a whole, and toward forming numerous worker commissions (*commissões de trabalhadores*) to drive out those men most closely identified in the minds of lower-level public employees with the New State—the directors-general and the directors of administrative services. The exiting of these middle managers during 1974–1976 was not so much a question of timidity as it was a quite correct perception on their part that they constituted visible objects against which popular hostility could be vented. From the standpoint of the left-wing parties, their removal was an essential part of the move to capture control of the state apparatus quickly and decisively.

The immediate impact of these developments was to accelerate greatly the fragmentation of the administrative system, a process already in progress under Caetano. In an effort to bring into positions of authority a new group of technicians accountable to himself and independent of the Salazarites, Caetano had relaxed some of the control and regulatory functions of the Presidency of the Council of Ministers. As he attempted unsuccessfully to establish his own power base, he also weakened the authority of many of the old-line directors. Failing to establish an effective new framework for policy coordination and execution, Caetano had hastened the process of disintegration. Various bureaucratic components within the regime already had established the primacy of their own dynamics before April 25. The removal of any semblance of authority from the top in the aftermath of the military coup, combined with the struggle for control of the government among competing military and civilian factions and mass upheaval from below, quickly pulverized what coherency was left in the old administrative system. A host of public organizations emerged, some with greater amounts of internal coherency, others with less—but there was no overriding authority to give them direction.

Still, not everything changed at once and to the same degree. Throughout the period of greatest crisis (1974–1976) virtually no changes were made in the organization or the personnel of the Ministry of Foreign Relations, except to add diplomatic representation in the Eastern bloc countries. All six provisional governments shared the same foreign policy commitment: the desire to present an image to the outside world of Portugal's unaltered alignment with the West and its participation in the North Atlantic Treaty Organization. Accordingly, the ministry continued as before to function through the same two basic directorates-general, *política* and *economia*.

Similarly, while there were certain superficial changes of a structureal nature in the economic ministries, no attempt was made to alter their operations in the least. The immediacy of the economic crisis and rising inflation made the various ministers and secretaries of state who entered and exited from the six provisional governments extremely reluctant to complicate further their already difficult tasks by bringing about bureaucratic disruptions in the functioning of their offices. Such was the case with the newly formed Ministry of Commerce and Tourism. Essentially all that occurred there was that the old State Secretariat for Commerce in the Economy Ministry received ministerial status, while tourist services in the Secretariat for Information and Tourism in the Presidency of the Council of Ministers were transferred to the new Commerce Ministry. The remainder of the Information Secretariat became the new Ministry of Social Communications, and its operations were quickly expanded as military and civilian radicals sought to establish a new state monoply and control over the mass media.

Two other instances of minimal change in the overall structure of state administration warrant mentioning. The juridical foundations of public bureaucracy in Portugal today are the same basic laws that were established in 1926 and 1927 and perfected in the early 1930s, when Salazar embarked on a policy dedicated to rooting out all residual influences of the parliamentary republic of 1910. Similarly, legal arrangements established for local government during the New State continue in effect. What is essentially an administrative apparatus, designed as an extension of state authority into community life, continues to provide the setting for local politics. It is into these imperfect bureaucratic structures, intended as devices for dividing authority at the local level, that new forms of political party representation and accountability have been channeled. Capable of incorporating expanded representation, they were never intended to function as a framework within which issues and the needs of the citizenry would be resolved at the local level.

Although there has been, then, significant continuity in some public organizations, it is important to recognize that change has occurred in other structures. Four of the New State's ministries were dismantled; another six have undergone substantial modification; and one entity has been so greatly altered that it must be considered a new public organization.

Neither the Overseas Ministry nor the Ministry of Corporations had a place in the new order. As a result of decolonization the former passed out of existence, except for a small directorate charged with handling details related to the independence of the overseas territories. Into the old Overseas building in Restelo went the newly formed Council of the Revolution. In the Ministry of Corporations those services linked to corporate concepts of the state were dismantled, while others involving labor relations lost their old regulatory functions and were regrouped into a new Labor Ministry under secretariats of state for labor and employment. Those activities originally defined as belonging to social security were transferred to the Ministry of Social Affairs (Health), while public housing services became part of the responsibilities of the Public Works Ministry.

Less extensive were changes in the old Ministry of Economy, which had been an imperfect amalgamation resulting from the merger of Commerce and Industry with Agriculture in the late forties. Under the new order, the formation of three new ministries—Commerce, Industry, and Agriculture—gave formal status to what was already operational reality. In an effort to provide greater coherency successive governments did transfer parallel services belonging to other ministries to Commerce and to Industry. And in one short-lived experiment separate ministerial status was given to external and internal commercial activities; it ended with the decision to return to a single commerce ministry. What was accomplished, then, was the bringing together of the state's regulatory and promotional activities affecting industry and commerce, and the granting of full autonomy to Agriculture. Under the old regime, agriculture had been consistently placed on the sidelines, while priority had been given to commercial and industrial activities.

Major alterations also occurred in the Ministério da Marinha (Navy), where military and civilian activities related to the sea had long been linked together. In subsequent reorganizations, military functions were separated and transferred to the Ministry of Defense, where the navy became a state secretariat along with the army and the air force. Fishing operations were transferred to the newly created Ministry of Agriculture. The division administering the country's merchant marine became an office under the authority of the Transportation Ministry, while shipping activities tied to foreign trade were assigned to the Commerce Ministry.

Of all the ministerial changes, the most important were those involving agriculture. With the creation of a new agricultural ministry and the bringing together of related public sector operations (such as the new Institute of Agrarian Reform), Agriculture was expanded from 4 into 40 distinct bureaus. A real attempt was made to develop an extensive field apparatus, and attention was focused on setting up agricultural departments in various areas of the country. For the first time farmers in remote rural areas came into contact with agricultural extension agents. It is important to single out the 1975 reforms in the Agricultural Ministry as the first major step by the state to modernize Portuguese agriculture.[6]

Nevertheless, it should surprise no one that the new Ministry of Agriculture has emerged as a highly politicized entity. After all, it has had to act under contradictory pressures. In the south substantial portions of agricultural land were occupied by day laborers, and their occupations have been stridently defended by the Portuguese Communisty Party (PCP). In the conservative north the peasantry continues to look with suspicion on state activities as guises for altering current landholding patterns.

Although this is a complex sitution that cannot be easily summarized, insight can be gained into some of the problems by conceiving of agricultural operations as being divided among three sets of contending political forces, each involving internal and external alignments. The focus of leftist, and particularly PCP, influence was to be found in the Agrarian Reform Institute until the Institute's dismantlement under the Sá Carneiro government (1979–1980) and the inauguration by that government of a policy of returning major portions of occupied land to its original owners. The expansion of the old directorate-general of agricultural services into an operation involving a much more active extension program, with regional delegations, is closely identified with the Socialist Party of Portugal (PS). Because these activities probably cannot be separated from PS endeavors to develop more solid grassroots support outside the major urban areas, it is not surprising that once Soares passed into the opposition and Sá Carneiro became premier, subsequent attempts to develop an agricultural extension program nearly came to a standstill. Technical services are much more likely to be dominated by old-line conservative bureaucrats and supported by political groups on the right. These right-wing clientele groups are centered largely in the north, where small landowners desire greater technical services and state assistance but resist any and all suggestions to modify the present land tenure system.

In the technical services area the core bureau is the Directorate-General for Water Resources and Agricultural Engineering (DG/HEA), an expanded bureau formed out of the old Directorate-General for Hydraulic Services in the Public Works Ministry. It was an autonomous junta for a brief period after the revolution, before emerging in its present form. If extension services are identified in the eyes of many outsiders with the Socialist party, others view the DG/HEA as an example of a new type of bureau operation which has emerged in post-1974 Portugal. For all effective purposes it has been captured by the clientele group most interested in its operations, the Confederação de Agricultura Portuguesa (CAP). A conservative interest group identified with northern small landowners and with political ties on the right, CAP has taken an immediate and direct interest in the bureau's operations, out of which a very close set of internal and external relations has developed between the two organizations.

In passing, brief mention should also be made of the other ministries in which modifications have been made. The Ministry of Social Affairs is the old Health Ministry, to which social welfare and social security responsibilities have been transferred. The Public Works Ministry now handles public housing programs. The Ministry of Finance and Planning contains what were originally two distinct organizations. In the early stages of the revolution the planning office (the Secretariado Técnico) was given distinct ministerial status, but later it was decided that planning and finance would be better off as a single organization. The old Presidency of the Council of Ministers today is no longer a ministry, but a small staff unit at the service of the prime minister. The Ministry of National Defense is the consequence of the merger of the old Army Ministry with staff units originally in the Presidency of the Council of Ministers; it is under the jurisdiction of the minister of national defense (a minister previously located in the prime minister's own office) and the Navy. The reorganized Ministry of Education now administers cultural affairs previously handled through the Presidency of the Council of Ministers. Like Agriculture, Education has become highly politicized because of the turbulent nature of its immediate environment.

Structural changes in the central ministries, however, are only part of the alterations in Portugal's public bureaucracy. To them one must add expansion in the number and kinds of enterprises under state control, major turnovers in executive-level personnel, and a dramatic increase in the number of people employed by the state. When all of this is taken into account, it should be obvious that the coherency established for public administration by Salazar has been decisively broken. The role of public bureaucracy in that bureaucratic-authoritarian regime was primarily regulatory; after the April 25 revolution public bureaucracy ceased to have this function. Cut loose from its previous hierarchical controls, the Portuguese public sector was caught up in the same turbulence and uncertainties that characterized all of Portuguese life from 1974 to 1976.

Expansion of the Public Sector

It was in this setting that the Portuguese state acquired—without much planning and thought—organizations engaged in all sorts of economic activities that had previously been in private hands. The old regime certainly had been involved in the economy and had had its state enterprises, but these activities had been linked to the preservation of private enterprise and to the use of state resources to promote and defend established economic interests. After April 25, especially during the more radical phases of the revolution (1975), the *Gonçalvistas* in command moved to confiscate the economic resources held by persons identified with the old regime. The nationalization of banks and insurance companies generated panic among many managers and owners of private firms. With their emigration and the abandonment of their places of work, the state acquired firms it had had no intention of seizing. These developments contributed a good deal to the confusion and disorder characterizing the public sector during the immediate post revolutionary period.

After 1975 Portuguese authorities issued a series of decree laws (*decreto-leis*) and other governmental regulations designed to establish some sort of legal coherency for the public sector. The key law was *decreto-lei* no. 46/77, which sought to establish general dividing lines between the public and private sectors. While there is no other single comprehensive piece of legislation ordering the public sector, attempts have been made to bring together the basic legislation in a format that would establish more clearly for all the organization of the state's newly acquired economic activities. At the moment the best of these is the *Legislação de Direito Económico*. A compendium, it pulls together basic legislation regulating approximately 100 public enterprises under the state's jurisdiction and 200 private businesses in which the government possesses significant ownership.[7]

Current Portuguese practice distinguishes among six types of public sector activities: public enterprises per se (state economic organizations whose finances and management belong entirely to the government), firms in which state intervention has occurred (*empresas intervencionadas*), firms seized by their workers, corporations (*sociedades anónimas*) in which the state now has a participatory interest, firms in financial difficulty that have passed into the state sector, and firms which have gone bankrupt and become state property. While such public enterprises as Portuguese State Airways (TAP) and the State Railways (CFE) antedate the revolution, banks and insurance companies nationalized in 1975 also now belong to this category of state firm. These organizations are completely state owned and state run. In contrast, the state has intervened in firms of the second category in what is defined as the public interest (i.e., as a representative of the community or nation, in the belief that there are interests beyond those of the owners which warrant representation); these have become mixed enterprises in that private capital continues to participate in their operations.

The last four categories all derive from situations in which owners and managers at some point after 1974 abandoned their enterprises. The first of these includes firms in which worker commissions have actively intervened and taken control of the enterprise. The second entails those major corporations to which the state has appointed administrators to oversee operations because it was felt that private interests alone should no longer make basic decisions affecting the national economy. To the last two categories belong enterprises where the owner either liquidated all readily available assets and left the country with them; or, when accounts were held abroad, transferred the assets to his or her own personal accounts; or simply abandoned the whole operation. In these instances the firms could no longer function as viable financial operations: either bankruptcy was impending or had actually occurred.

Complementing legislation has been the establishment of a government organization—the Instituto de Participação do Estado—to oversee these activities, and the assignment by decree law of various state enterprises to those central ministries whose activities are most closely linked to their operations. Without entering into the details of this state sector, an idea of its size can be gained by consulting data acquired by Harry Makler in 1976 and 1977, when he returned to Portugal to determine the status of the 306 enterprises he had first studied in 1965. These represented 20 percent of all enterprises employing from 50 to 499 persons (small enterprises), 54 percent of those employing from 500 to 999 persons (large enterprises), and 100 percent of those employing 1,000 persons or more (giant enterprises).[8] As can be seen in table 10.1, intervention and nationalization were confined mostly to the larger enterprises, and at no time passed the 50 percent mark.

Public sector policy since 1974 has been far from consistent; its fluctuations follow the ascendancy of the left in the early years of the revolution and the subsequent revival of the right. Until 1976 interventions and the placement of governmental representatives in firms were identified with the *Gonçalvistas*—military and civilian radicals in com-

TABLE 10.1
Postrevolutionary State Intervention in Portuguese Private Enterprise (in percentages)

Size of Enterprise[a]	Firms Put Out of Business	Firms Nationalized	Firms Subjected to Intervention	Firms Unaffected
Small (N = 176)	6	2	8	84
Large (N = 130)	2	15	25	58
Giant (N = 69)	—	19	27	54

SOURCE: Harry M. Makler, "The Portuguese Industrial Elite and Its Corporative Relations: A Study of Compartmentalization in an Authoritarian Regime," in Lawrence S. Graham and Harry M. Makler, eds., *Contemporary Portugal: The Revolution and Its Antecedents* (Austin, 1979), pp. 156–157.

[a] Small firms = 50–499 employees; large firms = 500–999 employees; giant firms = 1,000 or more employees.

mand of the Second, Third, Fourth, and Fifth Provisional governments. For the most part these men aspired to the creation of state socialism. Following the collapse of the *Gonçalvistas* and the consolidation of a middle-of-the-road civilian regime in the form of the First Constitutional Government under the Socialists, further nationalizations and interventions ceased, and personnel identified with the Socialist party moved into public sector management positions. More recently, under the technocratic cabinets of the Third and Fourth Constitutional governments, the shift has been toward a policy of requiring that enterprises in the public sector pay their own way. Officially this has been termed a policy of deintervention (*desintervenção*). But in actuality, since 1976 there has been little if any denationalization of enterprises acquired by the government, few government representatives have been removed, and there has not been a decline in participation where interventions have occurred.

Current priorities center on reducing the deficits with which these organizations have been operating, stabilizing their managements and operations, and returning them to productive operations. Beyond this it is difficult to generalize about such organizations since their operations, personnel, and dynamics very widely from one firm to another. What is new is the presence of labor unions, pressing for higher wages and employee fringe benefits. In some enterprises these changes have been absorbed effectively into the firm's operations; in others, such as TAP and CFE, labor disruptions have led to a decline in services, frequent strikes, and an increase in excess personnel. Frequently cited is the case of the State Railways, which have taken on large numbers of new employees in the interest of providing jobs for unemployed workers; but this one case does not speak for the state sector as a whole.

Public Personnel Changes

No assessment of the impact of the revolution on public administration in Portugal would be complete without more explicit reference to the people employed by and charged with management responsibilities in the public sector. It is in the personnel rather than in formal structures that the changes inaugurated can be most accurately perceived. In any discussion comparing public personnel before and after 1974, the significance of breaking the hold of directors-general and directors of administrative services over day-to-day administration must be singled out. Were it not for these decisive changes—first isolating and getting old-regime directors to resign, and later bringing in new directors (especially persons identified with or sympathetic to the Socialist party during the First Constitutional Government)—considerable credence could be given to those Portuguese nationals who state that public bureaucracy has changed little from New State days. By now, through various devices, most of the old-regime men have been replaced.

Some of the impact of such changes is hidden by the fact that the various governments in power since the initial coup have all respected existing legal norms. Outright firings did not take place. However, respect for legal regulations prohibiting removal without just cause has not prevented these governments from instituting changes by other means—primarily through the use of decree law to create new offices or to change office titles, and thereby appoint new personnel to head the programs of interest to the new governments. Even though some former officials are returning to civil service jobs now that normalization is in progress, they do not seem to be reentering strategic positions.

At the same time, one should not overlook the fact that there has been little real change in the actual operation of individual ministerial units. The rapid turnover in ministers, secretaries of state, and undersecretaries in what were six provisional governments (1974–1976) and four constitutional governments (1977–1980) was not conducive to the establishment of a new mechanism for policy coordination and execution. This situation did not change during the period when the president named technocratic cabinets without the support of the major parties in Parliament; nor did it change under the conservative Sixth Constitutional Government of Sá Carneiro. In such a setting government offices are much more likely to continue to follow their own internal dynamics, as they did before 1974 and as they have been doing since. Internal to Portuguese public bureaucracy are many unresolved conflicts among government personnel: some retain a militant, revolutionary orientation; others are more moderate; and increasingly some old-regime bureaucrats have begun to speak out again (if they survived without exiting from the organization), while others who left under pressure have returned to the ministries to reclaim employment by the state, in accord with their rights and privileges as full-fledged civil servants (*funcionários públicos*).

One often hears references to a deterioration in the quality of public services that has accompanied the politicization of public bureaucracy. In such cases it is necessary to distinguish between social class background and level of administration. From the viewpoint of the public that receives services or needs to extract goods from the central government and its district-level field offices, much of the old climate of indifference toward unknown outsiders continues, while ready access exists for those perceived to be influential and conservative. Compounding this situation is a popular resentment of bureaucrats as representatives of the old regime, and a preference on the part of popularly elected local officials to go their own way, especially if they do not belong to the current governing alliance. Local-level bureaucracy, in contrast, is markedly public-oriented, but its technically competent officials are few and funds are in short supply. While the limited number of interviews conducted by the author in Lisbon in March 1979, preliminary results from field work at the district level in fall 1980, and random conversations with local residents in 1979 and 1980 do not permit further generalization, the theme of deteriorating public services arose frequently enough to suggest that many people perceive a real decline in the quality of such routine operations as garbage collection and mail delivery since the revolution; such perceptions, however, must also be seen in the context of expanded expectations following the entry into power of democratically elected governments at the national and local levels.[9]

If the emphasis before 1974 lay on control and regulation through public bureaucracy, and civil servants were expected to follow norms of personal sacrifice to serve the greater interests of the state, the emphasis since 1974 has fallen on the payment of more adequate salaries, the increase of fringe benefits, and the opening up of employment opportunities to far more people. One might go so far as to suggest that one of the primary functions of public bureaucracy since 1974 has been to provide employment and security in the context of an economy incapable of providing new jobs for large numbers of people. If this is indeed the case, it becomes important to determine how much public employment has increased during these years. Those on the political right accuse the Socialist party of bringing in hundreds of militants as directors-general, subdirectors-general, and administrators of state enterprises. Others lay the responsibility for providing hundreds of new jobs at relatively low levels in the public sector (especially in the state enterprises) at the feet of the *Gonçalvistas* in the provisional governments. Still others call attention to the large number of civil servants formerly employed overseas who have been incorporated into the home services.

What is the size of Portugal's public bureaucracy? Accurate figures for total public sector employment before or after 1974 do not exist. Before 1974 the government did not include in its figures those employed in public enterprises. Since 1974 accurate information on employment in state enterprises has simply not been available. Recognizing these limitations, one can obtain an approximate idea of the bureaucracy's size by looking at the number of people employed by the central government (i.e., the mainline ministries) and its extensions outside Lisbon. The last general census of public employees before the revolution (1968) reported a total of 160,919 persons in the central ministries, 2,757, in Juntas Distritais and Juntas Gerais (various governmental boards at the national and regional levels), and 44,105 functionaries in local government—a total of 207,781. According to figures provided by the State Secretariat for Public Administration (SEAP), this total had increased to 320,000 by 1975 and to 378,000 by 1978. For 1979, in what is considered to be the most reliable general survey since the revolution, the total reported was 384,082. Breakdowns of this latter figure show 314,757 employed in the central ministries, 7,513 in the newly formed autonomous regional governments of the Azores and Madeira, and 61,812 in local government.[10]

Random interviews with people centrally involved in post-1974 changes in Portugal's civil service identified another way to estimate the bureaucracy's size. They suggested that SEAP figures for 1975 and 1978 be compared with gross domestic product (GDP) figures published in the 1978 World Bank report on Portugal. The figures are reproduced in table 10.2. The report states that more than half of the growth in GDP between 1973 and 1977 was concentrated in the public administration category. What is interesting is the bank's statement that, while some of this growth reflects a real increase in government services, much of it is to be attributed to the cost of absorbing former colonial civil service employees. The World Bank figures support the view that one of the most striking changes in the Portuguese public bureaucracy since 1974 has been the dramatic increase in the number of public employees; but where they have come from and where they have been employed is difficult to ascertain.

Further research into the area of public employment uncovered three additional breakdowns of civil service data. In 1979 SEAP reported 205 directors-general, 410 subdirectors-general, 615 directors of services, and 810 division heads. Estimates made that same year of the number of overseas civil servants incorporated into the home service ranged between 35,000 and 45,000. SEAP would restrict the range to between 35,000 and 40,000 but the previous minister of administrative reform places his estimates higher: at 45,000. Whichever is the more reliable figure is unclear, but what is certain is that by 1979 this process of reintegration had come to an end. The third set of figures, also collected in 1979 but not published until 1981, shows the largest concentration of government employees to be in three ministries: the Ministry

TABLE 10.2
Gross Domestic Product Growth by Selected Sectors
(in percentages)

	1968–73	1974	1975	1976	1977	1973–77 Annual Average
Agriculture	−0.8	−1.9	−2.7	1.5	−10.0	−3.5
Industry[a]	10.0	4.0	−8.5	3.3	10.3	2.0
Construction	12.5	3.5	−15.8	5.0	11.0	0.4
Public Administration[b]	8.8	14.6	19.7	30.4	0.0	15.7
Other services	5.9	−4.7	−4.6	12.9	8.0	2.6
GDP at factor cost	6.9	1.8	−4.0	8.6	5.7	2.9
GDP at factor cost without public administration	6.6	0.4	−7.0	6.2	6.8	1.4

SOURCE: The World Bank, *Portugal: Current and Prospective Economic Trends* (Washington, D.C., 1978), p. 4. Reprinted by permission.
NOTE: In discussing the meaning of this table, the World Bank report makes the statement that "perhaps the most striking figures in Table 1 relate to the expansion of *public administration* at the rate of nearly 16 percent per annum since 1973" (p. 7). It accounts for the quantum jump in the number of public sector employees (the "public administration") in terms of the incorporation of civil servants returning to Portugal from the former colonies, new ad-hoc hiring to "mop up part of the lay pool of open unemployment," and the "expansion of Government activities and services in post Revolution Portugal" (pp. 7–8).
[a] Includes manufacturing, mining and electricity, gas and water.
[b] Also includes defense, health, and education.

of Education and Culture (131,123), the Ministry for Social Affairs (81,637), and the Ministry of Agriculture and Fishing (19,998).

While these figures only give an approximate idea of the total number of people employed in the public sector, they do establish quite clearly a numerical increase since 1974 in those on the public payroll. Still, a couple of clarifications need to be made. Approximately one-third of the increase comes from personnel transfers, if one considers the fact that those paid through pre-1974 overseas budgets were after all already employees of the Portuguese government. Also, these figures consider public school teachers and health personnel (nurses as well as doctors) to be part of the personnel of the central government. Finally, nearly a quarter of the increase is to be found at the local level where municipal officials in many small- and medium-size towns could provide basic urban services for the first time.

Although Social Democratic Center (CDS) party leaders are quick to accuse the Socialists of placing their own people in positions as directors-general and administrators of state enterprises, it is not possible to establish the number who actually took office during the First Constitutional Government. The same problem occurs when one looks for figures pertaining to the appointment of civil governors, the representatives of the central government designated by the Interior Ministry; again, other parties call attention to the fact that during the First Constitutional Government the Socialist party named its own people to these positions, and that the only changes made during the Second Constitutional Government, when the CDS was in coalition with the PS, was to assign the former a few governships in the north and center (notably Aveiro). By 1980, however, it had become accepted practice for the government in power to designate civil governors. Accordingly, no Socialist governors remained, and in their place were found a majority of Social Democratic Party (PSD) appointees and a minority of either CDS affiliates or independents who supported the PSD-CDS coalition constituting the Sixth Constitutional Government.

Comparing SEAP figures and statements regarding their accuracy with newspaper accounts of *saneamentos* (purges of civil servants identified with the old regime), one can conclude that very few removals actually took place in the civil service. As a matter of fact, the commission set up for this purpose did more to protect the rights and tenure of middle-range Portuguese civil servants, who were under attack by lower-level employees through the instrumentality of worker commissions, than it did to remove people from office. After November 25, 1975 (the point at which the *Gonçalvistas* were ousted), the commission ceased to have a real mission; it was gradually phased out during the first part of 1976.

The rapid expansion in state employment, coupled with the politicization referred to earlier, has made it difficult for ministers, secretaries, and undersecretaries of state to feel that they can rely upon the employees under their jurisdiction. Accordingly, it has become the general practice for each new ministerial team, on taking office, to enter with its own staff (down to the level of typists), dispatch its own work, and deal directly with the issues brought to its attention through its own people. In such a setting there is a great deal of redundancy, with jobs and functions frequently being duplicated at the top because of the feeling that one really cannot count on the political loyalty of the civil servants below.

The politicization of public organizations, the difficulty of coordinating government policy at the top, and the problems created by the lack of organizational coherence within the mainline ministries have been reflected to some degree in the increase in the size of Portugal's governing teams between 1967 and 1979. In the Portuguese context, the concept of a governing team is an old one that has continued to prevail since 1974. Involved in the "government," then, are not just ministers, but also secretaries and undersecretaries of state. Whereas the stability

TABLE 10.3
Size of Governing Teams, 1967–1976, as an Index of Administrative Coordination Problems

		Total Number of Appointments[a]
Prerevolutionary Portugal		
The New State		
Salazar's last government:	1967–68	29
The Caetano governments:	1969–72	32
	1973	31
	1974	35
The Revolutionary Era		
The Provisional governments, 1974–76		
First (Palma Carlos, Prime Minister)		39
Second (Vasco Gonçalves)		47
Third (Vasco Gonçalves)		54
Fourth (Vasco Gonçalves)		66
Fifth (Vasco Gonçalves)		47
Sixth (Pinheiro de Azevedo)		40
Postrevolutionary Portugal		
The Constitutional governments, 1976–79[b]		
First (Mário Soares, PS)		62
Second (Mário Soares, PS/CDS coalition)		54
Third (Nobre da Costa, technicians)		46
Fourth (Mota Pinto, technicians)		52

SOURCES: Lawrence S. Graham, *Portugal: The Decline and Collapse of an Authoritarian Order* (Beverly Hills and London; 1975), p. 31; various newspaper clippings taken from the Portuguese press, notably *Expresso*.

[a] These totals include the prime minister, cabinet ministers, secretaries of state, and undersecretaries of state. The concept of a governing team has a particular meaning in the Portuguese context. It involves not just cabinet ministers, but all those appointed to key administrative positions in accord with this established nomenclature. Individual premiers are free to expand or reduce these appointments according to their needs and priorities. Over time this institutionalized practice has become a fairly reliable index of the organizational choices made from government to government. The term "government" in this case is synonymous with "governing team."

[b] The First and Second Constitutional governments were party governments, formed by Soares first from within his own party and later from the coalition of the Socialist party with the Social Democratic Center party. The Third and Fourth governments consisted of people without party affiliation.

of the New State years made possible smaller governing teams, since 1974 the practice has been to use much larger teams in an attempt to establish control over a political and administrative system that has moved in a variety of directions and which has been difficult to coordinate and control. Figures for the 1967–1979 governing teams are given in table 10.3.

Another indication of the degree to which the Portuguese civil service has changed is to be found in the number of public employee unions which have emerged: 44 to date. These organizations are of the most diverse sort. Some are highly specialized and are linked to specific professional fields, while others have much broader bases. Only a few are identified or affiliated with national organizations. Most reflect associations of particular groups of public employees who reacted to the radicalization of the civil service in the 1974–1976 period by banding together to oppose the actions of worker commissions. One example of the plurality of new organizations and associations in the civil service would be the formation of rival unions for local government employees. The older, larger, and more radical union is the Sindicato Nacional dos Trabalhadores dos Serviços Municipalizados (SNTSM); it is an affiliate of the country's major labor confederation, Intersindical, which is PCP-dominated. In contrast the Sindicato dos Trabalhadores da Administração Local (STAL), created in reaction to stances taken by SNTSM, is smaller, less radical, and identified with the União Geral dos Trabalhadores (UGT), the Socialist party labor federation.

The spontaneous appearance of employee organizations in the public service would have been unheard of before 1974. Although worker commissions are disappearing as the influence of the radicals wanes, public sector unions (*sindicatos*) are likely to remain. Not only do the unions have a continuing interest in organizing employees in state enterprises, but also many, if not most, people employed by the central government have found it to their advantage to band together to press for their own rights and prerogatives and to defend their own interests. A cursory glance at the list of 44 *sindicatos* in appendix 10.1 makes apparent the small size and fragmentary organization of many of them. But it is worth noting that a pluralism has emerged within the public sector, reflecting worker and professional interests independent of state interests, that over time will probably undergo greater consolidation. Absolutely none of this activity can be categorized under the corporatist label, the form of worker organization promoted under the New State.

A final change concerns the formation of technical assistance groups to work with local governments. Legislation provides for the organization of 38 Gabinetes de Apoio Técnico para as Autarquias Locais (GATs) throughout the country. Established within Portugal's national planning system, a pre-1974 creation, and subordinated to regional planning offices, each group consists of five or six members and is designed to work with between six and eight local municipal councils. In an environment in which there have been so many changes and uncertainties, and in which the reorganization of local government continues to be debated nationally, GATs have the potential of getting on with the extension of basic municipal services throughout the country without further delay. Thereby they may help to meet at least part of the pressure placed on local councils for immediate improvements in water supply, sanitation, housing, and a host of other public services long absent from so much of rural and smalltown Portugal. At the same time they represent an innovative approach to resolving in part two related problems: first, rigidities in governmental structure at the national and local levels, which provide no easy way to bridge the gap between central government services and newly autonomous local governments; and, second, utilization of surplus government personnel—former overseas civil servants and recent university graduates without prospects for employment in the limited private sector.

The Overall Picture

In conclusion, while actual organizational structures have experienced little real change, bureaucratic behavior has undergone a decisive alteration. The buildings and the offices are the same; the same legal precepts are utilized; the designations for internal departmentalization show little change, except for a new title here and there; and administrative services to the public probably have declined. But the old compliance patterns stressing respect for one's superior and service to the state in exchange for a limited salary and minimal fringe benefits, as well as conservative values and behavior patterns, have all disappeared. New personnel have entered who are identified with political perspectives and outlooks impossible under the old regime; lower-level bureaucrats have found new opportunities to move ahead and to voice their opinions; competent professionals have survived, and probably improved their status and income; and old-regime bureaucrats find themselves ill at ease and constantly threatened by the new environment. Although new norms regulating the work place in the public sector have not appeared, the old standards and expectations, with their emphasis on order, deference, regulation, and control, are gone. With these changes the central direction and rigid hierarchy of the New

State's administrative system have vanished. In the aftermath of the revolution public sector organizations, ranging from central ministries to newly acquired state enterprises, have been much more inclined to follow their own internal dynamics and to interact more openly with their new-found political clienteles.

In these circumstances issues of administrative reform have once again come to the fore. But the needs and expectations are far different today from those of the past. The last round of administrative reforms in the early seventies represented a feeble attempt by the Caetano government to relax the more rigid control characteristic of the Salazar era, to move into positions of authority younger men with more professional training who would be attuned to issues of economic development, and to create a setting for modernization without dismantling the bureaucratic-authoritarian system through which Salazar had consolidated his rule. In contrast, the present environment is one in which, with the cohesiveness of the old administrative system gone, new patterns of compliance, authority, and behavior must be developed. The seriousness and the depth of the country's economic crisis has dramatized the need for a public bureaucracy capable not only of contributing to economic development and modernization, but also of actively stimulating productivity in the nation's agricultural, commercial, and industrial sectors.

In this regard, the immediate problem—the conversion of the functions of public bureaucracy from control to promotion and development—is little different from the problems faced by public bureaucracies in so many other countries around the world. Coupled with the need for a developmentally oriented administration is the political imperative of decentralization. No one has yet attacked successfully the problem of how to reconcile the cost of expanded services and their more equitable distribution with more effective use of limited resources. On the one hand, commitment to grassroots democracy means the involvement of more people in government at the local level, the provision of basic public services hitherto unavailable outside the major cities, and an improvement in the quality of life at the periphery. On the other hand, Portugal's limited resources and its modernization needs in industry, commerce, and agriculture argue for central planning, controls over popular demands, and concentration of investments in selected sectors.

The call for administrative reform in the late seventies differed little from the call of the early seventies. The Caetano government and the Third and Fourth Constitutional governments each signalled the importance of administrative reform for their regimes and set up secretariats for administrative reform. Each was equally ineffective. Before 1974 administrative change was impossible without altering decisively the political power relationships in the old regime. Today the difficulties of instituting reform arise from the opposition of vested interests in the political parties and in the public bureaucracy. Many party leaders are unwilling to attack the problem because change would upset the current division and distribution of resources, while many civil servants see in administrative reform the risk of new disruptions in the public service and intrusions into their bureaucratic domains at a moment when normalization is returning.

Leaving development priorities aside for the moment, it is difficult to imagine how the bureaucratic decentralization Portugal needs so greatly is to be achieved. When it comes down to specific and concrete measures, one must ask where governmental reformers will find the political support needed when virtually all current politicians—whether of the center, left, or right in their political orientation—have been reluctant, on receiving power, to redistribute resources. It is for this reason that there are those in Portuguese public life who have concluded, after wrestling with the current multiparty system (which is strong on representation, but weak in its capacity for structuring a viable national government capable of making and implementing policy), that a strong presidential system will be essential before decentralization can be attacked effectively. Other needed reforms, which are intimately tied in with politics and current political power arrangements, are a reduction in the number of public functionaries, greater stability and more incentives for executive-level personnel, and improvements in the quality of public services. Even more important, given the urgent need for development, is the creation of a public bureaucracy which can take an active role in the economic modernization that must now begin in agriculture, and that must be accelerated far more rapidly in industry and commerce.

To attack effectively problems such as these requires not only systemic change, but the introduction of very different concepts in preparing people for civil service work. Two partial strategies already in the process of implementation in Portugal represent encouraging movements in this direction. One is the endeavor to get more professional and technically competent state employees out into the field and into contact with local groups needing services (viz., the expansion of agricultural extension services and the use of GAT teams to meet more immediately the needs of local government). The other is the formation of a national school for administration, charged with the responsibility of training a new generation of civil servants who will be better able to contribute to the developmental needs of the state and to build a public service more supportive of democratic governance. But unless there is more rapid movement toward the development of an administrative system congruent with representative government and capable of implementing new economic and social programs, consolidation of a stable and meaningful democratic order will prove difficult, if not impossible.[11]

Appendix 10.1
Public Service Unions
(sindicatos)

Federação Nacional dos Sindicatos dos Trabalhadores da Função Pública (National Federation of Public Service Employee Unions)

Associação Sindical dos Magistrados Judiciais Portugueses (Union Association of Portuguese Judicial Magistrates)

Sindicato dos Adidos da Função Pública do Distrito do Porto (Union of Public Services Aides in the Porto District)

Sindicato Nacional dos Agentes Técnicos Agrícolas (National Union of Agricultural Technical Agents)

Sindicato dos Construtores Civís (Union of Civil Construction Employees)

Sindicato de Delegados do Procurador da República (Union of Delegates of the Attorney General)

Sindicato Nacional dos Enfermeiros Diplomados (National Union of Nursing School Graduates)

Sindicato dos Enfermeiros da Zona Norte (Union of Nurses in the North)

Sindicato dos Profissionais de Enfermagen Zona Centro (Union of Nursing Professionals in the Central Zone)

Sindicato dos Enfermeiros da Zona Sul (Union of Nurses in the South)

Sindicato dos Engenheiros do Norte (Union of Engineers in the North)

Sindicato dos Engenheiros da Região Sul (Union of Engineers in the South)

Sindicato dos Engenheiros Técnicos Agrários (Union of Agricultural Technical Engineers)

Sindicato dos Engenheiros Técnicos do Norte (Union of Technical Engineers in the North)

Sindicato dos Engenheiros da Região Sul (Union of Engineers in the South)

Sindicato Nacional dos Médicos Veterinários (National Union of Veterinary Doctors)

Sindicato dos Músicos (Union of Musicians)

Sindicato dos Professores da Zona Norte (Union of Teachers in the North)

Sindicato dos Professores da Zona da Grande Lisboa (Union of Teachers in Greater Lisbon)

Sindicato dos Professores da Zona Centro (Union of Teachers in the Central Zone)

Sindicato dos Professores da Zona Sul (Union of Teachers in the South)

Sindicato dos Professores da Região dos Açores (Union of Teachers in the Azores)

Sindicato dos Profissionais de Enfermagem do Distrito do Funchal (Union of Nursing Professionals in the Funchal District [Madeira])

Sindicato Nacional dos Profissionais de Psicologia (National Union of Professionals in Psychology)

Sindicato dos Quadros Técnicos do Estado (Union of Employees in the State's Technical Services)

Sindicato dos Técnicos Paramédicos do Norte/Centro (Union of Paramedical Technicians in the North and Central Zones)

Sindicato Nacional dos Técnicos dc Topografia (National Union of Technicians in Topography)

Sindicato dos Trabalhadores da Administração Local (Union of Employees in Local Administration)

Sindicato dos Trabalhadores das Administrações e Juntas Portuárias (Union of Employees of Port Authorities and Commissions)

Sindicato dos Trabalhadores da Câmara Municipal de Lisboa (Union of Employees of the Municipal Government of Lisbon)

Sindicato dos Trabalhadores Consulares e das Missões Diplomáticas na Europa (Union of Employees in Consulates and Diplomatic Missions in Europe)

Sindicato dos Trabalhadores da Direcção-Geral das Contribuições e Impostos (Union of Employees in the Directorate-General for Contributions and Taxes)

Sindicato dos Trabalhadores da Função Pública Zona Centro (Union of Public Service Employees in the Central Zone)

Sindicato dos Trabalhadores da Função Pública Zona Norte (Union of Public Service Employees in the North)

Sindicato dos Trabalhadores da Função Pública Zona Sul (Union of Public Service Employees in the South)

Sindicato dos Trabalhadores da Função Pública Região da Madeira (Union of Public Service Employees in Madeira)

Sindicato Distrital dos Trabalhadores Judiciais do Distrito Judicial de Coimbra (District Union of Judicial Employees in the Coimbra Judicial District)

Sindicato Distrital dos Trabalhadores Judiciais do Distrito Judicial de Evora (District Union of Judicial Employees in the Evora Judicial District)

Sindicato dos Trabalhadores Judiciais do Distrito Judical de Lisboa (Union of Judicial Employees in the Lisbon Judicial District)

Sindicato Distrital dos Trabalhadores Judiciais do Distrito Judicial do Porto (District Union of Judicial Employees in the Porto Judicial District)

Sindicato dos Trabalhadores dos Registros e do Notariado (Union of Civil Registry Employees)

Sindicato dos Trabalhadores de Saúde e Segurança Social da Região Norte (Union of Health and Social Security Employees in the North)

Sindicato Nacional dos Trabalhadores dos Serviços Municipalizados (National Union of Employees in City-Run Municipal Services)

Sindicato dos Trabalhadores Sociais (Union of Employees in Social Services)

SOURCE: State Secretariat for Public Administration (SEAP).

Notes

For funding to return to Portugal in March 1979 I am indebted to the Gulbenkian and Earhart foundations. Unless otherwise noted, all references to current data refer to information available at that time.

1 For the purposes of this paper "public administration" refers to the management and operations of large-scale complex organizations in the public sector; "public bureaucracy" is a shorthand device for referring both to a particular set of public organizations centered in the executive branch of government, with various amounts of autonomy, and collectively to the people within them who fulfill specific roles; and "administrative system" stands for a particular combination of public organizations and the interaction patterns established among them as a consequence of variations in political regime types.

2 Jorge Campinos, *O Presidencialismo do Estado Novo* (Lisbon, 1978).

3 The importance of the Presidency of the Council of Ministers in contrast to the peripheral nature of the Council of Ministers under Salazar is generally not well understood by analysts of the New State, except for Campinos. See, for example, Paul H. Lewis, "Salazar's Ministerial Elite, 1932–1968," *Journal of Politics* vol. 40, no. 3 (Aug. 1978) p. 629.

4 Campinos, *O Presidencialismo,* pp. 174–176.

5 Marcello Caetano, in collaboration with Diogo Freitas do Amaral, *Manual de Direito Administrativo,* 1 (Lisbon, 1969), pp. 304–306.

6 Details regarding the reorganization of the ministry and the status of Portugal's agricultural sector are to be found in the World Bank report, *Portugal: Agricultural Survey* (Washington, D.C., 1978).

7 Artur Anselmo de Castro (Filho), José António Pereira da Silva, and Rui Afonso, eds., *Legislação de Direito Económico* (Lisbon, 1978). My source for these estimates of the number of public sector firms comes from a

personal communication from Frank Sherwood, member of a team of U.S. public administration specialists contracted to review Portugal's current administrative situation in March 1979.

8 Harry M. Makler, "The Portuguese Industrial Elite and Its Corporative Relations: A Study of Compartmentalization in an Authoritarian Regime," in Lawrence S. Graham and Harry M. Makler, eds., *Contemporary Portugal: The Revolution and Its Antecedents* (Austin, 1979), p. 161.

9 Readers should be aware of the difference between the two research trips on which these generalizations are based. The March 1979 trip was confined to two weeks of field work, the maximum time I could be gone from teaching responsibilities in the United States. In order to obtain information for this chapter the technique of confidential elite in-depth interviewing was utilized. Interviews were confined to knowledgeable persons in Lisbon, either in the government currently in power or outside of government but in positions of import. Fall 1980 research extended from September through December, and interviewing was both more extensive and more structured. The focus was on government authorities involved in development-oriented programs at the district and local levels in three representative areas: the Braga district in the Entre-Minho-e-Douro region, the Viseu district in Beira Alta, and the Evora district in the Alentejo.

10 Instituto Nacional de Estadística, Serviços Centrais, *Inquérito Inventário dos Servidores do Estado, 31 de Dezembro de 1968, Continente e Ilhas Adjacentes* (Lisbon, 1970), pp. 3–17, and "O distrito de Lisboa tem mais funcionários públicos do que a Suiça: Um inquérito feito aos recursos humanos da Função Pública. . . . ," *Expresso*, Apr. 11, 1981, pp. 29–R ff.

11 This chapter was first prepared for the June 1979 meeting of the Conference Group on Modern Portugal. On returning to Portugal in the fall of 1980 for new research, I reexamined the original paper in the light of the current administrative situation, only to find little significant change. While government by the PSD/CDS Democratic Alliance, with Francisco Sá Carneiro as prime minister in the Sixth Constitutional Government (1979–1980) had produced political stability, public administration remained in exactly the same position it had reached in 1979. By November 1980, on the eve of Sá Carneiro's tragic death, almost all of the GATs were in operation, although they were varying widely in their impact. In the same month the National School of Administration's inauguration finally took place, with its first formal classes scheduled for early 1981.

11 *Harry M. Makler*

The Consequences of the Survival and Revival of the Industrial Bourgeoisie

In every sphere, the bourgeoisie edged its way back. Thus, the workers were carried, step by step, toward governmental coalition with the bourgeoisie.
—Felix Morrow, *Revolution and Counter Revolution in Spain*

Soon after Portugal's revolution of April 25, 1974, there were definite signs that the country's new political forces—the Armed Forces Movement (MFA) and the First Provisional Government—were going to reorganize industry and move against the industrial bourgeoisie. The immediate closing of the stock exchange froze more than two billion dollars of privately owned wealth. The country's first postrevolutionary constitutional law (published on May 14) and the program of the First Provisional Government (published as *decreto-lei* 203/74 on May 15) stated that any protectionism, conditionalism, or favoritism restricting equality of opportunity for the economic development of the country would be eliminated, that there would be an intensification of public investment, that there would be reform of the credit system and the banking structure, and that the nationalization of investment houses, banks, and credit agencies would occur. General António de Spínola, seen by many to be allied with the country's large consortia, in his presidential inaugural address on May 15, 1974, said that "it is necessary to accelerate the rhythm of economic expansion, guaranteed within the principles of democratic order, to achieve the complete syndical liberty of the workers and owners [of production], dismantle the old corporative 'control' and annihilate its strangulations, and create an appropriate climate for the creation of political parties and economic associations."[1]

When the First Provisional Government took office, led by Spínola, the state's intention to intervene in the economy became quite clear when he spoke of the necessity of controlling prices, eliminating land speculation, and establishing agricultural cooperatives. However, there were few moves to implement these policies. Despite the anti-capitalist and anti-imperialistic climate, actual controls and regulation of industry and the industrial bourgeoisie were not imposed until late November 1974, more than six months after the revolution.

Neither the First Provisional Government nor the Second were destined to survive. Spínola was gradually forced to relinquish his rule to the MFA. General Francisco de Costa Gomes, General Vasco dos Santos Gonçalves, Major Otelo Saraiva de Carvalho, and Major Melo Antunes assumed power. These individuals gave a different tone to postrevolutionary Portuguese politics, supposedly more reflective of the "true face" of the MFA. According to one observer, the Communist party had succeeded in infiltrating the military, Portugal's labor federation (Intersindical), the country's mass media, and communications, and had taken control of hundreds of municipal councils throughout the country. Managers of both Portuguese and foreign companies in Portugal were purged by Communist-led worker commissions, and some industrial commercial enterprises were taken over.[2]

Regardless of these activities the rhetoric of the first two governments was conciliatory, stressing national, if not class, unity. Even after striking employees forced the government to assume control of Lisbon's larger water company (Companhia das Aguas de Lisboa) on May 21, 1974, the government "lacked the courage to employ the word 'nationalization,'"[3] and on July 18 General Vasco Gonçalves, the Second Provisional Government's prime minister, regarded as an ally of the Communists, noted that while Portuguese economic policy and the state had to be responsible to the Portuguese people and particularly to its underprivileged, it was also necessary that the state cooperate with private initiative in the reconstruction and modernization of the economy. His ambiguity was clearly apparent in his inaugural address:

> On the part of the government we will do all to keep a climate of confidence that the private initiative requires . . . as of now [that sector] will be an integral part of the superior national interests. . . . Effectively, the program of the Armed Forces Movement does not permit radical or revolutionary transformations of the socioeconomic structure of Portuguese society. However, neither from the letter nor the spirit of the above program can one conclude that it would be impossible to adopt measures considered necessary to accelerate socioeconomic progress, to raise the living conditions of the Portuguese people to approximate the levels of others in Europe.[4]

By the end of the summer Spínola was forced to resign. His appeal to the "silent majority" to rally against the totalitarian extremists and his policy to delay the independence of Portugal's African territories had won little support and, if anything, had strengthened the left.[5] Vasco Gonçalves and Alvaro Cunhal, the leader of the Communist party, were quick to emphasize that the attempted coup on September 28 was a fascist plot supported by the country's capitalists.

While financial capital had already been curbed through the nationalization of some banks, attacks against the industrial bourgeoisie and measures to control industry soon followed. However, from the beginning they were hesitant and selective. For example, on October 18 the MFA created a committee directed by Major Melo Antunes to develop a plan of economic and social action, but it soon became apparent that serious divisions and uncertainties existed within the military on basic economic issues and the role of national and international capital in the country's recuperation. While the MFA stressed bureaucratic and legal reforms and an "anti-monopolist campaign against large capitalist groups and large rural landowners who continue to retain economic power and are disturbing the orderly process of democratization,"[6] it seemed to avoid condemning all capitalists, noting that only a few had engaged in economic sabotage. Nevertheless, the MFA called for the effective control of basic economic activities and the intervention of the state in such activities, while questioning the intervention measures which had already been taken.[7] Some in the MFA[8] insisted that the development, execution, and administration of the plan be diverted from the "traditional bureaucratic mechanisms of the ministries, and especially the Ministry of Economics, and handled directly by the prime minister [Vasco Gonçalves] or a minister without portfolio."[9]

Despite legislation which defined the means by which the state could intervene in industry (*decreto-lei* 660, November 25), the MFA was becoming increasingly impatient. Leftists within the MFA blamed the lack of interventions on Major Melo Antunes; he was suspected of directly collaborating with technocrats, Socialist party sympathizers, and representatives of foreign interests who wanted to base the recovery and growth of the Portuguese economy on international public and private investment—those who obviously did not want to frighten foreign investors by advocating complete state control of the economy.[10]

Opposition to Melo Antunes' program was voiced by the MFA. On December 6, its Assembly of the 200 (Assembleia dos Duzentos), after hearing Antunes report, moved that "necessary measures . . . be rapidly formulated to integrally complement [Antunes'] program, specifically those [measures] that encompass an anti-monopolist strategy and are in the service of the working class."[11] Seven days later, as if to confirm the motion, the military security forces imprisoned some leading directors of several banking and credit institutions (e.g., Intercontinental Bank). Because of various delays and amendments, two more months elapsed before the program was officially published by the *Imprensa Nacional* on February 21, 1975.

These delays and amendments were indicative of the splits within the military and the uncertainty about the appropriateness of *estatização* ("statization") of the economy. A few days later, in a nationally televised address, Melo Antunes reflected this equivocacy in presenting his program. While appealing to the working class primarily by assuring the continued intervention by the state in the economy and worker participation in the control of industrial enterprises, Antunes carefully avoided antagonizing the industrial bourgeoisie. At one point he said that socialism is not incompatible with a plural society . . . in a plural society politically well organized in terms of the organization of production based on a socialist model, there exists a large zone of activities that can be exercised by private initiative . . . I believe that to construct an original model of socialism we cannot in any way dispense with the role of the middle class and if this political power [the government] is ready to launch this project [it has] to do it in strict alliance with various elements of the middle class."[12] Even Vasco Gonçalves, a strong proponent of complete state control of the economy, continued to favor a strict alliance between factory workers and the mass of the workers in general "without necessarily involving the marginalization of the middle class."[13] Debates on state intervention and the roles of various classes in the new society continued. These influenced both intervention policy and practice in the months that followed.

The Laws of Intervention

Well into 1975 there were pronouncements about the class structure, debates about who was a member of the proletariat, who was a fascist, who was undermining the revolution, who should participate in building a new Portugal, and so on. While there had been some strikes, work stoppages, and takeovers of some national and international commercial and industrial enterprises within a month after the revolution, the state's legal moves were directed against the banks and credit institutions, and were aimed at "the ten families" who presumably controlled the entire Portuguese economy largely through international subsidies. Sparked by banks' moves to withdraw credit from smaller enterprises, which would undermine the country's gross national product and aggravate growing unemployment, the Council of Ministers began on July 27, 1975, to discuss the nationalization of the country's issuing banks: the Bank of Portugal, the Bank of Angola, and the Overseas National.[14] Six weeks later (September 13), under *decreto-leis* 450, 451, and 452, the first legislation permitting the state's intervention (*decreto-lei* 540–14/74) in other financial institutions (e.g., commercial banks, loan companies) followed. Under this law the finance minister (José Silva Lopes at the time) was empowered to intervene in the administration of an institution, suspend management, or temporarily stop any activity which threatened its normal operation, the normal conditions of the monetary exchange, or the financial market.[15]

The first "nationalization," already mentioned, had occurred in late June 1974. Lisbon's old water company had been the first enterprise occupied by the workers (on May 21), less than a month after the revolution. By assuming control of the finances and administration of the entire company and its projects, the government had virtually nationalized the company, although it was apparently hesitant to label its actions as "nationalization" at the time.[16] Four more months would elapse before the government actually created a public company and specified its form of intervention.[17]

Decreto-lei 660/74, which was to have the most impact on the industrial structure, was enacted in late November 1974, six months after the revolution and following six months of uncertainty. By then the firmly entrenched military was strongly influenced by the Communist party, which was attempting to build its constituency within the working class. *Decreto-lei* 660 established the norms and conditions of the state's intervention in the economy. Although similar to *decreto-lei* 540, its predecessor, law 660 also applied to enterprises which were "not functioning in terms of normally contributing to the economic development of the country and for the satisfaction of the greater interests o the national collectivity. . ."[18] It specified eight conditions as indicators of abnormal functioning: (*a*) lockouts or dismissal (or the threat thereof) of a large number of employees; (*b*) abandonment of premises; (*c*) significant or unjustified decapitalization; (*d*) embezzlement of funds; (*3*) reduction in volume of production not justified by the market; (*f*) unjustified increase in general and administrative expenses; (*g*) refusal or delay in performing executive functions; and (*h*) other fraudulent or negligent executive conduct.

Most of these conditions referred to acts that would be committed by one person, presumably the head of an enterprise. The law thus seems to have been directed more against specific individuals—in this case industrialists—rather than the enterprise, its divisions, or other officers of the organization in question. Indeed, even before the unsuccessful rightist coup of March 11, 1975, the bourgeoisie were pinned against the wall. New laws pertaining to minimum wages and working conditions had created serious difficulties for a backward and incompetent capitalism that was accustomed to the protection of public powers. Subject to the Ministry of Labor's partiality toward the workers in contract arbitration, a strong anti-capitalist attitude on the part of the government, and the MFA's "cultural dynamization" program, many among the industrial bourgeoisie became alarmed. They ceased to invest, tried to export their capital, or tried to avoid complying with the laws. According to one observer, "the bourgeoisie were deviating because they were trapped and trapped because they were deviating."[19]

While other parts of *decreto-lei* 660/74 described the methods and forms of intervention and deintervention, in this first industrial intervention law more concern was demonstrated with the moral health of the industrial bourgeoisie than with the economic viability of their enterprises.[20] After March 11 and the entrenchment of the left, intervention legislation was replete with vicious attacks on the character and criminality of the industrialists.[21]

Interventions and nationalizations increased throughout 1975. By the spring of that year railroads, maritime transportation, the airline, petroleum and steel refineries, and tobacco companies had been nationalized, and they "dragged in a myriad of small and medium size enterprises" which were economically dependent on these basic industries.[22] Companies belonging to the large consortia (e.g., Empresa de Cimentos de Leiria of the Champalimaud group[23]) and those in the country's principal sectors (e.g., electrical machinery and fishing) had been intervened. In most cases the board of directors (*conselho da administração*) was suspended and a new one was appointed by the government. For example, on April 11, 1975, in suspending the board of Eduardo Ferreirinha e Irmão, a large northern motor and machinery manufacturer, the Council of Minister's resolution said that

> it has been known for a long while that Eduardo Ferreirinha e Irmão [Company] has had financial and administrative difficulties, since it has been the recipient of [the] continuous support of collective groups who are intimately connected with the state, such as the National Development Bank, the Portuguese Financing Company [which holds 26 percent of its capital], and the Fund for Export Development, which has cosigned significant loans. [Since] its situation has worsened during the past two months, through the mechanisms of *decreto-lei* 660/74 it is considered essential that the state should intervene in this enterprise. For these and other reasons the Council of Ministers on April 4, 1975, resolved that (1) all present administrative members of the enterprise be

suspended, (2) a three member administrative committee be named, (3) one member of this committee will perform the duties of president, (4) the Portuguese Financing Company and the National Development Bank will guarantee an immediate credit to cover back (owed) salaries, [and] (6) [*sic*] within six months the (new) administrative committee will present a detailed study, specifying the financial needs of the company.[24]

In this case there was an obvious concern with appeasing the workers, even if it meant dipping into the state's coffers—i.e., the National Development Bank. There were other instances in which intervention was more extensive and enabled the government to demonstrate its concern for law, order, and morality. When the Empresa de Cimentos de Leiria was intervened, for instance, its directors were suspended (and in one case imprisoned), their property and bank accounts were seized, and they were subject to judicial policy investigation. The government announced that

The Council of Ministers through the Ministry of Industry and Technology has become aware of desertion and escape to unknown parts of members of this enterprise's council of administration. . . . Being certain that such conduct will deliberately create turmoil in the eyes of the public and may also disorient other entrepreneurs, and also taking into consideration that such conduct is unfavorable to the national economy and that it does not aid the process of democratization . . . [it] has decided to take the following precautions: (*a*) suspend the managerial members of the firm . . . (*d*) freeze the property of the present administrators of the Empresa Cimentos de Leiria as well as those belonging to their consorts, [and] (*e*) determine an immediate investigation by the Judicial authorities of any criminal acts for which these administrators might be responsible.[25]

António Champaulimaud, the firm's president, though not cited specifically, had fled to Brazil. Apparently angered by his action, the government also authorized their new appointees to assume the administration of other companies in the Champalimaud group (section D of the resolution).

In the case of the country's largest textile mill, Empresa Textil Manuel Gonçalves, the act of intervention (February 3, 1976) noted that the firm's head, Manuel Gonçalves, owed the firm 91,000 *contos* (approximately 3,181,181 U.S. dollars in 1974), that there were private vouchers totalling thousands of *contos*, and that there was evidence of other embezzlement.[26] The government ordered the suspension of the enterprise's directors, a thorough investigation of its financial activities, and a new fiscal and commercial plan to be elaborated. Because of its national and regional social and economic importance, as well as its profitability, the Gonçalves textile firm became the subject of considerable controversy.[27] While Manuel Gonçalves was briefly imprisoned and then fled to Spain, within four months he had returned to the firm. On June 22, 1976, the government restored his ownership.[28]

During the summer and into the fall of 1975 intervention laws became more rigorous. One law (*decreto-lei* 222-B/75)[29] institutionalized the precautionary measures that could be imposed on the industrial bourgeoisie (as in the case of Cimentos da Leiria), while another (*decreto-lei* 597/75, promulgated on October 17),[30] enabled the state to quickly intervene in and appoint new directors to an enterprise upon the joint authorization of the finance and one other (appropriate) minister.[31] As a result the rate of interventions doubled, coinciding with the Communist party's attempt to maintain its control. However, divisions within the military were widening, and soon culminated in the dismissal of Vasco Gonçalves as prime minister.

Rollbacks and Deintervention

Vice Admiral José Pinheiro de Azevedo, who was politically more moderate, was invited to form the Sixth Provisional Government during the first week of September. His new cabinet contained four military men and three civilian independents, with the remaining posts apportioned according to the results of the April election: four Socialists, two Popular Democrats, and only one Communist.

Early in October the United States and the European Economic Community made loans to Portugal. In the national assembly (Assembleia Constituinte) debates about limiting nationalization, state control of the economy, and the indemnification of the agricultural and industrial bourgeoisie began. Throughout October and November the government thwarted Communist attempts to take power.[32] Among the most notable instances were the reduction of leftist control of the mass media and communications (e.g., the destruction of Rádio Renascença, the Catholic Church's radio station, which leftist groups such as the UDP, MES, and PRP controlled), and the replacement of four leftist civil governors with moderates (in Lisbon, Braga, Faro, and Castelo Branco). It was also apparent that the government was increasingly intolerant of demonstrations and strikes, and increasingly willing to use force against the left. All of this climaxed when a leftist military coup was crushed on November 25 by troops commanded by more moderate military leaders. As one scholar has noted, "a swing to the right ensued . . . The viability of a coherent radical stance within the military thus became as remote after November 25th as that of the *Spinolistas* had proven to be after March 11th . . . The revolution had come full circle. Into the vacuum left by the exit of the radicals came the moderates, now joined by many of those who earlier in the year could be identified as centrists."[33]

Intervention policy was seriously questioned, though interventions continued. The economy was crippled by widespread unemployment (aggravated by *retornados* from Portugal's former African territories), galloping inflation, lack of capital formation and investment, wage demands that far surpassed productivity, the loss of traditional markets (e.g., Angola), and a balance of payments deficit that was rapidly reducing Portugal's traditionally strong reserves. Just before the national elections in April 1976, Mário Soares, the Socialist party leader, declared that "the first thing that must be said to the Portuguese people, and we Socialists say it, is that there will be no more nationalizations. It is necessary to encourage the private sector and allow private management to work in safety."[34]

Within a few weeks following the Socialist election victory, intervention legislation was revised and a new law (*decreto-lei* 422/76) revoking the previous intervention laws (*decreto-leis* 660/74, 222/75, 597/75, and 631/75) was passed. Briefly, law 422 was much more explicit; it had 26 articles, compared to the 11 of law 660, its main predecessor. A good portion of the new law described the means for deintervention, another section dealt with the liability of intervened firms, and still another discussed the conditions of returning a firm to its original owners if, under intervention, its financial and economic equilibrium had be restored.[35] Noticeably absent from law 442 was any leftist rhetoric about monopolistic, self-interested capitalists, or even indirect aspersions on their characters, such as those of law 660, in which one provision had associated embezzlement with the industrial bourgeoisie. What the new law emphasized was that state intervention in private industries (*a*) must constitute a "perfectly adequate instrument for the dynamics of the socialization process, but it cannot be changed in practice into, or be construed, as an indirect process of nationalization; (*b*) must be seen as an exceptional practice, and only exercised when all other financial and economic *saneamento* (purging) has been exhausted; (*c*) can only occur to avoid an industry's dissolution, its bankruptcy, or the harming of the national interest (e.g., aggravation of the balance of payments deficit, an unemployment crisis, or [the disturbance of] regional equilibrium)."[36]

Interventions did not suddenly subside with the new legislation, with politics of a more moderate hue, or with the country's slow economic recovery, which began in 1977. Nor were there many deinterventions. Clearly the intervention and nationalization policy carried out during the year and a half that the left was in power had substantially changed Portugal's industrial structure and restricted the role of the industrial bourgeoisie. While there have been some tallies made of the employees and economic sectors affected by the interventions and nationalizations,[37] an analysis of the impact of state intervention on industrial structure and the industrial bourgeoisie remains to be done. By focusing on a representative sample of the leaders of Portugal's larger industrial enterprises, it is hoped that the following section will constitute a step in that direction.

The Impact of Intervention on Industry

A survey conducted in 1965 of a sizeable sample of larger Portuguese industries (industrial elites) and data gathered from manufacturers' associations and government agencies during the summers of 1976 and 1977 provide the data base necessary to analyze the impact of the state on the industrial bourgeoisie.[38] In July 1976, and again in June 1977, I returned to study the status of the 306 enterprises (whether intervened or not) and their leaders (their whereabouts). The Associação Industrial Portuguesa and the Associação Industrial Portuense (the manufacturers' associations of Lisbon and Porto, respectively) provided assistance. Data were also collected from the Instituto das Participações do Estado (the Institute for State Participation); from government legislation and from daily reports of official governmental activities, as reported in the *Diário do Governo* (later, *Diário da República*); and by telephoning companies directly. A year later, in June 1977, data on the profits and losses of each enterprise in the three years immediately preceding the revolution were sought (and eventually obtained in December 1977) from the Ministry of Finance's taxation department.

In the analysis that follows, some structural characteristics of the enterprises, and the career patterns, attitudes, and beliefs of the industrial elite, are correlated with data on interventions and the status (or whereabouts) of the industrial elite in order to determine which enterprises were intervened or nationalized and which industrial elites left their positions. Then, by an examination of labor relations and profit/loss data, the social and economic rationale for the state's intervention in an enterprise is determined. Finally, deintervention and the return of capitalism is briefly discussed.

Overview

In a previous study of the Portuguese industrial elite, I established that the Salazar/Caetano regime had recruited technocrats from managerial positions of the larger, modern sector companies in Lisbon, and through its corporative system had marginalized the propertied industrialists, the wealthier founders, heirs, and owners of the traditional sector, and the technologically backward enterprises, many of which were situated in Portugal's north.[39] Although rhetoric and legislation ten years later suggested that the same propertied class was still the target of state control and marginalization, my recent study of the industrial elite and their enterprises indicates that the tables had turned. Others bore the brunt of the political order that emerged soon after the revolution of April 25.

From the broadest perspective, 27 percent of Portugal's enterprises and 19 percent of its industrialists had been directly affected by the state's postrevolutionary intervention policy. Eight percent of the enterprises had been nationalized or had become public companies, 15 percent had been intervened financially and/or administratively, and 4 percent were no longer in business (table 11.1). Among the industrialists, 19 percent had quit their positions (of these 2 percent had been purged), 8 percent had retired, and 16 percent had died (table 11.2).[40] Many of those who had quit their positions migrated to Latin America, especially Brazil, where they apparently had little difficulty in locating lucrative positions.

Focusing on enterprises, table 11.1 indicates that larger enterprises and those in central Portugal were more likely to have been nationalized and intervened than smaller enterprises or those in northern Portugal. Indeed, the larger the enterprise the more likely that it had been nationalized; this was particularly true if the firm was situated in central Portugal. Larger enterprises in central Portugal tended to belong to the economy's newer, more modern sectors, and state intervention was greater in the modern sectors of services, chemicals, steel, and metal products than in the country's traditional sectors of textiles, construction, and nonmetallic minerals. Correspondingly, the percentage of nationalization was higher among technologically complex enterprises, particularly among those that employed a greater proportion of superior and intermediate technicians. The state had moved against the bulk of the technocratic class, most of which was employed in the new sectors. By controlling these sectors the state was attempting to restructure the national economy and at the same time to placate workers' demands.

Calculations suggest that what happened to the industrialists largely mirrored what happened to their firms.[41] The size of an enterprise correlated directly with whether an individual continued to function as a director of the firm (table 11.2, pt. A). For example, in small enter-

TABLE 11.1
State Interventions in Portuguese Industrial Enterprises by 1976
(percentage distribution)

	Nationalizations	Interventions in					No Interventions	Not in Business	Total
		General	Financial	Board of Directors	Management	Other			
Total	8%	6%	4%	2%	2%	1%	73%	4%	100%
(N)	(23)	(18)	(12)	(6)	(7)	(2)	(224)	(14)	(306)

	Nationalizations	Interventions in	No Interventions	Not in Business	Total (N)
Size of enterprise[a]					
Smaller	2%	8	84	6	(176)
Larger	15%	25	58	2	(130)
Giant	19%	27	54	—	(69)
Location[b]					
Northern Portugal	2%	11	79	8	(165)
Central Portugal	14%	18	67	1	(141)
Size and location					
Larger in Central Portugal	23%	23	54	—	(73)

Selected sectors					
Services	44%	8	48	—	(25)
Chemicals	20%	8	72	—	(25)
Metals[c]	2%	19	77	2	(51)
Textiles	—	12	75	13	(72)
Construction	—	—	91	9	(34)
Traditional/modern sectors and date of foundation[d]					
Traditional: founded before 1928	5%	18	69	8	(88)
Traditional: after 1928	5%	8	82	5	(112)
Modern: before 1928	15%	18	67	—	(48)
Modern: after 1928	21%	10	67	2	(58)
Technological complexity[e]					
Technologically complex (T+)	14%	15	69	2	(134)
Technologically noncomplex (T−)	2%	16	76	6	(172)

[a] Smaller = 50–499 employees; larger = 500 or more employees; giant = 1,000 or more employees.

[b] Northern Portugal = Aveiro, Braga, Oporto districts; central Portugal = Lisbon, Santarém, Setúbal.

[c] Includes electrical and heavy machinery, steel, and metal products.

[d] Traditional = mining, nonmetallic minerals, ceramics, glass, cement, wood, cork, foodstuffs, beverages, textiles; modern = steel, heavy metal products, electrical machinery, chemicals, services, paper products.

[e] Technologically complex (T+) = enterprises above the mean in number of superior or intermediate technicians or both; technologically noncomplex (T−) = enterprises below the mean in number of both superior and intermediate technicians.

TABLE 11.2
Percentage of Portuguese Industrial Elite
Who Quit Their Enterprises by 1976

	Quit	Still There	Died	Retired	Total
Total	19%	57%	16%	8%	100%
(N)	(60)	(173)	(49)	(24)	(306)

	Quit %	Quit (N)
A. Selected structural characteristics[a]		
Size of enterprise		
y Smaller	15	(144)
Larger	43	(89)
Giant (1,000 or more employees)	55	(44)
Location		
Northern Portugal	18	(139)
Central Portugal	37	(94)
Size and location		
Larger in central Portugal	54	(46)
Selected sectors		
Services[b]	54	(11[c])
Metals	28	(43)
Textiles	25	(64)
Construction	21	(24)
Chemicals[b]	7	(14[c])
B. Selected biographical characteristics[a]		
Socioeconomic origin		
Upper class	46	(92)
Middle class	22	(100)
Lower class	21	(33)
Geographic mobility		
Natives	25	(142)
Migrants	24	(72)
Foreign-born	42	(19)
Social Mobility		
Upward	32	(85)
Static	25	(100)
Downward	15	(46)
Education		
High school or less	16	(129)
University or more	38	(104)

TABLE 11.2 (continued)

	Quit	Still There	Died	Retired	Total
Total	19%	57%	16%	8%	100%
(N)	(60)	(173)	(49)	(24)	(306)

	Quit %	(N)
Ownership and control		
Founder	18	(84)
Heir	21	(80)
Owner-manager	32	(38)
Manager	52	(31)
Public office: before 1974		
National level	63	(8[c])
Municipal level	8	(25)
Other government	29	(14)
None	26	(186)
Corporative and public office: before 1974		
Corporative and public	20	(33)
Public[d]	23	(26)
Corporative	22	(50)
None	28	(133)
C. Selected attitudinal and behavioral characteristics		
Organizational control, authority, and managerial style		
Committees share in decision making	33	(106)
Only industrialist involved	20	(122)
Delegated authority	32	(142)
Concentrated authority	22	(94)
Special problems handled by committee	33	(106)
Special problems handled by industrialist only	20	(127)
Industrialists characterized themselves as		
Inspecting/supervising	21	(48)
Giving orders	22	(68)
Planners	32	(38)
Policy/norm makers	30	(38)
Confirming decisions of others	33	(15)
Enterprise's major problem viewed as		
Manpower	18	(61)
Internal reorganization	28	(18)
Fixed capital expenditures	26	(42)

TABLE 11.2 (continued)

	Quit	Still There	Died	Retired	Total
Total	19%	57%	16%	8%	100%
(N)	(60)	(173)	(49)	(24)	(306)

	Quit	
	%	(N)
Competition	38	(29)
Financial	29	(24)
Productivity problems attributed to		
Lack of employee interest/initiative	17	(30)
Employee "mentality"	13	(23)
Poor organization and equipment	37	(19)
Employee inexperience	42	(50)
Attitudes toward strikes		
Unfavorable	24	(191)
Favorable	42	(33)
Labor disputes resolved		
Direct collaboration or bargaining	21	(145)
Corporative or government resolution	35	(43)
Labor court case results		
Favorable to enterprise	26	(39)
Unfavorable to enterprise	51	(33)
Foreign capital participation and receptivity		
No participation and not favorable	23	(20)
No participation but favorable	27	(30)
Participation and favorable	35	(176)

[a] This table excludes 49 persons who died and 24 who retired.

[b] Half had retired or died in these sectors.

[c] Limited number of cases permits only tentative observations. Ten of the original 18 in this group had died or retired.

[d] Eighteen individuals, or nearly half of this group, had died or retired.

prises (50–99 employees) only 15 percent of the industrialists had quit, compared to 43 percent who had quit in the large firms; in the giant firms (1,000 or more employees) more than half had quit.[42] Regionally, too, the difference is remarkable. Among the large enterprises (500 or more employees) in central Portugal, 54 percent of the industrialists had left, while in the north the majority still held their positions, particularly in the outlying districts of Aveiro and Braga. However, four of the five industrialists who had been purged from their factories were from this region; textile magnate Manuel Gonçalves was one of the four.

Among the principal industrial sectors, services (e.g., public utilities, transportation) saw more than half (54 percent) of their industrialists leave—a proportion approximately double that of any other sector. When most service enterprises were nationalized in the spring of 1975, their boards of directors and top executives were replaced by state appointees. When an enterprise was affiliated with one of the large consortia, its leading industrialist left long before nationalization occurred. For example, José Manuel de Melo, the head of Sociedade Geral de Comércio, Indústria e Transportes, the country's largest shipping company, fled Portugal in the fall of 1974 with other owners and top executives of Companhia União Fabril (CUF), Portugal's largest consortium.

Part b of table 11.2 identifies those industrialists affected by intervention according to their biographical characteristics. The impact on the upper classes is vivid. Calculations show that the higher the socioeconomic class origin of an industrialist, the greater the likelihood that he had left his firm. But the more upwardly mobile also were more likely to have quit than those who were downwardly mobile. A number of the upwardly mobile were *comprador* industrialists, that is, loyal hirelings of the large consortia—middle class in origin, university educated, sons of the *petite bourgeoisie*. Others were state *compradores*, who had moved from assistant professorships (usually in law) in the university into deputy and (later) full cabinet (or national-level) positions, and then had been recruited to direct consortia-owned firms or had been appointed *administrador delgados* (delegate administrators).[43] Statistics pertaining to ownership and control and to public office (table 11.2, part B) corroborate this pattern. A much larger percentage of managers (52 percent) than owners of production —i.e., founders (18 percent), heirs (21 percent), and owner-managers (32 percent)—and a larger percentage of national-level politicians who held office before 1974 (63 percent) than municipal office-holders (8 percent) or non-office-holders (26 percent) had left their enterprises and positions.

Other calculations show that managers had received the highest salaries among the industrial bourgeoisie. When originally interviewed in 1965 most were making between $17,500 and $35,000 in U.S. dollars annually, whereas most founders reported earning $9,000 or less a year. Not long after the revolution a maximum allowed income of $12,000 U.S. dollars a year, from all sources, was established by the government. Considering what the income level of the same managers must have been by 1974, it is not difficult to explain why they left their positions.

Those who had held corporate office before 1974 were, on the other hand, among the more tenacious. Designed early in Salazar's New State to regulate economic life, the corporatist system became an object of unofficial and benign neglect on the part of both the industrial bourgeoisie and the state.[44] While it certainly was bypassed by the larger industries and consortia that had direct access to the state, it served as a placating, buffer institution for the propertied industrial elite—the less educated, the founders, heirs, and owner-managers of traditional, technologically noncomplex enterprises. These were neither the industries nor the bourgeoisie that the left was interested in containing. Although the corporatist system was dismantled soon after the revolution, those industrialists who held corporative office did not fall with it; this fact attests to the innocuousness of the system under Salazar and Caetano.

However, the firms of ex-corporative leaders did not entirely escape intervention. Indeed, the extent of administrative and financial intervention in such firms was relatively high, suggesting that corporative officers might have been so involved in corporative affairs that they neglected their enterprises, or that they might have become politicians in attempts to revive their failing businesses. The enterprises of many corporative leaders were economically stagnant and managerially backward, partly as a result of their direction by heirs who were more interested in public esteem than in business.[45]

In summary, it was *not* the propertied, traditional sector elites that the postrevolutionary government moved against, but their polar opposites: the managers of large consortia-owned enterprises in the modern sectors, whose firms were nationalized and who, in turn, left their positions. Under the new regime the technocrats and their modern sector firms were marginalized and controlled. In a sense the hunters became the hunted. But did they deserve to be attacked? Was state control purely ideological, or was it justified in terms of actual exploitation or mistreatment of employees? Was it imposed on enterprises which had been experiencing economic, financial, and/or administrative difficulties? Or was it a measure to restructure the economy?

Leadership Style

During the Salazar/Caetano regime labor was unorganized and the labor unions (*sindicatos*) had little power. There were strikes and work stoppages, but since most were illegal they were forcibly put down by the federal police and were rarely publicized. Conflicts over wages, hours, and working conditions, if not resolved within the enterprise, were presented to the labor courts by a union for adjudication. In the typical firm power was concentrated in the hands of a few at the top, and there was little willingness to delegate it to others, especially to those at lower administrative or production levels. Working conditions were generally grim, and few enterprises paid their employees or provided benefits above what the law required. More than two-thirds of the enterprises were family owned, and employee relations tended to be paternalistic. Industrialists even in larger firms of this type devoted most of their time and energy to giving orders, inspecting the factory daily, supervising production, and resolving disputes. In contrast, the modern nonfamily firm was usually directed by hired managers—power was delegated, the organization was defined, lines of authority were clearer, and there were policies, rules, regulations, and plans.

Much of the earlier intervention legislation and leftist ideology dwelt on the internationally dependent, amoral, capitalist domination of the working class, and proposed instead worker participation in an economy in which there were no divisions between the ruled and the rulers. What is of interest is whether the industrialists who quit were "democratic" in managing their firms and "liberal" with their employees, or whether they were "authoritarian," dictatorial, and exploitative, mirroring the outgoing regime itself. My earlier study of the Portuguese industrial elite examined managerial style, organizational control, authority, labor relations, and attitudes toward strikes; part C of table 11.2 relates these topics to industrialists who left their enterprises.

Contrary to what we might expect, calculations indicate that the firms which remained intact were not those headed by "democratic," tolerant industrialists but those in which power was concentrated, and in which employees were closely supervised and likely to be blamed for lack of productivity or profits. Such surviving enterprises tended to be directed by captains of industry, by self-made men, or by founders.

Industrialists who involved others in key decision making, or permitted divisions and departments to negotiate with one another, or whose boards of directors delegated authority to management, were more likely to have left their firms than those who closely held the reigns of power or those who carefully scrutinized all operations of their enterprises. That is, those firms in which there was some semblance of "participatory democracy" were more likely to lose their chief executive than those that were ruled by one individual.

This pattern was also apparent when "styles of management" were examined. Industrialists who indicated that they spent most of their time and energy establishing norms and policies for their firms, or in public relations and other external activities, or rubber-stamping the decisions of others saw their enterprises intervened and were more likely to have quit than those who saw themselves as involved in the actual operations, giving orders, and personally inspecting their factories. For example, while most (about 80 percent) of those who said that they continuously inspected their factories were still in the enterprises, smaller proportions remained of those who devoted most of their time to planning, confirming the decisions of others, or external activities.

When industrialists were questioned about problems facing their enterprises or their labor relations, the pattern that emerged was similar. Those concerned with internal problems such as manpower, internal reorganization, and fixed capital expenditures were still at the helm, while those who were worried about external problems such as competition, financial concerns, and government restrictions had left or had seen their firms intervened. Industrialists who believed that labor problems and lack of productivity were a result of poor equipment, poor organization, or employee inexperience were more likely to have left than those who directly blamed their employees for such problems on the grounds of lack of discipline, interest, initiative, or loyalty.

The *linha dura* (hard-line) approach was most vivid in attitudes toward strikes and courtroom confrontations. Industrialists who opposed the right to strike were more likely to have remained than those who favored it. And those who were willing to bargain directly with their employees in the event of a conflict were still there, rather than those who favored resolution by the government or its corporative organizations. In the courtrooms the industrialists who tended to win judgments brought against the enterprise by its employees or their *sindicatos* were most likely to have remained. Other calculations show that fewer of their enterprises were intervened or nationalized, while quite the opposite was true for those who lost their cases. It is possible that the enterprises of those who lost had more militant and/or better organized employees; indeed, even under Salazar it was known that the metallurgical workers' *sindicato* was particularly strong in the larger and more technologically complex firms.

It appears that industrialists who were more authoritarian, had more interaction with their employees, and exercised closer supervision were more likely to sustain their positions through the revolution. In enterprises where the organization was more democratic and the ambience more "liberal," the distance between the ruled and the rulers was greater and resulted in less interaction, a situation which the mass of the Portuguese workers might have disliked or might not have been prepared to accept. These findings coincide with studies of leadership style in American, Japanese, and Peruvian factories.[46] While closeness of supervision was negatively correlated with satisfaction among American workers, in Japan and in Peru a positive correlation was found. However, as observations in Japan have shown, as the values of a country become more democratic and as its industrial and economic structure alters, increasing dissatisfaction with paternalistic leadership styles, conditions of employment, and organization of production result.[47]

It is debatable whether, in postrevolutionary Portugal, managerial style, closeness of supervision, paternalism, etc., affected the ownership and control of production. In the larger factories in central Portugal the workers were more organized, more militant, and more politically conscious. In smaller enterprises and in the north, paternalism and loyalty characterized industrial structure and relations. However, when these workers perceived that their employment and wages would be compromised because owners began to threaten (or to act upon threats of) abandonment or closure of their enterprises, or when the state refused to intervene or nationalize (i.e., secure or underwrite) a sector or an enterprise, the workers took control. But one gathers that this was an act of last resort. Indeed, it has been noted that in most of the factories the workers soon delegated management to the more skilled, the more educated, or even to the former managers.[48]

Economic Viability

Enterprises were intervened regardless of their favorable labor relations and participatory democracy. One could argue that such actions were contradictory to the ideological basis of intervention policies, but that they were consistent with leftist efforts to restructure the economic order of the country. Furthermore, it was not the inefficient enterprises or those suffering losses that were intervened, but the profitable ones. A profitable firm contributes to the gross national product, provides employment, and in a poor, industrially immature country such as Portugal would most likely represent progress toward modernity. But the profit and loss figures in table 11.3 indicate that profitability was not the principal determinate of intervention or nationalization. Profit and loss figures supplied by Portugal's Ministry of Finance reveal that only 20 percent of the enterprises reported losses from 1973 through 1974, and that in 1974, when the country experienced numerous political disruptions, only 25 percent of the enterprises were in the red.[49] The fact that the majority of the intervened enterprises I studied had been profitable in the two years immediately preceding the revolution, and in 1974 as well, suggests that many interventions were unjustified under the terms of *decreto-lei* 660, and that the entire process of intervention had been a move of the leftist government against the bourgeoisie.

Table 11.3 shows that it was the "bigger fish" that the left was after, particularly those firms located in central Portugal and in the modern sectors. For example, among the giant profitable firms intervention was greater than among profitable firms smaller in size. The difference is apparent when the service sector (public utilities, transportation) is compared to textiles. Thirty-nine percent of the profitable service enterprises were intervened (most were nationalized), compared to only 11 percent of the profitable textile enterprises. The fact that textiles are

TABLE 11.3

Portuguese Industrial Enterprises That Had Profits or Losses between 1972 and 1974, by Nationalization and Intervention

(percentage distribution)

	Nationalization	Intervention	No Intervention	Not in Business	Total
Profitable enterprises	83%	65%	85%	17%	80%
(N)	(18)	(34)	(152)	(6)	(210)
No profit/loss information (N)	5	11	72	8	96

	Interventions[a]		No Interventions		Total[b]
	Profits	Losses	Profits	Losses	(N)
Size of enterprise[c]					
Smaller	8%	4	76	13	(106)
Larger	30%	11	50	9	(98)
Giant	28%	18	50	4	(50)
Location					
Northern	12%	4	71	13	(99)
Central	24%	11	56	10	(105)
Size and location					
Larger in central Portugal	33%	16	43	9	(58)
Selected sectors					
Services	39%	23	31	8	(13)
Chemicals	32%	—	58	11	(19)
Metals	18%	9	59	15	(34)
Textiles	11%	4	75	11	(47)
Construction	0%	—	77	23	(13)

TABLE 11.3 (continued)

	Interventions[a]		No Interventions		Total[b]
	Profits	Losses	Profits	Losses	(N)
Traditional/modern sectors and date of foundation					
Traditional: founded before 1928	19%	8	63	11	(65)
Traditional: after 1928	7%	6	75	12	(69)
Modern: before 1928	25%	16	41	19	(32)
Modern: after 1928	32%	3	61	5	(38)
Technological complexity					
Technologically complex (T+)	24%	6	58	12	(83)
Technologically noncomplex (T−)	14%	8	67	11	(121)

NOTE: When the number of cases is less than 20, observations are tentative.

[a] Includes nationalizations (i.e., 18 cases on which profit/loss information was reported).

[b] Excludes those enterprises on which no profit/loss information was provided between 1972 and 1974, and those which were no longer in business.

[c] Smaller = 50–499 employees; larger = 500 or more employees; giant = 1,000 or more employees.

located mainly in the north and services in central Portugal (especially in Lisbon) accounts for the regional discrepancy, and illustrates where the left's attack was concentrated. Had I included figures on the magnitude of profits they would undoubtedly show that the left was not only containing the largest firms, but that in doing so it was strengthening its financial power. Most smaller enterprises, although profitable, were not intervened.

The impact of intervention on the industrial bourgeoisie does not alter when the profitability of their enterprises is introduced as a factor. Table 11.4 shows that, holding profits constant, the higher an industrialist's social class of origin and the higher his educational attainment, the more likely he was to leave his firm. Even when factors of enterprise size or sector were introduced, the pattern remained; that is, although social class and educational attainment correlated positively with enterprise size, greater proportions of the upper class and the more highly educated quit. The managers, or *comprador* class, were the most typical in this respect. Regardless of profitability, this was the group that left. Although many were the victims of nationalization, many also fled in 1975 before the intervention period. In contrast, founders and heirs remained. Heirs seemed to be the most tenacious, since despite losses a number of them remained in their firms. One wonders whether this was due to loyalty to the family firm, lack of qualifications for employment elsewhere, or reticence about working or engaging in business with other families.

That profitability bore no relationship to the organizational control and authority patterns is apparent in part B, table 11.4. Industrialists who were inclined to delegate authority, saw themselves as policy formulators, and were more concerned with competition and the organization of production than with manpower problems were more likely to have quit than those who kept tight control over their enterprises and tended to deal directly and personally with their employees, clients, and government officials. It might be said that they tenaciously guarded the property to which their livelihood and success were intimately bound. Different circumstances prevailed among the non-owners of production, the managers of enterprises in dynamic sectors (often subsidiaries of large consortia). These individuals could afford to be more liberal in their ideas or in their largesse: all they could lose was their jobs, and since they were equipped with university training and industrial experience they were still employable elsewhere in the Latin world. We could say that they were more cosmopolitan than owner-industrialists, and the political roles played by managers illustrates this characteristic. Those who held multiple political offices (e.g., both corporative and ranking government positions) were more likely to have witnessed their enterprise's intervention and to have quit themselves; they were, so to speak, caught up and swept away. But their return was imminent. The Portuguese economy had been weakened and was recovering very slowly. The new Socialist government did not have a sufficient strength and organization to launch an effective economic policy. It was torn between appeasing factions of the left and the right at home and courting Western Europe and the United States abroad.

Conclusion

In the wake of the interventions industry was bearing the brunt of political instability. It was faced with frequent work stoppages, internal disorganization, raw material shortages, the loss of markets, severe import tariffs and restrictions, and rising labor costs. In view of these problems there was little inclination to invest. In 1976, for example, investment as a percentage of GNP was down to 10 percent, compared with 22 percent in 1975, the year of greatest political uncertainty in Portugal. Government strategy to encourage investment seemed to echo

TABLE 11.4
The Portuguese Industrial Elite Who Quit or Remained, by Profits and Losses of the Enterprises, 1972–1974
(percentage distribution)

	Quit		Still There		Total
	Profits	Losses	Profits	Losses	(N)
A. Selected Biographical Characteristics					
Socioeconomic origin					
Upper class	21%	11	52	16	(73)
Middle class	13%	10	71	6	(62)
Lower class	4%	4	78	13	(23)
Social mobility					
Upward	16%	10	66	8	(62)
Static	18%	11	57	14	(73)
Downward	4%	4	74	17	(23)
Education					
High school or less	9%	5	76	10	(79)
University or more	22%	14	50	14	(79)
Ownership and control					
Founder	10%	4	80	6	(50)
Heir	14%	9	60	17	(58)
Owner-manager	15%	15	63	7	(27)
Manager	30%	17	34	17	(23)
Geographic mobility					
Natives	14%	8	66	12	(95)
Migrants	15%	8	60	17	(47)
Foreign-born	25%	19	56	—	(16)
Public office: before 1974					
National level	29%	29	29	14	(7)
Municipal level	6%	6	83	6	(18)
Other government	30%	10	50	10	(10)
None	15%	9	63	13	(123)
Corporative and public office: before 1974					
Corporative and public	0%	22	64	14	(14)
Public	25%	5	65	5	(20)
Corporative	13%	8	63	16	(38)
None	16%	9	63	12	(83)

TABLE 11.4 (continued)

	Quit		Still There		Total
	Profits	Losses	Profits	Losses	(N)
B. Selected Attitudinal and Behavioral Characteristics					
Organization control and authority and managerial style					
Committees share in decision making	17%	13	65	5	(77)
Only industrialist involved	14%	6	62	18	(78)
Delegated authority	20%	13	58	9	(55)
Concentrated authority	11%	7	67	15	(97)
Special problems handled by committee	17%	13	65	5	(77)
Special problems handled by industrialist only	14%	6	62	18	(81)
Industrialists characterized themselves as					
Inspecting/supervising	13%	6	72	9	(32)
Giving orders	7%	7	66	20	(41)
Planners	26%	9	61	4	(23)
Policy/norm makers	16%	16	55	13	(31)
Confirming decisions of others	22%	11	55	11	(9)
Enterprise's major problems viewed as					
Manpower	6%	6	71	18	(34)
Internal reorganization	13%	20	60	7	(15)
Fixed capital expenditures	17%	7	67	10	(30)
Competition	18%	18	45	18	(22)
Financial	6%	19	69	6	(16)
Productivity problems attributed to					
Lack of employee interest/initiative	6%	6	89	—	(18)
Employee "mentality"	13%	—	67	20	(15)
Poor organization and equipment	27%	13	47	13	(15)
Employee inexperience	15%	15	61	9	(33)
Attitudes toward strikes					
Unfavorable	14%	9	66	11	(123)
Favorable	22%	15	48	15	(27)

TABLE 11.4 (continued)

	Quit		Still There		Total
	Profits	Losses	Profits	Losses	(N)
Labor disputes resolved					
Direct collaboration	13%	8	67	11	(97)
Corporative or government resolution	15%	12	62	11	(26)
Labor court case results					
Favorable to enterprise	28%	8	56	8	(25)
Unfavorable to enterprise	36%	18	41	5	(22)
Foreign capital participation and receptivity					
No participation and not favorable	13%	9	66	12	(115)
No participation but favorable	15%	10	55	20	(20)
Participation and favorable	22%	11	61	6	(18)

the past: it was strong-armed, austere, and fraught with contradictions. One policy involved increasing social security contributions and imposing forced savings in order to raise a quarter of a billion dollars, while another limited annual wage increases to 15 percent when inflation was still hovering around 30 percent. To prepare the economy for European Economic Community participation, still another policy assured generous loans for imports of capital goods, mechanization, and administrative modernization; but the loans were undersubscribed by some of the country's leading sectors because they were prevented from dispensing with surplus labor and its costs.

The Socialist government, well aware that confidence in the economy must be restored, attempted to modify legislation enacted in 1975 which nationalized banks and certain industrial sectors, restricted foreign investment, and gave workers such an extensive degree of control that entrepreneurship was stifled. But the government moved slowly, stymied by factions even within its ranks who argued that sufficient time had not elapsed to test the effectiveness of industrial reforms and state control of the economy.

By early 1976 those who had fled were being invited to return. The deintervention of Textil Manual Gonçalves in February of that year was indicative of the new policy. In this and in other firms the workers refused to work any longer for the state-appointed representatives and threatened to strike. Many workers were terrified that their factories would close: they were aware that sales had slumped; that state-appointed managers and boards were frequently inept, inexperienced, and dependent on distant ministries for the smallest of decisions; that former clientele and suppliers rarely visited the factories, and that if they did happen to come *o patrão* (the boss) was not there to greet them. Demonstrating workers who had once shouted "The MFA and People are One" were clamoring "Boss, friend, the workers are with you!" In some northern villages local Communist party headquarters' were burned and leftist sympathizers were expelled from factories.

On April 25, 1976, two years after the revolution, *Le Monde-Manchester Guardian Weekly* speculated that "while it would be difficult just yet to rush into a hasty denationalization of the big trusts, it is, on the contrary, simpler to give back to the private sector businesses where the state, without actually taking over the capital, had stepped in to replace a management in exile or accused of economic sabotage . . . "[50] And in the late summer of 1976, Mário Soares, Portugal's newly elected prime minister, went to Brazil to persuade exiled industrialists to return to Portugal, and apparently promised them compensation.[51] Within a year a number of the country's larger enterprises had been returned to their original owners (e.g., C. Santos to Bernardo de Almeida (Caria), Guerin Ltd. to José Machado, Lusalite to the Abecassis family), and there were indications that even the chief executives of the largest consortia whose companies were nationalized would be returning to at least resume their posts.

In a little over a year the Portuguese state, dominated by the left, moved against the industrial bourgeoisie, controlling and marginalizing members of large consortia and their associates. This was achieved through legal measures and the creation of state organizations. But because of the political and economic inexperience of the population, the country's dependency on larger and more powerful nations, and the debilitating influence of Eurocommunism, private capitalism was destined to return. It has returned, however, to a more modern economy and a more politically conscious labor force. Should there be another revolution, all factions will be more tenacious.

Notes

Earlier versions of this paper were presented at the Ad-Hoc Committee on Economy and Society, Ninth World Congress of Sociology, Uppsala, Sweden, August 16, 1978. The section on "Social Change: Modernization and Development," was given at the American Sociological Association Meeting, San

Francisco, September 5, 1978. The first part of the data analysis ("Overview") is a modified revision of the "Postscript" previously published in Lawrence S. Graham and Harry M. Makler, eds., *Contemporary Portugal: The Revolution and Its Antecedents* (Austin, 1979), copyright © 1979 by The University of Texas Press, pp. 153–160, as were table 11.1 and part of table 11.2. I wish to thank the Humanities and Social Science Committee of the University of Toronto and the Scientific Affairs Division of the North Atlantic Treaty Organization for their travel grants. I am also grateful for the comments and criticisms of Antonio D. Borges, Dain Borges, Rosalinda Costa, and Philippe C. Schmitter, and especially for the revisions suggested by David L. Raby. Portugal's Institute for State Participation and the Ministry of Finances taxation department supplied much of the data on which this study is based; Stanford University's Center of Latin American Studies provided a quiet setting and *convivio* during the preparation of this essay. The support of these institutions and their staffs is appreciated.

1 Inaugural address of António de Spínola, May 15, 1974, as cited in Orlando Neves, ed., *Textos Históricos da Revolução* (Lisbon, 1976), p. 84.
2 Tad Szulc, "Lisbon and Washington: Behind the Portuguese Revolution," *Foreign Policy* 21 (Winter, 1975–1976), p. 26. Szulc indicated that workers' commissions were "nationalizing industrial plants, banks, businesses, hotels, and restaurants," but this did not occur until late in the fall of 1974.
3 Avelino Rodrigues Cesàrio Borga, and Mário Cardoso, *Portugal Depois de Abril* (Lisbon, 1976), p. 58. Other cases of strikes and take-overs of firms are described on pp. 57–59 of this book.
4 Inaugural speech of Vasco dos Santos Gonçalves upon assuming the post of prime minister of the Second Provisional Government, July 18, 1974, as cited in Neves, *Textos Históricos*, p. 101.
5 See the description of events and political group activities surrounding Spínola's attempted coup of September 28 in Rodrigues, Borga, and Cardoso, *Depois de Abril* pp. 84–95.
6 Translated and summarized from "Boletim do MFA" (Nov. 12, 1974), as cited in Rodrigues, Borga, and Cardoso, *Depois de Abril*, pp. 104–106.
7 Rodrigues, Borga, and Cardoso, *Depois de Abril*, p. 105.
8 Identified by Rodrigues, Borga, and Cardoso as the "progressives."
9 Rodrigues, Borga, and Cardoso, *Depois de Abril*, p. 107. Words in parentheses are mine. Presumably the minister without portfolio was the Communist party leader, Alvaro Cunhal.
10 Those representative of this view were Rui Vilar, José Silva Lopes, and Maria De Lurdes Pintassilgo, who were the ministers of economics, finance, and social welfare, respectively, and Erik Lundberg, a Swedish economist who had studied Portugal's economy (Rodrigues, Borga, and Cardoso, *Depois de Abril*, pp. 64–65, 106–107).
11 Ibid., p. 133. Translated and condensed from Portuguese.
12 Extracted from *Diário Popular*, Feb. 28, 1975, as reported in Rodrigues, Borga, and Cardoso, *Depois de Abril*, p. 135. Words in parentheses are mine.

13 Rodrigues, Borga, and Cardoso, *Depois de Abril*, p. 135. Tad Szulc also recognized differences emerging among various factions within the Portuguese military; see, for example, Szulc, "Lisbon and Washington." Splits continue to this day. There are debates in the Revolutionary Council over amnesty for counterrevolutionaries and former secret police agents.

14 Even before 1974 these banks were essentially controlled by the government, as their governors and vice-governors were government appointees. It would be interesting to study the minutes of the council to see the arguments pro and con nationalization. The minutes (or records) of Portugal's constitutional assembly, organized in 1975, would also be an excellent source, as they would reveal the position of each political party.

15 Decreto-lei, no. 540-A/74, *Diário do Governo*, serie I, no. 238, Oct. 12, 1974.

16 Rodrigues, Borga, and Cardoso, *Depois de Abril*, p. 58.

17 See Decreto-lei no. 553-A/74, *Diário do Governo*, serie I, no. 253, Oct. 30, 1974.

18 Decreto-lei no. 660/74, *Diário do Governo*, serie I, supl. no. 274, Nov. 11, 1974.

19 Manuel de Lucena, *O Estado da Revolução: A Constituição de 1976* (Lisbon, 1976), p. 241. Translated and condensed from the Portuguese.

20 *Artigo* 2 of the law specified that the government could begin an investigation whenever there was evidence of any of the conditions of abnormal functioning. However, the law did not describe how the government would learn of that evidence. As it happened, most intervention processes were initiated by employees or workers' commissions when they complained to the Ministry of Labor (interview with Nuno Brederode Santos, attorney, Portugal's Institute for State Participation [Instituto das Participações do Estado] June 23, 1977, Lisbon). If the charges or abnormalities were justified the government was empowered to either liquidate or declare the enterprise bankrupt, or to choose some form of intervention (*artigo* 3). These forms were (*a*) nationalization (which only occurred in mid-1975 and among certain sectors); (*b*) control of an enterprise's board of directors, usually through the appointment of state delegates to it, and/or complete suspension of the board; (*c*) suspension of one or more of an enterprise's directors and his (their) replacement by state appointees (this rule was extended to the managerial level eleven months later by *decreto-lei* no. 597/75); and (*d*) financial intervention either through loans obtained through the Ministry of Finance, or through direct participation of the state via shares (*artigos* 3 and 7). *Decreto-lei* no. 76-C/75, Feb. 21, 1975, specified that the state could appoint administrators in enterprises in which it held a minimum of 20 percent of the capital. Most enterprises which were intervened administratively were also controlled financially. Provisions were made for either permanent state control—that is, nationalization (*artigo* 5)—or the return of the firm to its original owners through deintervention (*artigo* 6).

21 See, for example, decreto-lei no. 132-A, *Diário do Governo*, serie I, Mar. 14, 1975, and decreto-lei no. 406-A/75, *Diário do Governo*, serie I, July 29, 1975, pertaining to agriculture and rural property intervention.

22 Manuel Lucena suggests that when smaller and medium sized enterprises were intervened it was because a number of the larger companies participated in their ownership. This was entrapment by association. (Lucena, *O Estado de Revolução*, p. 242).

23 The Champalimaud group was one of the largest economic consortia in Portugal. It owned or controlled other large industrial, commercial, and banking interests. Its head, António Champalimaud, was president of Sidurgeria Nacional, the country's steel refinery. Immediately after the 1974 revolution Champalimaud fled to Brazil, where he reportedly continued his entrepreneurial activities and investments.

24 Resolução do Conselho de Ministros, *Diário do Governo*, serie I, no. 85, Apr. 11, 1975. Translated and condensed from the Portuguese. Words in parentheses are mine.

25 Resolução do Conselho de Ministros, *Diário do Governo*, serie I, no. 96, Apr. 24, 1975. Translated and condensed from the Portuguese.

26 Resolução do Conselho de Ministros, *Diário do Governo*, serie I, no. 194, Aug. 23, 1975.

27 See, for example, *Trabalho Colectivo dos Trabalhadores Ameaçados de Despedimento pela Administração da Textil Manuel Gonçalves, S.A.R.L.: "O Caso dos 17 da Textil Manuel Gonçalves"* (Porto; 1976).

28 Resolução do Conselho de Ministros, *Diário do Governo*, serie I, no. 28, Feb. 3, 1976. A case study of this intervention and deintervention would be invaluable to an understanding of political and economic events, both nationally and regionally, in this period. Of course, the political climate changed in Portugal. When Gonçalves fled to Spain radicalism was at its height; when he returned much more moderate forces were consolidating their power.

29 Decreto-lei no. 222-B/75, *Diário do Governo*, serie I, no. 109, May 12, 1975.

30 Decreto-lei no. 597/75, *Diário do Governo*, Oct. 28, 1975.

31 Usually this was the minister of industry and technology, but it could be the minister of labor (in the event of labor protest) or agriculture.

32 It is debatable whether the Communist party was attempting to take power during the last quarter of 1975. After April 1975 the Communist party had become impotent, perhaps not through any weakness of its own, but because of numerous internal conflicts which had been unleashed through "the collapse of the entire institutional and ideological structure of the old regime. . . ." (Bill Lomax, "Ideology and Illusion in the Portuguese Revolution: The Role of the Left," which appears as chapter 5 of this volume, see also Jean-Pierre Faye, *Le Portugal d'Otelo* [Nottingham, England, 1976]).

33 Lawrence S. Graham, "The Military in Politics: The Politicization of the

Portuguese Armed Forces,'' in Lawrence S. Graham and Harry M. Makler, eds., *Contemporary Portugal: The Revolution and Its Antecedents* (Austin, 1979), p. 250.

34 Henry Ginger, *New York Times*, Apr. 3, 1976.

35 Decreto-lei no. 422/75, *Diário da República*, serie I, no. 126, May 29, 1976.

36 Decreto-lei no. 422/75, p. 1215. Translated and paraphrased from the Portuguese. Words in parentheses are mine.

37 Gabinete de Estudos, Planeamento e Organização, Ministério do Trabalho, *Nacionalizações e Outras Intervenções Até 22 de Setembro de 1975*. Serie Relatório e Análises 3 (Lisbon, 1976).

38 A more detailed explanation of the research design and sampling procedures appears in Harry M. Makler, *A Elite Industrial Portuguesa* (Lisbon, 1969), appendix A.

39 Harry M. Makler, ''The Portuguese Industrial Elite and Its Corporative Relations: A Study of Compartmentalization in an Authoritarian Regime,'' *Economic Development and Cultural Change* vol. 24, no. 3 (April, 1976).

40 As far as I know, none of the industrialists were killed as a direct result of the revolution or its aftermath, although it is believed that some suffered cardiac arrest, nervous breakdown, and/or became alcoholics.

41 There were deviations from this pattern that will only be alluded to in this essay. Fifteen percent, or 34 of the 233 active industrialists, quit their enterprises, although their firms were not intervened, and 9 percent, or 20 industrialists, saw their enterprises intervened but remained at their posts.

42 Among the giant enterprises, 23 percent of the industrialists that I interviewed in 1965 had died. This is understandable, as the average age of this group was older than the average age (53 years) for the entire sample. Age and size of enterprise varied directly.

43 Makler, ''Portuguese Industrial Elite,'' p. 513.

44 Ibid., p. 524.

45 The relationship between familism, inheritance, and economic growth has been the subject of considerable study (see Charles P. Kindleberger, *Economic Growth in France and Britain* [Cambridge, Mass., 1964]). It is also plausible that more corporative leaders' firms faced economic and financial difficulties, and that in an attempt to resolve these they sought corporative office.

46 W. F. Whyte and L. K. Williams, ''Supervisory Leadership: An International Comparison,'' *Proceedings of the Thirteenth International Management Conference* (1963); Robert E. Cole, *Japanese Blue Collar: The Changing Tradition* (Berkeley, 1971), pp. 81–87, 179–183; Kunio Odaka, ''Traditionalism, Democracy in Japanese Industry,'' cited in Neil J. Smelser, *The Sociology of Economic Life* (Englewood Cliffs, N. J., 1976), pp. 116–117.

47 See, for example, the discussion of the structural factors that reduce lifetime commitment in Japanese factories in Robert M. Marsh and Hiroshi

Mannari, "A New Look at 'Lifetime Commitment' in Japanese Industry," *Economic Development and Cultural Change*, vol. 20, no. 4 (July, 1972), pp. 661–630.

48 Lomax, "Ideology and Illusion."

49 No profit/loss data was furnished for 32 percent, or 96, of the 306 enterprises studied; therefore they are excluded from the analysis. The figures for 1972 through 1974 were averaged and a variable was created which reflected the existence of profits or losses, rather than their magnitude.

50 Dominque Pouchin, "Portugal: The End of an Exile," *Le Monde-Manchester Guardian Weekly*, Apr. 25, 1976.

51 "Out of Exile: Portuguese Businessmen Back on the Job as the Government Returns Their Firms," *Wall Street Journal*, Jan. 13, 1978.

PART 4
THE LIMITS OF CHANGE IN A DEPENDENT NATION

12 *José Medeiros Ferreira*

José Medeiros Ferreira

International Ramifications of the Portuguese Revolution

The revolution of April 25, 1974, overthrew a political regime which had maintained neutrality during the Second World War. Originally overlooked because of Salazar's later collaboration with the Allies, this neutrality was disguised further by the colonial war, a contemporary expression of that same neutrality. For this reason, no one in Portugal has yet attempted to understand the international ramifications of the April 25 revolution from the perspective of that neutrality. In a way, only in 1974, with the overthrow of a nationalist dictatorship and with decolonization, did the ultimate consequences of World War II reach Portugal. In this regard, the Salazar dictatorship was truly a unique case among the NATO nations.

Thirty years after the war, the consequences of the April revolution gave rise to some rather special developments:

1. The events of the Portuguese revolution took place in the midst of the formalization of East-West detente as expressed at the European Conference on Security and Cooperation (1973–1975), but not without introducing a somewhat disconcerting element into East-West relations
2. They demonstrated how the demarcation of spheres of influence can occur because of unforeseen circumstances, and thus how the Portuguese Communist Party, in its bid for power in 1974–1975,

adopted its political stance in affirming its continued loyalty to the USSR in an area traditionally under western influence

3. They made it possible for the German Federal Republic to take a more active political role—virtually inconceivable a few years earlier—and to establish a significant presence on the Iberian peninsula
4. They brought about the transition to independence for the Portuguese colonies in Africa, rapidly and without any plan, through the breakdown of the colonial administration, and thereby benefitted the development of Soviet-Cuban influence in Africa
5. They triggered an intense internal debate in Portugal concerning the major options open to Portuguese foreign policy, thus underscoring the importance of the international aspects of the revolution of April 25.

The Major Portuguese Foreign Policy Options

For Portugal, international relations constitute an essential affirmation of its status as a sovereign state. Unlike those of other nations, Portuguese foreign relations are not a secondary consideration, for they occupy a "geometrical" position—one that is centric in terms of measuring influences and relationships—in which they either strengthen or weaken national sovereignty. In the same way, it can be said that the revolution of 1974 was also given definition by the way its position in the international community evolved. It is not an exaggeration to state that the greater part of the world attention focused on the Portuguese experience stemmed much more from the general importance attributed to the final shape of Portugal's foreign policy than to any real interest in the effects of the regime's economic and social policy on Portuguese society.

At the time it was overthrown the dictatorship was proudly alone—as Salazar might have put it—or, more prosaically, the regime found itself with little, if any, support. In the process, it destroyed, in the worst conceivable manner, what was after all a poorly conceived strategy for universally affirming Portugal's individuality. Salazar had been hostile to the United Nations and had resisted its pressures to decolonize. He had sought allies in the solitary states of South Africa and Rhodesia to be able to pursue his colonial war in Africa.

In contrast, the program of the Armed Forces Movement (MFA) proclaimed a series of principles favoring peaceful foreign relations: in its conduct of foreign affairs, "the Provisional Government will be guided by the principles of independence and equality among individual states, non-interference in the internal affairs of other countries, and the defense of peace, through expanding and diversifying its international relations on the basis of friendship and cooperation." In a special opening line to this paragraph, it was stated that "the Provisional Government will honor its present treaty obligations."[1]

In a proclamation read to the nation on the morning of April 26, General Spínola, as president of the Junta of National Salvation, referred briefly to respect for international commitments, but said nothing more on the matter. Such international commitments, it was understood, included continued Portuguese participation in NATO.

The most significant foreign policy implications were to be found, however, in another point of the MFA Program, where it is stated that the provisional government will establish "the basis of an overseas policy conducive to peace."[2] There the new regime confronted the great problem of decolonization, which would have a decisive influence on Portuguese life during the entire revolutionary process.

The establishment of diplomatic relations with the Soviet Union was effected quite easily. Relations with the Eastern European countries, with the exception of Albania, were normalized during the first months of the revolution. It was also possible to reestablish contact with the majority of African countries, and with the Third World in general. This was a task which the first several provisional governments accomplished to their satisfaction. The normalization of diplomatic relations with the People's Republic of China did involve some difficulties, which were not resolved until 1979, but the delay by the Chinese was unnecessary considering the unilateral recognition accorded to the People's Republic by the Portuguese government in January 1975, which acknowledged Peking as the sole representative of China. Several Arab and African countries also showed themselves to be reluctant to extend diplomatic recognition to Portugal—being worried, on the one hand, about the internal situation in Portugal, while being suspicious of the decolonization process on the other.

That widespread liberalization of Portuguese politics, however necessary, did not come to constitute a strategy for international relations, if one understands the term "strategy" to imply a choice of priorities. A better indication of Portugal's new strategy, perhaps, was to be found in the remarks of Mário Soares to the General Assembly of the United Nations in September 1974, when, as minister of foreign affairs, he took the opportunity to summarize some of the foreign policy orientations of revolutionary Portugal. In this declaration, loyalty to NATO, reinforcement of the Luso-Brazilian community, and closer relations with the United Kingdom, Spain, and the United States stood out just as much as the promise of defining a realistic policy vis-à-vis the countries of the Third World and active collaboration with the United Nations and other organizations of international cooperation—a type of collaboration that had been conspicuously absent during the previous colonialist and dictatorial regime.

Curiously, as a consequence of modifications brought about by the events of September 28 on the nature of the April 1974 revolution, the direction of Portuguese foreign policy became more confused and decision-making centers more numerous. Actually, indecision about both the type of regime to be established and the direction to give to decolonization encouraged competition among institutions, sovereign organizations, and individuals concerning the conduct of foreign policy.

The dispersion of its international contacts deprived the Portuguese state of a coherent global outlook for its foreign affairs. At the same time, these developments were seen by other states as an indication of greater openness to their interests. The whole process of foreign policy development became entangled in a deaf and mute battle over the major Portuguese foreign policy options.

While the official texts and public declarations were unanimous in the proclamation of the basic principles that were to govern the attitudes of the revolutionary government in the international community, there were forces that sought to redefine, or question, Portugal's traditional place in the international order. First of all, the Eastern European countries were presented as a viable alternative for trade and economic cooperation, should the internal evolution of the revolution lead to a break in Portugal's ties with the West. Such an illusion, based on a particular type of decolonization favorable to Moscow, would only have resulted in jeopardizing the realistic relations Portugal had established with that group of states—countries which were obviously incapable of fulfilling the alternative role. In the meantime, another option appeared: that of favorable relations with the Third World, especially with the countries emerging from Portuguese decolonization. This option had first arisen as an authentic metamorphosis from the anti-European approach taken by Salazarism; after the attempted right-wing coup of March 11, 1975, it served as a hindrance to, or a check on, the pro-Soviet tendencies of several high-ranking leaders. It was called in Portugal "the Third World option."

It was not until the First Constitutional Government took power in June 1976 that these diverse foreign policy proposals were superseded by a more global and complete conception of foreign policy: Portugal's European option was combined with the special relationship it enjoyed with other Portuguese-speaking countries, on the grounds that Portugal was essentially a European and Atlantic nation.

The Impact of Decolonization

We cannot understand the total significance of the different foreign policy approaches without referring to their implications for the process of decolonization then in progress. It had been evident for quite some time, and particularly since the emergence of the armed struggle in the colonies at the beginning of the sixties, that Lisbon was a prisoner of what was occurring in Africa. It can be said without fear of error that the dictatorship lived out its last twenty years searching for a solution to the problems in Africa—a solution it was incapable of finding. Lisbon, rather than being the capital of a colonial empire, was instead subjugated to it.

If we examine the MFA program and General Spínola's theses, we find that even after April 25 numerous and divergent forces were contesting the continuation of an integrated policy for Lisbon, Bissau, Maputo, and Luanda; the essential differences concerned the relative importance attributed to these capitals. Spínola was attempting to extricate Lisbon from the bind in which Salazar and Caetano had placed it, wanting to give it an important role in his project for a new federal community. Melo Antunes wished to see a nonaligned, tropical Luanda/Maputo axis emerge on which Lisbon would have to rely and, in a certain way, follow. Vasco Gonçalves gave encouragement to the more pro-Soviet theses of decolonization, in which Lisbon would fit into a "web" joined to Moscow via Maputo and Luanda.

It is appropriate at this point to ask what were the positions of the United States and the other Western nations at this critical juncture in Portuguese history. We can summarize by saying that they supported the efforts of democratic forces in Portugal to establish a liberal political regime, but that they showed themselves singularly unaware of the problems facing Lisbon with respect to decolonization. Generally speaking, Portuguese decolonization was viewed with sympathy by the Western nations, without their showing, however, any solidarity with the small nation then in the throes of a revolution.

General Spínola, president of the Republic at that time and therefore a well-qualified observer, provides an enlightening account in his book *País sem rumo* (Nation without aim) of his July 19, 1974 meeting with then President Nixon in the Azores. One can conclude from that account that Nixon was unaware of the problems facing Portugal in the decolonization process, and that he gave little importance to Lisbon's part in this process. The attitude of the Soviets appears to have been quite different, in that they directed their efforts in Lisbon toward influencing the advancement of independence for the Portuguese colonies in a way that would be most favorable to Soviet interests.

The isolation of Portugal during the decolonization process was a result of an erroneous assessment of the African situation by the Western countries, since it is evident that the Soviet Union was able to become involved in Africa after the independence of these nations. The negative combination of short-term egoism with a superficial assessment of the situation in Nixon's case had the effect, quite likely, of significantly weakening Portuguese influence in Africa. In short, the Portuguese decolonization process demonstrated conclusively the nonexistence of a Western policy regarding Africa. Yet the position of certain African countries clearly showed the need for a unique policy by Portugal in dealing with that continent.

Later relations between Portugal and Africa were in fact characterized by their distinctiveness and by the emphasis placed on bilateral relations between Portugal and the new African states. Their distinctiveness resulted from the idea that a democratic Portugal meant that future relations between Europe and Africa could be more innovative and mutually advantageous than these relations had been in the past, at least until the Lomé Convention.[3] The emphasis on bilateral relations grew out of recognition of the political and cultural differences between the Portuguese-speaking countries and the rest of the nations of Africa. Thus the results of decolonization, some of which are still unforeseen, had a marked influence on the delineation of Portuguese foreign policy.

Another decisive influence was the evolution of the internal socioeconomic situation, which profoundly affected the type of regime that was emerging out of the revolutionary process. Socioeconomic developments demonstrated that a small nation in the middle of Western Europe was able to determine its own evolution autonomously, resisting any possible foreign interference that was contrary to the will of the nation. Such autonomy indicated how important the internal social configuration was in the final resolution of the political crisis.

The Transcontinental Perspective

The revolutionary period formally ended with the ratification of the constitution in April 1976, and with parliamentary and presidential elections in April and July of the same year. The coming to power of the First Constitutional Government in July 1976 provided the opportunity for affirming a new direction in foreign policy. This was expressed in the program submitted by the government to the National Assembly—a program that showed an obvious preoccupation with demonstrating the truly complex nature of Portuguese foreign policy. The multiplicity of factors which had to be taken into account—such as

Iberian issues, and emigrant communities scattered throughout many countries in Europe, on the American continent, and in Africa—immediately gives us a feel for the transcontinental dimension of Portugal's international relations, then as now.

It is worth noting that Portugal's privileged position in the Atlantic, now increased by economic zones restricted to the Continent and to the Azores and Madeira islands, gives Portugal a vast and important area of maritime sovereignty intersected by major navigational routes, which imposes an obligation to participate in the Atlantic Alliance. Portugal's recent revolutionary experience has demonstrated the possibility of political, social, and economic transformation without the rupturing of either mutual respect or Western security. The United States discovered to what extent the Portuguese revolution could be important for the defense of human rights, and its solidarity has been evidenced by the financial aid put at the disposal of Portuguese authorities, especially since 1977.

In accord with the transcontinental perspective of Portuguese foreign policy, within which the creation of African-European solidarity has had a preponderant place, the First Constitutional Government showed great interest when invited to the Conference of Non-Aligned Countries convened in Sri Lanka in August 1978—an interest that was increased by the active participation of the new Portuguese-speaking nations of Africa. That government also was able to normalize relations with more than twenty of the nonaligned nations.

But the most important turnabout of all effected by the First Constitutional Government concerned the European option. The immediate effect of taking that option was the conclusion of several agreements with the European Economic Community (EEC) on September 20, 1976, at which time, as Foreign Minister, I had occasion to announce that Portugal was going to request admission to the community. Two days later I was present in Strasbourg to officiate at Portugal's admission as the nineteenth member of the Council of Europe.

The request for admission to the EEC, which was made on March 29, 1977 was preceded by careful diplomacy that culminated in visits by Prime Minister Mário Soares and the minister of foreign affairs to the capitals of the nine full members. Without a doubt, it was the most politically significant occurrence within the context of the government's European option. The request for membership was made on the basis of the following assumptions:

1. that the present community would be expanded (a point then under discussion)
2. that there would be an affirmative response from the EEC

3. that Spain would be admitted later
4. that a formal transition period of adequate duration would be allowed to enable Portugal to adjust to EEC rules.

Those assumptions which were open to confirmation (1 and 2) have by now been realized. Portugal is currently negotiating with the EEC in the expectation that those remaining (3 and 4) will be implemented. In any event, the country is operating under the assumption of future EEC membership.

Pursuit of the European option was never meant to signify the subordination of Portugal's policy of rapprochement with Portuguese-speaking countries—Brazil, Guinea-Bissau, Cabo Verde, São Tomé e Príncipe, Mozambique, and Angola. The equal commitment to the development of mutually beneficial relationships and to the utilization of the Portuguese language in international organizations remains. In short, after the presentation of the First Constitutional Government's program, the problem of Portuguese foreign policy options has been not so much one of conception, but rather one of execution.

Conclusion

All that has been said emphasizes the fundamental importance of the international aspects of the Portuguese revolution, especially in the period between 1974 and 1976. We can conclude that the April revolution marked the end of an attitude of indifference toward Portugal, and of the insignificance of Portugal in the evolution of Europe, in the North Atlantic, and in the world. The indifference and insignificance assigned to Portugal allowed the dictatorial regime to maintain a policy of isolationism in the context of the World War II world. After April 25, with the attention given by the great powers to the political struggle in Portugal and to decolonization, concern was focused on the possible worldwide strategic consequences of the Portuguese revolution.

This essay reflects the point of view of one who, through a ministerial position in the First Constitutional Government and other experience, has had an in-depth look at the international aspects of the Portuguese revolution. It is possible that this view needs to be expanded through collaboration and discussion with outside observers. In this regard, some themes for further reflection might be considered:

1. What new perspectives in the understanding of contemporary international relations does the Portuguese revolution open up?
2. What is the true degree of autonomy that smaller nations enjoy in determining their foreign policies?

3. What importance do internal factors have in determining the foreign policies of these countries?
4. What have been the effects of the Portuguese revolution on East-West relations?
5. What are the international consequences of the decolonization of the former Portuguese territories?

These are but a few of the questions raised by the Portuguese revolution which demand joint reflection.

Notes

1 "Programa do Movimento das Forças Armadas," in *Leis Fundamentais da República Portuguesa* (Lisbon, 1974), pp. 22–23.

2 "Programa," p. 23.

3 The Lomé Convention, which was completed on January 15, 1975 and signed in Lomé, Togo on February 28 that year, was a five-year trade and aid agreement negotiated between the European Economic Community (EEC) and 54 Atlantic-Caribbean-Pacific countries (referred to frequently as the ACP countries). Not only did it propose a plan for helping these developing countries to stabilize vital export earnings, but it also gave these countries duty-free access to the EEC for all manufactured and most agricultural products (ed.).

13 *Alex Macleod*

The French and Italian Communist Parties and the Portuguese Revolution

The eighteen-month period that constituted the revolution in Portugal coincided with a crucial moment in the evolution of the Communist movement in Western Europe, which affected in particular the French and Italian Communist parties. Given the important role played by the Portuguese Communist Party (PCP) in the revolutionary process, it would have been difficult for these two parties to ignore the Portuguese situation in the best of times. However, much more was at stake than simply lending support to a brother party. Portugal represented a test both for socialism in general and for the credibility of Western European communism in the months before the newspapers began to talk of "Euro-communism."

Less than seven months before the Armed Forces Movement (MFA: Movimento das Forças Armadas) gave the final push to an already tottering dictatorship the European left, and especially the Communist parties of France and Italy, had suffered a serious setback with the overthrow of the Popular Unity government of Salvador Allende in Chile. The French Communist Party (PCF: Parti Communiste Français), after more than ten years of campaigning, had committed the French Socialist Party to a common program, signed in June 1972, which bore resemblances to the strategy that had ended in disaster in Santiago on September 11, 1973. The Italian Communist Party (PCI:

Partito Comunista Italiano) had gone even further than the PCF in its support for the Allende regime, having long ago opted for the "parliamentary road to socialism." The presence of a strong Christian Democratic Party in Chile had given the Italian party an even greater interest in the outcome of the Allende experiment than the French party had. Neither the PCI nor the PCF could therefore afford a defeat for a revolution so much nearer home to them both.

During 1974 and 1975 Western European Communism was undergoing long-term changes which the Portuguese situation could retard, accelerate or possibly stem, depending on the actions of the Portuguese Communist Party and the reactions of those Communist parties most likely to share in power in their own countries. On the one hand, the international Communist movement was being transformed as the major nonruling parties began to reassess their own roles within it, and above all their relationships to the Communist Party of the Soviet Union (CPSU). Since 1956 the PCI had seriously questioned its traditional relationship with the CPSU, and in the late sixties the PCF also began to revise its ties with the Soviet party. The PCP remained well behind both of the other parties in its conception of the international Communist movement. On the other hand, the French Communists were following the example set by the Italians: they were changing the PCF into a mass party by opening its ranks more easily to new members, and were attempting to project a much more favorable image among the electorate.

Superficially the Portuguese revolution served as a mirror, bringing out the differences between the French and the Italian Communist parties and highlighting ambiguities which remained within the French party despite its claims to having changed. It is easy to point to the PCI's calls for caution and its public criticisms of the excesses of the Portuguese Communists, and to compare the PCI favorably with the PCF, which showed its true "Stalinist colors" by supporting Alvaro Cunhal even when his Portuguese Communist Party was displaying little regard for those principles of democracy that the French party was defending so vehemently at home. Yet this comparison does no more than beg the question. Since 1945 the French party had amply illustrated its rejection of the Leninist-type tactics adopted by the Portuguese Communists, as well as their tendency toward adventurism. Obviously the explanation for the different attitudes of the French and Italian parties must be sought elsewhere than in the PCF's hypothetical taste for a nonparliamentary path to socialism.

More than anything else, the Portuguese revolution revealed the different factors that contribute to the forming of policy within Western

Communist parties. In the PCF and the PCI the revolution clearly brought out the delicate balance which both parties must maintain between the demands of their respective domestic situations and those inherent in their membership in the international Communist movement. Against this background, this essay will first analyse the reasons why the two most important Western Communist parties adopted apparently different positions toward the role played by the Portuguese Communist Party in the Portuguese revolution. Since the international context within which the French and Italian parties acted influenced not only their positions but that of the Portuguese party as well, this analysis will be followed by a rapid review of the wider setting within which the three parties were acting between April 25, 1974, and November 25, 1975—i.e., from the fall of the Caetano regime to the attempted left-wing coup at Tancos, which sealed the effective exclusion of the PCP from power.

The revolution also contained a second series of lessons for those communist parties about to embark on the road of Eurocommunism—a strategy which was dependent on good relations among themselves and their socialist allies and rivals. At a time when the revolution was seriously threatened, the French and the Italian left showed themselves incapable of even minimum joint action or a common position toward a third party. In the long run, the acknowledged impotence of the united left proved to be the most telling result of the revolution for the PCF and the PCI, and therefore merits some reflection in its own right.

The PCF, the PCI and the Changing Portuguese Scene

Basically, the reactions of the French and the Italian Communist parties to the events that followed the coup of April 25, 1974 evolved as the different phases of the revolution developed. From the time of the fall of the Salazar-Caetano dictatorship to the attempted coup by General António Spínola with the "march of the silent majority" on September 28, 1974, both parties remained in general agreement, and sought to discover the exact nature of the process taking place in Portugal. They lent their support to the PCP which acted largely as a moderating influence in the first phase of the revolution. During the next period, which lasted until the abortive right-wing putsch of March 11, 1975, the Portuguese Socialist and Communist parties began to intensify their rival bids to lead the revolution. The PCP moved closer to the Armed Forces Movement, and forced a bill through the cabinet and the Superior Council of the MFA which gave the Communists control of the trade unions. This change brought out the first public divergences over Portugal in the PCI and the PCF.

The differences became more open and more clear-cut during the third phase, which ended in August 1975 with the ousting of General Vasco Gonçalves from the premiership of the short-lived Fifth Provisional Government—a government which was supported only by the PCP and its allies in the MFA. The third phase was a period of acceleration or radicalization of the revolutionary process that resulted in a defeat for the PCP. The Italians publicly criticized the Portuguese Communists for abandoning the parliamentary road to socialism and for allying themselves too closely to the MFA. The French, on the other hand, refused to condemn the PCP, defended many of its actions, and upbraided the Italians for openly attacking a brother party in its hour of difficulty. During the fourth and final stage of the revolution, from the end of August to November 25, the French and the Italian parties had no need to differ about a revolution that had failed, at least from the point of view of the Portuguese Communists; the PCF and the PCI showed more interest than the PCP in picking up the broken pieces of the revolution. The failure did not mean that Portugal had been simply forgotten or that it did not remain a bone of contention between the Italian and the French Communists. But by then the problem had been transferred to the left at large, and it was the general conception of Socialist-Communist relations that had become the subject of discord.

The Portuguese revolution raised a number of practical and theoretical issues for Western European Communists on which they tended to disagree in degree, if not in principle. Essentially it posed four questions. First: What is the nature of the revolutionary process in a Western European country, and can that process possibly assume relatively peaceful forms? Second: What constitutes an appropriate and acceptable means for defending a revolution? Third: How may the demands of a truly revolutionary process be reconciled with the principles of pluralism and freedom: Fourth: Do Communist parties have a duty to publicly criticize the actions of a brother party when its actions appear to contradict those principles which are upheld at home? Western European Communists were grappling with the problem of the practical meaning of revolution in a situation in which traditional Leninist tactics and strategy had largely lost their relevance.

The French Communist Party tried to avoid answering these questions directly by insisting on the obvious fact that Portugal was not France, by defending each party's right to adopt its own road to socialism, and by refusing to publicly condemn a brother party in the name of proletarian internationalism. This last point is important. The French party did not necessarily appreciate the general direction taken by the Portuguese party, though it strongly sympathized with the PCP's difficulties and saw resemblances to PCF positions at home in Portuguese voluntarism and the claim to a vanguard role. In a book published by the official PCF publishing house, Les Editions Sociales, in early 1976—i.e., once the revolution was dead—the French party criticized many aspects of the revolution, including the adventurism and the sectarianism of the PCP.[1] By then French Communist Party had put an end to its quarrel with the French Socialist Party, had gone through its Twenty-Second Congress, and had opted for an autonomist line within the international communist movement. Its criticisms could no longer harm the actions of its Portuguese brother.

For its part, the Italian Communist Party, long-time champion of the autonomy of each communist party, tended to measure the Portuguese situation in terms of its own conception of Socialism, or rather in terms of its own view of the growing body of general principles which were beginning to constitute a Western European Socialist model. In Italy the right wing and the Christian Democrat press, anxious to scotch the strategy of the historical compromise, seized upon all the mistakes of the Portuguese Communist Party to tar the Italian Communit Party with the same brush. The PCI was painfully aware of the strong connection between the success or failure of Socialism in Portugal and the prospects for Socialism in the rest of Western Europe. The PCF, however, pretended to remain blissfully insensitive to the wider implications of the Portuguese revolution for the rest of the Western Europcan left.

As the situation developed in Portugal, the disagreement between the Italian and French parties focused on several main topics: the Portuguese party's tendency to analyze events as though Portugal was a member of the Third World; the PCP's close alliance with the MFA; the consequences of the PCP's emphasis on its role as a vanguard party; the process of radicalization of the revolution; and the Portuguese Communists' oversimplification of Portugal's choice between fascism and their particular conception of Socialism.

During the first months of the revolution the French and Italian Communist parties limited their comments to general expressions of satisfaction at the fall of the oldest remaining dictatorship in Western Europe. Part of the reason for this circumspection lay in their more immediate domestic preoccupations; however, much of it also stemmed from their difficulties in trying to gauge the situation in Portugal. Traditionally they both mistrusted the army as an institution, which was equated in their own countries with the more reactionary elements of society. Such distrust explains why they tended to play down the role of the military in the overthrow of Portugal's old regime, claiming, for example, that the army had simply given "the final shove to a worm-eaten regime, hated by the masses, which had no support in the country."[2] Unlike the French Communists, the Italians never showed any enthusiasm for the alliance between the MFA and the PCP, and constantly called for a return to civilian rule as quickly as possible. Though neither the French nor the Italian parties considered an army to be an instrument of democratization over a long period of time, the PCF was much more prepared than the PCI to use an army to protect a Communist revolution in its early stages, and went along with the Portuguese party on this question.

The Italians expressed their particular concern over the tendency to institutionalize the MFA, especially after the attempted March 11, 1975 coup, and regretted the PCP's support of this process. They saw the dangers of creating dual sources of power—a situation they considered unstable and harmful to the revolution, which needed above all "an authority which is strong because it is democratic, i.e., based on a solid and extensive foundation of agreement."[3] The French, on the other hand, saw a positive side to the PCP/MFA alliance, and claimed that it represented a source of strength, not weakness; the two forces complemented one another and the revolution needed them both: "To advance the Portuguese revolution will have to borrow from the capital of consciousness accumulated by the Communist party. The forces of the people need, for their part, the militant and conscious guarantee of the Armed Forces Movement."[4]

In his later assessment Jacques Frémontier, the PCF analyst of the revolution, admitted that the Portuguese Communist Party had made a mistake in allying itself too strongly with the Armed Forces Movement, and thus had prevented the PCP from coming closer to the Socialists.[5] It is difficult to know whether this opinion represents second thoughts on the part of the French party, or the PCF's private view of the alliance at the time it was in effect. It should be remembered, however, that the PCF has rarely shown favor to uncontrolled adventurism.

Behind the Italian insistence on a rapid return to "normality" lay a much deeper concern. They worried about the Third World tendencies of certain leading elements within the MFA, which had also infected the PCP.[6] The French undoubtedly shared this concern but preferred to remain silent, indicating embarrassment over the Portuguese party's sense of perspective. Later Frémontier remarked that "the African or third-world illusion'' had done much ''to cause the Portuguese revolution to go off the rails.''[7]

The debate on the PCP/MFA alliance and the subsequent adherence to a Third World model that it implied did not raise immediate serious differences between French and Italian Communists. This was not the case with the question of the PCP's role in the leadership of the revolution. The French still clung to the traditional doctrine of the vanguard position which all Communists were purported to assume in a revolutionary situation. They therefore sympathized wholeheartedly with the PCP's claim to such a position among the Portuguese political parties, despite the ambiguity of its relationship with the MFA. The Italians, on the other hand, had long since adapted their interpretation of the vanguard of the proletariat by introducing Gramsci's concept of ''hegemony,'' and by their own version of an alliance strategy. The historical compromise, the latest edition of that policy, could hardly come to fruition if the party insisted on a clean-cut dominant position with the alliance. At the international level the Italians had been moving closer to Western Europe's Socialist and social democratic parties and could not allow the actions of the Portuguese Communists to destroy these efforts. It is by no means surprising, then, that the Italian Communist Party quickly reminded the PCP of the existence of the Socialists, and mentioned that the Socialist party already occupied ''a considerable place in Portuguese life, with [the support of] a large section of public opinion . . . and with the organizing work already begun.''[8] The Italians also based their attitude on what they considered a realistic assessment of the Portuguese situation before the elections of April 1975—an evaluation which led them to believe that the balance of forces did not warrant the PCP's optimistic estimation of its own importance.

The visit of French and Italian delegations to Portugal in November 1974 illustrated their different emphases and the different degrees of harmony that existed between the Portuguese Communists and their French and Italian counterparts. The French delegation was led by Georges Marchais, general secretary of the PCF, who reiterated his complete support for the PCP at a public rally held in Lisbon's Sports Palace. The Italians sent a member of the PCI secretariat, Ugo Pecchioli, who was a highly placed leader but not the general secretary. Unlike Marchais, the head of the Italian delegation went out of his way to meet representatives of other parties, including the Portuguese Socialists, whose relations with the Communists were already becoming more and more strained.

It is in their final communiqués that one finds significant differences between the French and the Italians concerning Portugal. In their joint declaration the PCF and the PCP stressed the "perfect agreement of both parties on all questions examined" and reaffirmed their solidarity. A key part of the document expressed their identity of views on the international Communist movement and their desire for unity "on the basis of marxism-leninism and of proletarian internationalism, in agreement with the principles defined in the Declaration of the Moscow Conference in 1969."[9] Since the Italian Communists had refused to go along with most of the Moscow document, the gap between the PCI and the French and Portuguese parties on a major question of policy was evident.

The PCI/PCP communiqué made no reference to any general agreement on all topics discussed, which leads one to suppose that their discussions had limits that both recognized. As for the question of relations within the international movement, the two parties simply expressed their "desire to contribute to the strengthening of the international communist and workers' movement," a phrase sufficiently vague as to be almost meaningless. At the same time, presumably at the insistence of the Italians, the text alluded to the PCI's contacts with "vast sectors of Portuguese politics,"[10] making it clear that the Italian party had no intention of restricting its Portuguese relations to the PCP. The French, on the other hand, never gave the impression then or at any other time that they would support directly or indirectly the Portuguese Communists' rivals.

A month later the French and Italian parties were to receive a practical test of their allegiance to the Portuguese party. In December the provisional Portuguese government of Vasco Gonçalves presented a bill giving the monopoly of labor representation to a single union, Intersindical, which was already much under Communist control. Understandably, the PCP welcomed such legislation; the Socialist Party of Portugal did not. In France most of the press and the political parties took the Socialist party's side on the issue. The French Communists, isolated within the political system since they initiated a polemic against the French Socialists in early October, felt no particular need to join the opinion of the majority. During January 1975 the official PCF daily, *l'Humanité*, published a series of articles sent by its special correspondent in Portugal, who presented the new measure in a favorable light. The Italian party, still at a relatively early stage of the debate on the historical compromise, first indicated its displeasure by restricting the information on the bill in its own paper, *l'Unità*, to that sent by news agencies, without attempting to defend the bill. Once the decision to adopt the bill had been ratified by the MFA and the provisional government, the PCI publicly denounced it. In an interview on television in late February, Enrico Berlinguer, general secretary of the party, acknowledged that the Italian Communists had a difference of opinion with the Portuguese over the question of Intersindical, but did not go into details. It was left to another PCI leader, Carlo Galuzzi, to explain that the party did not fully understand why the Portuguese Communists chose "to support the conception of a single union imposed by the law, something which is in opposition to our pluralist view. . . . [Pluralism] appears to us as an essential factor in a democratic process which is inseparable for us from the struggle for 'socialiam.'"[11] The events that followed the attempted right-wing coup of March 11 in Portugal brought the differences between the PCF and the PCI much more into the open.

The Impact of the March 11 Coup

From the viewpoint of the Italian Communist Party, the March 11 coup and the ensuing radicalization of the revolution could not have come at a less opportune moment. The PCI's Fourteenth National Congress, which was to debate and finally ratify the historical compromise, was scheduled for March 18, and general administrative elections lay only three months away. The congress had hardly started when it was announced that the Portuguese Council of the Revolution had suspended two far-left parties and the small right-wing Christian Democratic Party, whose leadership had been suspected of participating in the counterrevolutionary coup. The Italian Christian Democrats, who had sent a delegation of observers, (led by the arch-foe of the historical compromise, Senator Amintore Fanfani) to the PCI congress, seized this opportunity to officially withdraw their delegation on the grounds that the Italian Communist Party had refused to condemn such an antidemocratic act. The PCI waited until the end of the congress to give both the Christian Democrats and the Portuguese Communists its opinion on the latest developments in Portugal. Its spokesman on foreign affairs, Giancarlo Pajetta, had given a hint of what that opinion would be in a speech in which he compared the fall of fascism in Italy and Portugal: his party had followed certain basic principles, namely, the widening of the antifascist alliance and the maintenance of the democratic framework; from their experience Italian Communists had learned that in order to keep the framework of democracy and to struggle for national independence they must refuse to keep their party and their country "away from international political reality."[12] Though indirect in this speech, Pajetta's criticism of the PCP's actions constituted one of the central themes of the Italian analysis of the

Portuguese revolution's mistakes. It was left to Enrico Berlinguer, in his closing speech at the Congress, to explicitly condemn not only the outlawing of the Portuguese Christian Democrat Party but also the direction the revolution was taking.

The French Communist Party did not share the scruples of its Italian counterpart, and thought that on the whole the revolution was right to take precautionary measures against those whom *l'Humanité* called "the nostalgics of the old regime."[13] The French made no immediate mention of the position taken by the Italians, despite the presence of a journalist from the official PCF newspaper at the PCI congress. It took almost three weeks for the French party leadership to announce publicly that it did not agree with Berlinguer about the Portuguese situation and to accuse him of meddling in the affairs of the PCP.[14] The Italians immediately replied in an editorial in *l'Unità* that the respect of each party's autonomy did not prevent Communists from expressing "judgements on important events which happen in other countries and which preoccupy the workers and public opinion."[15] The incident went no farther, but with the development of the situation in Portugal other topics of disagreement soon appeared.

It would be fastidious to enumerate all the points on which the Italian and the French Communist parties continued to take opposite sides during the following five months. An analysis of their reactions to two of the most important Portuguese issues of the period—the elections of April 25, 1975, and the *República* affair—will suffice to underline their fundamental differences of approach.

Two Views of Portugal's April 25 Elections

Like the PCP, the French Communist Party mistrusted the possible results of an election called so soon in a country which had recently come out of 48 years of dictatorship. The French therefore welcomed the signing of the "platform of constitutional agreement" by the MFA and the six leading political parties—a platform which limited in advance the significance of the upcoming elections, and acknowledged the MFA's claim to the role of "motor of the revolution." The people would choose the members of a constituent assembly, not the members of a future government.

The Italians dismissed such a view as completely unrealistic. As Romano Ledda, special correspondent for the PCI theoretical journal *Rinascita*, pointed out, the campaign had mobilized too many people and had brought about such a confrontation that the importance of the event could not be ignored.[16] But the PCI, looking beyond the dynamics of the election campaign, insisted on the legitimacy that the results would give to all Portuguese parties, not just to the Communists and Socialists. In other words, the Italians hoped that the elections would supply the means for a return to a parliamentary-type regime and would result in the army being sent back to the barracks. Undoubtedly, the Italians also believed that the outcome would make the Portuguese Communist Party more realistic in its assessment of the situation and in its actions.

The election results, which gave just above 16 percent of the vote to the PCP and its ally, the Portuguese Democratic Movement, disappointed the French Communists, who had certainly hoped for a better showing for their Portuguese comrades. In their comments the French emphasized the ambiguity of the results and above all the equivocal behavior during the campaign of the main victor, the Portuguese Socialist Party. The French disappointment showed itself in the relative discretion that the party press demonstrated in its largely factual account of the results, and in the absence of any public declarations about the results by its leaders.

Clearly the outcome of the election corresponded with the hopes and expectations of the Italian Communists. *L'Unità* published two editorials congratulating the Portuguese people for having given massive support to democracy, and suggested that thanks to the conclusive success of the two main left-wing parties the revolution had a firm basis from which to proceed.[17] It was the Italian turn to show apparent naivety, given the strained relations between the Portuguese Socialist and Communist parties, which the elections had only exacerbated. Since naivety is not among the PCI's principal characteristics, one can only assume that it was advising the Portuguese Communist Party to heed the message of the results, and was also saying something to the Italian electorate, which was only one month and a half away from administrative elections. The Portuguese Communists took little notice of the warning, and in fact stepped up their bid to implant the revolution and to diminish the power of the Socialist Party.

Two Views of the República Affairs

The *República* affair, which came to the fore in the middle of May constituted another battle in the growing rivalry between Portugal's Communist and Socialists. In many ways it was decisive, and the PCP came out the loser.

Essentially, the suspension of the pro-socialist daily *República* by the Portuguese Council of the Revolution on May 20, after the printing staff had decided to occupy the paper's premises, began as an ideological difference over editing policy between the editors and the printers—all of whom were members of the Communist-controlled Intersindical, but *not* necessarily of the PCP. The issue was quickly transformed into a general debate over the principle of freedom of the press, and the Portuguese Socialist Party seized this opportunity to present itself as the injured party and to attack the Communists. The latter found themselves in a difficult position, brought upon them by the far-left majority in the printers' general assembly. Either the Portuguese Communists condemned the occupation of the newspaper and allowed themselves to be outflanked on their left—a situation no Communist party accepts easily—or they defended the occupation and left themselves open to the attacks of the Socialists. In view of the radicalization that had taken place since March 11, it was unlikely that the Communists could have chosen the former course without surrendering once and for all the civil leadership of the revolution to the Socialist party.

More than any other incident of the Portuguese Revolution, the *República* affair brought out clearly the intricate relationships between the domestic and international interests of the Italian and the French Communist parties. It broke out at the very moment when the French Communist Party proudly published a "charter of liberties," which was intended to confirm the party's total commitment to those basic civil liberties associated with Western democracies, and which the Italian Communists had already been defending for some years. Since on one level the *República* affair raised the problem of freedom of the press the PCF found itself in a tight corner, and in a situation that the French Socialist Party considered too good not to exploit. In Italy, with the June 15 elections looming ever closer, it was not the time for the Italian Communists to give free ammunition to either the Christian Democratic Party or the Socialist party (which rightly feared that it could suffer badly at the polls if it did not check the Communists' rising popularity). Within the international Communist movement, discussions concerning an upcoming Berlin conference of European Communist parties were entering a critical state, with the French and the Italians taking opposite positions on the role of the CPSU in the movement (see page 314).

The difficulty of the French Communist Party's position forced it to deal with the affair at two separate levels. On the one hand, it gave public support to the Portuguese Communists by attempting to minimize the importance of the event and to lay the blame for the deterioration of the political situation in Portugal on the Portuguese Socialists. On the other hand, the French Communists privately disapproved of the PCP's handling of the affair, but did not make their position known until after the event. The French Socialist Party, by standing solidly behind Mário Soares, the Portuguese Socialist leader, brought the problem directly into the French political arena, where it became one more element in the ongoing polemic of the French left.

The French Socialists had decided to back Soares after the leaders of the six Socialist parties of southern Europe (those of France, Spain, Portugal, Italy, Greece, and Belgium) met at Latché, France, at the end of May. Soares assured Mitterrand, the French Socialist leader, that the Socialist Party of Portugal wanted to follow a union of the left strategy. French support for the Portuguese Socialists then became a way of telling the French electorate that a Socialist party could both compete with Communists and form an alliance with them without yielding any significant ground.

Rather than get caught on the losing end of a debate about principles with the French Socialists, the French Communist Party tried to reduce the *República* affair to the dimensions of a labor dispute which the French and Portuguese Socialists were needlessly exploiting for their own ends. The most striking attempt to minimize the issue came from the PCF's leading union spokesman, Georges Séguy, who was general secretary of the Confédération Générale du Travail. After a short stay in Portugal at the beginning of June, Séguy announced at a press conference that in his view the affair constituted nothing more than "a case of a classic labor conflict."[18] This became the party's official line, but no other Western Communist party, except the PCP, bothered to publish Séguy's analysis. In fact, well before the visit of the French labor leader to Lisbon, an Italian union close to the communists—the Confederazione Generale Italiana del Lavoro—had issued a communiqué expressing its "intense preoccupation with certain recent episodes which, while threatening to aggravate the contradictions and to weaken the democratic forces, upset values such as political pluralism and freedom of the press which are essential in any democratic régime."[19]

It is interesting to examine the reasons why the French privately disapproved of the PCP's handling of the affair. The criticisms were addressed not so much to the questions of principle involved as to the tactical and strategic errors that had been made. Even Séguy admitted that one could "question the method" chosen by the printers. But it was two months after the event before the French Communist press made any mention of a mistake on the part of the Portuguese Communists. The theoretical organ of the PCF's central committee, *France Nouvelle*, acknowledged that it had been an error to attempt to remove *República* from socialist hands, and linked the incident to "the hardening of cleavages within the MFA and to the conflict of powers that it brought about."[20]

It was left to Jacques Frémontier to analyze the problem fully. In his view it had been a mistake to hand over the management of the paper to a workers' assembly which could so easily be manipulated.[21] However, he found that the affair reflected a more basic problem in the revolutionary situation: the left had been overrepresented in the media, giving a false impression of the balance of forces, misrepresenting the ideological debate within the country, and preventing the achievement of the ideological hegemony which every revolution demanded if it was to progress.[22] As for the role of the Portuguese Communist Party in the *República* affair, Frémontier made a severe indictment: "Perhaps it would have been more efficient, given the balance of forces, not to have offered the forces of reaction such wonderful pretexts to accuse the revolution of pure and simple theft or of brainwashing? . . . Perhaps it would have been more political, for the Communists, to have disassociated themselves clearly and firmly from those who multiplied provocations and adventures and who never stopped attacking them?"[23] In this passage, as elsewhere, the author echoed a frequent criticism leveled by the PCF at its Portuguese brother in private and by allusion. The Portuguese party had allowed itself to get involved in fruitless competition with the far left, and had therefore gone further than wisdom suggested.

Unlike the French, the Italian Communists squarely discussed the question in terms of principle, and did so very publicly. From the beginning of the affair the PCI had proclaimed that the principle of pluralism was at stake. The Italians strove not to be identified in any way with the actions of the Portuguese Communists, as was made clear in an interview given by Berlinguer to the noncommunist newspaper *Il Corriere della Sera*. The party's general secretary, listing the disagreements between the PCI and the Portuguese revolutionaries, included the *República* affair, claiming that the attitudes of the revolutionaries contrasted with "what we think about democratic freedoms, pluralism and alternating majorities," and adding that his party's conception of progress toward Socialism in democracy was "very different from the one which inspires the Portuguese Communists."[24]

A week later the Italian weekly *Europeo* published a conversation between Alvaro Cunhal and the journalist Oriana Fallaci, in which the Portuguese Communist leader expressed his general disdain for bourgeois democracy.[25] Since the conversation appeared in print only a week before the Italian elections, the PCI had to prevent the article from becoming valuable ammunition for its opponents. *L'Unità* immediately published an editorial by its director dissociating the Italian party from the views of the Portuguese Communists, and Berlinguer announced publicly that the article in *Europeo* represented a "vision which is profoundly different from the one we have."[26] Although Cunhal denounced the article for exaggerating what he had said, it can be safely assumed that the Italians were not convinced that the general tenor of the interview did not really reflect the thinking of the PCP.

Understandably, the *República* affair and the diverging stances taken by the two major Western European Communist parties had repercussions at the international level. The Portuguese Communists did not appreciate the attitude of the Italian party, and accused it of electoral opportunism. Cunhal administered a lesson in comradely behavior by waiting to comment on the Italian position until after the June 15 elections, at which time he accused the Italian Communists of not taking into account the effect their criticisms could have on the internal Portuguese situation—i.e., for reasons of electoral gain, the Italian party had objectively aided the enemies of the revolution. On the other hand, Cunhal wrote a special message to the French party, thanking the PCF for its "positions of fraternal solidarity."[27] The Italians remained unrepentant and maintained their right to judge in a "just internationalist spirit, without avoiding in any case an open and fraternal confrontation of criticism and self-criticism."[28]

During the summer of 1975 the course of the revolution changed dramatically. With the rise of more moderate elements within the MFA, supported by the Socialist Party of Portugal, the Communists and those who backed their conception of the revolutionary process became more and more isolated. The weakening of the PCP's position was highlighted by the outbreak of a series of anti-Communist riots in July and August in the northern and central regions of the country, which had shown little or no support for the Communists during the elections. This new situation changed the perspectives of the French and Italian Communists. It was no longer a question of debating the merits and demerits of the PCP's action; it became urgent to save as much of the revolution as possible. As we will see, when the Portuguese Communists began to be slowly but surely removed from positions of effective power after the summer of 1975, the parties of the southern European left were unable to come to any agreement on the practical steps that should be taken to defend the revolution. But first, it is important to understand what was happening to the French and Italian Communist parties during the revolution in order to appreciate both how much had changed within the left in France and Italy and the limits of those changes, which the Portuguese revolution made so apparent.

The PCF and the PCI in a Changing Communist Movement

At the time of the first months of the Portuguese revolution, the French Communist Party had been going through a major internal crisis, which could best be described as a "crisis of identity." At home it had been making a conscious effort to woo the so-called "new middle classes" of engineers, technicians, and executives. The campaign to enlist the support of these different social groups, or at least to neutralize their opposition to the party, consisted in playing up the strategy of a union of the left, in creating an image of a party attached to the values of cultural and intellectual freedom, and in opening its ranks to prospective new members and to interested observers. This effort was both a direct response to the PCF's slipping electoral support and to the challenge of the French Socialist Party, which had become completely revitalized since François Mitterrand had taken over its leadership in 1971. At the international level, the PCF had begun to reconsider seriously its relationship with the Communist Party of the Soviet Union and its traditional acceptance of Soviet and Eastern European-style Communism, which found so little favor with the French electorate.

These changes had provoked a deep internal debate, which had been sharpened by the results of the national presidential election in May 1974. In the election the French Communist Party had thrown its full support behind the candidate of the united left, François Mitterrand, who came within a hairbreadth of winning. Analysis of the electoral results indicated that the union of the left strategy had brought benefits almost exclusively to the Socialist party. The results of six by-elections for the National Assembly, held at the end of September 1974, confirmed this assessment. To head off criticism of the new path it had taken and to maintain internal party cohesion, the PCF leadership launched a bitter attack against the Socialist party in October 1974, accusing it of moving to the right; this campaign was to last for almost a year.

The polemic with the Socialists in France meant that the PCF had little choice but to support publicly the actions of the Portuguese Communist Party, especially when PCP relations with the Portuguese Socialists became increasingly tense. To do otherwise would have only provided ammunition to the internal critics of the PCF leadership and further endangered party unity.

In Italy, a fragile political situation could only strengthen the inclination of the PCI to adopt an attitude of prudence and moderation throughout the whole period of the Portuguese revolution. High unemployment and an annal inflation rate well above 20 percent reflected the vulnerability of an economy which had been shaken by the oil crisis of 1973. The bomb attacks of right-wing terrorists and a new phase of activity by the Red Brigades emphasized the endemic weakness of the Italian state. Finally, various spokesmen of the United States government clearly indicated that that country was determined to keep Communists out of any national Italian government.

It was also during the Portuguese revolution that the Italian Communist Party was trying to implement a new strategy, which had originated in the lessons it had drawn from the Allende experience in Chile. In a three-part article published in *Rinascita* in September and October 1973, Enrico Berlinguer had analyzed the failure of the Allende government and had concluded that for Italy to avoid the danger of a reactionary coup, supported by certain segments of the middle classes, Italy's Communist party must seek a "historical compromise" with the country's major party, the Christian Democrats. However, the Christian Democrats, still smarting from their defeat on the referendum on divorce in May 1974, and controlled during this period by their right wing, displayed little enthusiasm for a form of coalition which would mean sharing power with Italy's second largest party in terms of votes and its largest party in terms of organization and membership. The PCI was not about to allow the actions of the Portuguese Communist Party to upset a long-term strategy which depended on convincing a recalcitrant prospective ally and a wary electorate that it had nothing in common with either the methods or the view of society so strongly propounded by the PCP.

The revolution also had its repercussions within the international Communist movement, and brought out the diverging conceptions of "proletarian internationalism" held by French and Italian Communists. Traditionally the doctrine of proletarian internationalism implied recognition of the undisputed leadership of the world Communist movement by the CPSU and adherence to the Socialist model presented by the Soviet Union and Eastern Europe. For years the French Communist Party had paid mainly lip service to the supremacy of the Soviet model, but had almost always given its unqualified backing to the Soviet party's claim to leadership of the Communist movement. The PCF also interpreted proletarian internationalism to mean that a Communist party should always refrain from attacking a brother party, unless that party had infringed the rules of proletarian internationalism. Thus the French Communists resented Italian criticism of the Portuguese Communist Party, claiming that this constituted an unwarranted interference in the PCP's domestic affairs. The Italian Communists utterly rejected such a restrictive view of party relations, and suggested that they had both a right and a duty to "fraternal criticism" of another Communist party when its actions ran counter to the principles defended by the PCI.[29]

During 1974 and 1975, the whole question of proletarian internationalism became a vital issue in the Communist movement as the parties of Eastern and Western Europe prepared for the European Communist conference scheduled to be held in East Berlin in December 1975. This conference, which finally took place in June 1976, was seen by the Soviets as an instrument for reasserting their leadership over the international Communist movement. Initially this position was supported by the French, but it came under strong attack from the Italians, who advocated the right of each Communist party to act as it thought fit without taking its cue from the CPSU. In August 1975 it became clear that the French had suddenly decided to side with the Italian Communists in the debate over the content of the preparatory document for the conference. The reasons for this switch are by no means obvious, though it did represent an important step by the French party on the path it had been taking since the early 1970s.

The Soviets expressed their anger in a strongly worded article written by Konstantin Zarodov, chief editor of the Soviet-controlled journal of international Communism (known in its English language version as *World Marxist Review*), and published in *Pravda*. Without naming any party in particular, Zarodov attacked those who sought to drown communist parties in an "ideologically amorphous organization, in any type of union created according to the formula: 'unity at any price.'"[30] The rapid reaction of Georges Marchais showed that the cap fit. Within two days of the publication of the Zarodov article, the French Communist leader proclaimed at a press conference that his party's policies were made in Paris, not in Moscow, and that the PCF would only sign a preparatory document "if it corresponds to the policy of the French Communist Party."[31]

The immediate consequence of the PCF's change of sides was a return to a more cordial relationship between the French and Italian Communists—a relationship which had suffered during the period of public divergence (from January to August 1975) over the Portuguese revolution. By November 15, 1975, the two parties had signed a joint declaration in which they announced their agreement on a series of principles that were to form the basis of Eurocommunism.

The rapprochement between the PCF and the PCI did not mean, however, that the two parties really saw eye to eye over the fate of the revolution in Portugal. With the downfall, at the end of August 1975, of the government of General Vasco Gonçalves, which was made up almost entirely of representatives of the Portuguese Communist Party and its sympathisers, the PCP had been effectively dislodged from power. For three more months the Portuguese Communists attempted to exert pressure on the government and on the MFA. Then an ill-organized uprising of far-leftist paratroopers at Tancos on November 25, 1975 gave the PCP's opponents the opportunity they had been waiting for to clip the wings of the Portuguese Communist Party once and for all by implicating it in the preparation of the last-ditch stand of those who thought that the revolution had slipped too far to the right. During those three months a more open debate on Portugal took place among the parties of the southern European left. This debate reflected the changed climate in the relations between Socialists and Communists in France and Italy, but it also emphasized the fundamental differences that remained.

The French and the Italian Left after the Fall of Gonçalves: Agreement to Disagree

Throughout the period from April 25, 1974, to November 25, 1975, the Western European socialist and social democratic parties, in contrast to the Communist parties, found little difficulty in giving their full backing to the Socialist Party of Portugal. The presence of important Communist parties in France and Italy added a complicating factor to the attitude that the Socialist parties of the two countries could adopt toward Portugal, especially as in both countries the Socialist parties advocated either tactical or strategic alliances with the Communists.

In France a move was being made by mid-1975 to overcome the deep divisions in the left which had appeared since the PCF had launched its anti-Socialist campaign in October 1974. The three partners of a leftist alliance—the Communists, the Socialists, and the small left-wing radical movement—met in mid-August to discuss their differences. Little progress was made, however, and they could only register their disagreement about Portugal, restricting themselves to declaring a mutual preoccupation with the anti-Communist riots still raging in the north and center of that country.

As we have seen, the Portuguese situation had provided the French Socialists with an opportunity to demonstrate their capacity to resist any Communist onslaught on an important question of principle. But the French Socialist leader, François Mitterrand, also had problems of internal discipline to solve. The Socialist party's left wing, which constituted about 25 percent of the membership, had begun to criticize the unconditional support for Mário Soares that the leadership had publicly professed since the *República* affair in May 1975. The pressure on the leadership of the French Socialist Party was compounded by the attitude of the majority in the Socialist International to which it belonged. Dominated by the West Germans, the British, and the Scandinavians, this official body of the international Socialist movement disapproved of alliances between Communists and Socialists. Furthermore, West German Socialists had strongly committed themselves, both politically and financially, to aiding the Socialist Party of Portugal. To relieve the strong pressures from home and abroad the French Socialist leadership played a delicate balancing act, which consisted of taking a hard line toward Portugal's Communists and of maintaining its loyalty to the union of the left policy in France. In practical terms, this meant that the French Socialist Party could talk with the PCF about Portugal, deplore anti-Communists excesses, and get involved in any attempts to reach a compromise between Communists and Socialists in Portugal, but without condemning or criticizing publicly the Portuguese Socialists.

The French Communist Party, which had been subject to a very different set of pressures than the Socialists, reaped benefits from its unwavering support of the Portuguese Communist Party. It had reassured party militants that despite changes within the party, it remained true to its fundamental principles. At the international level, the constant show of solidarity with the Portuguese Communists, which continued right up to, and beyond, November 25, 1975, probably made the switch to the Italian position during the preparatory stages of the Berlin conference more palatable to the Soviets.

In Italy, relations between Communists and Socialists had not been affected by the Portuguese revolution, since there had been so little that they could disagree about. The Italian Socialists had little reason to antagonize the PCI. That the Italian Socialist Party represented a force on the decline was confirmed by the administrative elections of June 15, 1975;[32] it had been part of the coalition government led by the Christian Democrats, and had gained little from the experience. The Italian Communist Party, which had been winning ground as the leading party of the opposition and was now actively pursuing the strategy of the historical compromise, had no desire to see the decline of the Italian Socialist Party accelerate: a further weakening of the Socialists' position would make the historical compromise much more difficult to achieve, since the Christian Democrats would be even less inclined to negotiate with a sole representative of the Italian left. Moreover, the

PCI leadership still had to contend with an important segment of the party membership which had accepted the historical compromise with great reluctance, and which still preferred a strategy based on a solid Communist-Socialist alliance.

The growing tensions within Portugal during the summer of 1975 gave the two Italian parties an opportunity to publicize a rapprochement beneficial to both sides. On August 15, 1975, the Italian Communists and Socialists issued a joint appeal to the democratic parties in Portugal to come to an agreement based on "the recognition of the popular representation as it was expressed during the vote for the constituent assembly."[33] This was a purely verbal operation: no attempt was ever made to mobilize public opinion in Italy or abroad to defend the Portuguese revolution.

The most telling illustration of the limits of left-wing unity in southern Europe came with the reactions of the Communist and Socialist parties to a proposal made by Mário Soares at the end of August 1975. The Portuguese Socialist leader called for a meeting between the Communists and Socialists of France, Italy, Spain, and Portugal, ostensibly to discuss both the worsening situation in Portugal and the more general question of the means for "advancing together toward socialism."[34] Such a conference would have exerted further pressure on the Portuguese Communist Party at this critical time by emphasizing its isolation within the European left. It is difficult to believe that Soares seriously hoped or wished to achieve anything more substantial.

The leader of the Socialist Party of Portugal pursued his idea further in October by sending out official invitations to the other seven parties concerned. Not surprisingly, the Portuguese Communist Party declined the invitation. Alvaro Cunhal, the PCP's general secretary, explained why in an interview with the official weekly of the French Socialist Party, *L'Unité*, by declaring that while the Portuguese Socialists "were not trying to solve the concrete problem of the march toward socialism in our country with the Portuguese Communists, they want to go and discuss this problem at the international level with other Communist and Socialist parties."[35] The French Communists, undoubtedly wishing to show more degree of flexibility to the rest of the French left without reneging on their commitment to the PCP, announced their agreement with the proposal "in principle." They hedged their acceptance by refusing to discuss any common approach toward strategy, on the grounds that the differences among the four countries concerned precluded any possible coordination of strategy.[36] The French Socialists, of course, had given an unqualified yes.

As for the Italian Communists, they had shown an immediate interest in the project and had published an official acceptance even before the invitations had been sent out. For the PCI the proposed conference represented a further step in its general policy of bringing the Communist and Socialist parties of Western Europe closer together. The Italian Communist Party paid little attention to the ambiguity of the whole exercise, perhaps because it knew full well that neither the French nor the Portuguese Communists would let the meeting take place. Clearly the question of Portugal was not uppermost in the Italian Communists' thoughts; without even mentioning the Portuguese situation, Enrico Berlinguer explained to the French Socialist weekly that the conference "could allow a useful discussion of the problems of the struggle for socialism in Western Europe."[37]

The Soares proposal can hardly be termed a lost opportunity for the European left, since it was not presented in a way that could have led to the slightest hope of success. Rather, it reflected the state of division within the left at that time, and showed that even at a moment of deep crisis the divergences of outlook and interest could not be surmounted, despite the heavy price of failure.

Conclusion

The debate over Portugal contained all the seeds of the ambiguities of Eurocommunism. In the final analysis, each party evaluated the situation in terms of its own interests and not in terms of the future of Socialism in Western Europe. The Italian Communist Party discussed the Portuguese revolution and the questions of principle that it raised partly because the domestic political scene prevented it from acting otherwise. In doing so it was able to clarify its positions on certain vital issues, and asserted the priority that it attached to its domestic interests over the restrictive demands of the international Communist movement, as interpreted by the Communist Party of the Soviet Union and its supporters. For the French Communist Party a different set of principles was at stake. It found much greater difficulty in solving the contradiction between its adherence to the international movement and the needs of the internal French situation. To a certain extent a different set of pressures produced a different series of answers. The Portuguese revolution clearly showed that despite the convergence between the French and the Italian parties which had become evident over the previous five years, they remained very different and could react in strikingly dissimilar ways.

Notes

1 Jacques Frémontier, *Portugal: les points sur les i* (Paris, 1976).
2 Jean Lévy, "Le Portugal a l'heure de la liberté," *France Nouvelle*, May 14–21, 1974, p. 21.
3 Romano Ledda, "L'anomalia del caso portoghese," *Rinascita*, March 18, 1975, p. 18.
4 Jean Gacon and Henri Nédélec, "Comment se construit la démocratie," *France Nouvelle*, April 21–27, 1975, p. 18.
5 Frémontier, *Les points*, p. 87.
6 An extract from an editorial in *l'Unità* sums up the Italian position on this point: "By its complex social articulation, its political and geographical configuration, its economic relations, its historical traditions, the international framework within which it is situated, the links between its political forces and those of other countries, there can be no doubt that the prospects for Portugal are to be seen in the orbit of Western Europe; and within this same orbit one must then consider the forms and methods of a possible development in the direction of socialism." (Luca Pavolini, "Ancora sul Portogallo," *l'Unitá*, July 29, 1975).
7 Frémontier, *Les points*, p. 25.
8 Ennio Simone, "La via dei comunisti portoghesi," *l'Unità*, July 7, 1974.
9 For the complete text of the PCF/PCP communiqué, see *l'Humanité*, November 14, 1974.
10 For the PCI/PCP declaration, see *l'Unità*, November 22, 1974.
11 Interview with Carlo Galuzzi published in *L'Espresso*, March 9, 1975, p. 26.
12 Speech of Giancarlo Pajetta, in *XIV Congresso del Partiti Comunista Italiano, Atti e Risoluzione* (Rome, 1975), p. 480.
13 *L'Humanité*, March 20, 1975.
14 In a television interview with Georges Marchais; see *l'Humanité*, April 9, 1975.
15 *L'Unità*, April 9, 1975.
16 Romano Ledda, "Portogallo: l'ora del voto," *Rinascita*, April 9, 1975, pp. 5–6.
17 See *l'Unità*, April 27 and 28, 1975.
18 *L'Humanité*, June 4, 1975.
19 *L'Unità*, May 22, 1975.
20 *France Nouvelle*, September 1, 1975, p. 20.
21 Frémontier, *Les points*, p. 157.
22 Ibid., pp. 169–170.
23 Ibid., p. 168.
24 *Il Corriere della Sera*, June 1, 1975.
25 Oriana Fallaci, "La parola a Cunhal," *Europeo*, June 13, 1975, pp. 40–42.
26 *L'Unità*, June 11, 1975.

27 *L'Humanité*, June 4, 1975. Cunhal's comments on the PCI were published in *l'Unità*, June 24, 1975.
28 *L'Unità*, June 24, 1975.
29 See, for example, the editorial by Giorgio Napolitano, "L'internazionalismo del PCI," who explained that the PCI had deliberately chosen to view the Portuguese situation" in the light of our 'positions of principle'" (*Rinascita*, April 4, 1975, p. 3).
30 K[onstatin] Zarodov, "Leninskaia strategiia i taktika revoliutsionnoi borby," *Pravda*, August 6, 1975.
31 *L'Humanité*, August 9, 1975.
32 In the elections for the Chamber of Deputies in May 1972, the PCI took 27.1 percent of the vote and the PSI 9.6 percent. In the administrative elections of June 1975, the PCI share of the vote rose to 32 percent and that of the PSI to 12 percent. (*Le Monde*, June 23, 1975).
33 *L'Unità*, August 15, 1975.
34 *Le Monde*, August 23, 1975.
35 *L'Unité*, October 17–23, 1975, p. 19.
36 George Marchais in *L'Humanité*, October 23, 1975.
37 *L'Unité*, October 24, 1975, p. 18.

14 *Paulo de Pitta e Cunha*

Portugal and the European Economic Community

Three countries of southern Europe are involved in the second enlargement of the European Economic Community (EEC)—Greece, Portugal, and Spain. Their applications for full membership, in accordance with article 237 of the EEC treaty, were presented in June 1975, March 1977, and July 1977, respectively.

A treaty establishing an association between Greece and the Community was concluded at the beginning of the sixties. It provided for the setting up of a customs union, the harmonization of agricultural policies, and financial support for the economic development of Greece.

Portugal, one of the founders of the European Free Trade Association (EFTA), is linked to the European Economic Community through a free trade agreement for industrial products. The initial agreement of July 1972—to which were annexed tariff reductions concerning a number of Portuguese agricultural exports—was revised and enlarged in 1976. It makes provision for dismantling trade barriers affecting exports from the EEC to Portugal, and includes such new areas of cooperation as technology, financial aid, and the positions of migrant workers.

Between Spain and the Community a simple preferential agreement was established in 1970. It contains some tariff concessions, but falls short of a free trade system.

In the case of Greece, application for EEC membership developed logically out of the treaty of association. That treaty was frozen by the Community, except for features directly concerned with trade, during the period of the military dictatorship in Athens. But for Spain and Portugal, the step toward membership amounted to a major change in the course of their external relations. This was made possible by the establishment in both countries of democratic pluralistic regimes of the Western European type.

Following the conclusion of successful negotiations between Greece and the EEC, the conditions for the accession of the new member were laid down in a treaty signed on May 28, 1979. However, negotiations on the Portuguese and Spanish applications are still at a preliminary stage, after having been officially launched in October 1978 and February 1979, respectively.

As far as Portugal is concerned, the discussions held so far have aimed at identifying the main problems arising from the formation of a customs union and a common external policy, as well as working out specific matters pertaining to the European Coal and Steel and Atomic Energy communities. While negotiations regarding agricultural policy have begun, the problems are so great that no immediate large-scale changes will be made. In the meantime, the Portuguese government has applied for changes in the schedules of the free trade agreement currently in force, and has received approval for them. They include a temporary freeze on dismantling tariffs at the stage presently reached, and making use of the clause which allows for the protection of new industries beyond the time limit of December 31, 1979. The EEC Commission has prepared an extraordinary program of support for the Portuguese economy, taking into consideration the fragility of its structures and the need to improve its chances of withstanding the shock of competition that will come with economic integration.

There is no doubt that the application to join the Common Market reflects a far-reaching decision taken by the Portuguese government with the overt support of the three largest political parties (Socialist, Social Democrat and Centrist), and without direct opposition from the Communists. At the basis of this decision was a major political factor: the desire to strengthen pluralist democratic institutions. These institutions had been set up in Portugal in the aftermath of the April 25, 1974, military uprising, during a period of intense social and political disturbance, in which either a Communist takeover or an authoritarian military regime seemed not unlikely.

The severing of ties with former colonies—especially Angola and Mozambique—contributed further to Portugal's firm intention of sharing a European destiny. Because there is a strong consciousness of national identity among the Portuguese, great enthusiasm for participating in the building of a European political union of a supranational or federalist character could not be expected. But having returned once again to the European fold, and brought to a close the long historical cycle begun with its overseas discoveries, the Portuguese are now in need of a new national purpose. Given present circumstances, it seems entirely natural that the search for a new destiny should lead to involvement in the process of Western European integration. Not only does Portugal belong to Europe geographically, geostrategically, and historically, but it must also face the economic realities of trade relations, capital, and labor transfers—all of which are focused primarily on Western Europe.

The alternatives entail considering less realistic and more extreme solutions: adoption of a model of total isolation (along the lines of Albania), absorption into the Third World bloc of countries, or maintenance of the present pattern of external economic relations, as reflected in the free trade agreement with the EEC. But the latter choice—a type of purely commercial or "negative" integration—is not suited to a country like Portugal, because it lacks the concept of solidarity inherent in the process of integrating economies with different levels of development. Considerable attention is being given in the EEC to the problem of Portugal's choices, and is reflected in the concern, shared by various European institutions and the governments of the Nine, about the capacity of Portugal to withstand successfully the impact of accession. Any solution short of full membership in the EEC would fail to meet Portugal's need to define a new sense of national purpose and to consolidate its democracy. These needs are at the core of the decision to apply for EEC membership.

From an economic standpoint, joining the EEC may prove to be a catalyst for the sorely needed rationalization and modernization of crippled industrial and agricultural structures. Whether Portugal becomes a member of the European Economic Community or not, a great effort must be made to overcome Portugal's economic retardation so as to extricate the country from its present low standing among Western European nations. By entering the EEC—provided the concern for solidarity in the process of integration is honored—Portugal will become the recipient of real resources transferred into the country through Community funds. Moreover, it is expected that fixing of well-defined timetables for the process of joining the Common Market will turn out to be an incentive for the modifications needed in the structure of the Portuguese economy.

As a result of world expansion, which seemed relentless during the sixties, and the reservation of unsophisticated overseas market for Portuguese exports, the basic fragility of Portuguese economic structures remained somewhat concealed in the period before April 1974. Stagnation in agricultural production, duality in the area of manufacturing (whereby a very large proportion of small-sized enterprises, incapable of surviving competition, were maintained through protective measures), disorganization in the public administration, and the inefficient management of the economy (within the framework of a market-oriented system subject to inconsistent state interference, and not endowed with the traditional growth factors of a capitalist environment) constituted fundamental shortcomings. The unfortunate concurrence of the Portuguese revolution with the 1974–1975 world crisis dramatized these weaknesses.

The effects of sharp deterioration in trade, the loss of guaranteed overseas markets, and the sudden disruption of productive structures under the attack mounted against the foundations of the private enterprise system combined to create an alarming situation for the Portuguese economy. These events imposed severe stress on Portugal's external accounts, and a stabilization program had to be devised and negotiated with the International Monetary Fund. This program, however, through restraining domestic expenditures, made the objective of catching up with the EEC economies all the more difficult.

The decision by the Portuguese government to apply for Common Market membership, taken in the first quarter of 1977, was the consequence of neither a well-prepared, conscious effort to appraise the costs and benefits of joining the EEC, nor of a full discussion of the implications of such a major step for overall Portuguese policy. It seemed to be taken for granted that the European option would only bring advantages for Portugal: acceptance by the Nine as the next EEC member was seen as a sort of prize awarded for the establishment of democracy in Portugal. Such an oversimplified way of looking at the problem of accession to the Common Market must, of course, be supplanted by a more conscientious and precise endeavor to assess the consequences of EEC membership. Once the present round of negotiations is completed and a more distinct picture regarding involvement in the Common Market is obtained, the Portuguese people should be called on to ratify—through their political representatives or, if constitutionally feasible, by means of a referendum—the historic decision to join the European Economic Community. The importance of this issue cannot be minimized.

Application for membership on the basis of article 237 of the EEC treaty precludes the possibility of establishing an intermediate stage between the present situation and accession itself. Thus there is no possibility of a kind of pre-accession period that could be used to prepare Portugal for the transitional period. In considering the second enlargement of the Community, the European commission proposed a common pattern for the three applicant countries: the negotiation stage is to lead directly to the accession of the new member, which is from then on entitled to participate in the institutions and policymaking operations of the Community; after a transitional period of five to ten years, counted from the time the treaty of accession enters into effect, the newcomer must conform entirely with the rules and policies already adopted by the Community, which constitute the *acquis communautaire*. This requirement was originally laid out at the time of the first enlargement, which involved the United Kingdom, Denmark, and Ireland. It was renewed in the formal statement issued by the EEC Commission on May 23, 1979, on the accession of Greece, and it will be maintained for Portugal and Spain.

Yet provision for a transitional period and the devising of ways and methods for the Community to provide assistance are of fundamental importance to Portugal. Unlike Greece and Spain, Portugal achieved political democracy during a revolutionary period in which a Western type of economic system was called in question and a somewhat original path toward Socialism proposed. For this reason we can easily understand why those who praise especially the realization of a socialist experiment are diffident about Common Market integration. Although the EEC treaty declares its neutrality with regard to property ownership (public or private), the dynamics of integration will no doubt require the approximation of the Portuguese economic system to that of all the other member countries—basically, a private enterprise, market-oriented system.

The predominance of "negative" over "positive" forms of integration into the EEC reinforces further the requirement of conformity. All of this is reflected in the formula for an "internal market," which has as its objective the suppression of barriers among the member states. The guiding principle of the Treaty of Rome is undoubtedly the regulation of the economy through the action of market forces. Although a type of "market socialism," and hence a possible alternative to private enterprise, can be conceived, it is true that all existing pluralistic democracies (including the Nine) are not only market systems, but also specifically private enterprise systems of the "mixed" type that include a relatively large public enterprise sector. A general requirement for Portugal's joining the EEC is to make the logic of the Portuguese economic system compatible with the logic of the Common Market.

Economic Problems Facing Portugal in Joining the Community

The Portuguese government declared at the beginning of negotiations with the EEC that no particular difficulties would be found in establishing a customs union for industrial products, in adopting a common trade policy, and in accepting the obligations of the Community to the rest of the world. As far as the free movement of goods is concerned, this opinion is based on the assumption that the application of the present free trade agreement will by itself have the same effect. Nevertheless, Portuguese experience with previous free trade agreements, even those including special schedules allowing for a slower pace for the dismantling of tariffs on Portuguese imports, does not seem to justify the optimistic view of the government.

In spite of nonreciprocal advantages contained in annex *G* to the EFTA convention, no spectacular modifications in the structure of Portuguese industry were achieved during the sixties. Similar advantages were included in the free trade agreement with the EEC, but the potential they represented for the modernization of the Portuguese industrial structure was again not realized. The latter agreement entered into force at the beginning of 1973, and its normal application was frustrated by the revolution. Portuguese private industry was faced with the basic problem of survival in the midst of turmoil in 1974 and 1975.

Renegotiation in 1976 of the 1972 agreement, and the new advantages consequently granted to Portugal, revealed the incapacity of Portuguese industry to comply with its obligations as initially laid out. Provisions were made for abolishing ahead of schedule EEC tariffs on Portuguese industrial exports, and the time limit for dismantling of tariffs in Portugal was extended. Recent applications made by the Portuguese government for a freeze in the process of dismantling the still-existing barriers only confirm the difficulties Portugal is having in reaching the free trade stage.

The adoption of the EEC external tariff will create problems for Portuguese industry because of differences in the structure of present Portuguese tariffs (established mainly on a specific basis) and the *ad valorem* principle followed by the EEC. In some industries the switch to the new system may imply a sizeable loss in the degree of protection that is assured by present Portuguese tariff structures.

As far as Community obligations affecting third countries are concerned, the assumption of EEC membership by Portugal may create serious problems for some Portuguese industries. These may arise because the EEC has adopted an attitude typical of highly developed countries in the granting of general preferences and in relations with the African-Caribbean-Pacific countries included in the Lomé Convention.[1] In the enlarged Community Portugal will lose the flexibility it now enjoys in setting up commercial relations with countries outside Europe. In some cases Portugal's present position as a beneficiary of the systems of general preferences granted by the highly developed countries will change as it moves into the much less comfortable position of a donor.

The adoption of a common agricultural policy will also involve difficulties for Portugal. But it must be acknowledged that subjection to Common Market rules in this sector will not hamper the desired policy of completely restructuring Portuguese agriculture, for this is a fundamental task whether or not the country joins the EEC. The necessity of complying with Community requirements in this area may even be a positive factor in making possible the quicker introduction of suitable policies. For some agricultural products Portuguese prices are at present fixed centrally through the action of state monopolies.These arrangements are inconsistent with Common Market schemes. In other areas of agriculture existing market procedures are defective and obscure.

As a result of the progressive devaluation of the escudo, agricultural prices in Portugal are now generally lower than the institutional prices of the European Economic Community. Serious attention should be given to the consequences of this exchange rate policy because the price difference for Portuguese agriculture may cause strong inflationary pressures in the Portuguese economy and adversely affect local living standards—although the difference will be favorable to the local farmer and, at the outset, to Portugal's balance of payments position.

Modifications in land ownership in the "operational area" of Portuguese agrarian reform—the region south of the River Tagus—have created a new type of collective structure of property to which there is no parallel in any of the EEC countries. While a portion of the land that was earlier put under collective ownership has now been returned to its owners, that part which remains under collective ownership has neither clear-cut legal status nor links to the state, since the government has refrained, mainly for political reasons, from participating in the internal organization or decision-making process of such units. With public subsidies restricted and their survival linked to their ability to function in a market economy, it is questionable whether such structures will remain viable enterprises, capable of withstanding competition and complying with Common Market principles and regulations.

Their present difficulties in the Portuguese economy suggest an even more difficult future in the context of Europe at large.

In sharp contrast to the land tenure situation in the south, where large land units predominate, the average size of privately owned farms in the remainder of the country is extremely small. There are few, if any, of the conditions necessary for supporting technical improvements and the introduction of new mechanized processes. In this regard, contributions from the guidance section of the EEC agricultural fund may be of great importance to Portugal.

For the present, the possibility of further emigration of Portuguese labor to the EEC countries should not be discounted. In negotiating Greece's accession, a longer period (seven years) was decided upon before introducing the free movement of labor than was the case in other areas, where the average transition period has been five years. The establishment of a timetable on this point is central to the essence of a common market. It will certainly be one of the most delicate problems in negotiations on Portugal's candidacy.

In the field of taxation, the main modification to be made during the transition period is the adoption of the value-added tax (VAT) in place of the single-stage, wholesale sales tax presently used in Portugal. This change will certainly create a number of problems for the tax administration, where some somber signs of disarray can already be perceived. The extension of the transitional period and the acceptance of several exemptions from rules established in the EEC's VAT system may facilitate Portugal's adaptation to the new system of indirect taxation.

It should be made clear that in becoming a member of the Common Market Portugal aims to bridge the gap between its economy and those of the highly developed countries of the EEC, instead of perpetuating the present disparity in levels of development and standards of living. But even with correct policies and adequate external support, this is a long-range objective. The main economic advantage Portugal may expect to obtain by joining the European Economic Community is external support for resolving structural problems in its economy. Such support will take the form of exceptional aid given with the objective of reducing regional disequilibrium in the enlarged Community.

In its formal statement (May 19, 1978) on the Portuguese application, the EEC commission stressed that the accession of Portugal would create the risk of aggravating the country's internal economic difficulties by eliminating enterprises that have not yet reached the necessary level of development, and by increasing regional differences. It concluded that accession to the Common Market should not be carried out in such a way as to imply too heavy a sacrifice for Portugal. This challenge can be met successfully only if, on the one hand, a huge effort is made in Portugal to clarify the rules of economic organization and to overcome structural deficiencies, and if, on the other hand, there is an adequate transfer of real resources together with technological support on the part of the Community.

As the Portuguese Gross Domestic Product (GDP) corresponds roughly to only 1 percent of the total product of the EEC, the impact of the accession of such a small national economy will not pose any particular problems for the Nine. But we must take into consideration the still rudimentary stage of the organization of EEC regional policy, and the lack, for the time being, of any real distributive effect in the Community budget. The McDougal Report on the role of public finance in European integration correctly warns of the risk of an unequal sharing of the advantages resulting from integration if appropriate guarantees are not forthcoming.

It must be acknowledged that over the next few years Portuguese economic structures may well be incapable of absorbing considerably larger transfers of real resources from Community funds than those which result from existing mechanisms. But the question remains whether the EEC at its present stage of organization possesses the capacity to fulfill efficiently its task of redressing differences in per capita national income. Moreover, such a task is essential if an adequate policy for regional equilibrium, covering the whole area of the Community, is to be established.

The progress recently achieved in the EEC in the area of "positive integration" may complicate the task facing the candidates for membership, since it implies further requirements of harmonization in economic conditions and policies. At present, because of its higher inflationary propensity and the consequent adoption of a sliding parity for the escudo, Portugal cannot consider becoming a member of the European Monetary System.

Nevertheless, the process of integration in Western Europe is not stagnant, despite a number of setbacks. The June 1979 direct elections for the European Parliament were a step on the way toward European union, even though no further powers have been granted to that institution. Over the next ten to twelve years new political and economic events may well influence the European Community and stimulate its further evolution. Accession to the Common Market, through the representation it assures in the institutions of the Community, is a condition for active participation in the decisions that will shape the destiny of Europe.

Post–1974 Political Changes Constraining Portugal's Admission

Constitutional Factors

As a consequence of the ambiguous character of the 1976 Portuguese Constitution, not only have different interpretations of its contents been put forward, but its interpreters have reached opposite conclusions as to the type of society it admits or advocates. The constitution reflects the influence of different ideologies and the impact of the political and social disturbances that occurred while it was being drafted.

Some constitutional interpreters who are in favor of the Western model of society have sought to demonstrate how, in this fundamental Portuguese law, aspects pertaining to the obligatory construction of socialism are subordinated to the "open power" concepts inherent in the Western democracies. They cite those clauses which assert the principle of political democracy (article 3, paragraph 3, and article 9, subparagraph *b*), affirm the participation of political parties in the organization of political power (article 47, paragraph 1), proclaim the right of opposition and the principle of democratic representation (article 117), and refer to pluralism as the fundamental principle of political organization (article 2).

Making an effort to free the constitution from constraints arising out of its Marxist origins, these interpreters extend their analysis to the field of economic organization. They maintain that the socialist model is subordinated to respect for the principle of efficiency. For example, they cite the presentation of the major functions of the state in article 81 (subparagraphs *a* and *b*), which refer to the increase in well-being, to economic stabilization, and to the full utilization of productive resources; they go on to note that reference to the promotion of socialist relations does not come until subparagraph *n*. They also call attention to references made in several clauses which show a regard for the Western model of society: the acceptance of private enterprise (article 85, paragraph 1), the limitation of the compulsory nature of the economic plan to the activities of the public sector (article 92), the very description of tax categories in terms of a system typical of market-oriented economies (article 107), the possibility of the private ownership of means of production (article 89, paragraph 4), the task of the state in assuring balanced competition among enterprises (article 81, subparagraph *j*), the possibility of devolution to the private sector of companies indirectly nationalized (article 83, paragraph 2), and the guarantee of land ownership for small and medium-sized farmers within the framework of agrarian reform (article 99, paragraph 1).

Such clauses are no doubt of great importance, forming the basis of a constitititutional practice which is being developed and which leans toward the Western type of economic society. But the series of clauses reflecting the direct influence of collectivist Marxist thought is much more impressive, dominating the exposition on economic organization and economic rights and penetrating into the area of fundamental principles. Moreover, even the above-mentioned clauses, which serve as the basis for a moderate reading of the constitution, contain an element of weakness. Private enterprise is restricted to a point where it has only an instrumental function in "collective progress." And the main objective of article 85 seems to be to establish the principle of refusing the access of private persons to certain sectors of economic activity, and to foresee state intervention in the management of private companies.

In the description of the three sectors of ownership of the means of production, article 89 attributes a residual role to the private sector, as a form of historically precarious property allowed only in the "transitional stage toward socialism." Even the economic plan and the tax system, while allowing some features of Western type economies, are subordinated to the overall objectives of "building up a socialist economy" (article 91) and "progressive and effective socialization of the economy" (article 105).

We may conclude that the consideration given to private enterprise and the private sector of the economy in the Portuguese Constitution is marked by a spirit of suspicion and provisional tolerance. The only clause that allows for the return of nationalized enterprises to private hands (article 83, paragraph 2) stresses the exceptional character of such an action, and action that would depend on a lack of interest in the integration of the enterprises in question into the public and cooperative sectors, and that would be conditional on the modest size of the enterprises involved.

In the lengthy enumeration of the main economic tasks of the state (article 81), no reference is made to creating incentives for the private productive sector. The dominant theme is socialization by means of nationalization, and repression of the formation of private monopolies (subparagraph *g*). Protection of private enterprise is granted only to those firms of small or medium size (subparagarph *j*). Unequal treatment of employers and workers is the logical consequence of this attitude to the private sector: "entities representing economic activities" are mentioned only once (when reference is made to the National Planning Council, in article 94, paragraph 2), but "organizations of the working classes," also mentioned in the same clause, receive full, separate consideration in the sections dealing with economic rights and the functions of the state.

The Socialist principle is so strongly emphasized in the constitution that it invades the area of the organization of political power through the requirement imposed on the government of implementing a policy in accordance with the objective of "building up socialism" (article 185, paragraph 2). Such a clause, without parallel in any Western constitution, poses the fundamental question of how to reconcile the democratic principle—which by its very nature allows for alternative of political programs—with the pursuance of the unidirectional objective of socialism. The clauses of the constitution that deal with the private sector and its involvement in productive activity show an unfavorable bias against this form of ownership, for it is placed under the threat of total extinction in the event of completion of a Socialist program. As the constitution regulates only the present-transitional stage toward socialism", it is obvious that such completion depends upon further expressions of popular will through elections. But the implicit admission that the suppression of private sector control over the means of production will be the outcome of successful pursuance of the objective of building up Socialism (solemnly proclaimed in article 2) surely intensifies the climate of discomfort in the private sector that has already arisen as a result of restrictions imposed on its activities.

Although the Portuguese Constitution does not embody an unequivocal concept of Socialism, it seems clear that a dominant role is conferred on the principle of collective appropriation of the means of production. This concept of socialization, which is reflected in the economic organization of the Soviet Union and Eastern Europe, and which strongly diverges from the reformist and moderate content of the social-democratic experience of the West, is apparent not only in the solemn proclamations in article 10, paragraph 2, and articles 50 and 80, but also in the emphasis placed on nationalization as the outstanding method of attaining the objective of socialization: nationalizations accomplished after April 25, 1974, are indeed referred to as "irreversible achievements of the working classes" (article 83, paragraph 1).

The constitution seems to be in favor of the worker-management type of socialism (article 90, paragraph 3; article 61, paragraph 2; article 83, last part of paragraph 2), but such a solution appears to be the outcome of a process that begins with state ownership of productive activities and that identifies itself with the Socialist model after the transitional state. The combination of the "revolutionary process" with the principle of collective ownership (article 10) and the declaration that social and economic organization is based on the "power of the working classes'' (articles 2, 80, and 90, paragraph 2) are along orthodox Marxist lines. This intent is not diminished through the quli-fication of that process as ''pacific'' and of that power as ''demo-cratic.''

We may conclude that the Portuguese Constitution displays a model of social and economic organization which, although temporarily allowing for the coexistence of public and private sectors, encourages the ''development of socialist production relations and the transfor-mation of the system of capitalist accumulation'' in order to create conditions for the exercise of the ''democratic power of the working classes,'' in accordance with the objective of instituting a ''classless society.'' Such a model is probably not very differnt from the Eastern European systems that existed during the period of revolutionary take-off (before the adoption of the Soviet model), in which private initiative was still tolerated. The nature ascribed to economic organization in the Portuguese Constitution thus is not adjustable to a market-oriented economy with a strong private sector, which is the system in the EEC countries.

It is, of course, possible to argue that the socialist principle is not incompatible with the allocation of goods and services through the market. But it is clear that the underlying principle is an all-embracing, strongly dogmatic view of socialism achieved ''through the transforma-tion of capitalist relations,'' in which the market principle comes under suspicion and the administrative regulation of the economy becomes paramount. Nowhere in the constitution can be found a single favor-able reference to regulation through the marketplace. On the contrary, state control is constantly mentioned, even in the field of international economic relations; article 110, for instance, seems to anticipate a regime of state controlled external trade.

While liberal principles predominate in the treatment of individual rights, liberties, and guarantees, in the field of economic organization and rights there is a clear disequilibrium between the emphatic ex-pression given to the principle of collective ownership and state control and the attitude of mere tolerance of or contempt for a market-oriented, free enterprise economy. Consequently, any attempt to find in the Portuguese Constitution a positive framework for the type of economic organization found in the EEC countries can only be frus-trating.

The Experience of the Economic System

But the political constraints placed on Portugal's economic system since 1974 that reduce its compatibility with the EEC are not limited to the new constitution. In addition to the text of this fundamental law, the experience of the economic system since 1976 must be considered in order to appraise Portugal's degree of conformity with the system in effect in the Common Market countries.

On introducing its program (August 1976), the First Constitutional Government stresssed the subordination of the establishment of socialism to the popular will, as shown in free elections. However, the collapse of the "traditional system" (based on the "blind forces of the market and profit") was taken for granted because of the extensive socialization of basic sectors in the economy. The program contained certain measures aimed at dynamizing the private sector, but its major emphasis fell on the consolidation of the public sector (although not as a result of further nationalizations) and on the development of the "social property" sector. Tolerance for a mixed economy was clearly characteristic of this "transitional period," as a step toward a fully socialized economy. Moreover, the "irreversible" nature of the great reforms brought about by the revolution (agrarian reform, nationalization policy, worker control) was underlined. No thought was given to the embarrassing question of how to reconcile the democratic and pluralistic principle with the alleged impossibility of a reversal in the process of socialization, and the prospect of accession to the EEC was not even envisaged.

The programs of subsequent governments reveal an entirely different attitude. The Second Constitutional Government (February 1978) defined the Portuguese economy as "a mixed economy with competitive coexistence between the institutional sectors," thereby assuring a synthesis of the planned and market mechanisms suited to the country's future membership in the EEC. Strong emphasis was placed on the major role of private enterprise in the development of the economy, and an effort was made to present the public sector as comparable, in its relative size, to its counterparts in other Western European countries. The Fourth Constitutional Government (November 1978) (the program of the Third is not relevant to this discussion, as it was rejected by Parliament) maintained and reinforced the orientation of its predecessors in favor of the conformity of the Portuguese system to the model of economic organization in Western European countries.

But while the Second Constitutional Government seemed to be satisfied with the degree of approximation to the mixed economy model already attained, the Fourth showed in its program a clear intention of introducing new measures. These were incorporated in order to clarify a still-blurred picture of the economic structure and to create the conditions necessary for the mobilization of private enterprise for the development of the economy. Specific mention was made of the reconversion of public enterprises; concerned with entry into the Common Market, the government expressed the view that these should be subsidized for social reasons only. Since these government programs were not rejected by a parliamentary vote, they acquired the character of major "political acts." Furthermore, the principles and orientations contained therein exerted a strong influence on the practical aspects of the Portuguese constitutional system.

As regards economic organization, the line followed by all successive constitutional governments (including the First, notwithstanding the rhetoric used in its program) showed a clear tendency toward adjusting to the mixed economy model of Western Europe. The more ideologically inspired features focusing on a "transitional stage" on the way to socialism were left somewhat by the way. But such developments have not followed a linear pattern; they have not been free of fluctuations reflecting the tensions prevailing among social and political forces in Portugal. For example, in the weeks preceding the fall of the Fourth Constitutional Government, Parliament adopted certain legal measures—in the context of nationalized enterprises and agrarian reform—which showed some degree of return to a socialist-collectivist way of thinking.

It is certainly too early to infer from the above-mentioned tendency toward the mixed economy model that a *contra legem* set of practices has been firmly established. And it cannot be concluded that practical economic developments have in effect abrogated the constitutional clauses which point to an economic system inconsistent with those prevailing in Western European countries, and logically incompatible with the Treaty of Rome.

Bearing in mind the implications of accession to the EEC, a strong case can undoubtedly be made for a revision of the constitution that aims at eliminating the present discrepancies in economic organization. Provided, however, that the tendency toward the mixed economy model is maintained and that a reversal of this now-dominant orientation does not occur, such a revision does not appear to be a formal prerequisite for accession to the Common Market. It is preferable to conceive of the revision as a necessary consequence of the movement taking place in Portugal toward a mixed economy model.

True, the public sector sharply increased its share in the nation's economic life following the nationalization of privately owned or mixed companies in the fields of banking, insurance, oil refining, chemicals, the production and distribution of electrical energy, mineral extraction, shipyards, transportation (railways, roads, airways, and marine), the mass media, tobacco, and beer. But this process was brought about by a shift in political forces that occurred in March 1975. The original intention was no doubt a radical transformation of the country's economic organization: movement toward collective ownership of the means of production was intended to be a decisive step in the direction of a centralized economy, in accordance with the strategy of a total break with a Western type market economy. Although the containment of this revolutionary process near the end of 1975 did not represent any spectacular reversal of the nationalization measures already taken or still under way, it did lead to the consolidation of the enlarged public sector and to a government commitment to refrain from further nationalizations.

Containment of the revolutionary process also established a new basis for a system of management for public enterprises, which allowed for their integration into the framework of a market economy. Such a system was established by *decreto-lei* (decree-law) no. 260/76, of April 8, 1976. Even though its preamble employs the Marxist rhetoric of the constitution, this law applies to state owned enterprises the same rules regarding conditions of competition that affect privately owned firms.

Notwithstanding its new dimensions, Portugal's public sector is not particularly large. The contribution of public enterprises to GDP was only 15 percent in 1976—a percentage that is not uncommon by Western European standards. In Italy, for example, where the state has developed significant enterpreneurial activities, their contribution to gross fixed capital formation is higher than it is in Portugal.

On one point, however, there is a remarkable difference between the public sector of the economy in Portugal and that of the EEC countries. While in the latter banking is basically a private sector or a dual (private/public) sector activity, in Portugal—as a consequence of the first wave of nationalizations—banking institutions became a defacto monopoly of the state. Only those banks with foreign-owned capital were exempted. The decision to exempt foreign-owned capital from nationalization measures, not only in the banking sector but also in the main industrial fields, was a distinctive feature of the Portuguese revolution.

As foreseen in article 85, paragraph 2 of the constitution, Law no. 46/77 of July 8, 1977, defines the basic sectors in which private enterprises are not permitted. One of these areas is the banking sector. Also included in the list of "fully closed sectors" are insurance, electricity, gas and water supply, and railways. At the same time, this law establishes a separate list of industries in which some types of association with private capital, especially foreign-owned, are admitted.

It has been argued that in the aftermath of the nationalization of the banks the economic system in Portugal has undergone a fundamental alteration. Such a statement implies that Portugal has actually adopted a new model that is suited to the transition to socialism, and which is no longer compatible with the market-oriented, private enterprise economy existing in Western European countries. Such reasoning is based on a hasty analysis of the consequences of the nationalizations process in Portugal. The intended departure from the pattern of Western economies did not proceed. Instead of becoming an instrument for the full socialization of the economy, nationalizations tended merely to constitute a partial solution within the framework of a market-oriented economy which continued to operate; private enterprise still dominates the manufacturing industries, with about 90 percent of the production, and more than 90 percent of the labor force and of the total exports in that sector). Moreover, no significant merger involving banking institutions has taken place so far. The prerevolutionary pluralist scheme has been maintained, and the lack of progress toward the monopolistic formula (which has been adopted in several branches of heavy industry and in transportation) may facilitate the opening-up of the banking sector in the future. By the end of 1980 there were signs that this may be a distinct possibility.

Certainly, the exclusion of private ownership from banking activity in Portugal may create some problems related to the "freedom of establishment" provided for in articles 52 and 53 of the EEC treaty. According to one interpretation of the principle of nondiscrimination embodied in the EEC treaty, any member state is entitled to reserve to public enterprises whole sectors of its economy. It is true that such sectors become inaccessible to residents in other member states, but what matters is equality of treatment between natives and foreign nationals within the Community. (This view was adopted in a decision of the EEC Court of Justice in *Costa* v. *Enel.*) In my opinion, the principle of nondiscrimination should be considered in a larger setting; in particular, it should be understood as implying a reasonable degree of reciprocity in the treatment accorded by each member state to the nationals of other member states.

From this standpoint, a violation of the nondiscrimination rules would appear evident if Portugal should insist after accession on reserving the banking sector to public enterprises, while all other member states maintain a system in which banking activities can be performed by private and public entities alike. Such a practice might even be considered discriminatory (in the sense of a kind of reverse discrimination). To deny private enterprise of national origin access to the sector in question, while admitting the continued existence of old established foreign-owned enterprises—as now happens in Portugal—would discriminate against private enterprise in Portugal.

In its formal statement on the Portuguese application to the EEC, the Commission stated that the extent of the public sector in Portugal and the nationalizations carried out do not conflict with the Treaty of Rome, "provided Community regulations in the various fields are complied with." Notwithstanding its neutrality on systems of ownership in member states, the EEC Treaty is directly concerned with the conformity of state enterprises to the rules on competition. Paragraph 1 of article 90, although somewhat redundant, expressly applies to such enterprises the general clauses regarding competition (articles 85 and 86).

At a minimum, then, further clarification of the Portuguese economic system will be required as a condition of Common Market membership. And it is virtually certain that Portugal will be required to renounce those practices which in a systematic way favor public enterprises that are in competition with their private counterparts. The fields of taxation and credit policy will be particularly affected. In short, not only will Portugal have to face up to serious economic problems in considering EEC membership, but it will also have to make major adjustments in its new governmental control over the economy.

Notes

1 See note 3 in chapter 12 for a brief summary of the Lomé convention (ed.).

15 *Douglas L. Wheeler*

The Revolution in Perspective: Revolution and Counterrevolution in Modern Portuguese History

But, even deeper than the literary artifice of Sebastianism, the Sebastianist conscience remains [in Portugal] as a permanent and instinctive condition. The myth of "the king who must return on a foggy morning" still today is a commonplace in our language. No one says this with seriousness, but the sentence is many times used to refer to an untranslatable state of the mind that consists of believing that that which one deeply desires cannot happen, but at the same time hopes that it will happen independently of our effort and without any connection with our responsibility.
—José Hermano Saraiva, *História Concisa de Portugal*

Historical Perspective vs. Presentism

The Portuguese revolution of 1974–1975 was not the first revolution to have failed in this old country, nor, in all probability, will it be the last. For following every "revolution," or movement of fundamental political importance that brought change, however temporary, there have been countermovements or counterrevolutions. Periods of great stress and bursts of energy have been succeeded by eras of more inertia and stagnation. Since the fall of the centralizing dictator, the Marquis of Pombal, in 1777, other revolutions of whatever sort have been opposed by counterrevolutions that undid the work of the previous movement. For the purposes of this essay, modern Portuguese history will include these revolutionary and counterrevolutionary movements and the associated political regimes: the Pombaline regime, 1750–1777, and an ensuing reaction; the 1820–1822 revolution, and the Constitutional Monarchy of 1834–1910; the Republican revolution of 1910, and the first Republic, 1910–1926; the dictatorship of 1926–1974; and the revolution of 1974–1975 that is the subject of this volume, and its aftermath up to late 1981.

Historical perspective has been lacking in analyses of what happened in Portugal in 1974 to 1975 and thereafter. In both the media and in more than a few scholarly discussions the study of historical example and precedent from revolutions in Portugal's long past has been surprisingly slight. In view of the fact that Portugal as a society, among all the southern European states between Lisbon and Istanbul, has the deepest attachment to the past and is the oldest nation-state in Western Europe with unchanged frontiers (its birth as a nation-state was in 1140), the presentistic biases of contemporary commentators are particularly inappropriate.

Whatever the explanation for this characteristic of the analyses of the 1974–1975 revolution, many treatises emphasize a welter of events and a few immediate causes, but eschew a look into history for longer-range, general causes. That discussions of the events of 1974–1975 in newspapers and on radio and television ignored recent Portuguese history is not surprising. Nor is it unexpected that scholars ignorant of Portugal's history and political culture, and intent only on untangling some months' events, would forget that Portugal has had previous revolutions. Then, too, there was the shock effect of the military coup of April 25, 1974, a surprising event which appeared to create a sudden chasm between the past and the present, and to impel Portugal without warning into the future.

Other factors are also responsible for the temporary triumph of presentism over genuine historical perspective. A significant portion of the material on the revolution that has appeared both in Portugal and outside has been either Marxist-Leninist in substance or in sympathy—that is, analysis dominated by exclusive attention to current socioeconomic conditions and class conflict. While history plays a role in this analysis, it is rigidly selective and can ignore causes which do not involve class conflict or dependency theory.

There is also a popular Portuguese movement, in reaction to the traumatic events following the 1974 coup, that ignores the recent past—the last decade or two—and looks to the nineteenth century and to the "ages of glory" of pre-1800 Portugal. Whether as an exercise in consolation, as vicarious emulation, or as entertainment, this reaction is most significant. For if it can tell us little about the immediate causes of post-1974 events and trends, it is most informative concerning Portuguese attitudes, beliefs, and behavior that are related to long-term causes. The evidence for the existence of this popular Portuguese reaction against probing the past to understand the present, and for the use of a popular history of "happier times" as a vast escape hatch (though, in fact, they were generally not happy at all), is abundant in the Portugal of the early 1980s.

Three examples can illustrate the tendency to escape the present.

First, the unusual popularity of a succinct history of Portugal—a best seller on an unprecedented scale for a public obsessed with reading novels and watching television: as of 1981, historian José Hermano Saraiva's *Concise History of Portugal* was in its sixth edition, with more than 75,000 copies sold. Also televised as a series of lectures, Saraiva's work concentrates on pre-1800 history. Second, there is a revival of interest in all of Portugal's nineteenth-century writers of note, and it is remarkable that they are all in print. The publication of new finds from great writers like Eça de Queiroz have generated intense public interest in rival editions and in dramatized versions for the theatre.[1] And third, there is a revival of interest in literature about travel and exploration in Portuguese Africa brought about by popular editions of classics—material which lay in dusty libraries even during the colonialist dictatorship of 1927 to 1974—and the cult of the epic poet Luís de Camões, whose death 400 years ago was celebrated with grand fanfare in 1980. Mention should also be made of the popularity of a multivolumed biography of Premier Salazar, as well as a growing cult of Salazar.[2]

While all of these factors help to explain why a professional historical perspective of the Portuguese revolution of 1974–1975 has been lacking among media analysts and the Portuguese public, they fail to help us understand why a number of historians' observations are infused with presentism, or why Portuguese political culture has been so often ignored as a factor. An important illustration of how a historian can ignore or neglect both a historical perspective and massive evidence in Portuguese political culture is found in a recently published paper which emphasizes immediate causes for the failure of the Portuguese revolution: (1) the leftists' neglect to remain allied with military radicals; (2) the crisis of African decolonization, especially in Angola; (3) Portugal's serious economic crisis and international pressures for moderation; (4) communist blunders; and (5) the effect of the 1975 constituent assembly election returns.[3] Toward the end of the article there is only a hint that political behavior and other tensions among elements of the Portuguese nation might have played a role in the failure. Ignoring the statements of Portugal's most astute observers, who subscribe to the idea of a Portuguese national character and a distinct political culture with deep roots in the past, the writer adds in an understatement, "In behavior and psychology, it is not yet clear how much really changed in Portugal, beyond the traumatic recognition, as revolutionary optimism evaporated, of the resilient power and divisiveness of class, regional, and personal antagonisms and jealousy."[4]

This essay will explore Portugal's modern history for a perspective necessary to understanding the problems of the Portuguese revolution of 1974 to 1975; if "the past is prologue," in the case of Portugal's greatest crisis of this century, a new prologue is required.

Four Historic Tensions in Portuguese Society

Richard Herr has suggested that there are three tensions in Spanish society which have encouraged political instability and the failure of liberal governments.[5] It will be useful to review four tensions of the same sort that have persisted in Portuguese society for more than a century and a half, because the evidence is substantial, more than seven years after the 1974 revolution, that these tensions not only persist, but played a significant role in the origins and course of the revolution, and that they help to explain its ultimate failure. The tensions are personalism, political and ideological factionalism, conflicting patterns of land ownership in different regions, and the conflict between Lisbon—the capital—and the provinces.

Personalism (modern, pessoalismo; *archaic,* personalismo)

Broadly, personalism is the predominance of individual or personal interests and actions over collective or national interests and actions. Personalism is manifested in politics and government on at least two different levels: the individual and the collective. On the individual level, the Portuguese often define personalism as "egoism" or "the vice of egotism," by which they mean that individual or self-centered interests prevail over the common good, and that personal interests conflict with civic-mindedness. This tension can be demonstrated with a range of cases, from those of petty bureaucrats and officials of the municipalities to those of the dictator, president, or premier of the country. Related to personalism at the individual level are an ancient pattern of patronage or clientelism, the small size of the society and the polity, and a dearth of leaders or activists. Also related is the tendency to "personal survival" or "situationism," whatever the regime in power; to survive in a country with a scarcity of resources, including employment, individuals will shift allegiances easily.[6] Personalism at the individual level has been reinforced by traditional Portuguese patterns of respect for masculinity and age.

Personalism at the collective or national level is the allegiance of the "political nation," of whatever size or however defined, not to issues or ideas or institutions, but to persons or personalities. At the mass level, personalism is a natural element of authoritarian rule, dictatorship, or one-man rule. In Portugal rule by kings or queens, or, after 1910, by presidents and premiers (including the dictator António de Oliveira Salazar), has been a common pattern. Popular history for the masses, whether describing the brief eras of more representative government or those under authoritarian prescription, often features "the great man" as a national savior or doer of great deeds. Personalism at the national level is demonstrated in folklore as well as in official circles and in scholarly treatises.

Related to this tension is a traditional phenomenon known as "Sebastianism," an atavistic, messianic form of popular nationalism which has roots in the sixteenth century, when Portugal's King Sebastian was lost during an expedition to Morocco—an event followed by the Spanish domination of Portugal (1580–1640). *Sebastianismo* is a kind of historic personalism which, despite its roots in earlier eras and its links with Portuguese Judaic messianism, has contemporary significance in Portuguese attitudes and behavior patterns. According to one of Portugal's most distinguished historians, Hermano Saraiva, Sebastianist feelings persist, and they can be interpreted as inimical to modernization and a sense of civic responsibility.[7] Sebastianism has been a feeling among groups of Portuguese—not simply the uneducated masses—that a person, a personal hero, a great man would appear miraculously to "save the nation" from the continuing national crisis (*crise nacional*).[8]

Political and Ideological Factionalism

As tensions, personalism and factionalism overlap, because to some extent personalism at the two levels discussed encourages factionalism. In both Portugal and Spain there has been a struggle between those holding differing ideas and concepts of how politics and government should be conducted: between those who desired liberal, parliamentary government and those who wanted authoritarian rule; between the clericals and the anticlericals; between republicans and monarchists; and between parliamentarians and presidentialists. Factionalism is the splintering of the "political nation" into small groups or parties that fight among themselves, and often fail to reach a consensus about fundamental issues.

The conflict that gives rise to factionalism may have its source in disagreement, dislike of personalities, or disputes about personal qualifications or issues. Infighting, bickering, and backbiting among Portuguese, on the individual level, have an ancient pedigree and are recorded in a vast literature. Sixteenth-century observers of the Portuguese scene mentioned *murmuração* (carping, backbiting),[9] and a criticism by the seventeenth-century sage, Father António Vieira, of "our disunity, our jealousy, our presumption, our carelessness and our perpetual concern for individual interests" is often quoted in discussions of fissiparous tendencies among his countrymen.[10]

At the level of national politics factionalism appears in an excessive fragmentation of political groups and parties, the instability of political parties—including frequent splits among parties—and the failure of coalitions of parties to endure or to remain stable. This tension has also worked against the strength of parties in opposition, and has weakened single parties which have achieved some dominance. The reasons behind such factionalism are various: ideological disagreements, personality clashes, opportunism, vested interests' demands, and the struggle for public office and its rewards.

Land Ownership Patterns, North vs. South

Differing patterns of land ownership in certain regions have also represented a major tension. In terms of land-ownership patterns, the Tagus River acts as a kind of dividing line between northern and southern Portugal. In general, northern land-ownership patterns are characterized by *minifundia*—small, uneconomical plots owned by small farmers—although there are exceptional subregional cases. Quite different is land ownership in the south (especially in the Alentejo province), where there are the *latifundia*—large estates owned by middle-class proprietors, some of them absentee, and worked by a poor, landless peasantry. Serious problems and conflicts have arisen from these land-ownership patterns: differences in the social and political attitudes of the northern small farmers who own some land and those of the southern landless peasants who have sought to acquire some of the land on which they toil; severe economic trouble in the areas of food production and employment; and pressures for a land-ownership revolution in the Alentejo, which have been exploited by both vested economic interests and rival political parties and unions.

The Capital vs. the Provinces

Miguel Torga, the poet, described this well-known and traditional tension as "a lack of harmony between the conscience of the country and of the capital."[11] There are other ways of describing the tension between hypertrophic Lisbon and the underdeveloped provinces which runs through so much of modern Portuguese history. It can be seen as an urban-rural conflict, or the attempt of Lisbon's urban elites, with their more progressive doctrines, to "civilize" or modernize the rural areas. It is also a conflict between a centralizing tendency characteristic of the seat of government, education, society, and culture and a struggle for decentralization by provincial elements—between "two Portugals."

Ever since Pombal's program of centralization in the eighteenth century, every political regime has attempted, at least at the time it assumed power, to grant greater autonomy to regions outside the capital. The attempts made to decentralize in 1910 to 1912, 1932 to 1936, and 1974 to 1976 largely failed, and even greater centralization followed. Among the aspects of this conflict are the scarcity of resources in a limited economy and the pressures for deciding how to make a fair division of those resources that exist. To some extent this tension, in which Lisbon as an urban, industrial, power center meets resistance to its policies and interests from other regions of Portugal, parallels the conflict in Spain between a less developed center and a developed, industrialized periphery.

Portugal's Political Regimes and the Four Tensions since the 1820 Revolution

Before we discuss the relationship between Portugal's revolutions, counterrevolutions, history post-1820 regimes, and the four tensions, it is essential to analyze the word *revolução* and associated political words as they are used in the Portuguese historical context. The word "revolution" in English, American, or even French historical experience usually means (in the political sense) a radical or fundamental change in political organization, as well as the overthrow of one government or system and its replacement by another.[12] During the period from 1870 to 1930, the most decisively formative period in Portugal's modern history, the Portuguese word *revolução* assumed a different meaning—a fact of real political importance. As military intervention in politics increased and coups became common events, *revolução* came to mean merely a military coup or insurrection and a change of government, rather than "fundamental political change." In common parlance, then, *revolução* did not imply a basic change of institutions, but only one more barracks action or *golpe de estado*. Although the word faithfully described what occurred during key changes of regime in 1820, 1834, 1910, 1926, and 1974, "revolution" usually described simple changes of government, the fall of cabinets, or attempted changes brought about by military "movements" organized by elements of the officer corps in league with political forces. The word *revolução* became corrupted within the urban political culture of Lisbon and Oporto, where more progressive doctrines were held, while in the other Portugal of the rural provinces the political vocabulary was different. To describe a "revolution" or seemingly fundamental change in political organization, words of provincial or rural origins were employed: *reviralho* (turnabout of politics), or *reviravolta* (political about-face), both words with roots in the vocabulary of the whirling, turning peasant dances of northern Portugal. It is significant that when referring to revolutionary threats from *oposicionistas*, regime spokesmen, including Salazar himself, often employed the provincial peasant vocabulary.[13]

The 1820 Revolution and the Constitutional Monarchy

The process that resulted in the establishment of a constitutional monarchy began with the 1820 revolution, which was sparked by a military coup and inspired by similar events in neighboring Spain. In a sense, the basic principle of the 1820 revolution was echoed in all subsequent revolutions: the popular sovereignty of the Portuguese "nation" was to replace the divine right of absolutist monarchical rule. The constitution of every historic regime since has included popular sovereignty as a guiding principle, and even the authoritarian New State (1926–1974) mentioned the idea in the 1933 constitution.

A functioning constitutional monarchy, however, was not established until 1834. This regime featured a political system of ineffective parliamentary government—what was, in reality, a pseudoparliamentarism. During most of the period between 1834 and 1910 the monarch enjoyed considerable power and played a central role in mediating among branches of government; with the 1826 charter as the dominant constitutional instrument, the monarch had the pivotal *poder moderador* (moderating power). Despite economic and social progress, the political system's stability disintegrated from 1850 to 1890, because it was based largely on artificial foundations: the general apathy of an illiterate peasant mass, and an increasingly centralized administration controlled by a narrow oligarchy. Periodic attempts at "regenerationism," or forms of national revival entailing progressive policies, were followed by periods of lethargy and inaction. The major political conflict at the national level concerned the division of powers between the executive and the legislative branches, between those who desired a strong executive or leader and those who wanted the Cortes, or parliament, to be dominant.

The four tensions assumed their modern proportions during this period. As the Constitutional Monarchy's artificial two-party system broke down after 1890, parliamentary government appeared almost totally discredited. Personalism and factionalism were the most obtrusive tensions present, and they were clearly demonstrated in the press and in Cortes debates, but the problems of land-ownership patterns and the cleavage between the capital and the provinces were also severe. Internationally and domestically, Portugal's economic and financial condition worsened in the final decades of the Monarchy, and thinkers called for drastic solutions to the national crisis of that day.

The First Republic

Enemies of the Monarchy and of the Church, the Republicans called for the establishment of a republic which would modernize the country by returning authority and power to the provinces and towns, political reform, developing the colonies in Africa, and secularizing and reforming education. When the Republicans assumed power after the revolution of October 5, 1910, they inherited a deadly legacy from the Monarchy: a poor, largely agrarian country with illiteracy at 79 percent and a long tradition of ineffective government.

The first Portuguese Republic (1910–1926) attempted to bring about a true revolution and to establish a democracy. Both attempts failed. The myth of the Monarchy as a means of national salvation was succeeded by the initially appealing myth of the Republic as a panacea for Portugal's woes. If anything, the tensions of personalism and factionalism grew worse, and parliamentary democratic government became severely discredited not only in the cities and towns, but also in the rural areas. While the first Republic was popular when it came to power, it became unpopular and was never an effective democracy—a result of restricted suffrage, periods of press censorship, and executive manipulation of the law. Military insurrection in the form of frequent *revoluções* (there were forty-five governments in only fifteen years and eight months) replaced elections as the common means of changing governments. This historic regime became what I have described elsewhere as a "standstill polity": a system beset by inertia, perpetual conspiracies, and crisis wherein significant reforms could not be introduced or carried out.[14]

The Republic failed to develop a workable parliamentary regime in which constitutional means would replace the use of force and conspiracy or threat to allow legal changes of government. One political party, the Democrats (the first party in Portugal's modern history with roots among certain elements of the masses in the towns and cities),[15] dominated elections and the parliament from 1911 to 1917 and from 1919 to 1926, but lost popularity and failed to execute needed social, economic, and political reforms. Despite their promises the Democrats did not enfranchise women, and, far from granting greater autonomy to the provinces, brought a greater concentration of power to Lisbon. By working a significant expansion of both the civil and the military bureaucracies—a legacy Salazar inherited and did little to change—the Republicans survived in power, benefiting from disunity on the right and impotence on the left. For all of their intentions and ideas, the Republicans' achievements were modest, except perhaps in some aspects of education, and the Democrats as a party gave a bad name to what the dictatorship's partisans later described as "demo-liberalism."

The Dictatorship

As the winds of fascism and dictatorship were beginning to blow in Europe, a military dictatorship replaced the first Republic in the summer of 1926, following a coup organized by junior officers who were united largely by professional grievances. The parliament was closed down and did not meet again for nearly nine years. If the partisans of dictatorship did not find a man on horseback to lead them (the generals available were either unable or unwilling to play such a role), they found instead a University of Coimbra professor, António de Oliveira Salazar, to reform finances. The son of Beira Alta peasant farmers, Salazar became premier in 1932 and dominated the running of government while a president—always a professional military officer (General Carmona, 1926–1951; General Craveiro Lopes, 1951–1958; Admiral Américo Tomaz, 1958–1974)—as chief of state remained more ceremonial than political. The dictatorship lasted forty-eight years, and was the longest surviving authoritarian regime in modern European history.

The dictatorship that called itself the "New State" was a strange amalgam of the old and the new, a counterrevolution and a conservative reordering of priorities. While some labels were new, the substance represented considerable continuity and tradition. Given the fact that much of the opinion available in its initial years viewed the dictatorship as a popular alternative to disorder and virtual bankruptcy, the regime enjoyed support in its early decades. The counterrevolution promised was not entirely delivered, because no one vested interest or clique persisted in holding the upper hand in a regime which revolved about one man and a few confidants, and which was based not on fascism or Catholicism, but on a modern form of absolutist statism with an elaborate defensive system.

Fearful of the effects of modern mass education as well as industrialization, the New State remained in power as long as it did for a number of reasons. It effectively co-opted large sections of the oligarchy and the middle classes through concessions and government employment, and it based Lisbon's hegemony on two traditional pillars on which the structure of the Constitutional Monarchy had rested for so long: the neutrality or apathy of the masses, and an increasingly centralized administration bound up in the toils of patronage and influence. The New State, however, systematized mechanisms for dominance or defense of the state that previous regimes had only initiated or planned: paramilitary defense forces tied to loyalty to the regime—the secret police, the Portuguese Legion, and the National Republican Guard; censorship of the media; controls on employment in the corps of teachers and over curricula in schools and universities; controls on employment in the government, through a vetting process which involved the secret police; control of the military through influence on recruitment, promotion, and salary, and through surveillance from within by means of an espionage system; an extensive propaganda program; control of labor and management relations through a corporatist system; and strict control of legislative and judicial branch activities by a watchful executive.[16]

The dictatorship's answer to the tensions of personalism and factionalism was to attempt to depoliticize society. Political parties were banned, and a controlled "movement," the National Union, filled with government employees and other loyalists, was allowed to present single-candidate lists in rigged elections. Depoliticization began to break down with the rise of militant oppositionist activity and Allied influences during World War II.[17] With the defeat of German and Italian fascism, the regime was forced to liberalize. In the elections of November 1945, there was a brief relaxation of censorship and of restrictions on oppositionist election activity, but repression was rapidly resumed, and Salazar's authoritarian attitudes and policies became less popular.

The New State's term for its program of reforms and its attempted counterrevolution against the first Republic was "the National Revolution," an example of semantic chicanery. In a sense the elite who surrounded Salazar—always the stern schoolmaster—represented a *reviravolta* of the provinces against Lisbon in the 1930s and 1940s; Salazar the provincial professor was to bring simple, rural order to the chaos of the great capital city. Schmitter has shown that the New State leadership of the 1930s was composed largely of "civil servants, technicians and professors of fairly provincial origins who, with the important exception of the financial sector, do not appear to have *initially* been controlled by or held accountable to either a liberal, internationally linked, modern industrial-commercial bourgeoisie or a conservative, provincially bounded, feudal-landed aristocracy."[18] A similar pattern was discovered by Braga da Cruz in a recent study in which he demonstrates that the elite of such Catholic organizations as the Centro Católico Português and the Centro Acadêmico da Democracia Cristã (CADC) reflected traditional petty bourgeoisie influence, and that leaders of the Catholic organizations had roots among small rural landholders north of the Tagus and had, through university training, achieved important posts in business and government.[19]

It cannot be said that the dictatorship did not attempt to come to grips with the four master tensions of Portuguese society. With their own self-interested interpretation of personalism and factionalism as they observed them under the parliamentary Republic, Salazar and his propagandists in part justified rule by force and paternalistic controls by citing the flaws of what they alleged to be Portuguese national behavior and character.[20] In many respects Salazar's cure was worse than the disease, for when freedom was achieved in 1974 these two tensions not only persisted, but had been inflamed by a half century of repression.

As for the problems of land ownership and Lisbon versus the provinces, the dictatorship's record was for the most part a failure. While agrarian conditions in 1974 were in some respects an improvement over what they had been in 1926, the need for a massive agrarian reform remained, both north and south of the Tagus; the misery of the landless peasants in Alentejo persisted, and only large-scale emigration to Western Europe, Africa and the Americas had brought necessary, if artificial, relief. As for closing the gap between Lisbon and the provinces, if any one fact—besides repression—characterized the dictatorship, it was a growth in administrative centralization. Authority, power, and resources accumulated in Lisbon, Oporto, and a handful of other large towns, while rural areas received little. One of the specific criticisms allowed by the more prescient of the businessmen who made fortunes under the New State was that Salazar neglected to develop the rural areas.[21] To what extent this was a deliberate policy, or the result of other causes, remains a matter of debate.

All this said, and taking into account the fact that Portugal was rather ineffectively governed between 1820 and 1926, it is probably true that between 1932 and 1950 Portugal was more effectively administered than ever before in her history. After 1950, the men who ruled the country and their regime were outrun by time and events. After 1950, the regime was forced by new international and domestic pressures to begin to reverse major policies, and to initiate programs which were in direct conflict with the doctrines with which it had reached power.

The doctrines and policies that had been sacred in the early decades were discouraging or limiting industrialization; balancing the budget;

reducing or eliminating foreign debt; imposing rigid censorship, and distrusting new media like television; placing the development resources more in Portugal than in the colonies; strictly limiting or discouraging foreign investment; and keeping the armed forces satisfied, but preventing them from sustained participation in a war outside Portugal's frontiers in the metropole or the islands. After 1950 the New State, for a number of reasons, altered or reversed every one of these policies, beginning with development plans in the 1950s for Angola and Mozambique, increased industrialization (albeit still on a modest scale), and the introduction of television (in 1957).

It was in the 1960s, however, that the most significant socioeconomic changes came, as Salazar and his circle aged and became less aware and less effective as administrators. The crucial watershed was the guerrilla war that Portugal began to fight in northern Angola in early 1961, which spread to Guinea-Bissau and Mozambique during the following three years. The government had to dispatch a considerable portion of the nation's armed forces to fight far away in tropical Africa, and Portugal was forced to mobilize the largest armed contingent in its modern history. During a war of thirteen years the country sustained more than 13,000 dead, and an unknown number of maimed and wounded—losses greater than those suffered by Portugal in World War I, or in any conflict since the Napoleonic invasions and the subsequent civil wars in the first half of the nineteenth century.

Other changed policies had their impact following the upheaval of 1961: greater resources were invested in the African colonies; in 1965 and 1966, Portugal's investment restrictions were greatly relaxed to encourage foreign investment at home and in the colonies; with the rising costs of the African wars and greater development at home, budget deficits grew along with the foreign debt. After 1968, censorship was somewhat relaxed. Finally, younger generations of officers serving in the African wars not only gained professional experiences unknown before, but came to nurse professional grievances against the regime—grievances that arose from the overseas war in which they were involved. They organized a military union or brotherhood, the Armed Forces Movement, which overthrew the dictatorship in a bloodless coup on April 25, 1974.[22]

The Revolution of 1974–1975

The 1974 revolution brought a fundamental change in political organization: an authoritarian regime was ousted and a democratic system—what some call the second Republic and others the third Republic[23]—was established. Following a pattern somewhat like the swinging pendulum of the French Revolution of 1789, but without the bloodshed,[24] the revolution of 1974–1975 went through several distinct political phases: a moderate phase, from April to September 1974; a radical phase, from September 1974 to November 1975; and, in response, an increasingly conservative phase that has continued to the present. The country's social and economic structures experienced accompanying fundamental changes, especially in 1975. During that year a radical cabinet nationalized all Portuguese banks and insurance companies, and more than two million acres of farmland south of the Tagus were forcibly occupied by individuals and by cooperatives.

A full discussion of what happened, and why, during the turbulent episodes of 1974 and 1975 forms the heart of this volume. Among the major causes that help to explain the radical leftist attempt at revolution, the derailment of that revolution, and the course of a move to the right and of a counterrevolution, personalism, factionalism, landownership patterns, and the conflict between Lisbon and the provinces have an important place.

Freedom brought Portugal the first opportunity to establish and keep a truly democratic regime. At first euphoria reigned, but soon wiser observers understood that despite the relative ease of overthrowing the West's oldest dictatorship, consolidating a true democracy would be difficult. The dictatorship had been a miserable school for freedom. In addition to being burdened with this deadly legacy of history, Portugal remained the poorest and least educated of Western nations. Illiteracy remained at least at 25 percent, and virtually every sector of government, society, and the economy required fundamental reform. Yet for the first time in history Portugal held truly free elections, and the popular response was massive. Voter turnout percentages were record-breaking: between 78 and 92 percent of the electorate turned out for the six general elections held between April 25, 1975, and December 7, 1980. With all citizens of both sexes over the age of 18 allowed to vote, six million voters out of a population of ten million participated. This was the clearest evidence that at least one aspect of Portuguese democracy was functioning.

In other respects, Portuguese democracy was not functioning as well. While the second Republic's political record was superior to that of the first Republic,[25] unsolved problems remained monumental. There was governmental and political instability: as of mid-1981, Portugal had thirteen governments (six provisional and seven constitutional) in seven years; the average life of a government or a cabinet was only seven or eight months. Severe personal and factional tensions had been the direct or indirect cause for the fall or resignation of each of the governments. By the summer of 1981 the thirteenth government, under Francisco Balsemão was experiencing pressures from within the governing Democratic Alliance—pressures based as much or more on personalities and factionalism as on substantive issues and ideas.[26] Political parties remained fragile and, with the exception of the Portuguese Communist Party (PCP), lacked efficient, strong organizations with well-established constituencies.

There was evidence that a major cause of continuing ineffective government at the national, regional, and municipal levels was an oversized inefficient bureaucracy. The bureaucracy of the New State, with only a few exceptions, remained intact after the 1974–1975 revolution, and actually increased in size.[27] This increase—a problem recognized but not addressed—was a result in part of the absorption of thousands of former state employees from Portugal's collapsed overseas empire, the civil service element of the *retornados* ("returned ones").[28]

To the credit of the fledgling second Republic, significant efforts were made to relieve the tensions of land ownership and Lisbon vs. the provinces. Compromise legislation in the Republican Assembly attempted to undo some of the damage done by the occupations of the *latifundia* in the Alentejo in 1975, but this region remained an agrarian disaster area. Seven years after the revolution the country still imported more than half of the food it consumed, and the need for agrarian reform both north and south of the Tagus had not been met.

As for the fourth tension, there is evidence that attempts to reduce the power and authority of Lisbon over the provinces made little headway, that overcentralization continued to be a critical problem despite progressive legislation. It was unclear just how effective a 1979 law granting local areas 18 percent of the national tax revenues (a first in Portuguese history) would be. The problem of overcentralization was recognized by many, but there was little agreement as to solutions.

Finally, and possibly most crucially, there remained the evidence that despite high voter participation in elections, public attitudes were severely divided over the suitability of democracy for Portugal. To a growing cult of Salazar and to the more positive aspects of the dictatorship could be added negative influences from Spain's faltering democratic system, growing disdain for politics and for politicians as a class,[29] and the increasingly appealing myth—nursed by a larger proportion of the public than many democratic observers would care to admit—that in Portugal democracy is responsible mainly for a disintegrating economy and for a license for communist skulduggery.

The historic four tensions of Portuguese society, then, were only inflamed by the half-century long dictatorship, and the successor regime, a novice democratic system, has had neither the time nor the resources to make much headway against them. While the second Republic, in contrast to the first, has the advantages of greater international support for Portuguese democracy, slightly more political stability, less public violence, greater literacy, and free elections, the future of Portuguese democracy remains uncertain. The extent to which its fate will turn on the condition of the economy as well as on mass public attitudes is a complex question that cannot be answered by statistics on elections and the gross national product. The proposition that preparation for democracy may be a long-term and not a short-term problem in Portugal was eloquently expressed in a statement by former Premier Mário Soares in a personal interview with this writer in 1977: "The revolution must begin in minds, and there must be a reform of the Portuguese mentality that will give it a more critical sense [that can] combat a tendency to emotional and emotive feelings rather than the rational."[30] Soares added that his solution to the problem was a long-range one which involved self-government, the growth of self-discipline, the fundamental reform of public education, and a critical sense that could see through slogans and demagogy.

The final analysis of the counterrevolution against the leftist revolution of 1974–1975 is left to the other authors in this volume, but something should be said about the extent to which the counterrevolution, which began with the elections of April 25, 1975, and continued with popular attacks on Communist party elements in northern Portugal in July 1975, was a mass provincial reaction against radical doctrines emanating from Lisbon. Phil Mailer describes how the revolution exhausted many persons, and how a "state of permanent stale mate" led to a reaction among the working masses. The revolution's radicals were bitterly divided, and a main point of dispute concerned whether the revolution should be centralized or decentralized and local. In the end the revolution was merely, in Mailer's words, "a still-born infant."[31] To this British libertarian radical, a mood of indifference became a key factor: "The discussions were lively, but it was all external to people's real life. It might have been happening in another world. In no way were the workers going to support one side or the other. After 20 months of the 'revolutionary process' and of leftist talk they had drawn one conclusion: revolution and counter-revolution were jobs for specialists. And anyway, they had to work tomorrow."[32]

Any future revolution in Portugal will have little hope of success unless its leaders and followers can take into account the bitter legacy of history and a complex national psychology.

New Research in Portuguese History: Constructing a Prologue to the Revolution

Stanley Payne suggested in his epilogue to *Contemporary Portugal: The Revolution and Its Antecedents* that "almost everything is yet to be done" in reconstructing the inner history of the dictatorship.[33] Although this remains true in part, some years later the results of fundamental historical research suggest that a substantial beginning has been made and that new paths have been broken.

The Portuguese revolution's effect on historical research has generally been positive, although official restrictions on public access to the documentation of the dictatorship have now been instituted.[34] The new freedom from censorship and the secret police spurred new activity among scholars, students, and journalists. While much remains to be done, new materials now available are sufficient to revise a number of standard history texts, to allow us to ask more probing questions, and, perhaps most important of all, to provide a decent but public burial for some old myths.

Historical research published since 1974 has not only demystified the propaganda of the New State on a number of questions, but has brought into disrepute some commonly accepted generalizations and conventional wisdom about twentieth century Portuguese history. H. V. Livermore's survey history of Portugal emphasized that economics and finance were at the heart of post-1910 conflicts;[35] this revised edition also concluded with the judgement that the 1974–1976 period was "the most calamitous period" in the country's history[36]—certainly an ahistorical and hasty judgement in light of earlier, more calamitous times in the sixteenth, seventeenth and early nineteenth centuries, not to mention the rigors of the 1915 to 1927 period. Recent studies by Manuel Villaverde Cabral and others shed a new light on earlier generalizations.[37]

It appears certain that the New State's carefully nurtured myth that the regime faced no real opposition and no real labor agitation until after 1961 has been laid to rest by new studies on Portuguese labor organizations, strikes, and other activity in the 1918 to 1930 period.[38] Recent publications by Campinos and former Premier Caetano place in doubt the often repeated beliefs that the Portuguese professional military have a tradition of unity, and that the military did not have serious conflicts with the civilian leadership of the regime between 1926 and 1958—i.e., before General Humberto Delgado's controversial candidacy for the presidency.[39] Both Caetano and Franco Nogueira document fully the anxious internal conflict over the 1951–1958 presidency and the possible future candidacy of Marshal Craveiro Lopes, an officer who clashed with Salazar.[40]

At the Second Meeting of the International Conference Group on Modern Portugal, held at the University of New Hampshire in Durham from June 21 to 23, 1979, a number of the papers on historical topics, which are not included in this collection, helped to complement the meeting's announced theme of "Continuity and Change" during the post-1910 period.

Maria Filomena Mónica's paper, "Moulding the Minds of the People: Views on Popular Education in 20th Century Portugal," was a resumé of major conclusions found in her doctoral dissertation, an edited version of which had been published in Portugal.[41] Its main contribution is an analysis of the debate within the dictatorship, between 1926 and 1938, concerning literacy, popular education, and the function of primary schools. Mónica discovered that the New State saw the primary school as an instrument to indoctrinate the masses with "the somewhat inchoate Nationalist ideology," that the regime disapproved of any learning experience which might be "denationalizing," and that the Ministry of National Education represented the most "centralizing" of systems in the regime's expanding bureaucracy. While the Republicans before 1926 saw the school as an agency with which to "spread Reason," the New State as well as its socialist and anarcho-syndicalist opposition viewed the school as an ideological weapon. Unlike the other participants in the school debate, who favored centralized "state" education, the anarcho-syndicalists desired a school system that would come under local, municipal, or community control.[42]

The paper by Manuel Villaverde Cabral, "The 'Seara Nova' Group and the Ambiguities of Elitism," analyzed the debate about the nature and destiny of Portuguese society within what became one of the key opposition intellectual groups after 1926. Cabral's exegesis, based on the 1921 to 1927 issues of the group's famous publication, Seara Nova, nicely punctures the myth that the Seara Nova group was a cohesive, democratic, and socialist element. With a considerable amount of ideological factionalism present, the group's ideas were vague and ambiguous, and could not be fairly described as socialist. Like most of the ideological elements which made up the disparate coalition of the regime's leadership and supporters, the Seara Nova group adhered to the concept of "national salvation" by elites. As an opposition group with an ideological base, Cabral suggests, the Seara Nova group was ineffective in providing a clear alternative philosophy to that of the New State.

This writer presented a report on research in progress rather than a formal academic paper: "A Rapaziada of Military Coup-Makers: Comparing the Military Generations of 1910, 1926 and 1974." Among the major points made by this brief analysis of the role of the military in Portuguese politics were that recently published memoirs of the 1974 coup leaders, including those of Major Otelo Saraiva de Carvalho, suggest that organizing the April 25 coup was difficult, despite the regime's weaknesses, and that several little-discussed factors conditioned how the professional officer corps responded to pressures to intervene in politics: almost superstitious attention to military rules, customs, and hierarchy; "situationism" and personalism; and generational conflicts among officers. My findings suggested that these factors, as much as ideology and class, played a key role in the origins and course of the coup plot, and that the neutrality of the majority of officers and units made the coup possible, rather than a mass adherence to the plot. Finally, the analysis pointed out that the official regulations of the Moçidade Portuguesa (Portuguese Youth movement) a paramilitary institution established by the dictatorship during its most fascist phase in 1936, demonstrate more of a Catholic than a fascist doctrinal influence; one important regulation required that the educational program of the movement feature the tenets of "traditional Christian education."[43]

Jaime Reis's contribution to the meeting was an important paper on agrarian history, "Making Loaves out of Tariffs: The Origins of Modern Cereal Protectionism, 1889–1914." Reis brilliantly combined an analysis of a national question with massive evidence from unpublished local sources; his use of rare family archives—the kind of sources seldom used in Portuguese history because of difficulty of access—establishes a basis for a revision of some commonly accepted generalizations about recent agrarian history. Reis's subject is also one of the most controversial topics in the economic history of the dictatorship, since practically every Portuguese political figure from Salazar to the present leadership of the second Republic has had to take a stand on the question of wheat production. Cereal tariff legislation between 1889 and 1914 formed the basis, as Reis suggests, "for all subsequent legislation on the subject down to the present day."[44] His paper showed that there is no easy answer to the question of legislating agrarian reform in the wheat-growing regions of southern Portugal, and that class analysis, applied to this aspect of economic history, can produce an unduly oversimplified picture. It is worth quoting his conclusion: the battle over cereal prices was less "of a confrontation between producers and consumers over the 'subsistence issue,' and far more . . . a fight between two sets of complementary producers [millers and the grain-farming sector] over the sharing out of the global profits . . . in the end there were no clear victors, except perhaps the labouring population of the 'granary' region of southern Portugal whose cash income from working in wheat production in per capita terms more than doubled,''[45] Contrary to what many have assumed from Salazar's day to the present, absentee landlords benefited less from cereal protection than some other groups.

Finally, two papers on aspects of American diplomacy in the 1961 to 1965 period offered important revelations about the dictatorship's negotiating position on Portuguese Africa's future, and about the role of the American intelligence organization, the Central Intelligence Agency (CIA), in a generals' plot against Premier Salazar. Richard Mahoney's paper, "The Kennedy-Salazar Skirmish over Portuguese Africa," and Michael A. Samuels and Stephen M. Haykin's paper, "The Anderson Plan: An American Attempt to Seduce Portugal Out of Africa,"[46] benefited from the authors' use of official, unpublished United States government documentation obtained through use of the Freedom of Information Act (FOIA). These papers provided analyses of previously secret government activity, based on American documents; with the exception of recently published selected memoirs by Franco Nogueira,[47] one of the participants in the negotiations at issue, Portuguese documentation is lacking.

Looking again at American efforts to move the dictatorship toward an acceptance of self-determination for Portuguese Africa—efforts which apparently were largely unilateral, despite the continuing influence of Great Britain, Portugal's oldest ally—gives a pervasive sense of déjà vu. In light of the disasters that befell Portugal and Portuguese Africa beginning in 1974, how big an "if" in history was the so-called Anderson Plan? Might this plan have eased Portugal's transition from an authoritarian to a democratic regime? Might it have helped to prevent a civil war in Angola and to moderate the subsequent revolutions in Portugal's African colonies?

The Anderson Plan, named after Admiral George Anderson, American Ambassador to Lisbon from 1963 to 1966, was presented secretly to the Portuguese government in September 1965, and was finally rejected by the Portuguese in March 1966. The plan's outline included: (1) the commitment of both Africans and Portuguese to a timetable for self-determination, leading to an internationally supervised plebiscite within eight to ten years; (2) African, American, and Western European guarantees that this timetable would be observed; (3) multilateral cooperation to bring about the end of fighting in Portuguese Africa during the transition; (4) African, American, and Western European support for a substantial economic and social development program in Portuguese Africa.[48] On two key assumptions the American and Portuguese viewpoints were not reconcilable: that African nationalism was (or would be eventually) invincible, and that African independence did not require some form of European supervision. Samuels and Haykin demonstrated clearly that moving both the Portuguese government and African nationalist groups to accept the plan was unlikely, though the implementation of the plan would have been a diplomatic revolution. The authors neglected a further, and possibly pivotal, "if": if the Portuguese government had publicly accepted this plan, could the regime have resisted a right-wing military coup, given the still-prevalent strength of the hard-line policy in the Portuguese political arena? The link between the overseas policy and the dictatorship's internal support underlay much of Lisbon's official position. It should be remembered, in this context, that only in the 1969 elections did the non-Communist opposition include self-determination for Africa in its programs. Implementation of the Anderson Plan might have exposed the Salazar regime to the dangers of a right-wing coup by generals and settlers similar to those experienced by De Gaulle's France from 1958 to 1962.[49]

Richard Mahoney's paper revealed the outlines of CIA involvement in a generals' plot against Salazar in April 1961. The key plotter was General Júlio Botelho Moniz, Minister of Defense and, ironically, one of the "young lieutenants" of the army which had overthrown the first Republic in 1926. Mahoney's account of the failure of Botelho Moniz' plot to overthrow Salazar peacefully, by having President Tomaz dismiss Salazar, showed that the CIA overestimated the generals' strength and nerve, and underestimated Salazar's personalism and influence among the elite.[50] From the available evidence, and despite wishful thinking in the Kennedy administration, a successful generals' coup against Salazar at that time would have been unable to effect needed reforms in Portuguese Africa. More likely a power struggle, civil strife, and the threat of Spanish intervention to forestall a leftist plot would have been the immediate results.

The Use of Government Archives

The papers presented at the Conference Group meeting in 1979 suggest the importance of using unpublished materials held in government archives to come to grips with the prologue to Portugal's most recent revolution. In the 1970s the significant research on the dictatorship centered (1) on certain classes, such as the industrial elite, and on policies and structures, such as corporatism;[51] and (2) on the general history of the regime from a comparative political perspective: that is, what type of regime was it? Fascist or otherwise? Interest in the comparative approach was sparked by scholars' curiosity as to why the New State had survived for so long.[52] In some respects the questions asked during this phase of research were ahistorical, at least in the context of Portugal's history. More relevant questions are: "What was the regime in its origins?" "Was there more than one distinct phase of this regime?" "How did the regime function from within?" While Schmitter's answers to the latter questions mark a beginning of the work that must be done, the fact remains that too much of the dictatorship's inner history is unknown, and that much of the research of the 1970s relied on secondary and tertiary sources and did not make use of such primary sources as unpublished government records. It also remains true that more than a few studies generalize about the entire era of the dictatorship from conditions found in the regime in the 1960s or the 1950s,[53] and ascribe unwarranted importance to the role of Salazar during a half century of authoritarian rule.[54]

Recent research by this writer in Lisbon archives points toward a reconsideration of conventional wisdom about the history of the New State. Studies of unpublished materials in the archives of the Ministry of Foreign Affairs and in the files of the secret political police,[55] and of records at the former Ministry of the Interior, provide a basis for revising current knowledge of, and for tentatively documenting, three aspects of the dictatorship: (1) the functioning of corporatism in practice, not in theory, during World War II; (2) during the same period, the basing of crucial decisions in part on the regime's assessment (a realistic one as it turned out) of Portuguese public opinion, as exemplified by decisions made in the diplomatic crisis over the wolfram question; and (3) the use of secret police investigations to obtain information about the regime's supporters and friends as well as its opposition—a practice that also reveals how the regime viewed the nature of Portuguese politics.

Concerning corporatism, Ministry of Foreign Affairs documents from 1942 to 1944 show that in a crisis the Salazar regime would bypass the corporatist system and eschew corporatist doctrine by the use of a policy of expediency. If the corporatist system did not function to insure "social peace," the regime employed other means to achieve this goal. A revealing case involved severe pressures on Portugal during Britain's economic blockade of Europe in World War II, when Portuguese factories required certain imported raw materials in order to remain open. The regime reacted quickly to any threats of unemployment, and even during this era it dreaded strikes among industrial workers in the Lisbon region. If the factories could be kept open with more work, serious industrial unrest, already threatened in 1942, could be prevented. When the powerful industrial conglomerate C.U.F. (Companhia União Fabril) urged the government to act to obtain essential raw materials—in this case, cocoanut meat—to prevent the closing of its factories in an area where many workers were under Communist party influence, the Salazar government made an urgent request, through the British Embassy and the Ministry of Economic Warfare in London, for the release of the raw material. The British feared that the cocoanut meat, if released, would be re-exported from Portugal to Nazi Germany. The outcome of the "cocoanut case" remains obscure, but whatever the decision made by the British authorities, who were hard-nosed in their attitudes to Portuguese complaints on economic issues, unprecedented industrial unrest increased in Portugal through the final years of the war. Played out in "confidential" documents,[56] this episode illustrates how the regime's major decision-making disregarded the corporatist structure and remained in the realm of secret requests, maneuvers, and influence at the highest levels.

A further insight into how corporatism functioned was discovered in secret police dossiers indicating corruption of leading corporatist officials, including that of the naval officer Henrique Tenreiro.[57] Future investigations should be concerned with the questions, To what extent was the corporatist system a useful means of personal enrichment for ambitious supporters of the dictatorship? Was such corruption present at a relatively high level of the regime as early as the 1940s?

A study of secret archival documents also affords a fascinating glimpse into how the dictatorship weighed pros and cons—including Portuguese public opinion—in arriving at an important decision about wolfram ore (tungsten) exports during World War II. Despite the New State's claims, following the victory of the Allies, that Portugal's foreign policy had been one of "collaborative neutrality,"[58] Salazar, as a tough-minded, determined foreign minister went to extremes to maintain a façade of legalism, absolute neutrality, and lack of overt favoritism to either set of belligerents. Records of 1944 negotiations over the continued export of wolfram ore to Germany shed light on the extent to which Salazar would go to please both the Axis and Allied sides simultaneously. Even this late in the war Salazar was obsessed with the fear that if Portugal did not continue to make wolfram available to the Germans, who urgently required it for heavy war industries, Germany might declare war on Portugal and order an air attack, if not an invasion. The section on "The Portuguese Position" in one important document reveals that regime leaders still feared German retaliation, and believed that they could not afford to make public the regime's secretly pro-Allied position—a position demonstrated by the document. This passage includes the pivotal point: "Politically, it is indisputable that with the solution of the wolfram question [we] should at all costs avoid a political, military or economic reaction from one side or the other. In the case of absolute necessity we must always sacrifice the German interest to the Allied interest. Since the entry of Portugal into the conflict through a German reaction would be absurd, we must take special care to avoid an attitude which would provoke her [Germany]."[59] Putting aside the regime's assessment of the important variable of a German threat, the evidence is substantial that its wartime policy was, in diplomatic terms, both pro-Allied and realistic.

Another episode in the wolfram crisis, as seen from in-house documents, demonstrates that at least Salazar and the monarchist Luiz Sampayo, secretary-general of the Ministry of Foreign Affairs, held no illusions as to the popularity of the dictatorship with the Portuguese public. When Salazar, under severe pressure from Britain to cut off all wolfram exports to Germany in the spring of 1944, refused to alter his policy beyond reducing German supplies of the strategic ore, British and Commonwealth statesmen from Churchill to Smuts began to apply even greater pressures. As these increased, Sampayo prepared an internal ministry memorandum on the options available to Portugal; Portugal would have to give in to one or more of three potential acts by Britain: severe economic sanctions; a threat to break off Britain's alliance with Portugal; or an appeal for cooperation under the alliance (as had happened a year before, when Portugal leased bases in the Azores to Britain). The memo concluded that only the third option was acceptable. The truth of the regime's vulnerability, and of its actual relationship with public opinion, despite all the propaganda to the contrary, is revealed in the memorandum's next passage, which implies that the dictatorship's stability would have been endangered if Britain had applied economic sanctions or had broken off the alliance: I [Sampayo wrote to Salazar] have no confidence that public opinion in Portugal will follow or support the Government for very long. The Portuguese public when it experiences the first sufferings will turn against the Government . . . ."[60] On June 6, 1944, following Britain's appeal to the alliance, Portugal decreed the official embargo of further production and exports of wolfram to *all* belligerents.[61]

What the regime's use of its secret police investigations reveals about the dictatorship's view of Portuguese politics and of its supporters and friends is illuminated in records stored in Lisbon and Caxias.

Some of these materials suggest that the regime had its secret police carry out surveillance on supporters as well as oppositionists, since the records include dossiers on leading figures who were close to Salazar—among them his friend and physician from Coimbra, Bissaia Barreto, and the Ambassador to London, the Duke of Palmella. The records also show that despite the dictatorship's much-discussed efforts at depoliticization and the banning of political parties, at least some regime supporters in the secret police recognized that parties existed secretly or underground, and that the regime could manipulate them. Most instructive is the fact that the secret police dossier of Salazar's close friend, confidante, and physician, Bissaia Barreto, refers to Barreto as "The Party of the Center";[62] this label suggests that even the police viewed Barreto as an interlocutor of importance who maintained a dialogue with more than one competing and antagonistic circle around Salazar and among diplomatic representatives, despite the fact that he, Barreto, had no official status.

From the evidence produced by the papers discussed, by recent research, and by a study of some unpublished records, the nature, functioning, and operating context of the dictatorship appear to be much more complex than many previous studies have acknowledged. Several conclusions are inescapable: the dictatorship, paradoxically and despite its longevity, confronted opposition and a host of crises before the end of World War II, when its capacity to respond effectively was intact. After the war the complexity of the political situation increased, while the regime's capacity to cope diminished.

Conclusion

While this volume concentrates on the 1974 revolution and its aftermath, this chapter has attempted to place the relatively recent episode firmly in historical perspective. As we have observed of Portugal and the Portuguese, despite the burst of energy during 1974 to 1976, tradition is persistent and, although there have been some changes, modernization is relatively slow. The focus of the last part of this chapter on key aspects of the inner history of the dictatorship of 1926–1974, the political experience that preceded the 1974 revolution, has been deliberate. The pivotal role of historical factors, including experience, attitudes, customs, and beliefs, cannot be overemphasized in the case of Portugal, a country where historical memory has an ancient pedigree.

Placing recent developments in Portugal in historical context continues to be essential for at least three reasons. First, as we have observed in this chapter and in others, the four classic tensions of Portuguese society have not disappeared but still exist. Analyses of these tensions, then, remain vital to an understanding of Portugal today. Of the four tensions of Portuguese society the most significant and all-inclusive in terms of Portugal's progress toward modernization is the conflict between Lisbon and the provinces, the rural-urban cleavage. No Portuguese revolution or counterrevolution can succeed without addressing this continuing problem and tension. It has deep roots historically in both Iberian nation-states: Portugal and Spain. What Richard Herr concluded in his study of modern Spain can be applied to modern Portugal: ". . . the alienation of the common people of rural Spain from the urban groups holding progressive doctrines, . . . was the most important cause for Spain's political instability in the last two centuries."[63]

A second reason for the use of historical analyses in the study of contemporary Portugal is found in the extensive evidence of continuing popular, semi-messianic, personal cults. This interesting phenomenon may well be only one aspect of the tension of personalism, already discussed, but it continues to have a bearing on Portuguese political attitudes and behavior. While modern forms of a kind of ancestor worship may remain among more than a handful of families, personal cults related to traditional, annual commemorations of deceased political figures and leaders are also important. Anniversary commemorations for deceased heroes continue to be held, however remote in time the death date of the cult subject. Cases in point are the annual masses and commemorative celebrations on the anniversary of assassinated leaders. Every February 1st, there are masses held for the souls of the murdered King Carlos I and his heir apparent, Luiz (February 1, 1908), in at least one Lisbon church. Despite the fact that President Sidónio Pais was assassinated as long ago as December 14, 1918, annual masses in his memory are said in several Lisbon churches. The cult of "Saint Sidónio" Pais goes beyond anniversary masses; it includes the sale of medals with a picture of Saint Sidónio sold in stores in poor urban and rural districts and regular visits to his burial place in Lisbon's National Pantheon by indigent Portuguese visitors who leave written letters by his tomb, pray, and ask for help from the deceased hero. In 1981 a journalist observed visitors to this burial place conversing with their cult subject, Saint Sidónio, and during the colonial wars in Africa (1961–1974), some Portuguese mothers came to his tomb to ask for the protection of their sons' lives in combat.[64] There is also a growing membership in an evolving cult of "Saint Salazar," the premier-dictator from 1932 to 1968.

A third important reason concerns a traditional problem in modern Portuguese history: public access to information on government activities. Even before the post-1926 dictatorship, governments favored authoritarian policies concerning public access to information on official activities and concerning censorship. The Aviz dynasty's policy of secrecy when dealing with information on exploration and discoveries overseas, the policy of *sigilo* (from the Portuguese word for wax seal, *sigilo*), was only the first of a series of authoritarian public information policies.

Although the 1974 revolution led to the abolition of official government censorship and there was greater freedom of information by 1980, there is evidence that relatively little has changed concerning official attitudes and policies on public access to government archival records. Given the vital nature of historical research into such records as essential in understanding Portugal today, continuing restrictions on access to government archival records represent a serious problem. Many who support a democratic system in Portugal would agree on the importance of a thorough study of the records of the dictatorship's government for the enlightenment of present generations. Yet in 1981 a government law was passed that decreed the papers of Premiers Salazar and Caetano would be closed to public access for 25 years. Remaining records of the official secret police can be consulted by scholars, once authorization is given, but wide-ranging, professional research in these records is limited because of several factors: (1) a poor filing system; (2) a lack of professional archivists' assistance; (3) the fact that an unknown portion of the records is missing, having been destroyed or taken away during the more anarchistic times of 1974 to 1975 following the revolution; and (4) an important group of records is not available to researchers because the material is being used as evidence in current court trials.

Even with the serious concerns about the continuing need to take the ever-present historical factors into account, the fact remains that there has been progress in historical research as in other aspects of Portuguese studies in recent years. In government and politics, as always, judgements must remain tentative and cautious. In one sense, the Portuguese revolution of 1974–1975 failed, but in another sense it has succeeded. A radical, Marxist-Leninist revolution collapsed, but some of the major principles of pluralist democracy were established. If, as one Portuguese historian wrote recently, Portugal's post-1820 history can be interpreted as "successive milennial movements,"[65] then the dreams of the 1974 milennial movement have in part come true: the Portuguese are living in greater political freedom than in any previous political system they have known. Preserving this precious result of the revolution will alone be a worthy revolution.

Notes

1 José Hermano Saraiva, *História Concisa de Portugal* (Lisbon, 1981). An adaptation of Eça de Queiroz's *A Tragédia da Rua das Flores* was staged in Lisbon in 1980–1981.

2 Alberto Franco Nogueira, *Salazar*, vol. 1. *A Mocidade e os Princípios (1889–1926)*, (Coimbra, 1977); vol. 2, *Os Tempos Áureos (1926–1936)*, (Coimbra, 1978); vol. 3, *As Grandes Crises (1936–1945)*, (Coimbra, 1979); vol. 4, *O Ataque (1945–1958)*, (Coimbra, 1980); vol. 5, forthcoming.

3 Kenneth Maxwell, "The Transition in Portugal," Working Papers, no. 81, Latin American Program, The Wilson Center (Washington, D.C., 1981), p. 55.

4 Ibid., p. 44.

5 See Richard Herr, *Spain* (Englewood Cliffs, N.J., 1970), p. 262; Douglas L. Wheeler, *Republican Portugal: A Political History, 1910–1926* (Madison, 1978), pp. 16–20; Richard A. H. Robinson, *Contemporary Portugal: A History* (London, 1979), pp. 32–34.

6 See Robinson, *Portugal: A History*, p. 33. A wise editorial comment on the occasion of the third anniversary of the 25th of April, 1974, in the April 25, 1977, issue of the weekly *Expresso* (Lisbon), also made comments critical of a new post-1974 situationism.

7 Saraiva, *História Concisa*, p. 168.

8 A continuing belief held by public opinion as well as by scholars in Portugal is that a "national crisis" persists, and that the revolution of 1974–1975 did not end it. A recent title by a former official of the Sá Carneiro Government of 1979–1980, who is also a professional historian, illustrates the belief: Vasco Pulido Valente, *Estudos Sobre a Crise Nacional* (Lisbon, 1980).

9 See C. R. Boxer, *Portuguese Society in the Tropics* (Madison, 1965), pp. 86–87, 146.

10 C. R. Boxer, ed., *Further Selections from the Tragic History of the Sea, 1559–1565* (Cambridge, 1968), p. 11.

11 Miguel Torga, *Portugal* (Coimbra, 1957), p. 115.

12 See Wheeler, *Republican Portugal*, pp. 322–324, for a glossary of Portuguese political words; see also standard dictionaries.

13 See Manuel Barreira, ed., *Dicionário De Português-Inglês*, 1st ed., (Oporto, n.d.). The use of the words *reviravolta* and *reviralho* is common in the reports and dossiers found in the secret police files. The root word is *vira*, a traditional peasant dance of the Minho district in northern Portugal; the dance is performed by a *viradeira* (see Wheeler, *Republican Portugal*, p. 324).

Premier Salazar's speech was sprinkled with provincial colloquialisms, as reported in a personal interview with Salazar by British diplomat and historian Marcus Cheke; the interview, of 40 minutes length, was held during November 1945 (Private Diaries of Marcus J. Cheke, 1945 to 1947, entry for January 1, 1946, courtesy of Lady Constance Cheke and Val Cheke).

14 See Wheeler, *Republican Portugal*, pp. 155–171.

15 Ibid., pp. 253–262; see also Douglas L. Wheeler, "Nightmare Republic: Portugal 1910–1926," in *History Today*, vol. 31, (London, 1981), pp. 5–10.

16 See Douglas L. Wheeler, *Safe House: Lisbon and the Secret War*, forthcoming. This study of the role of neutral Portugal in World War II includes material on the dictatorship during the 1926 to 1945 period.

17 See Franco Nogueira, *Salazar*, vol. 3, pp. 512–590, and early chapters in vol. 4; and Hugh Kay, *Salazar and Modern Portugal* (London, 1970), chapter 7, "World War."

18 Philippe C. Schmitter, "The 'Régime d'Exception' That Became the Rule: Forty-Eight Years of Authoritarian Domination in Portugal," in Lawrence S. Graham and Harry M. Makler, eds., *Contemporary Portugal: The Revolution and Its Antecedents* (Austin, 1979), p. 21.

19 Manuel Braga da Cruz, *As Orígens Da Democracia Cristã E O Salazarismo* (Lisbon, 1980).

20 Much of the propaganda and informational material of the New State referred to the belief that certain traits of what was alleged to be Portuguese national character made dictatorship a practical necessity. In later years, for a foreign audience, Salazar expressed similar views; see António de Oliveira Salazar, "Principles and Realities of Portuguese Politics," *International Affairs* (London), vol. 39, no. 2 (April 1963), pp. 169–183.

21 Personal interview by this writer with Baron Frederick Beck, Lisbon, October 17, 1979.

22 For a discussion of how leading members of the Armed Forces Movement organized the coup of April 25, 1974, see especially the memoirs of Otelo Saraiva de Carvalho, *Alvorada em Abril* (Lisbon, 1977).

23 The "third Republic" is the term used by historian José Hermano Saraiva in his best-selling *História Concisa de Portugal*, p. 359.

24 See Robert Harvey, *Portugal: The Birth of a Democracy* (London, 1978); The Times [London] Insight Team, *Insight on Portugal: The Year of the Captains* (London, 1975).

25 See Wheeler, *Republican Portugal*, concluding chapter.

26 *Expresso* (Lisbon), June 13, 1981, and later issues; *O Jornal* (Lisbon), July 17–23, 1981; *The Christian Science Monitor*, July 22, 1981.

27 *Expresso* (Lisbon), March and April 1981 issues.

28 See the Portugal Surveys for June 14, 1980, in *The Economist* (London).

29 Disdain for politicians can be found in the daily press, letters to editors, private conversations, and in Lisbon musical reviews.

30 From the sound track narration of the film "Portugal: A Past in Search of a Future," written and produced for educational audiences by Douglas L. Wheeler and Lu-Me Productions (Durham, N.H.), 1978.

31 Phil Mailer, *Portugal: The Impossible Revolution?* (London, 1977), p. 354.
32 Ibid., p. 335.
33 Graham and Makler, eds., *Contemporary Portugal*, p. 349.
34 A decree-law of 1981 closed for the next twenty-five years all public access to the archives of premiers Salazar and Caetano; these government records are now installed in the Biblioteca Nacional de Lisboa. See Joaquim Vieira, "Os segredos do salazarismo," *Expresso* (Lisbon), May 23, 1981, Revista section, pp. 31R–36R.
35 H. V. Livermore, *A New History of Portugal*, rev.ed., (Cambridge, 1977).
36 Ibid., p. 394.
37 Manuel Villaverde Cabral, *O Desenvolvimento Do Capitalismo Em Portugal No Século XIX* (Lisbon, 1976); Cabral, *Portugal Na Alvorada Do Século XX* (Lisbon, 1979); see also works by Cabral cited in José Hermano Saraiva, *História Concisa.*
38 António José Telo, *O Sidonismo e o Movimento Operário Português. Luta de classes em Portugal, 1917–1919* (Lisbon, 1977).
39 Jorge Campinos, *A Ditadura Militar 1926/1933* (Lisbon, 1975); Marcello Caetano, *Minhas Memórias de Salazar* (Lisbon, 1977); on the Delgado episode, see also Franco Nogueira, *Salazar*, vol. 4.
40 Marcello Caetano, *Constituições Portuguesas*, 4th ed., (Lisbon, 1978), pp. 111–115.
41 Maria Filomena Mónica, *Educação e Sociedade no Portugal de Salazar* (Lisbon, 1978).
42 Maria Filomena Mónica, "Moulding the Minds of the People," p. 35.
43 Lopes Arriaga, *Mocidade Portuguesa. Breve História De Uma Organização Salazarista* (Lisbon, 1976).
44 Jaime Reis, "Making Loaves out of Tariffs," p. 1.
45 Ibid., p. 52.
46 Samuels and Haykin's paper was published in a revised form with the same title in *Orbis, A Journal of World Affairs* (Philadelphia), vol. 23, no. 3 (Fall 1979), pp. 649–699.

Two other papers on historical aspects of American diplomacy were also presented: John Seiler, "The Azores as an Issue in U.S.-Portuguese Relations, 1961–1963"; and Jerry K. Sweeny, "The Luso-American Connection."

47 Alberto Franco Nogueira, *Diálogos Interditos. A Política Externa Portuguesa e a Guerra De África* 2 vols. (Lisbon, 1979–80).
48 Samuels and Haykin, "The Anderson Plan," p. 18.
49 See Alistair Horne, *A Savage War of Peace: Algeria 1954–1962* (London, 1979), chapter 21, "The Generals' Putsch."
50 Richard Mahoney, "The Kennedy-Salazar Skirmish over Portuguese Africa," pp. 28–32.
51 Harry M. Makler, "The Portuguese Industrial Elite and Its Corporative Relations," in Graham and Makler, eds., *Contemporary Portugal*, pp. 123–166; see also Lawrence S. Graham, "The Military in Politics: The Politicization of the Portuguese Armed Forces," in Graham and Makler,

eds., *Contemporary Portugal*, pp. 221–256; and Howard J. Wiarda, *Corporatism and Development: The Portuguese Experience* (Amherst, 1977).

52 Philippe C. Schmitter, *Corporatism and Public Policy in Authoritarian Portugal* (Beverly Hills, 1975); see also the study by João Medina, *Salazar e Os Fascistas* (Lisbon, 1978).

53 Douglas Porch, *The Portuguese Armed Forces and the Revolution* (Stanford, 1977); Rona M. Fields, *The Portuguese Revolution and the Armed Forces Movement* (New York, 1976).

54 António de Figueiredo, *Portugal: Fifty Years of Dictatorship* (New York, 1976). From the historical and journalistic literature on the dictatorship, especially that published since 1974, interpretations are all too often dominated by personalist biases.

55 From 1932 to 1945 the secret police were known as the PVDE (Polícia da Vigilância e da Defesa do Estado); from 1945 to 1969, when the Caetano government changed the name, the secret police were called the PIDE (Polícia Internacional e da Defesa do Estado), the name most commonly associated with this institution.

56 Files on Wolfram and England, negotiations, in records largely from the Department of Political Affairs (Repartição dos Negócios Políticos), Bibliotica e Arquivo do Ministério dos Negócios Estrangeiros, Lisbon (cited in this chapter as BAMNE).

57 Henrique Tenreiro dossier, records under General Staff of Armed Forces, Committee for the Extinction of PIDE/DGS and LP (Portuguese Legion), South Wing of Fortress-Prison, Caxias.

58 An early semi-official statement which sought to publicize the idea of "collaborative neutrality," as a pro-Allied, relatively open policy rather than the more complex policy it was in reality, is found in the 30-page pamphlet by Luiz Teixeira, *Portugal e a guerra. Neutralidade colaborante* (Lisbon, 1945).

59 Unsigned memorandum circulated within top levels of Ministry of Foreign Affairs, BAMNE, Repartição de Negócios Políticos, Processo no. 436.1, "Volframio. Inglaterra. 1944," dated March 2, 1944.

60 Luiz Sampayo to Salazar, in BAMNE, "Informação. Resumo. Parecer," dated May 19, 1944.

61 See Douglas L. Wheeler, *Safe House*, chapter 11, "Wolfram War."

62 Bissaia Barreto dossier, records under General Staff of Armed Forces, Caxias.

63 Herr, *Spain*, p. 283.

64 José Freire Antunes, *A Cadeira De Sidónio. Ou a Memória Do Presidencialismo* (Lisbon, 1981), pp. 31–33.

65 Vasco Pulido Valente, "A Trombeta Soará," in Vasco Pulido Valente, *O País das Maravilhas* (Lisbon, 1979), p. 347.

Index

JACKET DESIGNED BY CAROLINE BECKETT
COMPOSED BY THE NORTH CENTRAL PUBLISHING CO.
ST. PAUL, MINNESOTA
MANUFACTURED BY CUSHING MALLOY, INC.
ANN ARBOR, MICHIGAN
TEXT AND DISPLAY LINES IN TIMES ROMAN

Library of Congress Cataloging in Publication Data
Main entry under title:
Papers presented at the June 1979 meeting of the
International Conference Group on Modern Portugal.
Includes bibliographical references and index.
1. Portugal—Politics and government—1974- —Congresses.
2. Portugal—History—Revolution, 1974—Influence—Congresses.
I. Graham, Lawrence S. II. Wheeler, Douglas L.
III. International Conference Group on Modern Portugal.
DP680.I53 1982 946.9′044 81-69819
ISBN 0-299-08990-8